DATE DUE

OCT 2 1 1998			

Rebels and Rulers, 1500–1600

Volume I

Society, states, and early modern revolution
Agrarian and urban rebellions

Armed peasants carrying a banner with plowshare. Title illustration from a pamphlet of the German peasant war: *Action, order and instruction agreed upon by all companies and bands of peasants and to which they have together bound themselves*, 1525. In March 1525 the articles in this pamphlet established the revolutionary peasant organization, the Christian Union of upper Swabia (see ch. 7). (Courtesy of the British Library.)

Rebels and rulers, 1500–1660

VOLUME I

SOCIETY, STATES, AND EARLY MODERN REVOLUTION

AGRARIAN AND URBAN REBELLIONS

PEREZ ZAGORIN

CAMBRIDGE UNIVERSITY PRESS

Cambridge
London   New York   New Rochelle
Melbourne   Sydney

For Adam

Published by the Press Syndicate of the University of Cambridge
The Pitt Building, Trumpington Street, Cambridge CB2 1RP
32 East 57th Street, New York, NY 10022, USA
296 Beaconsfield Parade, Middle Park, Melbourne 3206, Australia

© Cambridge University Press 1982

First published 1982

Printed in the United States of America

Library of Congress Cataloging in Publication Data
Zagorin, Perez.
Rebels and rulers, 1500–1660.
Includes bibliographical references and
indexes.
Contents: v. 1. Society, states, and early
modern revolution – v. 2. Provincial
rebellion.
1. Revolutions – Europe – History – 16th century.   2. Revolutions – Europe – History – 17th
century.   3. Europe – History – 1492–1648.
4. Europe – History – 17th century.   I. Title.
D210.Z33   1982   940.2   81–17039
ISBN 0 521 24472 2 (vol. 1) hard covers   AACR2
ISBN 0 521 28711 1 (vol. 1) paperback

Contents

Contents

Volume II
PROVINCIAL REBELLION
REVOLUTIONARY CIVIL WARS, 1560–1660

Preface

If of the making of books on revolution there appears to be no end, this is because the subject of revolution continues to possess a compelling significance for contemporary historiography and other disciplines.

The present book is the product of a combined interest in the general and historical problem of revolution and in the society and civilization of early modern Europe. It has grown naturally out of my previous work devoted principally to the history of early modern England and to the English revolution of 1640–60. Its purpose is twofold: first, to add to the comprehension of revolution by means of a comparative treatment of the revolutions of the sixteenth and earlier seventeenth centuries in their appropriate context; second, to throw further light on the society that produced these revolutions and thus determined their character and limits.

In pursuing these ends, I have also sought to aid understanding by pointing out some of the misconceptions frequently found in discussions of revolution. A part of the reason for these misconceptions is explained in the first chapter. That one of their main sources is Marxism, however, has made it necessary for me to criticize in various places both the Marxist theory and Marxist interpreters of revolution. In my judgment, everything valuable and true in the thought of Marx himself has by now been fully assimilated into history and the other social sciences as their common property and resource. What still survives as "Marxism," therefore, is in the East a petrified philosophy maintained as official dogma by authoritarian regimes and in the West an intellectual pastime for professors and commentators ranged into rival doctrinal schools.

Although I have cited many texts in the following inquiry, the latter, owing to its scope, can hardly be based primarily on original documentary evidence. Rather, it must depend to a considerable extent on the writings relating to its subject by many previous scholars, older and more recent. During the past generation or so, however, an increasing number of historians have focused attention upon the revolutions of early modern Europe. At the same time, a wealth of research and numerous works of synthesis have greatly extended and deepened our knowledge of broad aspects of this period. This is an achievement in which American, British, French, and other continental historians have shared. I have made use of many of their contributions, which have helped to stimulate and direct my thinking and in other ways facilitated my task. Naturally, I am aware of the dangers I have run in traversing diverse areas in which I am not myself a specialist. Notwithstanding, I have deemed it worthwhile to accept them, in view of the intrinsic importance and interest of the themes embraced in this book.

Of the work's two volumes, the first contains general theoretical, methodological, and typological reflections, a conspectus of the revolutions of the time in the states to which the study is devoted, and an examination of their essential contexts, followed by a discussion of peasant and urban rebellion. The second volume deals with provincial rebellion and then with revolutionary civil war, which, as the most consequential type of revolution to occur in the sixteenth and seventeenth centuries, receives the most extended treatment.

One of an author's chief pleasures is to express his gratitude for the assistance that has made his work possible. The Institute for Advanced Study at Princeton, by granting me its membership and an enjoyable year's stay, permitted me to begin the research for this book. A part of my support at the institute was contributed by the National Endowment for the Humanities under Grant H5426. In 1975–6, while visiting as Clark Memorial Library Professor at the University of California at Los Angeles, I was able to make further progress. A fellowship at the National Humanities Center provided the opportunity to advance the work toward conclusion. My warm thanks are due all these distinguished institutions for their help. I am also grateful to the administration of The University of Rochester for its cooperation and to the various libraries and their staffs whose collections I have used. Once again I am much indebted to Mrs. Claire Sundeen for her invaluable secretarial service in the preparation of my manuscript.

My deepest obligation is to my wife, Honore Sharrer, and this book is dedicated to our son.

PART I

Introduction

I

The concept of revolution and the comparative
history of revolution in early modern Europe

I

There are at least two reasons that might be cited for undertaking the
historical and comparative investigation of revolution. The first is the desire to make a revolution, the second is the desire to prevent it. Perhaps
nearly everybody is susceptible to the one reason or the other, but there
is yet a third reason that gives the study of revolution a compelling interest
and significance, even though its appeal is doubtless much more limited.
This is that the understanding of revolution is an indispensable condition
for the fuller knowledge and understanding of society. Depending on how
we define it, revolution may be common or uncommon, frequent or rare.
But in the case of societies, nations, and communities that have experienced revolution, we cannot claim to understand them adequately without
understanding their revolutions. In a deep and therefore a nontautological
sense, it is true that every people gets the revolution it deserves and equally
true that it gets only the revolutions of which it is capable.

Well over a century ago, Alexis de Tocqueville, one of the best minds
that ever devoted itself to the problem of revolution, stated the rationale
for the comparative history of revolutions. "Whoever studies and looks
only at France," he declared, "will never understand anything, I venture
to say, of the French revolution."[1] Tocqueville's precept, however, has
been honored far more in the breach than in the observance. Despite the
general recognition of the need for systematic comparative treatment of
revolution, work toward this end has remained the exception and relatively undeveloped. The most obvious explanation for this lack is the formidable difficulty of any comparative investigation and the risk of superficiality it entails. Thus it is understandable that historians in particular,

---

This chapter is a revised version of an earlier paper, "Prolegomena to the comparative history
of revolution in early modern Europe," *Comparative studies in society and history 18*, 2 (1976).

[1] Cited in A. Gérard, *La Révolution française, mythes et interprétations (1789–1790)*, Paris,
1970, 111.

with their keen awareness of the inexhaustible richness of events, have mostly preferred to concentrate on the close examination of individual revolutions rather than spread themselves thin in the attempt to encompass the phenomenon of revolution in wider comparative terms. To this consideration, however, the most appropriate reply is that, regardless of the danger of superficiality, as well as egregious error, the risk of comparative treatment should nonetheless be accepted in the hope that the result may contribute somewhat to the better comprehension of a subject of fundamental importance.

Apart from the inherent difficulty of any comparative investigation of revolution, there is at the outset another, almost equally considerable obstacle to such a study in the utter confusion surrounding the idea of revolution itself. Clearly no comparative historical account of revolution is possible even in a limited context without a prior theoretical determination as to what is to be understood by revolution; yet on this essential question one finds a striking absence of clarity, consistency, and agreement. There is first of all the sheer luxuriance of terminology: revolt, rebellion, insurrection, rising, internal war, civil war, sedition, coup – are these to be considered synonymous with revolution or distinct from it? Second, there is the sheer variety of developments to which the word *revolution* is applied: the industrial, commercial, scientific, and educational revolutions; the neolithic, urban, agricultural, and population revolutions; the intellectual, managerial, military, and computer revolutions; the revolution of cubism, of rising expectations, of modernization; the sexual revolution – what have these in common, and how, amid such diversity, is the field of revolution to be delimited?

Perhaps it may be supposed that the prevailing incoherence results mainly from uncertainties of a theoretical character or from incomplete knowledge, but to think so would be an error. It is primarily due, rather, to the vast symbolic significance and exploitative potentialities that the idea of revolution has come to possess in the modern world.

Revolution may well be the most powerful myth of our time, as it is certainly the most pervasive. Instead of serving merely as the name or description of a certain class of events, it is a symbol of identification and demand, a declaration of normative preference, a vague composite of images and sentiments suitable to manipulation for various purposes, a fashion, and even an opiate. (Like religion, revolution too may be the "opium of the people.") Already in the French revolution, which first launched both the word and idea on their modern course, *revolution* became something to conjure with, a creed, a faith, a mystique.[2] It seized the mind of

[2] For a historical account of the idea and terminology of revolution with references to the literature, see Perez Zagorin, *The court and the country*, London, 1969, ch. 1; M. Lasky, *Utopia and revolution*, Chicago, 1976, esp. chs. 5–6 (a work replete with fascinating citations and

many like a religion, loomed gigantically in Europe as a threat or promise, and rose in the sky as the sign announcing a new humanity and a new world. This was recognized at the time by the great conservative thinker, Edmund Burke, who pointed out that the French revolution was not like any previous political change in Europe. He could compare it only with the Protestant Reformation. "It is a revolution," he said, "of *doctrine* and *theoretic dogma*. It has a much greater resemblance to those changes which have been made upon religious grounds, in which a spirit of proselytism makes an essential part," and its principle is such as "by its essence could not be local, or confined to the country in which it had its origin."[3]

Descending the decades of the long nineteenth century in Europe, with its frequent revolutionary outbreaks, the idea of revolution retained its grandeur. It spread to Spanish America, to Russia, and eventually to Turkey, Asia, and Africa. It stood as the supreme theme in the incalculably influential teaching of Marx, which aimed not merely to interpret the world but to change it. Innumerable groups arose consisting of men and women professionally dedicated to making revolution. Revolution became the myth of bourgeois nationalists, terrorist secret societies, communist sects, social-democratic parties, and anarchist movements alike. The victory of Lenin and the Bolsheviks in 1917 gave it a new access of strength and transformed it into a worldwide force radiating from Moscow. In 1930 an American communist writer proclaimed ecstatically in what must be regarded as a representative expression: "O workers' Revolution, you brought hope to me . . . You are the true Messiah . . . O Revolution that forced me to think, to struggle, and to live. O great Beginning!"[4] The legacy of 1789, of the nineteenth century, and of 1917 caused revolution to be seen as the redemptive act destined to liberate oppressed nations, classes, and all mankind.

Along with this glorification, though, this divinization of revolution, the term also proved to be infinitely expansible, a concept to be invoked by scholars and popularizers for any number of different purposes. Wherever it was sought to convey the impression of overwhelming progressive change or to place an approved stamp of novelty on something, *revolution* was seized upon as the most suitable description. When Arnold Toynbee in 1884 coined the phrase "The Industrial Revolution" for the title of his famous book, he had a serious scientific end in view and intended to designate changes that he regarded as a "single great historical event." Inevitably, however, the more widely *revolution* was appropriated, the more it

interesting suggestions); and F. Gilbert, "Revolution," *Dictionary of the history of ideas*, ed. P. Wiener, 4 v., New York, 1973.
[3] Edmund Burke, *Thoughts on French affairs* (1791), in *Works*, rev. ed., 12 v., Boston, 1867, v. 4, 318–19.
[4] Michael Gold, *Jews without money*, New York, 1945, 309.

lost any precise meaning. Moreover, it was too rich in possibilities not to be adopted for exploitation by entrepreneurs and salesmen of every sort. Thus, by a process the reverse of that in which it symbolized something grandiose and total, the term *revolution* also became vulgarized, trivialized, and debased. It could be used in reference to a new product, a new reducing diet, a dress style, or a piece of music – anything at all that one wished to present as modern and advanced.

Already before World War I, Karl Kautsky, the German social-democratic leader and theorist, had recognized that "socialism is accepted in the *salons*, there is no longer need of any particular energy, it is no longer necessary to break with bourgeois society, in order to bear the name of 'socialist.' "[5] By the 1920s, a similar fate had overtaken revolution. In 1926, the English writer Wyndham Lewis commented satirically upon the current modishness and respectability of revolution, "official revolution," he called it, which in intellectual and polite society had become as obligatory as evening dress. "Everyone who has money enough is today a 'revolutionary.' " By a paradox, he pointed out, only by being nonrevolutionary does one become an outsider.[6]

Since then, the degeneration and confusion in the idea of revolution have proceeded so far that today it has become unavoidable to speak of the banality of revolution. The last years have witnessed this condition at its most rampant in the prevalence of revolution as a fashion in the West adopted by a motley assembly of movements and individuals for diversion or profit. As a result, to hear anything described as revolutionary is a nearly certain sign that one is being offered a counterfeit. This state of affairs has been most incisively depicted by Jacques Ellul. Taken up in the consumer society, as he has noted, revolution exacts no price; it is a "popsicle," chewing gum to while away the time. Everyone makes revolution, from artist to businessman. It is merely an aspect of one's "life style," the product of boredom.[7] The observation of Tocqueville concerning Lamartine and 1848 in France – "se sont faits révolutionnaires pour se désennuyer" – has a far wider bearing at the present time than when he wrote.[8]

[5] K. Kautsky, *The social revolution*, 1902, cited by Wyndham Lewis, "The art of being ruled," in *Wyndham Lewis: an anthology of his prose*, ed. E. W. F. Tomlin, London, 1969, 103.

[6] W. Lewis, *The art of being ruled*, 1926, in Tomlin, 101–3. See the whole section, "The oppressive respectability of 'revolution.' " In Lewis's long war with intellectual orthodoxies, this was a regular theme (although it sometimes led him into dangerous and perverse opinions, like his flirtation with fascist doctrines). In 1952 he wrote, "A XXth century *esprit libre* would be a man who had liberated himself from the dead hand of the new" (*The writer and the absolute*, London, 1952, 153).

[7] Jacques Ellul, *Autopsy of revolution*, New York, 1971, ch. 4.

[8] The quotation comes, I believe, from A. de Tocqueville, *Souvenirs, Oeuvres complètes*, v. 12, but I regret that I have lost the reference.

The reigning confusion is strikingly visible as well in the political realm. When revolution began in France in 1789, it was partly inspired by the recent American war for independence, which caused the French to view the birth of the American republic as a new epoch of liberty. French revolutionaries of every stripe naturally conceived themselves, too, as the champions of liberty against despotism and vindicators of the imprescriptible rights of man. Thus the idea of revolution that spread from France over Europe seemed indissolubly linked with liberty – this indeed was a central feature in the revolutionary myth transmitted during the nineteenth century. But if the nineteenth century did not succeed in doing so, the experience of the twentieth has made the relation between liberty and revolution entirely problematic. Fascist movements such as national socialism willingly described themselves as revolutionary, and the revolution that carried Hitler to power in Germany led to the imposition of a brutal dictatorship, to genocide, and almost to the destruction of Europe's independence and freedom. Similarly, in Russia, in China, and elsewhere, despotic new states have emerged from communist and "people's war" revolutions whose rulers claim the revolutionary myth exclusively for themselves in order to build and extend their tyrannical dominion. All this not only has discredited the assumption that revolution and liberty go together but has subverted the once widely held belief that revolution is necessarily synonymous with progressive advance.

II

If the phenomenon of revolution is to be susceptible to historical-theoretical consideration, its definition and boundaries must be removed from the incoherence that besets them and given reasonable fixity and delimitation appropriate to their object. For this the first and main prerequisite is a break with the "spontaneous philosophy of the social world" that leads to the uncritical acceptance of "preconstructed objects" implicit in the usage spontaneously proposed by society itself. Historical agents, like people in their everyday lives, form diverse representations of things and relations, but the student cannot be content with these, lest he be induced to perceive reality merely as it "demands" to be. Precisely because revolution exists in the common vocabulary as the reflection of multiple and inconsistent conceptions and expectations, it is necessary to go beyond the latter in order to think about the phenomenon adequately. As a leading French sociologist has acutely remarked, if the inquirer submits to the given as such, negating himself "by refusing consciously to build his own distance from reality and the conditions for an adequate knowledge of it, he condemns himself to ascertain preconstructed facts which are imposed on him because he is not provided with the means of knowing the rules of their construction."[9]

Pursuant to this methodological dictate, a scientific approach to revolution would cut through the mythological disguises that enfold it (and whose origin or "rules of construction" the history of the idea and terminology of revolution serves to make clear) in order to reduce it to its proper signification. Let us note some of the more common errors deriving from this mythology, which exercises its spell as strongly on the learned as on the layman. One is the charismatic view of revolution, which restricts its meaning to something total, grand, and monumental. This results in the exclusion of various kinds of revolutionary occurrences from the field of revolution because they are held to lack the requisite amplitude, although the standard for determining the latter is purely arbitrary in accord with the predilections of the observer. It also leads to pointless debates, which are all too frequent, as to whether some particular event or change is "really" revolutionary, again depending on the varying predilections of the observer. The charismatic view is particularly reflected in Marxism, although by no means confined to it alone, and underlies numerous conceptions of revolution. Thus in a well-known formulation, Siegfried Neumann defined revolution as "a sweeping fundamental change in political organization, social structure, economic property control and the predominant myth of a social order [thereby] indicating a major break in the continuity of development." A similar description has been offered by S. P. Huntington: "A revolution is a rapid, fundamental and violent domestic change in the dominant values and myths of society, in its political institutions, social structure, leadership, government activity, and policies."[10] There would be nothing wrong with these statements if they were merely intended to designate a particular type of revolution that is historically the rarest, but as they stand they are unacceptable because they define out of existence those types of revolutionary events that do not conform to the totality demanded. It is merely a prejudice, however, that would limit the conception of revolution in this way.

Often connected with the charismatic view is an implicit tendency of an ideological character to introduce valuational beliefs into the conception of revolution so that only changes deemed progressive are considered revolutionary. In consequence, movements like national socialism may be excluded by some students from the comparative or theoretical analysis of revolution. Thus Barrington Moore in his well-known work, *The social*

---

[9] P. Bourdieu, "Structuralism and the theory of sociological knowledge," *Social research 35*, 4 (1968), 703, 697, 695. See also the theoretical-methodological observations in P. Bourdieu, J.-C. Chamboredon, and J.-C. Passeron, *Le Métier de sociologue*, 2nd ed., Paris, 1973.

[10] S. Neumann, "The international civil war," *World politics 1*, 3 (1949), 333n.; S. P. Huntington, *Political order in changing societies*, New Haven, 1968, 264.

origins of dictatorship and democracy (1966), treats Germany as a country in which revolution failed to occur (as would of course be true if one were referring to a socialist revolution) and is disabled by his progressive criterion from recognizing that the history of nazism belongs centrally to the phenomenon of revolution in the twentieth century. For analogous reasons, and in accord with their own self-serving ends, contemporary communist regimes denounce internal resistance to their rule as reactionary or counterrevolutionary, but despite such negative labeling, a violent attempt to dislodge or change these regimes would certainly, in any objective account, come within the domain of revolution.

A further pertinent instance is provided in the recent study of counterrevolution in modern Europe by Arno Mayer. Having acknowledged his adherence to the conviction that revolution means advance or progress, Mayer sharply distinguishes between it and counterrevolution, to which category he relegates fascism. Yet he notes that fascism "built controlled mass movements and terror units," gave dominance to a "distinct fascist political class," and imposed a new elite "in the sphere of politics and ideas." Moreover counterrevolution, he points out, "acquires a project and thrust that transcend the mere restoration of order and the *status quo ante.*" His analysis thus makes it apparent that in a *theoretical* context, revolution and counterrevolution may be structurally related or homologous.[11] And, in fact, the latter is a species of the former, its precise content varying by historical cases, so that any attempt to dissociate them can be based only on arbitrary normative grounds. It follows as a general methodological conclusion that revolution must if possible be constituted as a descriptive category free of ideological commitments and prepossessions if some of its essential features or phenomenal forms are not to be arbitrarily extruded.[12]

[11] Arno Mayer, *The dynamics of counter-revolution in Europe 1870–1956*, New York, 1971, 2, 22–3, 45. See also the discussion in ch. 3 on counterrevolution as a heuristic concept, in which the resemblance of counterrevolution to revolution is obvious. On the subject of nazism, Raymond Aron has described the arguments among Frenchmen in 1933 in Berlin, where he was then studying, as to whether Hitler's conquest of power was a revolution. How could such a noble term, some asked, be applied to events in Germany? In reply Aron inquires what more would be needed to qualify as a revolution than to have effected, as national socialism did, changes in ruling class, constitution, and ideology (*The opium of the intellectuals*, New York, 1962, 38). Ernst Nolte (*Three faces of fascism*, New York, 1966) also demonstrates in an extremely interesting way the the homology between fascism and revolutionary Marxism in spite of their radical opposition to one another.

[12] A contrary view is advanced by John Dunn, who declares, "there are necessarily ascriptive as well as descriptive components even in the very identification of a set of events constituting . . . a revolution," and "Revolution is an actor's concept, not a purely external, naturalistic identification." Hence he holds that "the value-free study of revolutions is a logical impossibility for those who live in the real world" (J. Dunn, *Modern revolutions*, Cambridge, 1972, ix, 226, 2). To this argument the best answer that can be given is that in the requisite sense the value-free study of revolution, although very difficult, is perhaps not altogether impossible and that every effort should be made to conduct the investigation on

9

Undoubtedly, the most frequent confusion arising from the mythology of revolution is the identification of the latter with any large-scale change as such. Thus for at least a hundred years, whenever historians or social scientists have wished to stress the significance of some particular change or development with which they have been concerned, they have usually denominated it as a revolution. In this way, an indefinite number of revolutions over the most varied fields have been invented, as the list of examples given earlier in this chapter illustrates.[13] It is noticeable, however, that these revolutions are seldom presented according to any precise criteria or even with any specific chronological limits. They may be gradual or incremental, they may last for decades or longer, they may even manifest themselves politically as peaceable reforms, yet the temptation to term such changes revolution has been irresistible. To cite a characteristic illustration, the reviewer of a recent history of the Meiji restoration of 1868 in Japan, which brought back the ancient monarchy to primacy and marked the inception of Japanese modernization, declared that "so great a transformation warranted the name of 'revolution.'" And indeed, this statement reflects a general tendency in Japanese historiography to consider the Meiji restoration and its sequel a revolution.[14] Hence Japanese modernization, even though it occurred more or less peacefully and under the auspices of a traditional, undisplaced governing class, was nevertheless a "revolution" because it was a transformation. One might well think, of course, that a fundamental problem to be explained in Japanese modernization is that it took place *without* a revolution. But to pose this question is necessarily to imply a different and more precise definition of revolution than mere large-scale change.

What is wrong with the conception of revolution as equivalent to major change or transformation is that it begs the question of when and under what conditions change becomes revolutionary. This constitutes one of the essential problems in the theoretical and comparative analysis of revolution.[15] But this problem cannot even be raised if revolution is taken to signify change as such, for then no logical basis is available for distinguishing revolution from its alternative, reform, or revolutionary from nonrevolutionary change. It is easy to see, however, why this confusion between revolution and change exists and what perpetuates it. The great prestige that the symbolism of revolution has acquired since the early

that basis. At any rate, there is no need for the student to consent to the self-conceptions and representations of the historical agents; for him the ideas of the agents are vital evidence, but they can never be the last word.

[13] See the preceding discussion in the present chapter.

[14] Review of W. G. Beasley, *The Meiji restoration*, Stanford, 1973, in *Times literary supplement*, Dec. 21, 1973, 1556.

[15] See T. R. Gurr, "The revolution–social change nexus: some old theories and new hypotheses," *Comparative politics* 5, 3 (1973).

nineteenth century has magnetized the imagination of historians, and the impulsion to appropriate this symbolism as metaphor has worked to powerful effect. Accordingly, to describe something as a revolution is to bestow upon it the ultimate benediction of importance. The word serves, so to speak, as a coronation that anoints the process to which it is applied with the charismatic properties of the revolutionary event. This accounts for the proliferation and variety of revolutions to be found in the textbooks and popular sociology, and although it would be a substantial contribution to clarity if scholars ceased gratuitously multiplying revolutions and reserved the conception for a clearly defined, reasonably well-marked class of events, there is little ground to expect that they will do so.

As far as the mythology of revolution is concerned, no thinker or school of thought has added as much to its substance as Marx and the Marxists. To speak of Marx as a myth maker is in no way to deny the value of the theory-rich contribution that he made in the course of his life to historical and sociological understanding. But Marx's formation took place during the 1830s and 1840s in an intellectual environment permeated by what Professor Talmon has called the "religion of revolution," of which the vital common denominator was "the expectation of and preparation for some inevitable, preordained, total change in the social order."[16] And, in Marx's mature thought, the result of a complex integration and transmogrification of Hegelianism, socialism, and political economy, revolution is envisaged as the driving force or "locomotive" of history and becomes a systematic principle of historical interpretation.[17] Moreover, Marx conceives the whole progressive movement of mankind *sub specie revolutionis* – a movement destined to realize itself by means of the proletariat in an eschatological breakthrough to a new human reality free of social antagonisms.[18]

In implanting the conception of revolution with his own philosophical and ideological leitmotifs, Marx was responsible for further confusions and, paradoxically, even for a reductionist theoretical formulation of the nature of revolution. For if Marx saw revolutions as grandiose movements

---

[16] J. L. Talmon, *Political messianism: The romantic phase*, London, 1960, 17–18. This work and its predecessor (*The origins of totalitarian democracy*, London, 1952) are indispensable to the understanding of the modern idea of revolution. See also the interesting remarks and citations in T. Schieder, "Das Problem der Revolution im 19. Jahrhundert," *Historische Zeitschrift 170*, 2 (1950); and R. Koselleck, "Die neuzeitliche Revolutionsbegriff als geschichtliche Kategorie," *Studium generale 22*, 8 (1969).

[17] K. Marx, *The class struggles in France 1848–50*, in *Selected works*, ed. V. Adoratsky, 2 v., New York, n.d. v. 2, 283. In *The German ideology*, written 1845–6, Marx and Engels characteristically declared that "revolution is the driving force of history" (Eng. trans., New York, 1939, 29).

[18] I take the description of Marx's world perspective as an "eschatology" from the sympathetic and well-informed study by S. Avineri (*The social and political thought of Karl Marx*, Cambridge, 1969, 250 ff.). For the same view, see also L. Kolakowski, *Main currents of Marxism*, 3 v., Oxford, 1978, v. 1, 309–10, ch. 16. This masterly work is now the best treatment of Marxist thought, both historically and philosophically.

and epochal turning points, as a phenomenon he nevertheless identified them exclusively with the class struggle and the class transfer of state power. Furthermore, in the interest of the materialist conception of history that he developed, he could derive revolution causally only from deep preceding social contradictions between the productive forces and the relations of production. It was these contradictions, according to him, that generated irreconcilable classes and class differences. Thus, for Marx, although revolution must finally express itself as a political act, it is in essence and of necessity social. Revolution is therefore understood in the Marxist perspective purely as social revolution, where *social*, moreover, has the exclusive and restricted meaning of class and class conflict. This meaning is of course also introduced into the Marxian definition of revolution as an implicit causal explanation.[19]

In 1848, in their *Communist manifesto*, Marx and Engels presented their most famous exposition of this view, in which they described the "more or less veiled civil war" of classes raging within society that then "breaks out into open revolution."[20] Nearly a century and a quarter afterward, the following exchange occurred between two of Marx's latter-day disciples, the late president of Chile, Salvador Allende, and Régis Debray, a French Marxist philosopher. To the question, What is revolution? both returned the well-worn conventional answer. Allende: "It is the transfer of power from a minority to a majority class." Debray: "It is the transfer of power from one class to another. Revolution is the destruction of the machinery of the bourgeois state and the replacement of it by another."[21] The same formula appears in a recent discussion of theories of revolution by a British Marxist who defines revolution as "a change in which decisive political and economic power passes from the hands of a declining ruling class which has outlived its day, into the hands of a new advancing class."[22] But this, of course, merely repeats the orthodox doctrine previously affirmed by Marx's great follower, Lenin, and by Lenin's great follower,

---

[19] See Marx's well-known statement of the materialist conception of history in the preface to *A contribution to the critique of political economy*, trans. from 2nd German ed., Chicago, 1904. The first edition appeared in 1859; the second, published by Kautsky, in 1897.

[20] Marx, *Selected works*, v. 1, 217.

[21] R. Debray, *The Chilean revolution: conversations with Allende*, New York, 1971, 116, 81. The principal theme of these conversations is whether Chile can achieve a peaceful transition to socialism. Debray's attitude is noticeably sceptical and appears to have been justified by the subsequent overthrow of Allende's government in a military coup and the tragic death of the president himself. A curious aspect of the discussion is Debray's intellectual condescension toward Allende.

[22] J. Woddis, *New theories of revolution*, New York, 1972. This work is a defense of the revolutionary record of the Communist parties and a critique of the ideas of Frantz Fanon, Régis Debray, and Herbert Marcuse. One of its main arguments is that these theorists either underestimate or have lost faith altogether in the leading role of the working class within the revolutionary process. The debate deals with the strategy and main forces in contemporary and future revolutions, not with the nature of revolution itself.

Mao Tse-tung. Thus in 1917 Lenin wrote, "The passing of state power from one class to another is the first, the main, the basic principle of a revolution, both in the strictly scientific and in the practical political meaning of that term."[23] Mao in his turn, denouncing revisionism, similarly declared in 1960: "Revolution means the use of revolutionary violence by the oppressed class. This is true of slave revolution; this is also true of the bourgeois revolution."[24] Such statements illustrate the persisting core of the Marxist tradition from before 1848 to the present, in which revolution is understood entirely as a class-determined phenomenon.

Although this conception has had exceedingly great consequences in the deeds that compose the history of the modern world and its revolutions, it has also been the cause of serious error and misunderstanding. Nowhere, in fact, is the fusion between the theory and mythology of revolution and the influence exerted by the one upon the other more apparent.

The Marxian view reductively subsumes all revolution under the single category of class struggle. Because it narrows the conception of revolution solely to social revolution in this class sense, its explanatory strategy has no choice but to force the universe of revolutionary occurrences into the same mold. Besides the inevitable distortions that result even in the treatment of revolutions where class conflict may predominate, it cannot account for revolutions that present a different origin or character. There have been many of these in the past and our own time, including some of great magnitude in the early modern era, like the English revolution of 1640. Referring to the problem suggested by the latter, Peter Laslett has asked "whether the word Revolution can justifiably be used of seventeenth-century England if anything of Social Revolution is intended." Between the sixteenth and eighteenth centuries, he points out, economic and social change was relatively slow and gradual and contained nothing that "would have led of itself to political crisis." Hence he denies that class struggle is the necessary cause of revolutions and also contends that " 'revolution' as meaning a resolution of unendurable social conflict by reshaping society as a whole" was "impossible in preindustrial times."[25] We need not accept this judgment in its entirety to recognize its pertinence and validity as a criticism of the Marxist position. The conclusion to be drawn, however, is not that there were no revolutions in preindustrial society but that Marx's theory of revolution is quite inadequate to deal with them on its own terms.

Needless to say, I am not here attempting to deny the importance of

[23] V. I. Lenin, *Letters on tactics*, in *Collected works*, v. 20, *The revolution of 1917*, New York, 1929, 119.
[24] Mao Tse-tung, "Long live Leninism," *Peking review* (April 1960), reprinted in *Essential works of Marxism*, ed. A. Mendel, New York, 1965, 545.
[25] P. Laslett, *The world we have lost*, 2nd ed., New York, 1971, 159–60, 167, 171.

class, which in some cases may be great. Rather, I wish to deny the assumption of its universality as a necessary explanatory principle in the theoretical and historical treatment of revolution, together with the further assumption that class and the social are identical; the latter can also refer to other human formations and collectivities that may be much more relevant in the understanding of certain revolutions, like those of early modern Europe to be considered in this book.

Marx's belief in the centrality of class originated partly in his interpretation of the French revolution, which he considered to be in essence a colossal conflict between feudal and bourgeois society. In forming this judgment, he was variously influenced – by Hegel, by the Saint-Simonians, and by post-1815 historians such as Mignet, Guizot, and Thierry, who had stressed class struggle in their writings.[26] As a result, the French revolution – the greatest so far to occur in Europe and the one with the strongest thrust toward universality in its principles and influence – acquired an exemplary or classical status in Marxist thought. It was elevated to the position of an ideal type or model of revolution and the revolutionary process, even though Marx also held that, owing to its bourgeois character, the French revolution merely enthroned a new class in place of the old and was destined to be surpassed by a future proletarian revolution that would end all class domination. Later, following the Paris Commune of 1871, certain of the latter's features became exemplary as well both for Marx and then for Lenin.[27] Nevertheless, the decisive role in Marx's general theory of revolution of his historical interpretation and image of the French revolution is obvious and has had lasting effects. Engels acknowledged this fact when he wrote of himself and Marx that

as far as our conception of the conditions and course of revolutionary movements was concerned, [we] were under the spell of previous historical experience, namely that of France. It was, indeed, the latter which had dominated the whole of European history since 1789 . . . It was therefore natural and unavoidable that our conceptions of the nature and the paths of the "social" revolution were strongly coloured by memories of the models of 1789–1830.[28]

[26] See Marx's letters to Wedemeyer and Engels referring to the importance of the French bourgeois historians in discovering the significance of class. He describes Thierry as the "father of the 'class struggle' in French historical writing" (K. Marx and F. Engels, *Selected correspondence*, New York, 1942, 56, 71). On the influence of these historians, as well as of Hegel and the Saint-Simonians, in the conception of the contrast between feudal and bourgeois society and the transition from the one to the other, see O. Brunner, "Feudalismus: Ein Beitrag zur Begriffsgeschichte," in *Neue Wege der Verfassungs – und Sozialgeschichte*, 2nd rev. ed., Göttingen, 1968.

[27] K. Marx, *The civil war in France*, in *Selected works*, v. 2. For Lenin's invocation of the lessons of the Commune, see especially *State and revolution*, 1917.

[28] See Engels, "Introduction," written in 1895, to Marx's *The class struggles in France 1848–50*, in *Selected works*, v. 2, 173–4.

Elsewhere he declared in the same vein:

France is the land where, more than anywhere else, the historical class struggles were each time fought out to a decision, where, consequently, the changing political forms within which they occur and in which their results are summarized have likewise been stamped with the sharpest outlines. The centre of feudalism in the Middle Ages, the model country of centralized monarchy . . . since the Renaissance, France demolished feudalism in the Great Revolution and established the unalloyed rule of the bourgeoisie in a classical purity unequalled by any other European land.[29]

The canonical importance accorded the French revolution as forerunner and model was equally present among the Bolsheviks. *Jacobinism* was a synonym for the centralism of the revolutionary party demanded by Lenin before and after 1905.[30] After 1917, the Bolsheviks had the image and lessons of the French revolution continually in mind. As one historian of the latter has written, there was a "permanent telescoping of the two revolutions in the consciousness of the Russian revolutionaries."[31] This is well seen in Trotsky, who referred repeatedly to France in his *History of the Russian revolution*. It was also natural that Trotsky under the sway of the French revolution should have equated Stalin's ascendancy with Thermidor, the symbol of Robespierre's overthrow and of the betrayal of the revolution.[32]

Despite the theoretical significance that he attributed to the French revolution, however, Marx never offered any adequate critical justification for regarding it as the exemplary case or model. Nevertheless, the conclusions he drew from it became a part of the mythology of revolution. Marxists found in the French revolution a pattern applicable to the analysis of revolution in general. In its substance and stages as a class struggle it was thought to provide a morphological structure under which the explanation of other revolutions could, *mutatis mutandis*, be subsumed. Of course, Marxists have not been alone in adopting this procedure. The ideal-typical character ascribed directly or by implication to the French revolution, however differently the latter may be interpreted, has been a noticeable feature of a great deal of thinking about revolution.[33] Marxism has merely

[29] See Engels, "Preface" to the 3rd German ed., 1883, of Marx's *The eighteenth Brumaire of Louis Bonaparte*, in *Selected works*, v. 2, 314.
[30] See Gérard, 80–1.
[31] F. Furet, "Le Catechisme de la Révolution française," *Annales E. S. C.*, *26*, 2 (1971), 259.
[32] See Gérard, 84. Isaac Deutscher, Trotsky's biographer and a Marxist historian of Trotskyist persuasion, has contended that every step in the history of the Russian revolution must be seen "through the French prism" (cited in Gérard, 84).
[33] A well-known example is Crane Brinton's comparative study of the English, American, French, and Russian revolutions (*The anatomy of revolution*, New York, 1938). The uniformities Brinton finds among these four revolutions strike me as largely extrapolations from the French case, without which it is most unlikely that he would have arrived at them. He explicitly refers to the French revolution as "a kind of pattern revolution" (ed. 1957, 3).

shared this assumption, albeit perhaps deriving the widest theoretical inferences from it. That such a view requires justification, however, or that the French revolution with all its importance may not be *the* paradigmatic form of revolution to which other cases either approximate or from which they deviate, has hardly ever been seriously considered.

In Marx's theory of revolution, there appears an intricate mixture of the factual-theoretical and the normative-ideological. To say that his thought was ever free of wish-fulfilling projections or ideological motives and prejudices would be wrong. All the same, full acknowledgment must be given to his claim that, in contrast to the ahistorical abstractions of German idealist philosophy, he based his own conceptions on the "real ground of history" and "actual social relations."[34] Furthermore, even if he regarded the French revolution as the classic and exemplary case, he nonetheless established his judgment of it by study of the historical materials such as were then available. In these respects, although his purpose was not only to understand revolution but to prepare men to make it, Marx may be said to have met the empirical requirements demanded of the theorist and historian.

What in Marx's thought originally possessed the living force of a great intellectual achievement, however, has long since tended to harden into a sterile orthodoxy. Like the materialist conception of history with which it is associated, his theory of revolution has itself been converted through his influence and by many of his followers into an extrahistorical abstraction and metaphysical philosophy of history. Instead of being taken as a hypothesis subject to testing, correction, and disproof, it has been made, mainly for political purposes, into an a priori presupposition through which the entire problem of revolution is approached and resolved. As one philosopher has rightly commented, the Marxian doctrine is frequently advanced "as a necessary truth which no future experience could possibly confute."[35] In applying it to specific examples of revolution, Marxist historical scholarship has too often had to impose a mutilating pressure on the facts and in the face of recalcitrant evidence to resort to excessively ingenious methods of interpretation, which cause its procedure to resemble the addition of epicycles to the Ptolemaic hypothesis in order to "save the phenomena." Insofar as it remains consistent with its own premises, however, the Marxist theory of revolution cannot overcome the reductionism inherent in its monocausal class explanation. For these reasons and in this sense, Marx's conception belongs under the guise of science to the modern mythology of revolution in which it is perhaps the most powerful ingredient.

[34] See *The German ideology*, 28, 29.
[35] W. H. Walsh, *An introduction to philosophy of history*, 3rd ed., London, 1967, 28.

III

A divine right of names does not exist, and definitions of phenomena are to be judged entirely by their clarity, utility, and convenience. For the comparative study of revolution we need a definition that will serve to distinguish revolutionary from other kinds of events, that will be sufficiently inclusive of these events whatever their type, scope, or historical period, and that contains no evaluative preferences or built-in causal theory. I therefore propose to use the following:

A revolution is any attempt by subordinate groups through the use of violence to bring about (1) a change of government or its policy, (2) a change of regime, or (3) a change of society, whether this attempt is justified by reference to past conditions or to an as yet unattained future ideal.

In this definition, government refers to personnel, such as monarchs and ministers; regime, to the basic form and institutions of government; society, to social structure and stratification, system of property control, and dominant values.[36]

Some comments on the corollaries and implications of this definition in relation to the purposes of a comparative historical study are desirable.

Far more revolutions have failed than succeeded, and, even when revolutionaries have gained power, they have rarely retained it for long or built durable regimes. Most of these cases have happened in this century, whereas the Netherlands revolt against Spain is an instance from the sixteenth century. Hence it is preferable for comparative purposes to base the concept of revolution on the occurrence of rebellion rather than exclusively on the nature of its outcome.

In connection with this problem, a recent analyst maintains that one of the essential aspects of revolution is a change of government, that is, a transitionary event at a specific moment of time. Without the latter, he believes, "no certain identification can be made of an earlier period of disaffection as . . . 'revolutionary.' "[37] This view, however, is only partially applicable at best. Some of the biggest early modern revolutions present a diffuse and episodic character as civil wars lasting many years. In these there may be no specific event of transition but instead the gradual assumption of governmental functions by rebels and the formation in stages of a de facto dual power. Other cases, like the English Pilgrimage of Grace in 1536, take the form of rebellion on a considerable scale, which

---

[36] Various definitions of revolutions are available, but there is no need to review them here. Many seem to me to be too exclusive, although I am aware that critics may accuse the one given above of being too broad. I have based it on the conception adopted by Chalmers Johnson (*Revolution and the social system*, Stanford, 1964; and *Revolutionary change*, Boston, 1966) and on suggestions in a private communication from Ted R. Gurr.

[37] P. Calvert, *A study of revolution*, Oxford, 1970, 4–5.

is then repressed after a few weeks or months. But in these instances, as elsewhere, the resort to organized forcible resistance to authority, irrespective of whether a change of government ensues, is evidence that we are in the presence of a revolution of some kind that may be pertinent to comparative study.

Violence as a means is a defining characteristic of revolution that distinguishes it from nonrevolutionary attempts at change.[38] To speak of nonviolent revolution is, as Chalmers Johnson has pointed out, a contradiction in terms.[39] To be sure, the notion of violence is hard to define precisely. According to Johnson, it is any action running counter to stable expectations "that deliberately or unintentionally disorients the behavior of others."[40] This seems too broad. The central element in violence is force and coercion, including imminent threat. If these are lacking, violence cannot be said to exist.

With violence in this fundamental sense, however, we can also associate what may be called "symbolic violence" – blasphemies in gesture, speech, and writing that, in deliberate transgression and reversal of prevailing social norms, are intended to destroy the sanctity or prestige of ruling persons and institutions and to proclaim the equality or superiority of subjects, the inferior, or the oppressed. Hegel declared that "once the realm of the imagination has been revolutionized, reality can no longer hold out."[41] Symbolic violence in this sense is a common feature of revolutions. The Paris crowd's contemptuous treatment of Henri III in 1588, which forced him to leave his capital, and the trial of Charles I by a court of his own subjects in 1649 are examples of symbolic violence. In the great wave of iconoclastic riots that broke out across the Netherlands in the summer of 1566, despite the actual physical attack on churches, the symbolic aspect was uppermost and formed the threshold to rebellion. Another notable instance is the behavior of Wat Tyler, the rebel leader, in his meeting with Richard II at Smithfield during the English agrarian revolt of 1381. According to the indignant monastic chronicler, Tyler took Richard's hand and shook his arm, called him "brother," and rinsed his mouth before the king "in a rude and villainous manner." Then, after sending for a jug of ale and drinking down a great draught, he mounted his horse in the royal presence.[42] Episodes like these, tending to corrode authority, show that

---

[38] Violence may sometimes also be an element in reform. This is stressed by A. O. Hirschman, who observes that violence "has in part the function of signalling protest to the central authorities," and that "an improvement in the signalling mechanism serves to increase pressure as much as an intensification of the problem" (*Journeys toward progress*, New York, 1965, 334, 335). As a means of reform, however, violence is likely to be quite limited, and its purpose is to secure the cooperation and compliance of elites and to accelerate the adaptive processes of the political system.

[39] Johnson, *Revolutionary change*, 7.   [40] *Ibid.*, 8.   [41] Cited in Avineri, 138n.

[42] See the contemporary texts in R. B. Dobson (ed.), *The peasants' revolt of 1381*, London, 1970, 164–5, 172.

symbolic violence can perform the disorienting function to which Johnson refers: In the words of a slogan posted in Paris during the student protest of May 1968, "L'insolence est une nouvelle arme révolutionnaire." In revolutions, however, violence is always coupled in some way with the reality or imminent threat of force and compulsion.

The aims and goals of revolution vary widely and affect its magnitude and scope. In the conception of revolution given here, these goals are specified in ascending order, with a change of government or its policy as the lowest and most limited and a change of society as the biggest. Each goal of larger magnitude will as a rule also encompass the lesser ones. Thus, a change of regime is likely to necessitate a change of government, and a change of society a change of government and regime. The different types of revolution may also bear a relation to the goals sought. A coup d'état, for instance, most commonly aims at a change in the personnel or policy of government, occasionally at a change of regime, and only rarely at a change of society.

In attempting to delimit the field of revolution, the question arises as to the latter's relation to riots as a lesser manifestation of collective violence, especially because historians of early modern revolutions occasionally confound the two. In his valuable study of the revolution of 1647 in Naples, Rosario Villari describes an earlier outbreak in 1585 in which the populace, provoked by a rise in the price of bread, lynched Giovanni Vincenzo Starace, a wealthy merchant and speculator.[43] In treating this incident as a revolt, as well as in the political significance he ascribes to it within the prehistory of the events of 1647, Villari greatly exaggerates its importance; in reality, it seems to have been merely a riot of a type that was exceedingly common in preindustrial Europe and that all urban authorities had to anticipate as a possibility in times of scarcity unless they took measures to expand grain supply or reduce prices.[44] Similarly, Professor Porchnev's account of popular insurrections in France in the first part of the seventeenth century also confuses riot with rebellion in some cases.[45] A French historian has used the term *microrevolt* for the small disturbances that were frequent in various regions of France at this period and were sometimes the forerunner to rebellion as well.[46] The Normandy rebellion of the Nu-pieds in 1639, for example, was preceded by riots against tax

[43] R. Villari, *La rivolta antispagnola a Napoli: le origini (1585–1647)*, 2nd ed., Bari, 1973, 33–58.

[44] In his famous novel, *I promessi sposi*, A. Manzoni gives a masterly description of a bread riot in Milan in 1629, which is a representation in fictional form of one of the classic types of disturbance at this period. See ch. 5 for a discussion of such outbreaks in relation to early modern revolutions.

[45] See B. Porchnev, *Les Soulèvements populaires en France de 1623 à 1648*, trans. from the Russian, Paris, 1963; the insurrections treated by Porchnev are discussed in chs. 7–8, dealing with agrarian and urban rebellions.

[46] M. Foisil, *La Révolte des Nu-pieds et les révoltes normandes de 1639*, Paris, 1970, 138.

officials in several towns, such as Rouen in 1634 and Caen in 1637.[47] But this endemic agitation and ferment of popular discontent dissipated itself in ephemeral outbreaks more often than it led to actual rebellion.

Admittedly, when we contemplate the states and societies of early modern Europe, in which subjects were still relatively unhabituated to the yoke of centralizing governments and the means for maintaining public order remained more or less exiguous, it may be difficult in certain instances to determine where small-scale rebellion as a manifestation of the general phenomenon of revolution shades off into riot. Nevertheless, theoretically and for comparative purposes the two should be distinguished. Moreover, this task is facilitated by the attention given in recent years to the historical investigation of crowds and riots, which has made it possible to understand them better.[48] In general, riots differ from rebellion in a number of ways. First, they are mostly spontaneous protests in which planning and organization are nonexistent or at a minimum. Second, they are usually of very brief duration, lasting a day or two at most. Third, their targets are picked for their immediate visibility, and their aims, if any, are often nonpolitical as well as of the most present and restricted kind. Fourth, as spontaneous outbursts of popular anger, their expressive function tends to predominate over any instrumental purpose. Because of these characteristics, riots should be considered as an independent phenomenon that occurs both within and separately from revolution and whose connection with the latter is therefore indeterminate.[49]

The preceding discussion leads to a final topic of importance that must be confronted in the comparative history of revolution, and this is the relation of revolution to rebellion. One of the ablest contemporary students of revolution has referred to the "now universal distinction between 'rebellion' and 'revolution' " yet is also forced to note the general confusion

[47] *Ibid.*, 141, 142; this revolt is discussed in chapter 9.

[48] See the broad survey by Charles Tilly, "Collective violence in European perspective," in H. D. Graham and T. R. Gurr (eds.), *The history of violence in America*, New York, 1969. Among the principal historical studies are those by G. Rudé; see "The pre-industrial crowd," in *Paris and London in the eighteenth century*, New York, 1973, for a general statement of some of his findings. He points out here that the food riot was the main type of disturbance in preindustrial society and believes that it occurred more often in villages and market towns than in cities. L. Tilly provides an analysis distinguishing several kinds of food riots in "The food riot as a form of political conflict in France" (*Journal of interdisciplinary history* 2, 1 [1971]). E. Thompson ("The moral economy of the English crowd," *Past and present* 50 [1971]) gives a vivid account stressing, as do other writers, the legitimating moral belief, such as "just price" or "just wage," that actuated the crowd. Among numerous kinds of riots in early modern Europe besides food and tax riots were xenophobic and iconoclastic riots. The latter, important in relation to such sixteenth-century revolutions as the French civil wars and the Netherlands rebellion, deserves much closer study; for a recent account, see N. Davis, "The rites of violence: Religious riot in sixteenth-century France," *Past and present* 59 (1973). Instances of both are discussed in Chapters 9, 10, and 11 in this book.

[49] It should also be noted that at some times and in some situations, as during recent years in the United States, riots may be connected with reform, to which they give an impulsion.

and uncertainty as to what is being distinguished.[50] This confusion is illustrated in the diverse practice of historians with regard to the problem. A recent work on medieval revolutions, for instance, speaks interchangeably of revolution, revolt, insurrection, and so forth; a reviewer of this same work, however, complains of such indiscriminate usage on the ground that "revolution" is a word "much richer in content" than the others.[51] A number of historians have stressed the need to differentiate rebellion from revolution in the context of early modern Europe. J. H. Elliott cautions against the danger of distortion in applying the concept of revolution to the revolts of the sixteenth and seventeenth centuries.[52] Roland Mousnier takes a similar view in his comparative study of French and other peasant risings of the seventeenth century and therefore characterizes these revolts as nonrevolutionary.[53] An analogous opinion is expressed by another historian of early modern France, who contrasts "mere rebellion" to "true revolution," the latter of which he considers to have been an impossibility in the early modern era.[54] As against these assertions, a historian of sixteenth-century political movements does not hesitate to speak of "revolution" and "revolutionary parties" in connection with the French wars of religion and the Netherlands rebellion,[55] and a recent history of the Scottish rebellion of 1638 against Charles I describes this event as a revolution and points out the "artificiality of trying to draw a line between rebellion and revolution."[56]

Not surprisingly, the terminology current in early modern Europe itself provides no guidance in adjudicating these differences or distinguishing

---

[50] Johnson, *Revolutionary change*, 135–6.

[51] See M. Mollat and P. Wolff, *Ongles bleus, Jacques et Ciompi: les révolutions populaires en Europe aux XIVe et XVe siècles*, Paris, 1970; and the review of V. Rutenberg, "Révoltes ou révolution en Europe aux XIVe–XVe siècles," *Annales E. S. C. 27*, 3 (1972).

[52] J. H. Elliott, "Revolution and continuity in early modern history," *Past and present 42* (1969).

[53] R. Mousnier, *Fureurs paysannes: les paysannes dans les révoltes du XVIIe siècle*, Paris, 1968.

[54] A. L. Moote, "The preconditions of revolution in early modern Europe: Did they really exist?" *Canadian journal of history 7*, 3 (1972), 212, 215. See also R. Forster and J. Greene (eds.), *Preconditions of revolution in early modern Europe*, Baltimore, 1970, who speak in the introduction to this collection of essays of certain revolts as having the potentiality to become revolutions. It is worth noting that under the influence of Marx and modern historians, African anthropologists have used the contrast, revolution–rebellion, in reference to African tribal conflicts. M. Gluckman, who has studied these conflicts, distinguishes revolution from rebellion on the following basis, namely, that rebellion is concerned with alterations in the personnel of social positions, not with the pattern of these positions themselves, whereas revolution derives from deep contradictions in social structure that must lead to a radical change in the pattern (M. Gluckman, *Order and rebellion in tribal Africa*, New York, 1963, intro., ch. 3). See also P. C. Lloyd, "Conflict theory and Yoruba kingdoms," in *History and social anthropology*, ed. I. M. Lewis, London, 1968.

[55] H. G. Koenigsberger, *Estates and revolutions*, Ithaca, 1971, ch. 9. The author does, however, distinguish rebels from revolutionaries in that the former aim only at capturing the existing state machinery, not at radical social change, as do the latter.

[56] D. Stevenson, *The Scottish revolution 1637–1644*, Newton Abbot, 1973, 315–16.

between revolution and rebellion.[57] *Revolution* at that period meant circular motion and was largely used in a cosmological context to describe the rotation (revolutions) of the heavenly bodies. When transferred to human affairs, the word continued to retain the idea of circularity and referred to the cycle of changes in states with its attendant upheavals. As yet, *revolution* was not associated with willed, conscious innovation or with progress. Not until the seventeenth century in any case was *revolution* much used in a political sense. The first rebellion in European history that actually became known to its contemporaries as a revolution was the English revolution of 1688; yet they still tended to conceive this revolution in cyclical terms as a *restoration* of a legal order that the deposed monarch, James II, had tyrannously violated. Other words for civil strife common in Western Europe during the sixteenth and seventeenth centuries all referred to forcible illicit resistance to authority and to the disturbances it provoked: thus, in France, for example, *sédition, rébellion, émotion, émeute;* in Spain, *alteraciónes* and *sucesos;* in England, rebellion, sedition, and also troubles.[58]

Obviously, the present distinction between revolution and rebellion is mainly intended to bring out certain features in revolutions after 1789 that are thought to have been absent or negligible in preceding centuries. Two such features frequently stressed are an ideology of innovation and progress on the part of rebels and their expression of a self-conscious will toward basic structural change and the creation of a new society. In contrast to these characteristics of modern revolutions, those of an earlier period of European history, it is held, lacked the aim of fundamental transformation and were dominated by conservative ideologies looking to the past rather than to the future and the goal of a new order. It is on such grounds that Ellul, for example, claims that "the phenomenon of revolution is without precedent in premodern history."[59]

[57] For the history of this terminology, see Zagorin, *The court and the country*, ch. 1; Lasky, *Utopia and revolution*, chs. 5–6; Gilbert, "Revolution."

[58] For examples of the French terminology, see Foisil, 136–8; and R. Mousnier, *Recherches sur les soulèvements populaires en France de 1485 à 1787: questionnaire* (Centre de recherches sur la civilisation de l'Europe moderne), Paris, n.d., 6; for Spain, *Diccionario histórico de la lingua española* (Academia española), *s.v.* "*alteración*" and the contemporary writings on the revolt ("*sucesos*") of Aragon in 1591, referred to in R. B. Merriman, *The rise of the Spanish empire*, 4 v., New York, 1918–34, v. 4, 571n., 605; for England, see, e.g., F. Bacon, "Of seditions and troubles," in *Essays* (1625).

[59] Ellul, 38. In insisting on the difference between revolution and rebellion, Ellul also reveals his affinity with the antihistoricist humanism of Albert Camus's *The rebel* (New York, 1956). Rebellion, for Camus, beyond the specific historical content it may contain, expresses man's capacity to pronounce a categorical "no" to oppression and to defy history and its supposed inevitabilities. Ellul in turn can thus contrast the professional modern revolutionary of the Leninist type, who has apotheosized the historical process as the guarantor of his acts, to the rebel, who lacks a futuristic consciousness of the new and represents the principle of rejection and spontaneous resistance. The contrast here in question, although valuable, is more philosophical than historical. The early modern era had its revolutionaries as well as

To be sure, there are significant differences between revolution before and after 1789 (broadly speaking) that it should be the purpose of comparative history to describe and explain. Although this may be so, however, these differences do not correspond to, nor are they illuminated by, the distinction between revolution and rebellion. Take the case of the conservative ideology previously cited, which I shall henceforth call the ideology of the normative past. In the first place, this is not the only sort of ideology to be found in premodern revolutions. The conception of a future new order as the goal and justification of revolution also sometimes appears, both in the religious form of millenarianism and in the secularized form of rationalistic and natural rights doctrines. In the second place, ideologies of the normative past, despite their backward-looking orientation, can lead both to innovative demands in rebel programs and to large-scale change. This is clearly shown by such cases as the sixteenth-century Netherlands rebellion, the English revolution of 1640, and the Castilian urban revolt of the Comuneros, about whose conservatism or modernity historians have argued.[60]

The truth is that the relation between conservative ideologies and innovation is much more complicated than is usually realized. An essential consideration to the understanding of this relationship is the fact of the unintended consequences of action, for demands and measures directed to system restoration or maintenance can unintendedly give rise to system innovation. As a theorist of economic development has remarked, "Efforts to maintain or restore a social organization or a way of life or a standard of living that is threatened or weakened have yielded unintended innovational change in modern societies."[61] The same observation applies as well to earlier societies and some of their revolutions. A further consideration in deciphering this relationship is the difference between manifest and latent function familiar from its use in functional analysis in sociology. Thus, to revolutionary actors, the manifest function of the beliefs they profess may be preservation or restoration; their latent function, however, even if the actors are unaware of it, may well be innovation.[62] Such discrepancies between the motivations of behavior and its function are com-

---

rebels, even if the making of revolution had not yet become a vocation or the mythology of revolution in its historicist form a dominant belief.

[60] For the debate concerning the revolt of the Comuneros, see J. A. Maravall, *Las comunidades de Castilla*, 2nd ed., Madrid, 1970; and J. Perez, *La Révolution des "communidades" de Castille*, Bordeaux, 1970. Several other early modern revolutions have been the subject of a similar debate over their conservative or modern character. The issue is further discussed in Ch. 8 of this book in connection with the Comuneros.

[61] A. O. Hirschman, *A bias for hope: essays on development and Latin America*, New Haven, 1971, 34–6.

[62] See R. K. Merton, *Social theory and social structure*, Glencoe, 1949, ch. 1, for an influential discussion of manifest and latent functions; and the more recent general account by M. J. Levy, *International encyclopedia of the social sciences*, v. 6, s.v., "Functional analysis."

mon in social life and help explain why the prevalence of a conservative ideology in revolution does not necessarily preclude the possibility of substantive change or novelty as its outcome.

The attempt to distinguish revolution from rebellion, notwithstanding that its aim may be to elucidate genuine differences, is misconceived because it is based on a logical blunder or category mistake.[63] It would distinguish the whole from one of its parts (and an ill-defined part at that), as one might try, for example, to distinguish violence from war or mammals from whales. Such a procedure is clearly futile.

Moreover, this attempt may be seen as a further consequence of the modern mythology of revolution, whose influence has proved so difficult to escape. It grows out of the belief, uncritically presumed by many historians and theorists, that the charismatic "great" revolution aspiring toward totality is identical with revolution itself or "really" revolution. This belief is false: When the phenomenon of revolution is properly conceived as a problem for comparative history and sociology, it is recognized to manifest itself in a variety of forms rather than exclusively as the so-called great revolution. There is also a highly questionable teleology and finalism implicit in the attempt to set revolution apart from rebellion. It presupposes a historical progression in which rebellion is merely a stage evolving toward revolution as a goal. Rebellion thus falls short of, and is a condition of inadequacy relative to, revolution.[64] It is difficult to see any justification for this presupposition. Obviously, societies with given social structures, economies, political institutions, cultures, belief systems, and so forth will produce certain kinds of revolution and no others. These revolutions should be examined in their own right and appropriately considered according to type, if possible. To view them as lower or higher stages in a sequence of progressive development is gratuitous and only means that the theorist or comparative historian has without realizing it subjected his own thought to the thought and consciousness of the modern, post-1789 makers of revolution, who have been primarily impelled by motives other than intellectual understanding.

A preferable procedure that avoids these pitfalls is to accept revolution as the generic class containing all revolutionary occurrences of whatever kind. There would then no longer be any question of the superfluous distinction between revolution and rebellion but rather the task of working out the different kinds or forms of revolution in accordance with ap-

[63] For the notion of category-mistake, the misallocation of something to an inappropriate category, see G. Ryle, *The concept of mind*, London, 1963, 16 ff.

[64] The anthropologist, M. Gluckman, has noticed the teleology of rebellion–revolution that is inherent in Marx's theory of revolution. He declares that, to Marx, "rebellion was . . . a step on the road towards total revolutionary class-consciousness and action, and was seen as part of a cumulative process" (Gluckman, *Order and rebellion in tribal Africa*, 10). The connection with the mythology of revolution is obvious.

propriate criteria. We are at present far from having an adequate typology or classification of revolutions. The type most commonly considered by students is that of the "great" revolution, which is the subject, for instance, of Crane Brinton's well-known comparative study, *The anatomy of revolution* (1938). In this work, which he intended as a contribution to social science, Brinton examined four "great" revolutions, the English, American, French, and Russian. But the characteristics and related criteria constituting the class of "great" revolutions remain obscure and undefined in his account; notwithstanding the uniformities he claimed to observe among the group of revolutions in question, it is noticeable that the American revolution differs very considerably from the French and Russian, as does also the English revolution in some essential respects.[65] If, therefore, all four belong to the class of "great" revolutions, it must be in spite of these differences. Brinton recognized that the sociology of revolution requires a careful discrimination of types, and in passing he mentions several, such as authoritarian, territorial, nationalist, colonial, and palace revolutions.[66] Nevertheless, these are presented as no more than desultory suggestions and are not developed.

Despite the widespread currency of the conception of the "great" revolution, there appears to be no agreement as to what it is or how its essential typological features are to be determined. The suggestion, for example, that the "Jacobin-communist" revolution is the fundamental type of the "great" revolution does not remove the difficulty because a number of revolutions usually accepted as "great" in some sense, like the Netherlands, English, American, Mexican, Algerian, or Turkish revolutions, can hardly be described as "Jacobin-communist."[67]

On the whole, therefore, it seems neither illuminating nor useful to think of the "great" revolution as a separate typological category. To do so is as if an earth scientist set on studying the variety of the world's mountains were to place certain of them in a class of "high" mountains irrespective of their geological history and structure. The result would be to overlook identities and differences to which height affords no key. An effective typology of revolution should take a number of criteria into account, and it might then be discovered that the "great" revolution, that is, the revolution of substantial magnitude and consequence, appears in more than one type.

In an adequate typology of revolution, moreover, the types sought would not be conceived as reified and static categories. Rather, they would ap-

---

[65] See for some of these differences, P. Zagorin, "Theories of revolution in contemporary historiography," *Political science quarterly 88*, 1 (1973), 31.

[66] Brinton, *The anatomy of revolution*, 21–4.

[67] On the "Jacobin-communist great revolution," see Johnson, *Revolution and the social system*, 45.

proximate more to structures or models describing a set of possible relationships between the features constituting the type, which in turn give rise to a determinate kind of action within particular societies. The question may be raised, though, whether revolution can be said to possess a structure. That the answer is yes is suggested, for example, by T. S. Kuhn's well-known work in the philosophy, history, and sociology of science, *The structure of scientific revolutions*. Even if one should hold, as I do, that the conception of revolution properly applies only to political and not to scientific or knowledge-producing communities, Kuhn's account seems nevertheless to confirm the possibility of envisaging a certain process of change as a structure appropriate to disparate empirical cases.[68] With regard to revolution as understood in this book, despite the presence in every instance of the contingent and unforeseen, it is also permissible to speak of structures. Not only can no revolution transcend the character of the society of which it is part, but every revolution is somehow inscribed by the character and limits of its society. There may thus be structures of agrarian or provincial or elite-led kingdomwide revolutions in early modern society that typological investigation could disclose. In an effective typology, the types or structures would not be universal; they would be historical and designed to illuminate the nature, forms, and boundaries of revolutionary action in particular societies with whose fundamental characteristics they would be coordinated. The development of typologies of this sort remains one of the principal desiderata for a better historical and theoretical understanding of revolution.

The enterprise to which the preceding discussion has been a prologue seeks to make some general sense and even to discern a kind of order in the revolutions of early modern Europe. Its scope in space and time is explained in the following chapter. Its main perspective, however, is that of comparative history, of which a modern German practitioner, Otto

---

[68] T. S. Kuhn, *The structure of scientific revolutions*, 2nd rev. ed., Chicago, 1970. The concept of a scientific revolution emerged in the eighteenth century as a borrowing from the political realm, which had in turn first taken the term *revolution* from science and cosmology; see I. B. Cohen, "The eighteenth century origin of the concept of scientific revolution," *Journal of the history of ideas 37*, 2 (1976). Although the historiographic notion of scientific revolution has long enjoyed canonical status, Kuhn is the first historian of science, I believe, who has taken the idea of revolution seriously enough to try to give it literal application to the community of scientists. Thus, there is a parallel between the central importance he assigns to the paradigm and paradigm conflict in the scientific community and the role of ideology in revolutionary conflicts. The parallel between his account of science and the field of revolution proper is further seen in his discussion of the "incommensurability" of paradigms and in the use of such terms as *crisis, commitment,* and *conversion-experience* to describe the episodes of basic advance ("paradigm change") in the growth of science. Such resemblances help to explain the vehemence of some of Kuhn's critics among philosophers and historians of science, who decry his view of science as abounding in irrationalist and relativistic consequences; see I. Lakatos and R. Musgrave (eds.), *Criticism and the growth of knowledge*, Cambridge, 1970.

Hintze, wrote: "You can compare in order to find something general that underlies the things that are compared, and you can compare in order to grasp more clearly the singularity of the thing that is compared, and to distinguish it from others. The sociologist does the former; the historian the latter."[69] This statement is unexceptionable, save for the division of labor it prescribes. I see no reason why the historian should not look for the general as well as the singular in the things compared. If doing so makes him a bit of a sociologist, so much the better.

In undertaking this comparative study of revolution, I have wanted to do justice to both the general and the particular within a certain spatiotemporal context. Revolution is an extremely complex phenomenon that has to be seen in light of the social and political order, economy, culture, and beliefs that shape it. As an act of revolt, it is also an elemental human fact, often moving and tragic, in which the capacities and passions of mankind are strongly displayed. It is essential for the comparative historian to keep both these views in mind and to strive to realize them both. In principle, I have endeavored throughout this work to avoid either excessive abstraction or overburdening detail. Although I have often alternated between the large and the small, macrocosm and microcosm, structure and event, my fundamental strategy has been to maintain a balancing middle distance as most appropriate for observing both general features and specific configurations in the interrelations between early modern society and its variety of revolutions.

[69] Cited in *The historical essays of Otto Hintze*, ed. F. Gilbert, Oxford, 1975, 23.

2

Conspectus, typology, causality

I

The revolutions selected for consideration in this book almost all occurred in the century and a half between the beginning of the sixteenth and the middle of the seventeenth century. Moreover, with the main exception of the German peasant war, they belong almost entirely to the history of three states: England, France, and the Spanish empire. The rationale for this choice of locale in space and time as the basis for a study of early modern revolutions is explained by a number of reasons.

Far across the abyss of time, before the French revolution and the emergence of industrial society, lies spread out and stretching backward into the past the Western Europe of the old society. Dominated in its polities by monarchies and princes and in its social structures by nobilities and aristocracies, still rural despite its great capital cities, still agricultural despite its commerce, manufactures, and bourgeoisie, this is the society that grew out of the feudal world and was eventually to be transformed during the nineteenth century into the industrial world. One phase of its life history, the last, which was disrupted by the French revolution, is usually known as the *ancien régime*. The whole of its history is commonly described as the early modern era, extending from about 1500 to the late eighteenth century and the outbreak of the French revolution.

Of this period it was the first half, broadly speaking, that witnessed the basic advances in the building of states, the introduction or growth of institutions designed to consolidate centralized government, and the decay of older institutions that stood in the way. This evolution, fundamental to the history of early modern Europe, was connected by mutual dependence with other momentous changes: the emergence of the Atlantic economy and the rise and decline of the inflow to Europe of the treasure from Spain's American mines; the recurrence of prolonged international wars on an unprecedented scale; the modification of social structures; the Protestant Reformation working out its consequences in manifold forms; and shifts and alterations in cultural ideals, belief systems, and values.[1]

In view of the vast movement of Europe in the sixteenth and seventeenth centuries, it is hardly surprising that both the largest number of revolutions of the early modern epoch as well as the biggest occurred during this period. The eighteenth century until near its end was much less subject to upheaval than the two preceding centuries; and within the latter it was the time span from about 1520 (the revolt of the Comuneros in Castile) to 1660 (the exhaustion of the revolutionary disturbances of the midcentury) that presents us with both the greatest frequency and the most important cases of revolution.

Between 1500 and 1660, the three states that occupied a paramount position as great powers in Europe were England, France, and Spain.[2] Their rivalries and alliances played the largest role in determining the pattern of European international relations; their conflicts were responsible for the biggest wars.[3] Individually, of course, as seen at the level of discrete events and succession of leading personalities as well as of particular institutional configurations, each of the three has a different and quite distinct history. But looked at in a wider view and at a certain level of generality, they present various common features, are seen to be played upon by similar forces and to undergo parallel experiences. This is the case not only because they belong to the same civilization and reflect its problems and characteristics as it emerged from the Middle Ages. (Here we may profitably recall Lucien Febvre's insistence in connection with the French Reformation that even its specificity and national traits are intelligible only in a European context, the countries of Europe, despite their originality and distinctive traditions at the beginning of the sixteenth century, having all shared a common spiritual culture for centuries.)[4] Also,

---

[1] Lord Acton's evocative description of the opening sixteenth century, even if somewhat hyperbolical, is in place here: "After many ages persuaded of the headlong decline and impending dissolution of society, and governed by usage and the will of masters who were in their graves, the sixteenth century went forth armed for untried experience, and ready to watch with hopefulness a prospect of incalculable change" ("Inaugural lecture on the study of history," *Lectures on modern history*, London, 1930, 4).

[2] The Ottoman empire, an extra-European great power pressing upon Central and Western Europe, may be left aside; so may the state created by the Austrian branch of the Habsburgs, which did not begin to attain great-power status until the latter part of the seventeenth century. The Dutch republic, which as a result of its commercial, maritime, and colonial ascendancy became and remained a great power in the seventeenth century, was born out of the revolution of the Netherlands against Spanish rule.

[3] See J. R. Seeley, *The growth of British policy*, 2 v., Cambridge, 1895. This work, now apparently rather neglected, remains one of the most interesting and illuminating discussions of the European state system and great-power relations in the sixteenth and seventeenth centuries.

[4] L. Febvre, "Une Question mal posée: Les Origines de la réforme française" in *Au coeur religieux du XVIe siècle*, 2nd ed., Paris, 1968, 58–9.

and in a more particular sense, the history of these states reveals to us every stage and all varieties of early modern political and social development. Correspondingly, therefore, it gives us also a substantial representation of the possible types and processes of revolution that are congruent with and consequent upon early modern political and social structures.

Let us cast a rapid glance at the monarchies of these states and their European dominions during this period, which begins with the three contemporaneous reigns of the Tudor Henry VIII in England (1509–47), the Valois Francis I in France (1515–47), and the Habsburg Charles I in Spain (1516–56).

In England, the Tudor dynasty continues to rule during the sixteenth century. The kings of England are also kings of Ireland, which has long been subject to the English crown. In 1603, at the death of Queen Elizabeth I, the Scottish Stuart dynasty succeeds the Tudors with the accession of James I, and England is thenceforth connected to Scotland by a personal union of crowns.

In France, the line of Valois kings occupies the throne until its extinction by the murder of Henry III, in 1589, when it is succeeded by the house of Bourbon in the person of Henry IV. The French monarchy, although ambitious for Italian conquest in the first half of the sixteenth century, fails in this attempt and has no kingdoms outside France under its rule. The state it governs expands mainly by internal consolidation and integration and by annexation on France's frontiers rather than by foreign acquisition or by dynastic association with other realms.

In Spain, kings of the Habsburg dynasty succeed one another during the entire period. Their state is the most farflung and the most diverse. Besides its enormous transoceanic possessions, Spain is also an empire in Europe. In peninsular Spain, Charles I (who is commonly known to history as Charles V due to his election in 1519 as Holy Roman emperor) is ruler of the kingdoms of Aragon and Castile, held through inheritance in a union of crowns. To these Iberian dominions his son, Philip II, adds the crown of Portugal in 1580. In the Pyrenees, the Spanish monarchy is master of the kingdom of Navarre. Outside the peninsula it possesses in Italy the kingdoms of Naples and Sicily, both derived through the crown of Aragon, and the duchy of Milan. As emperor and head of the Habsburg house, Charles I and V also links Spain to Germany and to his Austrian family possessions, but this connection does not outlast his time, after which the Spanish and the Austrian Habsburgs form separate branches ruling over his divided inheritance. Finally, in Northern Europe, Charles, as duke of Burgundy and by other titles, brings to the Spanish monarchy the lordship of the provinces of the Netherlands and of Franche-Comté. All these domains are politically distinct, possessing their own institutions and united only through the person of the sovereign to whom each owes allegiance. The Spanish monarchy must accordingly create institutions of imperial government in order to administer and coordinate its disparate realms.

II

Such is the site of the sixteenth- and seventeenth-century revolutions that may fall within our consideration. Next, we should try to gain a view of their occurrence and incidence in time and space.

At present, save in part for the work of Sorokin shortly to be noticed, there is not available any census of revolutions either worldwide or for a particular society and offering quantitative information on their various aspects and characteristics.[5] Even for our restricted period, insufficient and untrustworthy evidence would make it difficult to compile a complete census of revolutions along with accurate data on their duration, spatial extent, participants, goals, victims, and so forth. This difficulty is compounded by the fact that historians have failed to agree in their definitions of revolution or in their classification and description of its different types.

A few partial or general historical surveys centered upon the revolutions of early modern Europe exist and should be noted for the reader's benefit:

For Tudor and Stuart England, brief overviews of its rebellions have been given both by Fletcher and by Davies; they include most of the important cases and seek to bring out some of their general features and causes.[6]

For France, the main survey is Porchnev's, which is confined, however, to the earlier seventeenth century and omits a few considerable rebellions, like those of the Huguenots in the 1620s, presumably because they fail to qualify as *"soulèvements populaires."* Besides this general work, extensive and detailed surveys of French rebellions focused upon several provinces have been written by Bercé and Pillorget.[7]

---

[5] A census of twentieth-century revolution is contained in P. Calvert, *A study of revolution*, Oxford, 1970, app. A, which lists 363 revolutionary events between 1901 and 1960. Data on civil strife in 114 polities in the 1960s are collected in T. R. Gurr, "A comparative study of civil strife," in *Violence in America: historical and comparative perspectives*, ed. H. D. Graham and T. R. Gurr, Washington, D.C., 1969. See also the remarks in T. R. Gurr, *Why men rebel*, Princeton, 1971, 3, 3n.

[6] A. Fletcher, *Tudor rebellions*, 2nd ed., London, 1973; C. S. L. Davies, "Les Révoltes populaires en Angleterre (1500–1700)," *Annales E.S.C. 24*, 1 (1969).

[7] B. Porchnev, *Les Soulèvements populaires en France de 1623 à 1648*, trans. from the Russian, Paris, 1963; Y.-M. Bercé, *Histoire des Croquants: ètude des soulèvements populaires au XVIIᵉ siècle dans la sud-ouest de la France*, 2 v., Geneva, 1974; R. Pillorget, *Les Mouvements insurrectionnels de Provence entre 1596 et 1715*, Paris, 1975. V. L. Tapié (*La France de Louis XIII et de Richelieu*, Paris, 1967) has a useful review of the rebellions of Louis XIII's reign (1610–43). R. Mousnier, (*Fureurs paysannes: Les Paysannes dans les révoltes du XVIIᵉ siècle*, Paris, 1968) provides a review of seventeenth-century French peasant revolts in part 1. R. Bonney (*Political change in France under Richelieu and Mazarin 1624–1661*, Oxford, 1978, ch. 10) gives an overview of "tax" rebellions.

For Spain, the principal if not only survey is Elliott's, which deals in brief compass exclusively with the revolts of the 1640s in the Spanish monarchy.[8]

For the century 1560–1660 as a whole, an unsystematic review of Europe's revolutions is included in a general treatment of the age by Kamen.[9]

Finally, for the cluster of mid–seventeenth-century revolutions, although these have been discussed in several short interpretive studies, the only considerable survey remains the work of Merriman, which is also incomplete; it leaves out, for example, the Irish rebellion of 1641 and the revolt of 1647 in Sicily.[10]

Thus far, however, the sole attempt to present a census, classification, and comparative data on revolutions in a number of countries during many past hundreds of years and down into the twentieth century is Sorokin's, published in 1937 in connection with his magnum opus on sociocultural dynamics. This work, ostensibly a sociological treatise dealing with changes in group life on the largest scale, is in actuality a universal philosophy of history comparable to similar works by Spengler and Toynbee and ultimately to be judged by the same standards. Its data on revolutions, like its related data on wars and other phenomena, were compiled to test and confirm hypotheses on major fluctuations in societies, including the crisis and breakdown of our own contemporary "Sensate" culture. I shall be concerned here only with the much more modest subject of the figures relating to early modern revolutions in order to ascertain their possible usefulness to our inquiry.[11]

Sorokin does not speak of revolutions but of "internal disturbances in intragroup relationships,"[12] and hence his tables may include any event from a small disorder like a strike or riot to a major civil war, depending on whether the standard narrative histories he has used as sources happen to record it. In some instances, the tables erroneously list what is in essence a single event as separate lesser ones. Thus, the French wars of

[8] J. H. Elliott, "Revolts in the Spanish monarchy," in *Preconditions of revolution in early modern Europe*, ed. R. Forster and J. Greene, Baltimore, 1970.

[9] H. Kamen, *The iron century 1560–1660*, London, 1971, chs. 9–10. See also now Y.-M. Bercé's brief survey of European revolts of the period, *Révoltes et révolutions dans l'Europe moderne XVIe–XVIIIe siècle*, Paris, 1980.

[10] R. B. Merriman, *Six contemporaneous revolutions*, Oxford, 1938.

[11] P. A. Sorokin, *Social and cultural dynamics*, 4 v., New York, 1937–41; volume 3, *Fluctuation of social relationships, war and revolution*, part 3 and appendix, contains data and tabulations on revolution based on a study of twelve countries and empires from 500 B.C. to A.D. 1925. Sorokin declares that he has derived his conclusions from "an examination of some seventeen hundred disturbances – a number never approached by any other investigation" (398). In analyzing his tables, I have had the valuable assistance of my two former doctoral students, Dr. William Bidwell and Dr. Ruben Garner.

[12] Nevertheless, chapter 12 carries the title, "Methodological study of revolution," and Sorokin does not discriminate in his general remarks between internal disturbances and revolution.

religion, in reality one long revolutionary civil war punctuated by intermittent truces, become nine internal disturbances, the Fronde three, the
English revolution three. This contrasts, for no understandable reason, to
the enumeration of the revolt of the Netherlands as a single event from
1576 to 1609. In other cases, the reverse practice is followed by incorrectly
treating separate events as one, as with a number of localized French insurrections of the seventeenth century.[13]

With respect to completeness, the parts of the tables covering the century and a half of our study reveal a number of omissions. I shall not
attempt to list them because in later chapters I note the occurrence of the
several types of revolution, but I shall cite some examples.

The most numerous omissions relate to France. The detailed surveys
by Porchnev, Bercé, and Pillorget record many disturbances and revolts
that are not included in Sorokin's census. Among them are various agrarian (peasant) and urban insurrections, especially during the decades of the
1630s and 1640s, as well as such provincial rebellions as that of Languedoc
in 1632 and Normandy in 1639. In the case of England, the tables omit
the Western (Prayer Book) rebellion of 1549 and the agrarian insurrections
of 1607 and 1628. They also overlook the Irish rebellion of 1641, despite
their inclusion of previous (although not all) less important Irish rebellions
in the table pertaining to England. In the case of Spain and its possessions,
among the omissions are the revolts of Portugal in 1640 and of Naples and
Palermo in 1647.

The tables also contain a classification of the nature of each internal
disturbance according to its objectives, which are divided into five categories, such as political, social, and religious. It is unnecessary to review
the details of this classification, which is crude and unsatisfactory for typological purposes. Symptomatic of its defects is the fact that a majority
of events are placed in the fifth class, a catchall of "disturbances with a
specific objective" or "without any single dominant objective but with two
or more equally strong objectives."[14]

Apart from the census of disturbances, the most noteworthy feature of
Sorokin's tables is the assignment of a geometric average to each disturbance, combining its sociogeographic area, duration, proportion of population involved, amount and intensity of violence, and effects. The average expresses the magnitude of the disturbance and is used for comparisons
of the scale of revolutionary events over time and for particular countries.

This procedure gives an impression of precision or "scientific" measure-
ment that is quite unfounded because in many cases the geometric average
or magnitude is based on poor and insufficient data in the sources and on
sheer guesswork. As an absolute figure it is frequently unreliable, and as

[13] See *ibid.*, app. to pt. 3, tables for the respective countries.
[14] The basis of this classification is described in *ibid.*, 403.

an indicator of the relative importance of particular disturbances it can at times be highly misleading. To cite a few examples, in the table for France, "armed conflict at Paris and Lyon" in 1539 – apparently a printers' strike – has a magnitude of 12.16, which exceeds that of the first and second wars of religion (10.00 and 11.45), the revolt of 1615 in Languedoc (11.45), and the first Fronde (10.00). Similarly, for England, an "insurrection in northern Wales" in 1408 (Glendower's rebellion), with a magnitude of 28.44, exceeds the peasant revolt of 1381 (24.10), the biggest agrarian rebellion in England's history; and "a coup d'état in favor of Mary" in 1553 (referring apparently to the failure of the duke of Northumberland's attempt to prevent Queen Mary's succession) has a greater magnitude (7.36) than the Scottish revolution of 1638 (5.64).[15]

Generally speaking, Sorokin's graphs and tables do not contain any revelations. No trends or periodicities, as he points out, can be deduced from them, nor do they suggest any significant correlations. They may be helpful, however, in gaining an approximation of the number and frequency of internal disturbances – or at least those that a variety of detailed narrative histories deemed important enough to record for the countries tabulated. Several figures relative to the sixteenth- and seventeenth-century revolutions are worth noting.

Between 1500 and 1660, the total number of disturbances in the states that interest us is as follows, according to Sorokin's tabulation: England, twenty-five; France, twenty-five; and Spain, thirteen.[16] We have seen, however, that these figures contain some errors and omissions. The total for France therefore ought to be considerably larger, whereas that for Spain refers only to the peninsula, so that to it must be added the Netherlands rebellion from the table on the Netherlands as well as several other omissions from Spanish possessions already mentioned.

Looking at Sorokin's total measure of internal disturbances in Europe by centuries from A.D. 525 to 1925, one notes that the sixteenth and seventeenth centuries do not rank among the five most turbulent centuries (in descending order, the thirteenth, fourteenth, twelfth, nineteenth, and fifteenth).[17]

[15] Ibid., app. to pt. 3.

[16] These figures are derived from the tables for the respective countries in ibid. A comparison with the number of revolutionary events in the same countries from 1660 to 1800 shows the following:

	1660–1700	18th century
England	6	9
France	6	13
Spain	2	2

[17] Ibid., table 47, 471, 486. The same data indicate that the sixteenth century is the eleventh most turbulent, the seventeenth century the eighth most turbulent, and the eighteenth century the fourteenth most turbulent.

Nevertheless, for England the seventeenth century is estimated as the third most turbulent, its importance being highlighted by the fact that it contains the largest single disturbance in English history, the revolution of 1640 against the Stuart monarchy.[18]

For France, the sixteenth and seventeenth centuries are estimated as the fourth and fifth most turbulent of its history; moreover, the fifth and sixth largest disturbances belong to the years 1572–7 and 1585–93 of the civil war.[19]

For the Netherlands, the sixteenth century is one of the least turbulent (an observation Sorokin recognizes to be somewhat surprising), yet it also contains the largest single disturbance of the provinces' history in the rebellion against Spain.[20]

For (peninsular) Spain, also, the sixteenth century is one of the least turbulent, but the revolt of the Comuneros in 1520 is both the fourth largest disturbance in Spanish history as well as the largest single rebellion between 1500 and 1800.[21]

Finally, it appears from Sorokin's data that about 80 percent of the 1,544 disturbances from 500 B.C. to A.D. 1925 had a duration of less than a year. Further, "for the majority of countries taken separately the predominant type of disturbance is . . . of a few weeks' duration."[22] I see no reason to doubt the substantial correctness of this conclusion or its applicability to the revolutions of the early modern era, although there are of course very notable exceptions and the importance of a rebellion is not necessarily measured by its length.

Summing up, a brief conspectus of the course and highlights of revolution between 1500 and 1660 in England, France, and the Spanish empire shows that each was subject to a number of revolutions ranging in scale from small to very large and with some common types, as we shall see, occurring in all three. In England the largest rebellions of the sixteenth century were the Pilgrimage of Grace in 1536 and the Norfolk or Kett's agrarian rebellion in 1549. The biggest and most important of all came at the end of the period in the revolution of 1640–60, which was also associated with big revolutions in the two other kingdoms of the English crown, Scotland and Ireland. In France, which experienced by far the greatest number of rebellions, the biggest and most important of them occurred in two phases, separated by half a century, the first being the civil war of the later sixteenth century from 1562 to 1598, the second the Fronde in the years 1648–53. In between, and apart from these two largest upheavals, various other rebellions of a more limited character broke out with epidemic frequency in the earlier seventeenth century. In the Spanish monarchy, the biggest and most consequential revolutions were sepa-

---

[18] *Ibid.*, table 35, 439–40.   [19] *Ibid.*, table 31, 427, 429.   [20] *Ibid.*, table 41, 459–60.
[21] *Ibid.*, table 39, 454–55, and app. to pt. 3, table for Spain.   [22] *Ibid.*, table 50, 478–9.

rated both in time and in the dominions where they occurred. The first was the revolt of the Comuneros in 1520 in the kingdom of Castile, the very heart of the monarchy; the second followed half a century later in 1566, with the rebellion of the Netherlands. At the end of the period, an outburst of contemporaneous rebellions during the 1640s in Portugal, Catalonia, Naples, and Sicily was a symptom of the crisis of the Spanish state, which announced the decline of Spain as a European power.

Although it occurs outside the domains of the three monarchies, the German peasant war of 1524–5 should be added to our conspectus. It was the greatest agrarian rebellion of the early modern era as well as the biggest in the history of Western Europe, and as such it offers suggestive aspects for comparisons with other agrarian revolts of the time.[23]

Needless to say, I do not propose to consider all the revolutions that took place within the rule of the English, French, and Spanish crowns during the period. Such an undertaking would be impossible and, even if possible, probably of little interest. What is important is to ascertain the types or structures included in the spectrum of revolution in early modern society and to examine some well-selected cases in order to bring out comparative and individual features.

III

At first view, a bewildering multiplicity of revolutions within an almost infinite diversity of circumstances presents itself to the comparative historian of revolution in early modern Europe. Is it possible to discern in this multiplicity a limited number of types representing the general features, forms, and structures of revolutionary action at this period?

This, the typological problem, has always been of vital concern for the social sciences and comparative studies. Its centrality dates back at least as far as Aristotle's effort to systematize the classification of polities and constitutions, and today one of the important issues in political science continues to be that of defining the types and characteristics of democratic and totalitarian regimes.[24] Besides the development of typologies in the several social science disciplines, there has also been extensive theoretical discussion of the rationale of type constructs themselves, of Max Weber's conception of the ideal type as a method of sociological investigation, and

---

[23] Sorokin assigns the German peasant war a magnitude of 27.61, which makes it in his estimate the largest single disturbance in Germany–Austria between the later thirteenth century and 1918; see *ibid.*, table in appendix to part 3.

[24] See the unpublished paper by Juan Linz of Yale University ("Notes toward a typology of authoritarian regimes," presented in 1973 at a seminar at the Woodrow Wilson School, Princeton University), which contains a stimulating discussion of the typological problem in political science, along with ample references to the literature and a "suggested typology of political systems."

of typological constructs compared with models and model building and the respective properties of each in their representation of empirical reality and for use in research.[25] History, moreover, even when not primarily comparative, has found it impossible to dispense with typological analysis. In his discussion of institutions, social structures, and cultures, the historian has no alternative in the face of the "infinite manifold" of the real but to make use of typological concepts.

A number of typologies, both general and limited, have been suggested for revolution. Marxist theory and the historiography derived from it contain an unformalized typology of slave, serf and peasant, bourgeois, and proletarian revolution.[26] A typology of revolution proposed in 1964 by Chalmers Johnson includes six types: jacquerie, millenarian rebellion, anarchistic rebellion, Jacobin-communist "great" revolution, conspiratorial coup, and militarized mass insurrection. In a subsequent modification of this categorization, Johnson also proposed a fourfold typology of simple rebellion, ideological rebellion, simple revolution, and total revolution, a typology based upon the goals envisaged in the ideology connected with each type.[27] Among other suggested typologies are the following: personnel, authority, and structural revolution; abortive, moderate, and radical revolution; Eastern and Western revolution; social and political revolution.[28]

All these typologies are apparently intended as general or universal. For the revolutions of early modern Europe, however, the most influential typological category has been that of the bourgeois revolution as defined by Marx, which after stamping itself upon the French revolution, of which

[25] For Weber's view of the ideal type, see his *The methodology of the social sciences*, ed. E. Shils, Glencoe, 1949, 89 ff.; and the account of R. Bendix, "Max Weber," in *International encyclopedia of the social sciences*, New York, 1968, v. 16, 495, 499–500. An interesting critical discussion of Weber's typological ideas and of typological methods, their characteristics and limitations in general, based, however, it seems to me, on a too exigent notion of what sociology can accomplish, is given in P. Bourdieu, J.-C. Chamboredon, and J.-C. Passeron, *Le Métier de sociologue*, 2nd ed., Paris, 1973, 71 ff. and *passim*.

[26] Marx's typology of revolution is sketched in *The communist manifesto*. The later Marx and Marxist thought also recognized national independence and colonial anti-imperialist revolutions as types but sought to assimilate them to the prevailing categories of bourgeois (antifeudal) and proletarian revolution. This attempt has generated both an endless amount of theoretical scholastic disputation and important strategic-tactical consequences in actual twentieth-century revolutions.

[27] C. Johnson, *Revolution and the social system*, Stanford, 1964, pt. 2, *Revolutionary change*, Boston, 1966, ch. 7.

[28] These typologies have been proposed respectively by J. Rosenau, L. P. Edwards, S. P. Huntington, and M. Hagopian. For references to them, see Johnson, *Revolutionary change*, 141; P. Zagorin, "Theories of revolution in contemporary historiography," *Political science quarterly 88*, 1 (1973); and M. Hagopian, *The phenomenon of revolution*, New York, 1974, 101–6. T. Skocpol's comparative study of the French, Russian, and Chinese revolutions includes a discussion of social revolution as a type in chapter 1 (*States and social revolutions*, Cambridge, 1979).

it became the dominant interpretation, was then extended by Marxist writers to various revolutions of the sixteenth and seventeenth centuries as well. Accordingly, we have a number of these revolutions conceived by Marxist scholarship as either victorious or failed struggles by a nascent bourgeois social order against a reactionary feudalo-absolutist one. As a further development of the same typological conception we also have the view, which has recently become current in Marxist historiography in Eastern Europe, of the Protestant Reformation and the German peasant war as constituting the era of *"die frühbürgerliche Revolution."*[29]

Another early modern typology, based on a survey of the Netherlands and English revolutions, the Fronde, and the revolts of the 1640s in the Spanish empire, consists of great national revolution, national revolt with the potential to become a revolution, urban jacquerie, and secessionist coup.[30] An alternate classification, arising out of the examination of some sixteenth-century rebellions, adopts the two broad categories of conservative and modern revolution as its fundamental typological conception.[31] Much more restricted, in comparison, is a typology directed to German peasant rebellions of the later fifteenth and early sixteenth centuries, which classifies them as revolts in behalf of either past customary law (*das alte Recht*) or the divine law (*das göttliche Recht*). Some typological distinctions have also been proposed for the French peasant and popular revolts of the period.[32]

---

[29] For a general statement of this view, see the papers presented at the 1960 meeting of the historians of the German Democratic Republic (DDR) in G. Brendler (ed.), *Die frühbürgerliche Revolution in Deutschland*, Berlin, 1961. The main formulation is the contribution by Max Steinmetz, which contains the "theses" on the subject. A point of interest is Steinmetz's observation that Soviet scholarship as late as the 1950s did not treat the German peasant war as an "early bourgeois revolution" but placed it instead among peasant outbreaks ranging from the Jacquerie of the fourteenth century to the Taiping rebellion of the nineteenth, while seeing the Dutch revolt against Spain as the first bourgeois revolution, then followed by the English and French revolutions (*ibid.*, "Nachwort," 304n.). However, the germ of the treatment of the German Reformation and peasant war as a bourgeois revolution goes back to classical Marxism; see F. Engels's discussion to this effect in his "Introduction" (1892) to the English edition of his *Socialism: utopian and scientific* (1882).

[30] Forster and Greene, *Preconditions of revolution*, introduction.

[31] The typological distinction between conservative and modern revolution, with its implicit reference to the French and subsequent revolutions, has been particularly discussed in connection with the Castilian revolt of the Comuneros (see J. A. Maravall, *Las comunidades de Castilla*, 2nd ed., Madrid, 1970; and J. Perez, *La révolution des "comunidades" de Castille*, Bordeaux, 1970) and the Dutch rebellion (see H. A. Enno van Gelder, "De opstand tegen Philips II en de Protestantisering der Nederlanden," *Bijdragen voor de geschiedenis der Nederlanden 10*, 1 (1955), and the reply to this article by L. Rogier, "Het karakter van de opstand tegen Philips II," *ibid. 10*, 2–4 (1956), together with Enno van Gelder's rejoinder to Rogier, *ibid. 11*, 2 (1956).

[32] G. Franz, *Der deutsche Bauernkrieg*, 9th ed., Darmstadt, 1972, 1, for the German peasant revolts; both this and the suggested categorization of French peasant and popular revolts are discussed in Ch. 7 of this book.

Although something can probably be learned from all these typological ideas, it is at the same time apparent that they presuppose different or unspecified criteria and represent various levels of abstraction, rising from what seems hardly more than a description of individual events to very broad taxonomies. Moreover, even a cursory view shows that the general typologies omit some types and misconceive others, whereas those referring more directly to the early modern period suffer from such defects as incompleteness, excessive generality, or procrustean reductionism.

Whether a universal typology or structural model comprehending all the forms of revolution is attainable is a question I would prefer to leave open, despite my extreme scepticism on this score. The very real doubts that may arise concerning such a possibility, however, are aptly summed up by a historian of medieval revolutions who points out that "since the structures [of society] are not timeless principles, it is useless to seek after an abstract, timeless, synchronic structural model . . . of revolutions," of which the result would only be banalities.[33] A similar argument is advanced in a recent criticism of the sociology of revolution for "attempting to derive certain properties of revolutionary social change" rather than "to provide analysis specific to particular forms of society." "Is there any such thing," the same writer asks, "as *the* sociology of revolution? Rather, should we not simply develop different theories specific to different types of society?"[34]

Whatever the final verdict on such views may prove to be, the reservations they express do at least justify the importance of trying to discover the nature and characteristics of revolution in historically different societies and hence also of the search for the types of revolution in early modern Europe.

What, then, are the basic criteria to be looked for in the typological differentiation of early modern revolutions? They seem to me to consist of the following:

1. The socioeconomic position of the participants
2. The geographic extent or focus of rebel action
3. The aims and goals, implicit or explicit, of rebellion and the targets of rebel violence
4. The forms and degree of rebel organization
5. The rebel mentality, justifying beliefs, or ideology

Although most of these criteria are probably reasonably clear, some amplifying comments may be helpful.

The socioeconomic position of rebels refers to a variety of possible char-

[33] F. Graus, *Struktur und Geschichte drei Volksaufstände im mittelalterlichen Prag*, Sigmaringen, 1971, 27–8.
[34] J. Urry, *Reference groups and the theory of revolution*, London, 1973, 132.

acteristics, including status or class, kinship, occupation, and profession, as well as, more generally, whether revolutionary actors are drawn from elites, from inferior strata, or from both.

Geographic extent or focus is an essential criterion for early modern revolution, involving as it does not merely physical but political space. The kingdoms, states, and nations of sixteenth- and seventeenth-century Europe were as yet so imperfectly integrated politically and in other ways that local solidarities and communities, whether of villages, city, or town, province or region, could decisively affect the nature of revolution.

Aims consist of rebel grievances and demands, the possible generalization of demands into programs, and the changes that such demands envisage or imply. The targets of violence, whether persons or property and things, generally bear some relation or correspondence to the aims of the movement.

Organization is a relative phenomenon but is present in some degree, however rudimentary, in every revolutionary occurrence. Hence the criterion of spontaneity or calculation that has been suggested for the typological differentiation of revolutions is pointless, as spontaneity merely signifies a low or primitive level of organization.[35] The relevant question is that of organizational forms, coordination, and leadership, and here considerable variety is encountered in the different types of revolution.

Finally, mentality includes beliefs, values, and principles of right order in the world. The justifying claims or doctrines advanced in revolution will be a reflection or concretization of such conceptions. One may speak of mentality, however, when the actuating beliefs and values are comparatively loose, unsystematized, and only partially explicit. Ideology, in contrast, represents a much greater elaboration of belief into articulated systems tending toward completeness and integration in accordance with their basic principles. In this sense, although beliefs and mentality may be traceable in any revolutionary event, their development in the direction of an ideology is less frequent and more characteristic of some types of revolutions than of others.

In reviewing these criteria, it might perhaps be asked why, instead of those that have been indicated, we should not simply take the goals or magnitude of change sought by a revolution as its main or sole typological determinant. A glance at individual cases, however, indicates that no invariant connection exists between kind or scale of revolution and magnitude of envisaged change. Thus, a coup d'état, which is commonly regarded as the most limited of revolutions, can in certain instances aim not merely at changes in policy or government but at sweeping changes in regime or society. This is illustrated in the twentieth century by the mod-

---

[35] For spontaneity or calculation as a criterion, see Johnson, *Revolution and the social system*, 28, 30.

ernizing revolutions of Kemal Ataturk in Turkey and Nasser in Egypt, both military coups that initiated substantial social and political change.[36] Similarly, the English Catholic Gunpowder plot of 1605, which attempted the assassination of King James I and many Protestant notables, or the military coup in 1650 by the Stadholder William II, prince of Orange, against the autonomy and preponderance of Holland in the Dutch republic, may both be seen as implicitly intending changes in regime.[37] Moreover, the history of revolution in early modern Europe provides a number of cases of rebellions of different character that nonetheless demanded extensive political change. Since these differences are just as important in a comparative understanding of revolutions as are the goals sought, our typological criteria must take them into account.

Using the criteria that I have suggested, we can derive a limited number of types of revolution in early modern Europe.

1. Conspiracy and coup, limited largely to the action of noble and aristocratic elites

2. Urban rebellion, either by plebeian and inferior groups against urban elites and governments or by urban communities against external royal and state authority

3. Agrarian rebellion by peasants and others against landlord and/or state authority

4. Provincial, regional, and separatist rebellion by provincial societies or dependent realms against their monarchical state center

5. Kingdomwide civil war against monarchies based on noble and aristocratic leadership and involving the entire society

An additional candidate for possible inclusion is the millenarian rebellion, which is often conceived as a distinct type of revolution and has been the subject of considerable attention in recent years.[38] In the context of early modern Europe, however, I believe that the phenomenon of millen-

---

[36] A more recent example is the Peruvian revolution of 1968. The military junta that gained power in Peru by a coup d'état aimed to transform Peruvian society, and among its acts were various nationalizations and one of the biggest agrarian reforms in the history of Latin America. The fact that in Turkey, Egypt, and elsewhere military coups have been the means of significant change demonstrates that in some societies there are no forces or groups sufficiently strong and well organized to bring about revolutionary change other than armies and military elites.

[37] The coup of 1650 in the Dutch republic is discussed as a revolution by Merriman (*Six contemporaneous revolutions*, 71–88). See also P. Geyl's description, which brings out clearly the coup's political significance in the context of republican institutions and compares it with Charles I's attempt in 1642 on the opposition leaders of the English House of Commons (*The Netherlands in the seventeenth century: part two 1648–1715*, London, 1968, 13–19). A more recent account is H. Rowen, "The revolution that wasn't: The *coup d'état* of 1650 in Holland," *European studies review 4*, 2 (1974). Both coups failed, the Gunpowder conspiracy because it was detected beforehand, the Dutch coup of 1650 because William II's death a couple of months later undid its effects.

[38] For a discussion, see Zagorin, "Theories of revolution in contemporary historiography," and Ch. 6 in this book.

arian rebellion can be better understood as a projection within and modality of other types of revolution, and therefore I propose to treat it in that connection.

The discussion in subsequent chapters will be devoted to four of the five types of revolution listed above and will not include consideration of the conspiratorial coup. This is not because the latter was infrequent or necessarily insignificant. On the contrary. France in the earlier seventeenth century, for example, saw quite a few noble conspiracies, attempts at palace revolutions that sought not only the removal of ministers and favorites but also important policy changes, sometimes with foreign help. In England, besides the Gunpowder plot and some preceding Catholic and other conspiracies against the monarchy, the revolt of the earl of Essex in 1601, an abortive coup, was one of the most striking events of the close of Queen Elizabeth's reign: Essex had been the queen's favorite, and his downfall left a deep impression upon political men. In Spain, the conspiracy in 1641 by two great noblemen, the duke of Medina Sidonia and the marquis of Ayamonte, had nothing less in view than the establishment of Andalusia as an independent kingdom. But in spite of the interest of such cases of revolutionary coups, the other types of revolution are generally of greater consequence, and their examination is sufficiently demanding to justify our concentrating all our attention upon them.[39]

Something should also be said concerning the idea of the bourgeois revolution as a typological category, in view of its influence in discussions of revolution. As has been pointed out earlier, the "bourgeois revolution" achieved canonical status first of all in connection with the French revolution, a feat due mainly to Marx, although its origins can be traced at least as far back as the communist Babeuf's condemnation of the French revolution's limited character in the *Manifeste des égaux* of 1796.[40] Its substance is the portrayal of the revolution as the conflict and victory of the bourgeois class over the pre-1789 feudal-aristocratic society. Not only has this interpretation been enthroned as orthodoxy by a succession of twentieth-century French academic historians, including Mathiez, Lefebvre, and Soboul,[41] but it has also been adapted by Marxist scholars to several

---

[39] Although most revolutionary coups in the twentieth century have been dominated by the military, as in the majority of Latin American cases, the coups of early modern Europe were the attempts of dissident aristocrats. For the example mentioned in the text, see R. Mousnier, "The Fronde," in Forster and Greene, *Preconditions of revolution*, 137–8; S. R. Gardiner, *What Gunpowder plot was*, London, 1897; J. E. Neale, *Queen Elizabeth*, New York, 1957, ch. 21; A. Dominguez Ortiz, *Crisis y decadencia de la España de los Austrias*, 3rd ed., Barcelona, 1973, ch. 4.

[40] See Chapter 1 in this book; and D. Thomson, *The Babeuf plot*, London, 1947.

[41] See A. Cobban, *The social interpretation of the French revolution*, Cambridge, 1964, for illustrations and discussion. Typical is Lefebvre's remark that the French revolution "is only the crown of a long economic and social evolution which has made the bourgeoisie the mistress of the world" (cited in *ibid.*, 8, from G. Lefebvre, *Etudes sur la Révolution française*,

preceding early modern revolutions. Thus we are assured that the English revolution of 1640–60 was "the first complete 'bourgeois revolution' " decisive for future socioeconomic development, "a bourgeois revolution . . . of classical type" closely comparable to the revolution of 1789 and one that "set the stage for the industrial revolution . . . to come."[42] Similarly, the rebellion of the Fronde during Louis XIV's minority is pictured as a bourgeois revolution that remained abortive because the French bourgeoisie of the period betrayed its own historic mission by becoming feudalized.[43]

The claim by Marxist scholars that the English and French revolutions were decisive events for the emergence of a capitalist order is far more a matter of faith than of historical proof or probability. Of the English revolution the most that can be said is that, insofar as it contributed to the growth of political and religious liberty, it may also have contributed somewhat to the conditions favorable to subsequent British imperial and economic expansion. This, however, does not make of it in the requisite sense a "bourgeois" revolution.[44] Of the French revolution, Professor Cobban, one of the leading critics of the orthodox view, has pointed out that its beneficiaries were peasant proprietors, lawyers, *rentiers*, and the conservative propertied who successfully resisted the new economic trends. "Insofar as capitalist economic developments were at issue," he suggests, "it was a revolution not for, but against capitalism. This would . . . have been recognized long ago if . . . not . . . for the influence of an unhistorical sociological theory."[45]

The characterizations of the "bourgeois revolution" are commonly vitiated by their verbal equivocations and mechanistic class analysis. When used by historians of Marxist persuasion, feudalism and bourgeoisie, for instance, tend to become terms of almost infinite elasticity designating widely divergent conditions and groups. The alleged class dichotomy between the aristocracy and an increasingly wealthy, self-conscious bourgeoisie is not only false but also much too reductive and crude to serve as a guide to the complex social and economic realities of the *ancien régime* in France. As has been justifiably said of this description, "To fit in with the

Paris, 1954, 246). A. Soboul, *The French Revolution: 1787–1799,* New York, 1975, is among the latest general statements of the position.

[42] E. Hobsbawm, "The crisis of the seventeenth century," in *Crisis in Europe 1560–1660,* ed. T. Aston, New York, 1965, 53; C. Hill, "The English civil war interpreted by Marx and Engels," *Science and society 12,* 1 (1948), and *The English revolution 1640,* 3rd ed., London, 1955; M. Dobb, *Studies in the development of capitalism,* New York, 1947, 176. See also Engels's statement of the position in his "Introduction" to the English edition of *Socialism: utopian and scientific.*

[43] Porchnev, *Les Soulèvements populaires en France,* pt. 3, chs. 1–2.

[44] See also H. R. Trevor-Roper, "The general crisis of the seventeenth century," in *Religion, the Reformation and social change,* 2nd ed., London, 1972, 52–5, for an effective criticism of the Marxist conception of the English revolution as "bourgeois," and Ch. 12 of this book.

[45] Cobban, *The social interpretation of the French revolution,* 172.

theory, eighteenth-century France had to be envisaged as still basically a feudal society . . . regardless of the facts."[46] On analogous grounds, another historian of the *ancien régime* has pointed out the futility of continuing to explain the French revolution as "the triumph of an unidentifiable capitalist bourgeoisie over an unidentifiable feudal aristocracy."[47] Similar criticisms based on modern research have also caused the Marxian interpretation of the English revolution to fall into disrepute; for whatever the revolt against Charles I may have been, it was not a bourgeois revolution, if to say it was means that it was waged by a bourgeoisie against a semifeudal social and political order.[48] Equally in the case of the Fronde, to conceive it as a bourgeois revolution *manqué* is only possible, as one of its foremost students has demonstrated, by the doctrinaire forcing of facts into a theoretical straitjacket.[49]

What has been said in the previous chapter about the contribution of Marxism to the mythology of revolution applies no less to its idea of the "bourgeois revolution." If the latter still looms large in accounts of revolution despite its inadequacies, this is because its main function is less that of historical clarification than to serve a particular version of the meaning of history. In the guise of a "law" of social development determined by the class struggle, the "bourgeois revolution" assumes its place as a stage within a teleological progression necessarily leading to the proletarian revolution and socialism as the next stage. The "bourgeois revolution," as a historian of the French revolution calls it, is thus, "a metaphysical personage" that offers a "quasi-providential interpretation of events."[50] The teleology of which it is part, moreover, defines an ideal trajectory toward the future in relation to which persons and classes either fulfill or betray their "historic" mission, for this philosophy also pretends to know better than the historical actors themselves what their role, purposes, and aims should be. And it is surely only through devotion to the same philosophy that Marxist writers have ingeniously contrived to make the "bourgeois

---

[46] *Ibid.*, 169.

[47] P. Goubert, *L'Ancien Régime*, 2nd ed., Paris, 1969, 257. See also G. Taylor, "Noncapitalist wealth and the French Revolution," *American historical review 72*, 2 (1967), for a convincing critique of the interpretation of the French revolution as a bourgeois revolution. As he points out, "Between most of the nobility and the proprietary sector of the middle classes, a continuity of investment forms and social-economic values . . . made them, economically, a single group. In the relations of production they played a common role." Skocpol (*States and social revolutions*, 174–9) also presents some doubts about the "bourgeois revolution" thesis applied to France.

[48] See Zagorin, *The court and the country*, chs. 1–2, and L. Stone, *The causes of the English revolution 1529–1642*, London, 1972, 39–40, 54, 71–2.

[49] R. Mousnier, "Recherches sur les soulèvements populaires en France avant la Fronde," in *La Plume, la faucille, et le marteau*, Paris, 1970, for a convincing refutation of Porchnev's misconceptions.

[50] F. Furet, "Le Catechisme de la Révolution française," *Annales E.S.C. 26*, 2 (1971), 279. The whole essay is an acute criticism of the orthodox interpretation of the French revolution.

revolution" absorb within its elastic boundaries events as different in nature as the German peasant war and Reformation, the English and French revolutions, almost all the revolutions of 1848, the Risorgimento, the American civil war, the Russian revolutions of 1905 and February 1917, the Mexican revolution, and the precommunist phase of the Chinese revolution – a list that merely confirms its lack of usefulness as a type in the empirical comparative study of revolution.

The several properties and spectrum of characteristics of the types of early modern revolution outlined above will be considered later in connection with the discussion of specific cases. It should be pointed out, however, that in distinguishing one type from another I have not followed any rule or formula prescribing the proportions in which to weight or combine the requisite criteria; indeed, no such rule is or could be available for this purpose. The problem of the typological differentiation of the phenomenon of revolution in particular societies cannot be solved by a simple generalized procedure conducted to rule. Rather, it can be dealt with only by the informed judgment and insight of the historian bringing his knowledge to bear upon the complex nature and facts of these societies in order to discern the fundamental configurations of revolution inscribed within them.[51]

Furthermore, a typology consists of ideal types. It is therefore a set of constructions or, if one likes, "a coherent fiction to be measured against the real."[52] Each type is derived by a unilateral accentuation, a heightening, an abstraction of certain real properties in an intellectual operation that sets it a distance from the specific events known, for example, as the English revolution, the German peasant war, or the Netherlands revolt, to which it may refer and which the historian by a different intellectual operation is also able to bring before him in all their concrete particularity. Accordingly, in the type we obtain a constructed object, one to which no empirical case of revolution entirely corresponds, just as in many empirical cases there will be features associated with more than one type.

From this it will be apparent that I reject the typological approach commonly adopted in discussions of revolution, whereby a particular historical instance is treated as the privileged or paradigmatic case and so becomes the model in relation to which either revolution in general or some restricted class of revolutions is to be understood. This method seems to me arbitrary in that it can offer no adequate reason why one historical instance of revolution should be preferred as model to another.

---

[51] The place and importance of judgment, insight, and methods not generalizable in a manual of scientific procedure are clearly and profoundly brought out by K. Polanyi (*Personal knowledge*, London, 1958).

[52] See P. Bourdieu, "Structuralism and the theory of sociological knowledge," *Social research 35*, 4 (1968), 697.

If, as is frequently done, the French revolution is accepted as the model of revolutions, and if, in addition, as Brinton and many other writers have observed, it passed through successive stages from the rule of moderates to the rule of extremists, a reign of terror, and a Thermidorean reaction, then by extension the analogous sequence must be the case for other revolutions as well. As a result we see misguided efforts to trace out by means of strained arrangements of the facts the same succession of stages in such a revolutionary civil war of the sixteenth century as the Netherlands rebellion against Spain, where it scarcely applies and where the context also differs very markedly from that of the revolution in France. If the commencement of the revolt of the Netherlands is dated in 1566, with the great outbreak of iconoclasm and the first appearance of armed resistance to Philip II's government, then it began with an extremist phase, not a moderate one.[53] Moreover, the Netherlands rebellion as a whole presents to a certain extent an oscillation of phases, as illustrated by the moderate culmination in the Pacification of Ghent in 1576, rather than a steady intensification in a radical direction. I do not, to be sure, deny that revolutions have often displayed a tendency to develop toward increasingly extreme courses with concomitant changes in leadership. Nevertheless, such a sequence cannot be considered as either a law or the inevitable logic of revolution, to be imposed as a "fit" on every major revolutionary event.

The acceptance of some particular historical instance as the paradigm for revolution seems to me to miss an essential point concerning the nature of typological descriptions. To repeat, the type is a constructed or fictional class and is not identical with the real. Hence, with regard to the revolutionary civil wars of sixteenth- and seventeenth-century Europe, for example, the Netherlands rebellion does not constitute the type, any more than do the French wars of religion, the English revolution, or the Fronde. All of them share some basic properties of the type, which is nevertheless not equal to any of its cases.

By means of an appropriate typology, though, we can recognize in the revolutionary event as empirically presented the characteristics that cause it to belong to or approximate one type of revolution rather than another. And we can also ask fruitful comparative questions about variations and resemblances among cases of revolution of the same type as well as about possible parallels among revolutions of different types. In this connection

[53] See the discussion concerning the applicability of Brinton's model to the Netherlands rebellion by G. Nadel, "The logic of *The anatomy of revolution* with reference to the Netherlands revolt," *Comparative studies in society and history* 2, 4 (1960); G. Griffiths, "The revolutionary character of the revolt of the Netherlands," *ibid.* 2, 4 (1960); and I. Schöffer, "The Dutch revolt anatomized: Some comments," in *ibid.* 3, 4 (1961). Interesting observations and reservations about Brinton's and the French revolutionary "stage" or "phase" model are offered by Hagopian (*The phenomenon of revolution*, ch. 5).

we shall note again that we do not want our different types of revolution to be a reified or static set of classes. Instead, we should like them to signify, if they can, certain alternative structures of action and patterns of possible relations among the requisite criteria, which may in turn be co-ordinated with the conditions and processes in the world of early modern Europe out of which its actual revolutions were produced.

IV

Besides typology, there is another fundamental problem that the comparative historian of revolution can hardly hope to avoid: causality. Does the comparative study of revolution have available to it any adequate causal theory that will serve its explanatory purposes? Traditionally, causality is the question upon which most of the intellectual effort devoted to revolution has concentrated. From Aristotle to the present, philosophers, historians, sociologists, political scientists, economists, and psychologists have grappled with it; however, despite the useful ideas that their writings sometimes present, no general theory has so far been developed by which we could predict future occurrences of revolution, or, if we prefer a less exigent standard than prediction, from which the causes of particular past revolutions could be deduced.

Needless to say, the statesmen and thinkers who were the contemporaries and witnesses of, and sometimes actors in, our early modern revolutions were also preoccupied with their causes. The philosopher Francis Bacon, a servant of Queen Elizabeth and King James I, offered an inclusive list of the causes of rebellion in states: "innovation in religion; taxes; alteration of laws and customs; breaking of privileges; general oppression; advancement of unworthy persons; strangers; dearths; disbanded soldiers; factions grown desperate; and whatsoever in offending people joineth and knitteth them in a common cause."[54] Cardinal Granvelle, Philip II's trusted minister, saw the cause of the Netherlands rebellion in the discontent and ambition of a debt-ridden nobility bent on restoring its fortunes through revolt and innovation.[55] An English politican, Sir Edwin Sandys, pointed to the domain of what we would nowadays call *conjoncture* when, in warning of the effects of unemployment in the slump of 1621, he declared,

[54] F. Bacon, "Of seditions and troubles," *Essays* (1625).

[55] This was not only Granvelle's view but was also held by contemporary memoirists like Hopperus and Pontus Payen, who remained loyal to Spanish rule. Payen connected the emphasis on noble indebtedness and discontent to historical recollections of Catiline's conspiracy in republican Rome. I am persuaded that this explanation of revolution in the sixteenth and seventeenth centuries often derived from classical reminiscences and influences; see the remarks of these writers cited in E. Marx, *Studien zur Geschichte des Niederländischen Aufstandes, Leipziger Studien aus dem Gebiet der Geschichte*, v. 3, Leipzig, 1902, 112–14.

"*Bellum Rusticorum* in Germany proceeded from this, that the poor wanted work."[56] Under the heading of changes in states, the French jurist, Jean Bodin, the foremost scholar to deal with comparative politics in the sixteenth century, devoted a lengthy discussion to the causes of revolutions both ancient and modern.[57] Clarendon, a leading figure in the English revolution who was also its first great historian, ascribed its origin to a combination of causes, including religious hypocrisy, the ambition, pride, and folly of persons, and the mistakes of government and ministers.[58]

We could cull many other causal explanations of revolution from the literature of the age. For some we might also find adequate confirmation and a particular application. But in what sense can they serve a general explanatory function? At most such causal accounts are partial and contingent, true maybe for certain cases but not for others. Perhaps they could be absorbed into a comprehensive theory of revolution; in themselves, though, they are incomplete and have no theoretical standing.

Some who reflect on the subject might contend that the main obstacle to a causal theory of revolution lies in the extreme complexity of revolution itself, a characteristic that it shares, of course, with many other phenomena of social life. Others might add as a further obstacle the inefficacy of the methods the social sciences have so far had at their disposal to deal with problems of this order. Nonetheless, despite the admitted difficulties of the undertaking, there are a number of theories of revolution available in the social sciences today, and it is worth looking briefly at several to see what they offer to historical and comparative investigation.[59]

Among the theories professing to provide a causal explanation of revolution, three in particular deserve notice. One is Marxist historical materialism; another is structural-functional social-systems theory; and the third is the theory of relative deprivation. As the Marxist theory of revolution has already been the subject of critical treatment in both this and the previous chapter, it may be left aside and our discussion focused on the other two.

Theories that conceive society as an integrated functional whole, con-

---

[56] Sir Edwin Sandys, cited in J. Thirsk and J. P. Cooper (eds.), *Seventeenth-century economic documents*, Oxford, 1972, 1; for "*conjoncture*" and the economic context of revolution, see Chapter 5 in this book.

[57] J. Bodin, *Les Six livres de la république*, Paris, 1576, bk. 4, ch. 1. I use the English translation by Richard Knolles, *The six bookes of a commonweal*, ed. K. D. McRae (1606; reprint ed., Cambridge, 1962).

[58] Edward Hyde, Earl of Clarendon, *The history of the rebellion*, ed. W. D. Macray, 6 v., Oxford, 1888, v. 1, 1–4.

[59] For a survey and discussion, see Zagorin, "Theories of revolution in contemporary historiography"; L. Stone, "Theories of revolution" in *The causes of the English revolution 1529–1642*; and Hagopian, *The phenomenon of revolution*. Some of the writings cited in the following notes also contain useful analyses and criticisms of both older and more recent theories of revolution.

sensual in nature and based on shared values, have a respectable provenance in the sociological tradition of the nineteenth century and include among their exponents Max Weber, Emile Durkheim, and, more recently, Talcott Parsons. Applied to revolution, these theories are also assumed in such general studies as those by Edwards and Pettee, which identify the origin of revolution with "cramp" or "strain" in the ongoing processes and institutions of the social system, leading, if not corrected, to dissensus and violent conflict.[60] The same assumption, based on the notions of "structural conduciveness" and "strain," underlies the attempt by Smelser to explain revolution as a form of action subsumed within the still wider category of "collective behavior."[61] For the examination of this type of theory, a good example is provided by the work of Chalmers Johnson, representing as it does the most concentrated effort to solve the causal problem of revolution by means of structural-functional analysis.[62]

The central premise of structural-functional analysis is the conception of the functional social system as a state of homeostatic equilibrium. The causal process of revolution is accordingly held to begin with the inability of the system's adaptive and adjustive mechanisms to cope with changes in the environment or in values, whether these changes originate from within or outside the society. The result of this inability in asynchronization of different kinds, manifesting itself in disequilibrium and dysfunction. Should leaders and elites fail or refuse to take timely measures to restore equilibrium and reintegrate the social system, dysfunction will spread through various subsystems, giving rise to increasing protest and disaffection among the society's members. Multiple dysfunction and elite incompetence or intransigence thus create the potentiality of revolution. Whether the latter occurs or not will then depend on the intervention of some particular event acting as an accelerator or trigger, such as the incumbent regime's defeat in war or anything else that weakens its power and raises the confidence of its revolutionary opponents. Should such an event ensue, then revolution becomes highly probable or certain.

The incurable weakness in this explanation of revolution, which seems to me to make it a pseudo rather than genuine causal account, is the emptiness of the idea of a social system in equilibrium. By this I mean that its defect does not consist of some particular empirical inadequacy but in its

---

[60] L. Edwards, *The natural history of revolution*, Chicago, 1927; G. Pettee, *The process of revolution*, New York, 1938.

[61] N. Smelser, *Theory of collective behavior*, New York, 1962. A critique of structuralist-functionalist theories generally, including a discussion of both Smelser's and Chalmers Johnson's theories of revolution, is given in A. D. Smith, *The concept of social change*, London, 1973; see also B. Salert, *Revolutions and revolutionaries: Four theories*, New York, 1976, which deals with Johnson and several other writers, including Gurr, treated in the present chapter of this book.

[62] Johnson, *Revolution and the social system*; Johnson, *Revolutionary change*.

lack of content and the impossibility of specifying the criteria whereby the state of equilibrium and its opposite may be known. The anthropologist Lévi-Strauss has remarked, "To say that a society functions is a truism; but to say that everything in a society functions is an absurdity."[63] Some such error appears to be entailed in the conception of a society in equilibrium. When Johnson describes the nonrevolutionary society as a state of equilibrium, he only tells us that it functions – which we know already – but tells us nothing as to what equilibrium is. To be sure, he does propose several tentative indexes of disequilibrium, such as the rate of suicide or the "military participation ratio"; but there is not the slightest reason to suppose that these necessarily indicate either disequilibrium or a potential for revolution unless we have first accepted the theory they are intended to confirm.

It is apparent that a confusion exists here between the idea of the prerequisites of a society or social system as such, on the one hand, and of equilibrium, on the other. As an economist has pointed out in a decisive criticism of equilibrium theories in sociology, "Time and again it appears that the concept of equilibrium is extended so far as to become coterminous with that of organized society; what, then, is actually discussed is not so much a set of equilibrium conditions as a set of minimum conditions of social existence."[64] When we look at existing societies, however, what we invariably see is imperfect integration, numerous dysfunctions, and frequent failures in elite and governmental performance. The crucial problem, then, becomes to ascertain which of these engender the process of revolution and why. Unfortunately, Johnson's version of social-systems theory can provide no solution to this question because, in the absence of any determinate content or clear meaning for equilibrium, no inference to the relevant dysfunctions can be made. This failure, to my mind, vitiates the functionalist equilibrium model as a causal explanation of revolution.[65] What then may perhaps remain as an expedient is, first, to distinguish the long-range causes or preconditions of revolution from its precipitants or immediate occasions and, second, to identify the relevant social processes, institutional failures, patterns of conflict, and follies or injustices of rulers that comprise the revolutionary sequence in any particular

---

[63] C. Lévi-Strauss, *Structural anthropology*, New York, 1963, 13.

[64] Cited from Alexander Gerschenkron's critique of Parsonian theory by N. Smelser, *Essays in sociological analysis*, Englewood Cliffs, 1968, 218n. A similar confusion appears in Smelser's own description of equilibrium (*ibid.*, 211), which is in reality no more than the description or definition of a system.

[65] See the related criticism of Smith: "The trouble with the functionalist answer is that its alternative to equilibrium is the unstructured anarchy of anomie. Whereas what we discover repeatedly are patterns of group conflict and multiple tension and 'dysfunction,' rather than . . . synchronous equilibrium or normative breakdown" (*The concept of social change*, 120).

case. This procedure is unexceptionable and is widely used by historians and other students of revolution, but it is of a purely ad hoc character and has no deductive relation to the theory in question.[66]

More precise, by contrast, and less susceptible to these objections is the theory of relative deprivation (RD), which long before its recent appearance in generalized form was advanced by Tocqueville as a causal explanation of the French revolution. In his well-known work on the *ancien régime*, Tocqueville contended that an unprecedented increase in prosperity preceded the revolution of 1789 and that this promoted a spirit of unrest and discontent that was strongest in those parts of France that had experienced the most improvement. He connected this fact with the general observation that "it is not always when things are going from bad to worse that revolution breaks out. On the contrary, it more often happens that, when a people which has put up with an oppressive rule over a long period without protest suddenly finds the government relaxing its pressure, it takes up arms against it."[67] Implicit in this comment is the perception that a lightening of burdens arouses hopes and expectations that may exceed the possibility of gratification, in which case the consequence can be frustration, anger, and revolt. This view runs counter to a general tendency, reflected in Marxism and elsewhere, to connect revolution with continually worsening conditions of exploitation and oppression. In 1962, J. C. Davies attempted to formalize and combine both views in a theory proposing that revolution is probable when a lengthy period of economic growth and improvement is succeeded by a sudden halt and downswing, christened the J-curve. It is based on the assumption that a growth phase generates new wants and expectations, which are then abruptly disappointed as slump ensues. With the onset of the J-curve, an acute disparity develops between mounting expectations and the possibility of their satisfaction, which in turn makes revolution likely. Revolution is accordingly explained in this theory as the effect neither of prosperity and improvement nor of misery and oppression but of a particular sequence of the two.[68]

RD introduces a crucial psychological determinant between "objective conditions" and action by subordinating and relating the former to the

---

[66] Attempts to draw on Johnson's ideas in the historical explanation of revolution follow this procedure; see Stone, *The causes of the English revolution 1529–1642*. In a preliminary version of this essay, Stone ascribes its "theoretical framework" to Johnson; see Forster and Green, *Preconditions of revolution*, 65n.

[67] A. de Tocqueville, *The old regime and the French revolution*, trans. S. Gilbert, New York, 1955, 176–7.

[68] J. C. Davies, "Toward a theory of revolution," *American sociological review* 27, 1 (1962), and "The J-curve of rising and declining satisfactions as a cause of some great revolutions and a contained rebellion," in Graham and Gurr, *Violence in America*.

perception of the actors whose behavior is to be explained. Of the treatments of revolution from this standpoint, in which RD is conceived as the prime mover, the fullest and most lucid analysis has been given by Ted Gurr.[69]

Gurr's account is buttressed by a summary of findings by psychological experimenters that indicate a causal relation between frustration and violence – or, rather, a disposition of frustrated people to become violent in certain circumstances. RD is defined as a perceived discrepancy by individuals between their value expectations and their value capabilities, that is, between what they feel entitled to have and what they think they can obtain. The expectations subject to RD may include not only the values connected with economic security and material welfare (although historically these are what have been salient for most people) but also those pertaining to political status and participation and to personal development and moral beliefs. RD may occur either because expectations remain the same while capabilities decline (decremental deprivation), or because expectations increase while capabilities remain the same (aspirational deprivation), or, finally, because the two increase concurrently and then diverge as the J-curve sets in, making capabilities decline while expectations continue to rise (progressive deprivation). When any of these patterns prevails, men will express anger, frustration, and discontent. If RD becomes strong enough and is also focused on political objects, it can create a situation leading to violence and revolution. Whether this happens depends on different variables, including the scope (extent of people affected) and intensity (depth of their reaction) of RD, the legitimacy ascribed to regimes, the presence and influence of ideologies sanctioning violence, and the means of coercion available to incumbents and dissidents.

What can RD contribute to advance the causal understanding of revolution? Its main attraction is that it helps to explain the otherwise puzzling fact that an actual betterment of "objective conditions" can nevertheless sometimes increase rather than diminish discontent. For this reason it may be useful in trying to understand revolutions or protest movements that are known to have occurred during or following a period of improvement of any kind, whether in standards of living, social mobility, or political participation. To do this, it would not only need to determine what sorts of people feel deprived but would also probably need to make use of the related theory of reference groups, which has been devised to explain the mechanism of social influence through which individuals and groups acquire fresh wants and expectations.[70]

[69] T. Gurr, *Why men rebel*, Princeton, 1970.
[70] The idea of "relative deprivation" first appeared under this term in S. Stouffer et al., *The American soldier*, 2 v., Princeton, 1949. It was further generalized and connected with the theory of reference groups by R. K. Merton and A. Kitt. For a general account and discus-

An example of the implicit adoption of these theories for such a purpose may be seen in some of the uniformities Brinton claimed to find among the English, American, French, and Russian revolutions. One of these is that all four societies were "on the upgrade economically before the revolution came, and the revolutionary movements seem to originate in the discontents of not unprosperous people who feel restraint, cramp, annoyance rather than downright crushing oppression." Another uniformity is that the sharpest class antagonisms are felt by people "who have made money . . . and contemplate bitterly the imperfections of a socially privileged aristocracy . . . Strong feelings . . . are roused in those who find an intolerable gap between what they have come to want . . . and what they actually get." "Revolutions," Brinton further comments, "seem more likely when social classes are fairly close together than when they are far apart."[71] Although it is doubtful that the ascribed uniformities do in fact apply to all four cases, it is nonetheless apparent that, insofar as they hold, relative deprivation and reference group theory might help to explain them and that Brinton is making use of the two in his analysis.

In a similar way, the ideologies of the normative past that have been noted as frequent in medieval and early modern rebellions, in which rebels appeal for justification to a past state of affairs, could be interpreted in some instances as an expression of decremental deprivation. In this case, value expectations have not changed, but discontented groups perceive a decline in their customary value positions and capabilities. As Gurr points out, "Decremental deprivation is probably most common in 'traditional' societies and in traditional segments of transitional societies." He also speculates that, historically, it has been a greater source of collective violence than any other pattern of RD because "men are likely to be more intensely angered when they lose what they have than when they lose the hope of attaining what they do not yet have."[72] But it must be added as regards this particular pattern that decremental deprivation is merely a jargon term that obscures something more obvious and elemental; for what it signifies here is *absolute* deprivation, net loss, and oppression.

Although the theory of relative deprivation may offer some useful insights to the study of revolution, its value on the whole seems limited, and

sion, see "Reference groups," *International encyclopedia of the social sciences*, New York, 1968; and W. G. Runciman, *Relative deprivation and social justice*, Berkeley, 1966. An interesting variant and application of RD is presented in A. O. Hirschman, "The changing tolerance for income inequality in the course of economic development," *Quarterly journal of economics* 87 (1973), which focuses on the "tunnel effect." A recent discussion of these ideas in connection with revolution is available in Urry.

[71] Brinton, *The anatomy of revolution*, ed. 1965, 250–1. In this edition, Brinton takes cognizance of J. C. Davies' work of 1962, which he attempts to incorporate, but the same uniformities and underlying ideas appear in the original 1938 edition.

[72] Gurr, *Why men rebel*, 48, 50.

it clearly fails to qualify as a general causal theory. That revolutionaries are discontented people is a truism, if not a tautology; but, as Gurr remarks, "most discontented men are not revolutionaries."[73] Between mere discontent and revolution an enormous distance intervenes. How do men traverse it? What RD reveals is only the socially derived source of discontent in the individual that makes him feel deprived. From this point the explanation must extend in continually widening circles to account for the discontent of many individuals, for the fact that they act together, become violent, are not effectively repressed, direct their violence at political instead of other targets, and are eventually mobilized in revolution. At every step on the way diverse causes and influences come into play that will determine whether the outcome is revolution or not, causes connected with economic and sociostructural developments, perhaps, or with political conflicts and changes, or with beliefs and ideologies. Although one might possibly attempt to incorporate these variables in the form of probabilistic empirical hypotheses, as Gurr does, none is itself a derivative or inference from RD, which merely stands at the inception of the process. Thus, RD might at most state a necessary condition of revolution, but only one such condition, whereas additional necessary conditions would have to be sought elsewhere.

Moreover, the theory of relative deprivation is also too narrow, compared with the variety of facts likely to be needed by historians and sociologists of revolution for their explanations. On the one hand, we have the three patterns of RD, three only, answering no doubt to the desire for parsimony but telling us little in themselves until the requisite historical material is brought into consideration. On the other hand, we have the complication of processes and the dense sequential texture of events that form the actual genesis of revolution in particular cases. How can all these be contracted to the compass of RD without impoverishment and the loss of vital explanatory elements? How can even the attitudes, sentiments, and perceptions that motivate revolutionary actors be understood in the single and exclusive terms of one or another of the patterns of RD? Even in societies where "decremental deprivation" and ideologies of the normative past are more apt to occur, the beliefs and demands of insurgents are rarely altogether nostalgic and lacking in germs of novelty; often they present a combination of defensive – retrospective and aggressive – innovative themes in their programs. Thus RD might easily lend itself to use as a formula that merely oversimplifies the intricacy of the revolutionary phenomenon.

These reflections suggest some doubt as to whether it makes sense to envisage the possibility of any general theory of revolution. To qualify

[73] *Ibid.*, 355.

fully, such a theory would need to state both the necessary and sufficient causes of revolution such that the occurrence of the empirical conditions leading to revolution would be connected to their outcome by a universal causal law of the form: Whenever events and/or processes of the kind C, C_1, C_2, ... C_n, then Revolution, and whenever Revolution, then events and/or process of the kind C, C_1, C_2 ... C_n. Pretty clearly, a law of this nature seems unattainable, owing to the indefinite number and variety of causes required.

Nevertheless, a theorist might perhaps feel reasonably satisfied if he were only able to specify the necessary causes, treating the latter as invariant preconditions, while relegating the sufficient causes to the realm of precipitants that are likely to consist of unique occasions and contingencies not susceptible of generalized causal formulation. However, even with this approach, which has been advocated as the means to facilitate systematic causal investigation of revolution, the obstacles to a generalized theory of revolutionary preconditions remain insuperable.[74] Most writers on revolution have commonly recognized the necessity of multicausal explanations. Johnson is representative of this view when he states that the factors responsible for revolution "are as manifold as the elements comprising society itself" so that "the analyst must . . . make use of sociological, psychological, military, and economic, as well as political, concepts."[75] More significantly, perhaps, historians of revolution, from whose works nearly all our real knowledge of revolutions is obtained, use a diversity of particular causes, whether broad or narrow, in their explanations and rarely pretend to possess a general causal theory; nor do they consider their explanation of a revolution to be weakened or invalidated if it cannot be universalized or subsumed under an alleged general law of the causal conditions of revolution. How, then, can the multicausal analysis of the theorist and the singular explanations of the historian be integrated into a comprehensive theory of revolutionary preconditions?

To meet this difficulty, it is sometimes held that, because "many particular . . . conditions" may be connected with revolutions, the investigator "should stress broad propositions about social processes and balances that can comprehend a variety of such conditions."[76] Plausible as this recommendation may appear, it would still fail to achieve the purpose intended. For the more extended the propositions about social processes become, the greater the difficulty of bringing them into deductive or even close relation to the specific phenomenon to be explained. Broad-gauged propositions concerning social conflict, anomie, and violence may perhaps be

---

[74] H. Eckstein, "On the etiology of internal wars," *History and theory 4*, 2 (1965).

[75] Johnson, *Revolutionary change*, xi; see also Eckstein, "On the etiology of internal wars," 88.

[76] Eckstein, "On the etiology of internal wars," 34.

indispensable to explaining revolutions, but they may be equally necessary to explaining elections, strikes, suicide, crime, and war. They are too general to yield a statement of the preconditions of revolution. To be sure, they might lead us in the direction of some of these preconditions, but they would still have to be supplemented by less general propositions referring to revolutions exclusively. And the latter task brings us back to the same problem we started with of discovering all these propositions.

There is, then, reason for scepticism concerning the likelihood of a general causal theory of revolution. Perhaps the truth may be that no causal propositions exist that apply universally to all cases of revolution – at least none that are not at the same time either vacuous or trivial.

To pose the foregoing questions is to touch on widely discussed problems in the philosophy of science and history as to the place and function of general laws in historical explanation.[77] Without entering into the issues involved, which lie beyond our scope, I believe it is justifiable to point out that adequate explanations of revolutions are certainly possible despite the lack of a general theory of revolutionary causality. Such explanations will consist of an indefinite number of combinations of both singular and rather broad causal statements that are in principle subject to evidential tests. Or, as a recent writer has put it:

Such complex or macro-events as revolution must be explained in terms of the particularized grouping of lower-level features whose total makes up this revolution . . . A revolution is explained . . . when we have enumerated adequate sets of antecedent conditions with their respective empirical generalizations. The resulting explanation . . . is bound to be highly complex, but those seeking simplicity should study something other than the causes of revolution.[78]

In attempting to explain revolutions, there is also a use for limited theories that take account of distinct causes without presuming to universal status. A causal explanation, for instance, such as Brinton's, specifying "the transfer of the allegiance of the intellectuals" among the observed uniformities of revolution (this in turn presupposing a further theory about the role of intellectuals in maintaining political and social stability), may well be true of certain revolutions even if not of others.[79] Similarly, a recent study by Stone on the causes of the English revolution draws on a variety of theories in order to identify and explain the preconditions. Although this method may seem excessively eclectic, it is nonetheless impossible to

[77] Among the key contributions to this extensive literature are C. Hempel's "The function of general laws in history," reprinted in P. Gardiner (ed.), *Theories of history*, New York, 1959; and W. Dray, *Laws and explanation in history*, Oxford, 1957.

[78] Hagopian, *The phenomenon of revolution*, 123.

[79] Brinton, *The anatomy of revolution*, 251. In discussing the "transfer of the allegiance of the intellectuals" as a causal uniformity, Brinton makes his strongest case for it in connection with the French revolution, whereas his treatment of it in relation to the English and American revolutions is more tentative (*ibid.*, 39–49).

dissent from the author's conviction that "to explain in a coherent way why things happened the way they did has necessitated the construction of multiple helix chains of causation more complicated than those of DNA itself. The processes of society are more subtle than those of nature."[80] The same conclusion is expressed by a theorist in reference to modernization but also applies equally well to revolution: "The range of causal factors involved, the complexity of linkages to be traced, is on such a scale as to render any overall theory too general to be of value. Partial theories with restricted insights are all we can hope for."[81]

Finally, as regards the comparative history of revolution, it is surely not necessary to have uniform or identical causal explanations; resemblances and parallels will suffice. Comparative history merely presupposes that among the events, processes, and structures it selects for study there are to be found some correspondences, or some common and analogous features, the clarification of which will add to the understanding of the phenomenon in question.

---

[80] Stone, *The causes of the English revolution 1529–1642*, 146. Besides Johnson's, the theories Stone uses in this work include the J-curve, relative deprivation, and status inconsistency, the last proposed by G. Lenski as "a way of linking social and economic change to revolution" by showing that "a society with a relatively large proportion of persons undergoing high mobility is likely to be in an unstable condition" (*ibid.*, 125, 134, 54).

[81] Smith, *The concept of social change*, 94.

PART II

Revolutionary contexts

3

The society of orders

I

The society that the European revolutions of the sixteenth and seventeenth centuries occurred in and that entered into their nature and established their limits was profoundly different from our own. Not merely its main component groups were different, but so was the essential basis of its stratification. In our present conception or picture of society, we naturally tend to think first of economic classes and to consider class in this sense as the most important collectivity as well as perhaps the controlling reality in political and social action. Early modern society was not a class society, however, and therefore presented an alternative type of structure. Although latter-day historians who have written about this society have provided all the material necessary for its correct understanding, they have often failed to draw the full theoretical conclusions from their own descriptions. Hence confusion and disagreement as to the sort of society it was have persisted. But if we consider it systematically, it is evident that it was not homologous with the society destined to displace it after the eighteenth century and that it incorporated a differently determined structure.

In using the collective singular, "early modern society," I do not of course mean to imply that we might not equally well speak of "societies." Europe did, after all, consist of plural societies, and the distinctions among them also decisively affected their revolutions. We could not simply superpose an account of the English social order on that which enclosed the peoples ruled by the French or Spanish monarchies. But here, as everywhere in comparative studies, the critical consideration is the parallelism or resemblances evinced at a certain level of generality. Although specific distinctions may not be ignored, the main inclusive fact to be noted at the outset is that early modern societies possessed the common trait of being, under whatever modalities, societies of orders or estates dominated by nobilities and aristocracies.

In this society, the fundamental basis of stratification was status, which, assimilating and subordinating to itself other criteria of differentiation, designated the honor, dignity, deference, and esteem, or lack of them, attaching to particular positions and functions of groups and individuals. The resulting structure appeared as a complex gradation or hierarchy of various "orders," "estates," or "degrees" of men, the whole constituting a system that openly proclaimed its inequality.

The German sociologists Weber and Tönnies, attempting to bring out the central features that set off this society from others, and themselves born into a nation that preserved many of its vestiges, provide some observations helpful to its analysis.[1] Both distinguish it from a social organization based on classes, which are mainly economically determined collectivities created by common economic interest and conditions in relation to the market. "Class situation," suggests Weber, is ultimately "market situation," whereas status, in contrast, designates "every typical component of the life fate of men that is determined by a specific, positive or negative, social estimation of *honor.*" Status, he remarks, is manifest above all in a "specific style of life"; and he further notes that "with some simplification, one might say that 'classes' are stratified according to their relations to the production and acquisition of goods, whereas status groups are stratified according to their . . . *consumption* of goods as represented by special 'styles of life.' "

Besides these general observations, several others by these two writers may be mentioned as additional clues to the understanding of our subject. Tönnies comments that estates or orders have an organic relation to each other similar to the limbs of a body, whereas classes are engaged in contractual relationships. He also stresses the rigidity of estates compared with the "often extreme fluidity of classes." And he considers that ruling estates (*Herrenstände*) are the prototype of such a structure in their insistence upon noble status and honor. Both he and Weber draw attention as well to the strong tendency toward endogamous marriage within status groups displayed by this society. Moreover, Weber emphasizes the resistance to the parvenu and to "the pretensions of sheer property" or money as such. "If mere economic acquisition and naked economic power," he points out, "could bestow upon anyone who has won it the same honor as those who are interested in status by virtue of style of life claim for themselves, the status order would be threatened at its very root."

Finally, as still another depiction in similar terms of the structure of this

---

[1] The quotations in the following two paragraphs are from F. Tönnies, "Stände und Klassen," in A. Vierkandt, *Handwörterbuch der Soziologie*, 1931, and M. Weber, *Wirtschaft und Gesellschaft*, 1922, pt. 3, ch. 4, translated respectively as "Estates and classes" and "Class, status, and party," and included in R. Bendix and S. Lipset (eds.), *Class, status and power: a reader in social stratification*, Glencoe, 1953.

early modern society, we may cite the account given by a recent historian, Roland Mousnier, which, although referring primarily to France, has wider bearings and applications as well:

In a stratification by orders or estates, social groups are hierarchized . . . not according to the wealth of their members . . . nor according to their role in the production of material goods, but according to the esteem, honor, and dignity attached by the society to social functions which have no relation to the production of material goods.

He adds that, in France, honor and esteem went first of all to the profession of arms and the aptitude for command and protection resulting therefrom.[2]

These various characterizations by modern scholars afford a sufficient ingress to the broad understanding of the society in which our sixteenth- and seventeenth-century revolutions occurred. To make proper sense of it, we must take its structural principles and internal differentia as we find them and not, by a prior theoretical fiat, redefine and reduce them to something quite other than themselves. The latter procedure would give us only artificial social categories rather than the real groups and collectivities we need for our purpose, those whose actuality is attested in the contemporary evidence, who possessed a common consciousness and sense of identity, and who could thus at times attempt to exert a common will upon their world.

What conditioned the awareness of early modern societies and provided the framework for their members' political action and conflicts was, accordingly, a system of status defined in the main by a constellation of extraeconomic criteria, such as birth and descent, titles of honor, legal and customary privileges, lordship or other forms of authority over the land and its inhabitants, university education, office, and other varieties of service to the prince and his government. Wealth in this system had a dual place: First, it was the material basis for maintaining the honorable styles of life appropriate to the higher status positions; second, it was the primary means of mobility within the status hierarchy (a point to which we shall return). Besides aristocratic elites, the structure of orders encompassed the members of the professions, the higher and lower clergy, urban elites and occupational strata, the occupational functions connected with trade, merchandise, finance, the crafts, manufactures, and, finally, the

---

[2] R. Mousnier et al., *Problèmes de stratification sociale: deux cahiers de la noblesse pour les états généraux de 1649–1651*, Paris, 1965, intro., 14–15. Mousnier has devoted a number of writings to this subject; see, among others, "Problèmes de méthode dans l'étude des structures sociales des XVIe, XVIIe, XVIIIe siècles," in *La Plume, la faucille et le marteau*, Paris, 1970; *Les Hiérarchies sociales de 1450 à nos jours*, Paris, 1969; "Les Concepts d' 'ordres,' d' 'états' . . . à la fin du XVIIIe siècle," *Revue historique* 247, 502 (1972); and, for a compendious exposition, *Les Institutions de la France sous la monarchie absolue*, Paris, 1974, v. 1, *passim*.

peasants who fed the population, all of whom were hierarchically incorporated at levels prescribed by the dominant criteria.

The society of orders, which descends from the Middle Ages, was often pictured in the commonplaces of medieval thought as consisting of three great estates, those who pray, those who fight, and those who work (*oratores, bellatores, laboratores; Lehrstand, Wehrstand, Nährstand*). A leading student of the corporate life of the Middle Ages declares that "its social organization rested definitively on the priest, the knight, and the peasant."[3] But the traditional schema of the three estates, which endured into the Renaissance and the sixteenth century, was merely the most simplified and abstract representation of a medieval world actually far more intricate in its bewildering variety and differentiation.[4] Even more so was this true of early modern societies, subject as they were to powerful new economic and political pressures that modified both urban and rural life, as may be seen, for instance, in the microcosm of the provincial Beauvaisis in France, whose variegated structures have been so incisively revealed by its historian.[5] And despite the fact that the societies of orders also aspired to be ordered societies, they showed many signs of disorder, of thrusting movement, of mingle-mangle rise and decline of families and groups, which the prevailing status system was able nonetheless to contain within its mold. Hence they presented a complicated, multiple stratification among the innumerable ranks, communities, corporate bodies, functions, and occupations of which their various orders consisted. Contemporary thinkers reflected this complexity in their descriptions of their society, for within the schematism of status they usually portrayed it as a more elaborate organism than that of the three orders and as containing many estates and degrees.[6] The tendency of most of these thinkers was further to visualize the status hierarchy, in its essence if not necessarily in its actual operation, as a normative arrangement and moral community of interdependent functions and reciprocal duties that formed a body politic of common benefit to all its members, whatever their station. This conventional conception, with its static overtones and roots in traditional religion, cosmic assumptions, and philosophy, must be seen as an idealization and an ideology serving to palliate or justify the existing profound inequality. But the organic character and mutual dependence among the orders that contempo-

---

[3] E. Lousse, *La Société d'ancien régime: organization et representation corporatives*, Louvain, 1943, 103.

[4] See R. Mohl, *The three estates in medieval and Renaissance literature*, New York, 1933.

[5] See P. Goubert, *Cent mille provinciaux du XVIIe siècle*, Paris, 1968, an edition of the first part of the author's larger work, *Beauvais et le Beauvaisis de 1600 à 1730*, 2 v., Paris, 1960.

[6] For some English examples, see P. Zagorin, *The court and the country*, London, 1969, 23–5; and, for France, C. Loyseau, *Cinq livres du droit des offices, suivis du livre des seigneuries et de celui des ordres*, Paris, 1610, and the discussion in Mousnier, *Les Hiérarchies sociales*, ch. 6.

rary writers ascribed to their society does not mean, needless to say, that it was lacking in conflicts. On the contrary, its conflicts were many; indeed, from this point of view it can be compared, in a graphic phrase that has been used of early seventeenth-century France, with "a volcano with multiple craters."[7]

Important features of early modern revolutions, like the leading role of aristocracies and elites in all the great revolutionary civil wars of the period, are connected not in a contingent way but systematically and structurally, by a fundamental dependence and congruity, with the general properties of a society of orders. So when Fernand Braudel puts the question, for example, whether the social conflicts of the sixteenth century were class struggles, he answers negatively on the ground that there can be no classes without a corresponding class consciousness, which was lacking at the time.[8] That a consciousness of class was absent from the contemporary conflicts is largely true; but then we must immediately add the crucial proviso that what took its place was the consciousness of status such as a society of orders engenders and which had its own vital effects upon the latter's internal conflicts.

II

If we attempt a brief survey of some of the orders from the standpoint of our inquiry, we notice first, in place of highest estimation, the nobility. At this period, according to a Spanish historian, "there are fundamentally only two estates, nobility and plebeians,"[9] a statement that, although literally an exaggeration, serves nevertheless to point up the significance of nobilities in the states and societies of our sixteenth- and seventeenth-century revolutions.

When we speak of the nobility, however, we are dealing with a much diversified body containing numerous gradations of rank, power, and wealth and differing somewhat in different countries. We also meet both formal-juridical definitions of noble status, such as Marc Bloch held to be an essential condition for the existence of a *noblesse*, and informal-customary definitions.[10] The complexion of the noble order was modified, moreover, by the effects of social change such as has been noted in the case of France, which during the sixteenth century saw "a continual addition of newcomers who by usurpation and prescription, purchase of lands and noble fiefs,

[7]R. Mandrou, *Classes et luttes de classes en France au début du XVIIe siècle*, Florence, 1965, 26.
[8]F. Braudel, *La Méditerranée et le monde méditerranéen à l'époque de Philippe II*, 2nd rev. ed., 2 v., Paris, 1966, v.2, 78–9.
[9]J. A. Maravall, *La Philosophie politique espagnole au XVIIe siècle*, Paris, 1955, 281.
[10]J. Meyer, *La Noblesse bretonne au XVIIIe siècle*, 2 v., Paris, 1966, v. 1, 30.

military service, offices, and ennoblement, sought to unite themselves with the old nobility."[11]

Hence the reticulation of nobilities as well as their national and provincial variations. If we look at England, the nobility consisted, strictly speaking, only of the titular peerage, a legally defined, numerically small, hereditary status of the rank of baron and above, transmitted by male primogeniture. But in a wider sense it also included the gentry, the order of more eminent landed families immediately beneath the peerage, to which the younger children of peers (who in England, unlike many continental states, did not inherit their father's rank) also belonged and which contemporaries considered a lesser nobility.[12] Professor McFarlane, one of its historians, accordingly describes the English nobility as a *noblesse* whose "members cannot be contrasted with the gentry because they included them," the latter's privileges, however, being "tacit ones . . . without the sanction of legally defined status."[13] Furthermore, the peerage and gentry together constituted the aristocracy; and it is legitimate, I think, to refer generally to the ascendancy of aristocracies in early modern societies if, going beyond the purely juridical aspect of status, we take aristocracy to be synonymous with nobility in its broader social meaning at the time.

There were certain dissimilarities between continental nobilities and the English. For one thing, the former were more severely hierarchical and sharply differentiated. In England, the titular peerage and upper gentry formed a practically homogeneous social body by the later sixteenth century. In countries like France, the Spanish kingdoms, and the Netherlands, however, a small and powerful elite, the high nobility, which was frequently a court nobility, stood well above the rest at the summit of the noble order. In France it consisted of the princes of the blood, dukes and peers, and those known as *les grands* generally; in Castile and Aragon, of the lords who held the rank of grandees of Spain plus some other distinguished *titulos;* in the Netherlands, of the provincial governors and members of the famed knightly order of the Golden Fleece founded in the fifteenth century by Duke Philip the Good of Burgundy. Beneath these

[11] *Ibid.*, v. 1, 6; see also G. Huppert, *Les Bourgeois Gentilhommes*, Chicago, 1977, for the effects of social change and mobility on the French *noblesse*, including some anomalies of status.

[12] Sir Thomas Smith (*De republica anglorum* [1583], ed. L. Alston, Cambridge, 1906, 31 ff.) and Thomas Wilson (*The state of England* [1600], *Camden miscellany* 16[1936], 17) are two of numerous writers who regard the gentry of knights, esquires, and gentlemen as a lesser nobility. This was the common opinion of the time.

[13] K. B. McFarlane, *The nobility of later medieval England*, Oxford, 1973, 6, 7n., xxiv. McFarlane also remarks, "Arguably, tacit expectations rather than legal privileges or prohibitions dominated English notions of status," in contrast to other European states (*ibid.*, xxv).

lofty aristocratic strata descended lesser ranks and titles down to the *gentilhommes, caballeros,* and *hidalgos,* who were simply noblemen.[14]

Nobility originated in such manifold ways as prescription and long continuance of families in the noble way of life, royal creations, sheer usurpation that eventually gained acceptance, and the possession of offices conferring noble privileges on their occupants. The last method, wholly unknown in England and practiced somewhat moderately in the Spanish kingdoms, became most common in France through the crown's policy of granting nobility to various, principally judicial, offices acquired by purchase. As a consequence, the French noble order, besides other internal distinctions, displayed a structural peculiarity hardly paralleled elsewhere in importance, its division into a nobility of race or descent founded on the profession of arms, the *noblesse d'épée,* and a nobility of functionaries ennobled through office, like the magistrates of the Parlement of Paris and other administrative organs, the *noblesse de robe.* Despite their legally sanctioned personal noble status, members of the latter, which has been termed a *"noblesse de second rang,"*[15] were not accorded social recognition as noblemen. Thus, when a late sixteenth-century noble writer averred that "tout gentilhomme est noble, mais tout noble n'est pas gentilhomme," he was merely expressing in typical fashion the basic difference between the two kinds of nobility and the superiority felt by those of the sword toward those of the robe.[16] In conformity with this attitude, French social custom prescribed at least three generations as necessary for the creation of authentic nobility of race and *la gentillesse.*

As a sort of ultimate emanation of the status system enveloping early modern societies was the transverse line to be seen in every one of them, a line both actual and symbolic, which set off nobilities and aristocracies from the nonnoble and the inferior orders – *noblesse* or *gentilhommes* from *roturiers, hidalgos* from *pecheros,* gentlemen from the common people. This line, to be sure, was not drawn at the identical point in each society, and the prerequisites for crossing it might vary somewhat from one to another, but it existed in all as a pervasive feature of their social and political life. Those above it formed a small or tiny portion of the population of states, as some sample estimates for the early seventeenth century indicate: 4

---

[14] See Mousnier, *Problèmes de stratification,* introduction; A. Dominguez Ortiz, *The golden age of Spain,* New York, 1971, ch. 8, and *Las clases privilegiadas en la España del antiguo régimen,* Madrid, 1973, ch. 1, based on the same writer's *Sociedad española en el siglo XVII;* P. Rosenfeld, "The provincial governors from the minority of Charles V to the Revolt," *Standen en landen 17* (1959).

[15] Mandrou, *Classes et luttes de classes en France,* 65.

[16] See the quotation from P. Saint-Julien de Balleure, 1581, and remarks in H. Drouot, *Mayenne et la Bourgogne,* 2 v., Paris, 1937, v. 1, 71; Saint-Julien is also discussed by Huppert, *Les Bourgeois Gentilhommes,* 47–8.

percent or less in England, under 2 percent in France, 10 percent in Castile (probably too high a figure), 1 percent in Catalonia, 1 percent in the kingdom of Naples.[17]

Nobilities contained wide contrasts of wealth. At one extreme were the lords of great estates with many tenants and princely incomes; at the other, small gentlemen on modest domains, poor backwoods squires, and even what has been called in France and Spain a noble proletariat.[18] Such differences were certainly consequential in politics and society, yet the quality of nobility, if it did not abolish them, tended to transcend them by investing its possessors with a common superiority.

Passing in rapid review the accompaniments of noble or aristocratic status most pertinent to our purpose, there is first the prestige of the noble, the customary deference they received, and the highly envalued principles of lineage and honor they exemplified. Titles of rank, respectful forms of address, rituals of precedence, the cultivation of heraldry and genealogies, sumptuary laws restricting the use of rich apparel and similar luxuries in their favor, game laws, the practice of the chase, the duel as a point of honor, the carrying of swords, the display of their coats of arms in manor houses and churches, the wearing of their liveries by followers and dependents, family seats reserved to them in churches, as likewise their lavish tombs emblazoned with their arms – in these and a hundred other ways the social supremacy of nobility manifested itself.

Next, there were the multiple privileges nobilities enjoyed. Among the most tangible in many states was immunity from direct taxation, an exemption justified on the ground that noblemen served the body politic with arms instead of money. Thus in France and Spain they did not pay the *tailles* or *servicios* levied by the crown. In England the aristocracy, although relatively lightly taxed, had no fiscal privileges of this kind but possessed others, formal and informal, corresponding to its position. Peers alone had the right to sit in the House of Lords, for example, and in criminal cases had to be tried by members of their own order, while the gentry in numerous ways exercised local supremacy in their communities due their status. The law in general also tended to treat the noble differently from commoners, although privileges varied by country. Accordingly, they might perhaps be subject to special jurisdictions for their of-

---

[17] P. Laslett, *The world we have lost*, 2nd ed., New York, 1971, 27; J. P. Cooper in *The new Cambridge modern history*, v. 4, Cambridge, 1970, 17; Meyer, *La Noblesse bretonne*, v. 1, 56 (an estimate of the nobility of Brittany in the 1660s, placing it at about forty thousand, or 2 percent of the nearly two million inhabitants of the province); Dominguez Ortiz, *Las clases privilegiadas*, 26–7; J. H. Elliott, *The revolt of the Catalans*, Cambridge, 1963, 27, 66.

[18] Cooper, in *The new Cambridge modern history*, v. 4, 18; W. G. Hoskins, "The estates of the Caroline gentry," in W. G. Hoskins and H. P. R. Finberg, *Devonshire studies*, London, 1952; Dominguez Ortiz, *Las clases privilegiadas*, ch. 3, and *The golden age of Spain*, 113; Meyer, *La Noblesse bretonne*, v. 1, 21 ("une véritable plèbe nobiliare").

fenses or not be liable to arrest for debt, to torture, or to degrading punishments. Everywhere certain court and ceremonial offices, military commands and embassies, and places in central and local government were apt to be reserved to them, while in Catholic states, nobility, coupled in Spain with the further condition of *limpieza de sangre* because of the Spanish obsession with purity from Jewish ancestry, was often a prerequisite for high ecclesiastical preferment and admission to exclusive cathedral chapters, chivalric orders, and even some religious houses.

Third, there was the power nobilities exercised over peasantries and inhabitants of the rural countryside and villages. Even though no invincible obstacles prevented nonnoble people from buying seigneuries, noble fiefs, manors, and estates, and even though well-off bourgeois, officials, and others did so in growing numbers for profit and social advancement, the land in the main continued to be both owned and dominated by nobilities and aristocracies, including in some cases ecclesiastical landlords. It was perhaps only as a somewhat more emphatic expression of the normal condition that *"monsieur le gentilhomme"* in France could be pictured speaking of the peasants who owed him rents and corvées as *"mes subjects."*[19] Although the feudal regime and independence had succumbed by the sixteenth century to the superior strength of centralizing monarchies, landownership in early modern societies rarely had the character of a purely economic relation to land but was also likely to be associated with higher status and with some measure of authority over the land's inhabitants and cultivators. Exploitation, paternalism, and protection went hand in hand. Landlord power might even increase under centralized monarchy. By the sale of royal domains and villages in Naples and Castile during the earlier seventeenth century, Philip III and Philip IV of Spain transferred thousands of tenants and their communities to the direct control of other landlords. Alienation of crown lands in this way did not mean "refeudalization," as has been erroneously supposed. Inspired purely by the royal state's need for money, its main effect was the infiltration, expansion, and reinforcement of the noble order by an ennobled bourgeoisie of rich merchants and financiers.[20] The prerogatives of landownership varied, of course, with regions and states. Seigneurial dues or rights of jurisdiction over peasant communities, merely vestigial and of small and

[19] Bernard Du Haillan, *De l'estat . . . de France* (1580), cited by W. Church, *Constitutional thought in sixteenth-century France*, Cambridge, 1941, 242n. Du Haillan was one of the foremost historians and publicists of the age in France.

[20] See Villari, *La rivolta antispagnola a Napoli*, ch. 5, for the view that the integration of merchants and financiers, enriched by dealings with the state, into the Neapolitan baronage was a "refeudalization" and "feudal offensive." A. Dominguez Ortiz, referring to the alienation of royal lands, tenants, towns, and vassals in Castile to a diversity of buyers, noble and nonnoble, in the 1620s and 1630s, points out that this was not a "feudal reaction" (*The golden age of Spain*, 155–7).

declining account in England, were often of much more importance in France, Spain, and some of the German areas that were the scene of the great peasant war. English agriculture, moreover, had probably become more highly commercialized or capitalistic by the middle of the seventeenth century than anywhere else in Western Europe except the Dutch republic. But such contrasts did not diminish the nearly universal authority belonging to nobilities both as landowners and local governors over the rural population, tenants, and peasants. Especially noticeable in this respect was the exceptional position of the higher nobility: the *grands* with their possessions spread over the provinces of France; the ducal and princely owners of vast latifundia in peninsular Spain and southern Italy; the heads of the great aristocratic families of the Netherlands who held considerable portions of the land in some of the rich southern provinces prior to the revolt; the wealthier English peers and upper gentry possessed of large estates and revenues. Landed property on such a scale, frequently reinforced by entails to assure its continuance through generations, was likely to give its masters substantial territorial power and influence.

Finally, there was the universal phenomenon of patronage, seen not only among nobilities but equally in the relations between them and their inferiors. Appearing as a successor, more informal type of political-social authority after the demise of feudalism, divorced from tenure, fief, and homage, patronage was a pervasive characteristic of the age and the normal and natural accompaniment of the hierarchic structure of early modern societies. Idealized, it could be conceived, as it was by one Elizabethan thinker, as an essential attribute of an ordered polity: "Be this . . . the summe of all, that the commens winne the nobles with service, the nobles the commens with benevolences. They obey lowlye, th[e] other rule favourably. They strive to excell in iustice, th[e] other in obedience."[21] One of its principal effects was to foster the tendency toward vertical integration and the formation of solidarities between higher and lower status groups. The greatest patrons of all were kings in their dealings with their nobilities, councillors, officials, administrators, and bourgeois subjects, but the aristocratic order itself was permeated with patronage connections. Behind persons of the greater nobility and leading ministers of state usually stood extensive clienteles of bureaucratic, household, and estate officials, servants, followers, and dependents, lesser noblemen, kindred, and tenants. The bonds uniting these disparate elements were composed of both sentiments of loyalty and considerations of interest based on favors and benefits received and given – in short, of "*fidélité*," "faithful service,"

---

[21] Laurence Humphrey, *The nobles*, 1563, sig. d. iv–v. Humphrey was a leading Puritan cleric who had been a Marian exile.

respect for "ancient blood," and *"servicio y merced."*[22] In such ties lay an essential source of provincial and regional rebellion. But common religious or political sympathies could intertwine with them as well, in which case patronage might also become a factor in the development of broad-based movements of opposition and revolutionary change in church and state. Affiliations of patronage and clientage created constellations of power centered on illustrious noble families, like the princes of the house of Bourbon, whose name, as one of their enemies wrote, sustained the Huguenot cause in the French civil war.[23] For with rare exception it was nobilities who appeared as the natural leaders in early modern societies and whose prestige therefore played a major role in drawing subjects into resistance against divinely ordained kings.

III

Following nobilities, we must next glance briefly at the position of bourgeoisies and urban elites and orders, although again solely in those aspects essential to our inquiry. Here also we find heterogeneous elements, many distinctions connected with fortune and function, and variations among the early modern kingdoms. A common development in all that must be kept in mind, however, was the political decline and subjection of their cities. The forms and spirit of civic liberty and independence decayed or expired during the sixteenth century as state-building kings absorbed urban government and economic policy into the fabric of their rule. The world of the fifteenth-century Renaissance founded preeminently on the splendor of Italian and Flemish cities evolved into the world of the early modern monarchies founded preeminently on the luxury of royal courts. The old royal capitals, London and Paris, flourished as centers of the court and government of the Tudor and Valois sovereigns, with whose political interests the interests of their wealthiest bourgeois subjects were closely identified. Palermo and Naples, Milan and Brussels, became viceregal capitals of Spanish administration in Europe. Genoa, Antwerp, Lisbon, and Lyons acquired a new importance as international commodity and money markets serving the financial needs of insatiable Spanish or French masters. The cities of Castile were harnessed to the geopolitical strategy of the world monarchy of the Habsburgs Charles V, Philip II,

---

[22] See Mousnier, *Problèmes de stratification sociale*, 42–3; M. James, "The concept of order and the northern rising 1569," *Past and present 60* (1973), and *Family, lineage, and civil society . . . 1500–1640*, Oxford, 1974; Elliott, *The revolt of the Catalans*, 40–1; P. Lefebvre, "Aspects de la 'fidélité' en France au XVIIᵉ siècle: Le Cas des agents des princes de Condé," *Revue historique 250*, 507 (1973).
[23] B. Montluc, *Commentaires*, cited in J. Shimizu, *Conflict of loyalties: politics and religion in the career of Gaspard de Coligny*, Geneva, 1970, 130.

and their successors. Only in the Dutch republic, because it won its independence from Spain, did the cities preserve a portion of power in the political life of the state. Against this background, it is hardly surprising either that urban rebellions declined in frequency and consequence after 1500 by comparison with the preceding two centuries or yet that one of the greatest civil conflicts of the period was an urban revolution in Spain against the Habsburg monarchy, the revolt of the Comuneros.

Although cities may have differed considerably in their economic importance and occupational structure, in the kinds of commerce or manufactures in which they specialized, and in their attraction as centers of conspicuous consumption, they all tended to reproduce in their own particular environment the hierarchic pattern of the society of orders. It was as though the gene or cell bearing the latter's code transmitted to its urban progeny an identical principle of stratification. The governing bodies of urban communities, like the *échevins, consuls, jurats,* mayors and alderman, and *regidores,* usually consisted of small, self-perpetuating oligarchies of rich and prominent citizens. Pronounced inequality of political rights and privileges in municipal and guild affairs, extreme contrasts of wealth and poverty, and the ever precarious economic situation of the lower orders composed of miscellaneous tradesmen and artisans, semiskilled or unskilled laborers, and in the capitals and larger cities also beggars, vagrants, and lumpen elements lacking any settled occupation, all served to generate social tensions that could break out in plebeian revolt against urban elites or figure as an ingredient in other types of revolution. In some places, municipal offices conferred noble status or were routes to legal ennoblement, and the families of the uppermost level of citizens constituted urban patriciates or aristocracies. England was an exception to this, for the civic corporations of London and other towns were of a nonnoble character. In France, however, certain civic offices gave their possessors legal nobility, and in a number of Castilian cities the magistracies were the monopoly of *caballeros* and *hidalgos.* The administration of Naples was likewise in the hands of a citizen nobility. Both the capital and provincial towns in the Neapolitan kingdom, Barcelona, and other Spanish cities contained a separate estate whose members held the rank and title of "noble" or "honorable citizens." In some French towns, too, those belonging to the highest urban estate bore the appelation of *noble homme.*[24] Civic elites of this kind, displaying hereditary features and enjoying honorific privileges, merely illustrate in clearest form the general tendency of urban social structures

---

[24] R. Doucet, *Les Institutions de la France au XVIe siècle,* 2 v., Paris, 1948, v. 1, 363, 373–4, and see the whole of pt. 2, ch. 16, "La ville"; Dominguez Ortiz, *Las clases privilegiadas,* 52, 57, 124–9; Villari, *La rivolta antispagnola a Napoli,* 179–80; Elliott, *The revolt of the Catalans,* 68; Huppert, *Les Bourgeois Gentilhommes,* 16–19.

to replicate in their own milieu a type of differentiation modeled after the status system of the society of which they were part.

Coming to the bourgeoisies of the period, although we may be tempted to think of them as a commercial and industrial "middle class" placed between aristocracies and inferior groups, such a view is too gross to take account of the variety of stratification and estates the urban world embraced. Generally speaking, the term *bourgeois* had no specific economic correlate but, as the name and its medieval origins indicate, referred to the inhabitants of towns. More particularly, it designated a status: The *"bourgeois," "bürger,"* or *"burgess"* was a citizen, someone distinguished at a minimum from the unprivileged mass of townsmen by possessing rights of citizenship in the urban community.[25] Beyond this appeared other kinds of hierarchization. The bourgeois was nonnoble, yet, as we have seen, municipal elites in continental states occasionally incarnated an adaptation of the aristocratic principle. This made them something more than a bourgeoisie without merging them into the superior order of nobility founded on descent, land, and military functions. Similarly, the French *noblesse de robe*, because its members were apt to be of bourgeois ancestry, was a sort of severed limb of the bourgeoisie, legally ennobled yet considered disdainfully as bourgeois by the *noblesse d'épée*.[26] On the other hand, the term *bourgeois* in France frequently described an exclusive group of citizens "living nobly" on their incomes, practicing neither craft nor merchandise, who were eligible for town offices and had the right to be entitled *bourgeois* of their particular *ville*. This honorific distinction had no counterpart in English urban society, whose upper groups consisted of those in the most lucrative employments, notably merchants, a word that in the parlance of the time did not mean any kind of shopkeeper or trader but was usually limited to the men engaged in international and wholesale commerce.[27]

But the outstanding feature of urban structures was the clear demarcation between their elites, however constituted, and the remaining inhabitants of every condition ranging from middle and petty bourgeois strata of citizens and freemen of the guilds down to unprivileged and impoverished manual and wage workmen such as existed in the textile towns of the Netherlands and elsewhere. Always there was an *haute bourgeoisie*, like

[25] See P. Jeannin, *Les Marchands au XVIᵉ siècle*, Paris, 1957, 173–4; H. Pirenne, *Belgian democracy: its early history*, Manchester, 1915, 156–9; *The Cambridge economic history of Europe*, v. 3, Cambridge, 1963, 15.

[26] Mousnier, *Problèmes de stratification sociale*, 41; Mandrou, *Classes et luttes de classes en France*, 60. Huppert, *Les Bourgeois Gentilhommes*, is devoted to an examination of the status intermediate between the bourgeoisie and nobility in France, which he infelicitously and rather misleadingly calls a "gentry."

[27] Mousnier, *Problèmes de stratification sociale*, 41–2; M. Marion, *Dictionnaire des institutions de la France aux XVIIᵉ et XVIIIᵉ siècles*, Paris, 1923, *s.v.*, "bourgeois"; Zagorin, *The court and the country*, 122.

those known in Beauvais as *les familles*,[28] a sector that, although differing according to the characteristics of the urban, regional, and national economies to which it was related, contained the tax farmers, financiers, and contractors to royal governments, the capitalists and speculators whose prosperity was connected with economic privileges granted by the crown, the men of substance in the export business and foreign trade, the controllers and the larger middlemen of cloth and other domestic manufactures. It penetrated into the rural zones of cities and the hinterland beyond as purchasers of seigneuries, lands, and estates, as creditors of needy lords, gentry, tenants, and peasants, and as administrators for greater noble and ecclesiastical landlords. From it in France came also the main aspirants to ennoblement by way of office.

By the standards prevalent in the monarchical societies, bourgeoisies and businessmen followed pursuits incompatible with aristocratic existence. They worked, they bought cheap and sold dear, they were thought to gain their profit by cheats and deception – in short, they carried on a money-grubbing existence remote from the noble way of life. No one denied that they performed a function both necessary and useful to the body politic, but their occupations nevertheless made them socially inferior. In England, although a few of the greatest merchants acquired knighthoods, merchants and citizens as a whole were not accepted as gentlemen, and, because land was the true aristocratic vocation, those who lived in towns by trade or manufactures could not belong to the higher orders. The like was even more the case in France where, as Jean Bodin noted, trade derogated from honorable birth and nobility. Similarly in Spain, despite the fact that its noblemen, unlike those of Northern Europe, often deserted their country estates for urban palaces and many of the nobility dwelt in towns, a rooted prejudice existed against trade and *el deshonor de trabajo*, combined with the corollary belief that no one was noble who did not live from his rents.[29]

It is from this angle that we can best examine the relationship of bourgeoisies to aristocracies. Although the values of the age hardly allowed much merit to social mobility, preferring instead to emphasize the duties of every person in his station, social mobility was nonetheless a conspicuous feature of early modern societies. Moreover, it seems to have reached unprecedented proportions in the century and a half of buoyant conditions and inflation that followed the economic depression and contraction of the late medieval period. In England, the expansion of the gentry through

---

[28] P. Goubert, *Cent mille provinciaux*, ch. 10.

[29] Zagorin, *The court and the country*, 121–4; J. Bodin, *The six bookes of a commonweal*, trans. Richard Knolles, ed. K. D. McRae (1606; reprint ed., Cambridge, 1962), 400; Dominguez Ortiz, *Las clases privilegiadas*, 123; J. Lynch, *Spain under the Habsburgs*, 2 v., Oxford, 1965–9, v. 1, 107.

the rise of families, the more than doubling of the titular peerage from 1603 to 1641, and the general increase of honors and titles; in France, the broadened access to ennoblement through the ever-growing system of venality of office; in Spain, the profusion of royal grants and sales of *hidalguía;* in the Neapolitan kingdom the tripling of the titled baronage between 1590 and 1640 all attest to the fact.[30]

Riches, of course, played a basic part in this phenomenon. "Sir Money is a powerful knight," wrote Quevedo (1580–1645) of his Spain of Philip IV, and the poet Gongora (1561–1627) declared that coats of arms were made by *escudos* and dukedoms by ducats.[31] The relentless ambition of a climbing age lowered the barriers to becoming a gentleman in England so that, as one of the acutest Elizabethan observers pointed out, "gentlemen . . . be made good cheape . . . For whosoever . . . can live idly and without manual labour, and will bear the port, charge, and countenance of a gentleman . . . shall be taken for a gentleman"; although the same writer continued nonetheless to define a gentleman in the traditional way as one whom blood and race "doth make noble and known."[32] In France, the commoners who moved up the social ladder into the aristocratic order, hoping with the passage of time to achieve full recognized noble status, sprang from legal and commercial fortunes that could afford the price of ennobling offices in institutions such as the *parlements, chambre des comptes,* and other royal courts.[33] In Naples the risen men who bought demesnial crown lands and penetrated the nobility during the 1630s and 1640s with the titles of prince, duke, marquis, and count were tax farmers and financiers.[34]

In this way, loosened by inflation and lubricated by wealth, facilitated also by the financial needs of royal governments, the structure of the society of orders became less rigid, circulation within it more rapid, and vertical ascent more frequent than before, as the new wine of riches flowed more abundantly into the old bottles of status. One of the effects was the "treason of the bourgeoisie," to use Braudel's striking phrase.[35] For what

---

[30] See L. Stone, *The crisis of the aristocracy 1558–1641,* Oxford, 1965, ch. 3, and "Social mobility in England, 1500–1700," *Past and present 33* (1966); G. Batho in *The agrarian history of England and Wales 1500–1640,* ed. J. Thirsk, Cambridge, 1967, 290–305; J. H. Elliott, *Imperial Spain,* London, 1963, 104–5; Villari, *La rivolta antispagnola a Napoli,* 189–90. The subject of social mobility in relation to the context of revolution is further discussed in Ch. 5 of this book.

[31] Cited by J. Caro Baroja, "Honour and shame: A historical account of several conflicts," in *Honour and shame: the values of the Mediterranean society,* ed. J. Peristiany, Chicago, 1966, 105–6. Gongora's punning lines on the power of money are too witty not to be given in full: "Cruzados hacen cruzadas, escudos pintan escudos, y tahuros muy desnudos. Con dados hacen condados, ducados dejan ducados, y coronas majested. Verdad."

[32] Sir Thomas Smith, *De republica anglorum,* 38–40.

[33] Meyer, *La Noblesse bretonne,* v. 1, 200–2.   [34] Villari, *La rivolta antispagnola a Napoli,* 173.

[35] Braudel, *La Méditerranée,* v. 2, 68.

aspiring urban elites and bourgeoisies wanted most as a rule was to be received into the noble order. "The universal hunger for titles of nobility," with its deleterious contempt for commerce and manual labor, has been recognized as a prevalent trait of seventeenth-century Spain.[36] In France, "the ambition of every prosperous bourgeois," it has been said, was "to either buy or acquire some title of nobility"; and it has been shown in the case of the wealthy Beauvaisins how they purchased noble offices or tried to dissemble their commoner status by such pretensions as annexing to their family patronyms the names of seigneuries they owned, eventually dropping the former for the latter.[37] In England, where the superior orders were probably more open and the interrelations between aristocracy and commerce somewhat closer than in France or Spain, the most successful citizens and merchants did not create business dynasties but sought admission to the gentry, gained knighthoods and even a rare peerage, bought estates, and founded landed families.[38]

The temptation of bourgeoisies to the nobility and its way of life was strengthened by several factors. Even in the boom economy of the sixteenth century, the alternatives for capital investment were not so very numerous. Commerce was generally hazardous, and high returns on one enterprise might be followed by ruinous losses on another, whereas land, apart from its social prestige, remained the most reliable of investments. Or if not in land acquisition, then the bourgeois employed his capital in mortgages or usurious loans to hard-up landlords and peasants, or he invested in the state debt like the *juros* of the Spanish monarchy or the *rentes* of the Hotel de Ville of Paris, by which means he frequently became in any case a *rentier*.

Moreover, bourgeoisies were rarely united by any overriding common interests. Their economic horizon had hardly yet become the national market, which existed nowhere in the kingdoms of the sixteenth century, although England approached the nearest to it. The economies of states were subject to many internal barriers to freedom of trade, and the mercantilist policies of rulers were exercised through monopolistic privileges and restrictive practices in favor of special groups. Cities and economic associations were more often than not strong rivals and competitors with one another for markets and governmental favors, just as there was conflict and rivalry between town and country. Reflecting the sectionalism and particularist spirit in economic affairs, bourgeoisies, as Braudel has

[36] Elliott, *Imperial Spain*, 305; J. Vicens Vives, *An economic history of Spain*, Princeton, 1969, 339–40, 416–18.

[37] P. Goubert, *Louis XIV and twenty million Frenchmen*, New York, 1972, 48; Goubert, *Cent milles provinciaux au XVIIe siècle*, 381–2.

[38] Laslett, *The world we have lost*, 48–50; Stone, *The crisis of the aristocracy*, 39, 368–74, 534–5; and see for some qualifications to this view, R. Lang, "Social origins and social aspirations of Jacobean London merchants," *Economic history review*, 2nd ser., *27*, 1 (1974).

pointed out, lacked any consciousness of themselves as a class,[39] their closest attachment being as a rule to their own urban community, whose interests occupied a primary place in their allegiance. It was the city or, in the exceptional case of the Castilian revolt of the Comuneros, an alliance of cities, that formed the essential context of the political action of urban elites and bourgeoisies.

In view of all these circumstances, it makes little sense to speak of a class struggle between bourgeoisie and aristocracy in the period we are discussing. To do so is to misunderstand both the structure and the dynamics of early modern society. Not only have we to do with orders or estates rather than classes, but we may also wonder how it is possible, for instance, to see a bourgeois–aristocratic class conflict, as Professor Mandrou claims to do, in the relationship between *noblesse de robe* and *noblesse d'épée* in France, when the former of the two alleged opposing classes desired above all to assimilate with the latter. Thus, the "flight from bourgeois status," which Mandrou himself stresses as a feature of French society, vitiates this view.[40] Similarly, Professor Porchnev's reproachful criticism of the seventeenth-century French bourgeoisie for its "feudaloabsolutist" compromises is merely otiose because its behavior is sufficiently intelligible in the existing conditions.[41] Against these misconceptions, it is useful to point out that the early modern bourgeoisie was neither a class nor the bearer of a revolutionary vocation. As has been rightly said of the sixteenth-century merchant, he "was too concerned to make a place for himself in the established order to think of overthrowing it – or even to imagine that it could be overthrown."[42] Because social as well as political superiority lay in aristocracies, not bourgeoisies, it is to them that we must mainly look for the initiation and leadership of some of the greatest revolutionary conflicts in early modern societies.

IV

Finally, we come to the peasants and inferior population of the rural world, who made up the largest mass of the ruled in the states of our sixteenth- and seventeenth-century revolutions. Here generalization is even more

[39] Braudel, *La Méditerranée*, v. 2, 71. See also the unclear and inconclusive discussion of classes and class consciousness by F. Mauro, who seems to hold that there was an awareness of class but no class conflicts in the sixteenth century and that other solidarities outweighed those of class affiliation (*Le XVIᵉ siècle européen: aspects économiques*, Paris, 1966, 337–44).

[40] Mandrou, *Classes et luttes de classes en France*, chs. 2–3. There was certainly antagonism and rivalry between the military and judicial nobility, in part because the former believed the latter was acquiring a monopoly on the administration of the kingdom through the system of venality of office; this, however, was not a class conflict.

[41] B. Porchnev, *Les Soulèvements populaires en France de 1623 à 1648*, trans. from the Russian, Paris, 1963, pt. 3, ch. 2.

[42] Jeanin, *Les Marchands*, 176.

difficult than in the case of aristocracies and bourgeoisies due to the enormous range of local conditions influencing rural economic and social structures, about which we still know too little. Nevertheless, if we venture on such an attempt in order to extract what is pertinent to our inquiry, some broad common features appear. In sketching them it is advisable to refer to agrarian society rather than only to peasants, just as it is also preferable to speak of agrarian and not simply of peasant rebellion. For although modern anthropologists and students of revolution have debated the definition of the peasant, which they have conceived either widely or narrowly as their purposes require,[43] what should not be forgotten is that agrarian society not only was highly stratified but embraced many nonagricultural occupations. Rural villages everywhere contained small tradesmen, tavern keepers, drink sellers, and a variety of artisans like the carpenters, wheelwrights, ploughwrights, coopers, makers of wooden tools and implements, and other sorts of craftsmen indispensable to the needs of an agrarian economy. Moreover, textile and other industries grew up in the countryside or spread from the towns, providing secondary employment for poor peasants to eke out a livelihood.[44] So we need not be surprised to learn that Robert Kett, who led the Norfolk rebellion of 1549, the biggest English agrarian insurrection of the sixteenth century, was described in his indictment as a "tanner," any more than that Wat Tyler, a leader of the English peasant revolt of 1381, was a tiler, or that there were apt to be many village craftsmen among the multitudes that rose in agrarian rebellion.[45] Beyond this, agrarian society was not hermetically sealed off from the towns, and the larger peasant movements nearly always evoked supporting or parallel outbreaks in nearby urban centers, as happened, for instance, in the German peasant war of 1525 and had also occurred in earlier medieval agrarian rebellions.[46] For the country reached into the towns, which contained not only fields, gardens, orchards, and

[43] See G. M. Foster, "What is a peasant?," in *Peasant society*, ed. J. M. Potter, M. N. Diaz, G. M. Foster, Boston, 1967; E. Wolf, *Peasant wars of the twentieth century*, New York, 1969, xii–xv; H. A. Landsberger (ed.), *Rural protest: peasant movements and social change*, London, 1974, 6 ff.; and the valuable critical-historical discussion by G. Dalton, "Peasantries in anthropology and history," in *Economic anthropology and development*, New York, 1971.

[44] See A. Everitt, "Farm labourers," in Thirsk, *The agrarian history of England and Wales*, 425–9; J. Thirsk, "Industries in the countryside," in *Essays in the economic and social history of Tudor and Stuart England*, ed. F. J. Fisher, Cambridge, 1961; Goubert, *Cent mille provinciaux au XVIIᵉ siècle*, 150–1.

[45] F. W. Russell, *Kett's rebellion in Norfolk*, London, 1859, 158–9; R. Dobson (ed.), *The peasants' revolt of 1381*, London, 1970, 17–18. Kett, however, was also a well-off landowner.

[46] On the interaction between mediaeval agrarian and urban revolts, see M. Mollat and P. Wolff, *Ongles bleus, Jacques et Ciompi: Les Révolutions populaires en Europe aux XIVᵉ et XVᵉ siècles*, Paris, 1970, for examples and discussion, including the revolt of maritime Flanders of 1323–8, the French Jacquerie of 1358, and the English revolt of 1381. See also Ch. 7 in this book for further discussion of this topic.

livestock within their limits but often, as in sixteenth-century Montpellier, resident peasants and rural laborers, *"gens de bas estatz,"* who went out to work the surrounding lands.[47]

One of the most obvious characteristics of the peasant and rural populations of early modern societies was the social and economic inequality among them. This was not due to the differences between free and unfree status because by the sixteenth century the majority of peasants in Western Europe had thrown off serfdom and were personally free. Where serfdom persisted, as it did in several French provinces, in England as an increasingly rare exception, and in parts of southern Germany where the great peasant war broke out, it was an anomalous survival whose burdens had been attenuated and that was in practice more often an irritant than an oppression. Well-to-do bondmen were to be found both in England and among the Swabian peasants, and it has been shown that *Leibeigenschaft* among the latter did not necessarily spell meanness of condition.[48] Although the demand for emancipation figured in both the Norfolk revolt of 1549 and the German peasant war, serfdom was not the primary cause of either of these movements and especially not of the former, nor does it in any event provide a general clue to the social background of agrarian rebellion as a type of revolution during this period.

From one angle, what we mostly see in the rural world of Western Europe is the disappearance or advanced decomposition of the earlier condition of serfdom, with landlord incomes now based on pecuniary rents and the attachment of money dues and other obligations to land instead of persons. Full-fledged landownership was the exception in agrarian society, most peasants occupying their lands under different kinds of customary tenancies and leases granted by landlords subject to varying payments and conditions. They also still remained widely subject to the jurisdiction of the seigneury, the manor, and equivalent forms of lordship from which they held their lands, which regulated numerous matters pertaining to their holdings and interests and stood as perhaps the most direct and tangible manifestation of landlord authority. The different forms of

[47] See P. Clark and P. Slack (eds.), *Crisis and order in English towns, 1500–1700*, London, 1972, 6; E. L. Ladurie, *Les Paysans de Languedoc*, 2 v., Paris, 1966, v. 1, 337–8.
[48] Thirsk, *The agrarian history of England and Wales*, 267, 400; D. Sabean, "The social background to the peasants' war of 1525 in southern upper Swabia," Ph.D. thesis, University of Wisconsin, 1969, 132 and ch. 5 and "Famille et tenure paysanne: Aux origines de la Guerre des Paysans en Allemagne," *Annales E.S.C. 27*, 4–5 (1972). The main disability of serfdom among the German peasants studied by Sabean lay in the problems of land inheritance to which it gave rise. See also M. Postan's cautionary remarks against making servile status the main basis of analysis of the condition of the medieval English villagers (*The medieval economy and society*, Berkeley, 1972, chs. 8–9). On the survival of French serfdom, the *mainmortables*, to be found above all in Nivernais, Burgundy, and Franche-Comté, see Marion, *Dictionnaire des institutions*, 507–8, and Doucet, *Les Institutions de la France*, v. 2, 493–6.

occupancy and tenure, like the English freeholds, customary copyholds, and leaseholds, or the French *censives* and *metayage*, reflected a spectrum of property rights in land going from the short-term lease at one end to hereditary possession on fixed nominal payments closely approaching full ownership at the other, with many gradations in between. The system of unencumbered, absolute private property in land lay still in the future; however, there would seem to be little doubt from a legal standpoint that, provided they fulfilled their obligations to their landlords, many tenants could sell, bequeath, transfer, let, and sublet their holdings.[49]

Superimposed upon diverse patterns of tenure and occupancy appeared the most consequential feature of agrarian society, the widespread difference in the size of landholdings. After the depression and demographic decline of the late Middle Ages, which had resulted in abundant land available to peasants on comparatively favorable terms, the sixteenth century brought a rapid alteration of conditions, as under the dynamic charge of renewed population growth, price inflation, widening markets, and need for food the demand for land intensified and values rose. Thus the factors that fueled the economic advance of early modern Europe also led to further inequality among peasants and cultivators in the distribution of land. Regional studies of agrarian society have traced out a common evolution in this respect, one whose main trends consisted in mounting pressure on land whether manifest in the continued subdivision of holdings or in consolidation and the growth of commercial farming, an increasing proportion or majority of peasants without enough land to yield them a livelihood, and the expansion of the landless and of agricultural laborers accompanied by the long-run decline of real wages.

We may observe aspects of this development equally reflected in the "double impoverishment" in land and wages, combined with the extraction of higher rents, among the peasants of Languedoc;[50] in the pattern of land distribution in the Beauvaisis, where three-fourths of the peasants possessed scarcely a tenth of the land in the earlier seventeenth century and most held two hectares or less (under five acres), an amount insufficient for economic independence which condemned its occupants to

---

[49] B. Slicher Van Bath remarks on the gradations between ownership and tenancy "so subtle that it is sometimes difficult to know exactly where to draw the line" (*The agrarian history of Western Europe*, New York, 1963, 310). Of the French *censitaires* who held *censives* and resembled the English customary copyholders, R. Mousnier says that "in practice . . . *censitaire* property was little different from the absolute private property of post-Revolutionary times" (*Fureurs paysannes: Les Paysannes dans les révoltes du XVIIᵉ siècle*, Paris, 1968, 40). For a careful discussion of the nature and variety of English land tenure, emphasizing customary tenants' security of tenure, see E. Kerridge, *Agrarian problems in the sixteenth century and after*, London, 1960, esp. ch. 3.

[50] Ladurie, *Les Paysans de Languedoc*, v. 1, 326, and pt. 2, chs. 3–4.

grinding poverty and an incessant struggle to live;[51] in England, where the steady advance of commercial over subsistence agriculture produced an "ever-growing army" of landless or near landless farm laborers, equaling possibly a third of the rural population by the mid-seventeenth century, while the purchasing power of their daily wage had fallen by the period 1610–20 to less than half of what it had been 150 years before;[52] and in the upper Swabian peasantry, where demographic pressure and the resulting competition for land, already marked in the later fifteenth to early sixteenth centuries, forced the sons of tenants without prospect of land to become day laborers, promoted the economic cleavage of peasant communities, and aggravated tensions in the countryside.[53]

These differences stamped the stratification of the peasant and nonnoble orders whose position was tied up with landholding; they were a manifestation of "the brutal oppositions and innumerable nuances" that characterized early modern agrarian society.[54] Thus French rural structure has been pictured as a pyramid with a very broad base and slender apex at whose summit stood the big farmers and collectors of noble and ecclesiastical *seigneurs* occupying large leases, then followed by *laboureurs* owning a plow team and cultivating fair-sized or family farms, many *haricotiers, bordiers,* and the like poorer peasants on small holdings that provided a subsistence in good years, and at the bottom a mass of *manouvriers* with a cottage and perhaps a tiny bit of land who hired out as workers for the farmers and *laboureurs* or took alternative employment in local manufactures.[55] A corresponding structuring was common in the English rural social order, where the familiar status designations of yeomen, husbandmen, and laborers were related to land and borne by people whose socioeconomic position was clearly distinguishable from one another in the same village.[56] In Castile, with its big estates and latifundia, the agrarian order was apparently even more unequal than in France, consisting of a relatively small number of *labradores* or peasant tenants and leaseholders, few of whom were well off, and many *jornaleros* or day laborers; while in Catalonia the gradations went from the more prosperous peasant proprietors on secure tenancies and leases (*masovers*), to their subtenants and cottagers

[51] Goubert, *Cent milles provinciaux*, 184, and "The French peasantry in the seventeenth century: A regional example," in *Crisis in Europe 1560–1660*, ed. T. Aston, New York, 1965.
[52] Everitt, "Farm labourers," 462, 396–400; P. Bowden, "Agricultural prices, farm profits, and rents," in Thirsk, *The agrarian history of England and Wales*, 600–1; M. Spufford, *Contrasting communities: English villagers in the sixteenth and seventeenth centuries*, Cambridge, 1974, pt. 1, for a study of differentiation in landholdings in Cambridgeshire villages.
[53] Sabean, *The social background to the peasants' war*.
[54] Goubert, *Cent milles provinciaux*, 177.   [55] *Ibid.*, ch. 6; Mousnier, *Fureurs paysannes*, 36.
[56] Spufford, *Contrasting communities*, 38–9.

(*menestrals*), to the landless laborers.[57] There can be little doubt that, wherever we look in agrarian society, analogous configurations of this kind appear, although the extent of inequality and the nature of the groups involved differed by country and region.

These inequalities were decisive for the situation of rural common folk when faced with natural catastrophe, economic contraction, or growing pressure from the state or landlords. Living close to the margin of subsistence most of the time, the poorer peasants and agricultural laborers who had little land were terribly vulnerable in the event of any adverse development. In good years they could sustain themselves, find by-employments, pay their rents to landlords, their tithes to the church, and their taxes to the king – obligations that varied, needless to say, from place to place and were lighter, certainly as regards taxes, in England than in France or the possessions of the Spanish monarchy. But if the harvest were bad or should fail, if famine or scarcity ensued, if a trading slump caused unemployment, if big farmers turned away their laborers, or if in addition the state tried to increase exactions, then these humble people became the first victims, those among whom in times of disease the death rate soared as the infants, the sickly, and the old were carried off, while the living were reduced to extremes of beggary and hunger. Such were the conditions that regularly prevailed during recurring subsistence crises in France in the seventeenth century. Albeit here, again, we must allow for the possibility of differences because the demographic evidence suggests that by the same period the English peasants may have been more immune to the worst consequences of such disasters and therefore less likely to starve.[58]

In spite of its centrality to the understanding of peasant and agrarian society, however, there was no direct or necessary connection between the inequality of landholdings and agrarian rebellion, as in any particular case so many other factors were present to influence the former's effects. It is apparent, too, that prosperous and poor peasants alike may be susceptible to rebellion under certain conditions. The prosperous may be incited to revolt by threats to their position or their improving well-being, for example; the poor may do so if their oppression surpasses tolerable limits. Of the early modern agrarian rebellions, the German peasant war presents aspects closer to the first instance, whereas the numerous French peasant revolts in the earlier seventeenth century more nearly resemble the second. And in contrast to either of these cases, it is instructive to note that

[57] Lynch, *Spain under the Habsburgs*, v. 2, 5; Elliott, *The revolt of the Catalans*, 30; the main account of the "social cleavages" in peasant society in Spain is N. Salomon, *La Campagne de nouvelle Castille à la fin du XVIᵉ siècle*, Paris, 1964, ch. 7.

[58] Goubert, "The French peasantry in the seventeenth century: A regional example"; Laslett, *The world we have lost*, 120–1. For the persistence of famine in parts of England due to harvest failure and demographic surplus, see the illuminating study of A. Appleby, *Famine in Tudor and Stuart England*, Stanford, 1978.

Castile, whose landed regime was one of heavy inequality based on a "rural proletariat,"[59] had no agrarian rebellion in the sixteenth century.

There are, finally, two other features of agrarian society to be noticed from the viewpoint of our inquiry: the role of landlordship and the role of the village community. Both were basic poles within which the peasant life of the time was set, and they obviously existed in innumerable variations arising from distinctive regional histories and customs and from alternative types of landscape, settlement, and rural economy; but we are concerned only with a few widespread structural characteristics perceivable within these diversities.

Economic historians have tried to establish in detail the impact of the secular trends of the European economy in the sixteenth and seventeenth centuries upon the position of landlords and peasants. One of the critical problems is the degree to which the income of each was affected by the growing demand for land, the long-term inflation along with consequent changes in the ratio of specific prices, which frequently favored agricultural products, and the decline in the purchasing power of money. Connected with this are related questions such as how far tenants benefited from the unearned increment arising from fixed, traditional rents and rising prices and whether landlords in an inflationary age were able to alter tenancies and rents to their greater profit.

Apart from these questions, though, what must also be kept in mind is that the peasants did not encounter the landlord purely in his economic capacity as a recipient of rents or services or merely as a possible adversary over the distribution of an unearned increment or the surplus from peasant labor. They also met him, or at least were conscious of him, as a superior in a society permeated by the ascriptive values of birth, descent, and rank, in which they themselves were accounted of inferior or base condition. This landlord, moreover, if sometimes a bourgeois, a lawyer, or an official, was most likely to be a nobleman or gentleman, or perhaps an ecclesiastic or a religious body clothed in the privileges of the clerical order, as was often the case in the territorial patchwork of southwest Germany where the peasant war originated.

The situation was underscored by the survival of seigneurial institutions throughout Europe, which, if commonly much weakened and contracted from what they had been in the age of feudalism and serfdom, still performed a number of functions. The manor, *seigneurie*, *Grundherrschaft*, represented both a territorial unit or landed estate and a lord's legal jurisdiction over his tenants. To be a landowner in many cases thus meant lordship, and lordly possession of the soil meant a form of ascendancy over its inhabitants. As a juridical entity, the manor expressed the fact

---

[59] Lynch, *Spain under the Habsburgs*, v. 1, 111.

that the lord enjoyed a legal authority for certain matters over his tenants and that he retained the eminent domain of his estate, and hence that all tenancies, even those heritable or for life, were a usufruct for which dues were owed in acknowledgment that they derived from him. These dues consisted of rents in money and kind and usually included casual payments as well, like heriots and fines or premiums on entry or succession to the tenancy. Accompanying them might also go residual labor services such as a few days work at the harvest. Lords might still keep the monopoly of the mill, the winepress, or oven, which they leased out as a commercial privilege and tenants were obliged to use at a charge. Manorial courts held by lords as a rule no longer dealt with civil or criminal causes of substance, these having been removed to royal jurisdiction, but they had cognizance of petty disputes between tenants, the transfer and succession of holdings, the admission of tenants, and the enforcement of customs regulating tenants' rights individually and collectively in the lands of the manor.[60]

The above is to simplify a vast, difficult subject containing any amount of local differences that has never been comprehensively or comparatively studied. The essential point, however, is that landlords were connected to peasants by a social relationship at once paternalistic, even with benevolent overtones, and extractive or exploitative, insofar as they sought, whether for their greater profit or simply to maintain an accustomed standard of life, to alter traditional arrangements on their estates.

Typical measures of this latter kind by landlords were attempts to raise traditional old rents, entry fines, and payments, to appropriate lands subject to common rights of the community, to shorten tenancies, to convert customary tenancies to leases, to revive obsolete seigneurial rights, to take over tenancies themselves for commercial farming, and to circumvent manorial customs hindering these and similar policies, all of which reflected a modification of economic behavior at the imperatives of inflation and the expansion of the market sector of rural economies. The same imperatives were also producing greater economic inequality among peasants themselves. Yet, if the methods described gradually became more common, the paternalistic aspect of landlordship also remained significant, an aspect inherent in the landlords' role as manorial superior, patron and sometimes protector, dispenser of hospitality and charity, local dignitary, judge, or magistrate. And because landlords wanted their tenants' and peasants' loyalty, it must doubtless have influenced their economic conduct, too. Like upward mobility, so its reverse, the indebtedness, impov-

---

[60] For some indications on this subject, see Kerridge, *Agrarian problems*, pt. 1, ch. 1; Doucet, *Les Institutions de la France*, v. 2, 457–60; P. Goubert, *L'Ancien Régime*, 2nd ed., Paris, 1969, 81–5; F. Lütge, *Deutsche Sozial-und Wirtschaftsgeschichte*, 3rd rev. ed., Berlin, 1966, 211–17.

erishment, and decline of noble landowners, was a definite part of the social history of the early modern states. Even in England, where an inexorable shift to economic rents was evident by the 1590s, Tudor noblemen sometimes showed themselves reluctant because of paternalistic attitudes to increase their landed income at the expense of tenants, while the structure of rural society still remained patriarchal or paternalistic in the earlier seventeenth century.[61] Probably the description of English landlord–tenant relations at the time as "never wholly dominated by the ethos of the marketplace" also holds even more for other states and regions, where commercialization of agriculture had proceeded less far than in England.[62]

What we see, then, among landlords and peasants are interrelations of both deference and cooperation and of hostility and conflict in different shadings and proportions. Marc Bloch's well-known statement that "agrarian revolt seems as inseparable from the seigneurial regime as . . . the strike is from large-scale capitalist industry," although true, is therefore incomplete.[63] The revolt against the landlord nobleman was only one possible manifestation of agrarian rebellion. Another was the revolt against royal exactions or misrule, wherein peasants combined with landlords who might lead them, assist them, or give them covert support. The German peasant war was aimed primarily at landlords who also happened in many cases to possess immediate governmental powers over their tenants, but antiseigneurial, antinoble revolts were the exception in seventeenth-century France, where it was far more common for peasant rebels goaded to fury by royal fiscal exactions to be aligned with their landlords against the crown's oppression than to take up arms against them. And in other types of revolution in which peasants participated, we occasionally even find the peasant insurgents threatening local gentlemen and landlords with death unless they joined and led them.

As for the peasants themselves, the institution with which their own personal lives were most closely connected was the village community. Sometimes identical with, sometimes included in or overlapping the manor and the ecclesiastical parish, it played an essential role in administering many immediate concerns of tenants and villagers – the appointment of petty officials, the upkeep of the church, the supervision of rules for the use of common fields, woods, and wastelands, the preservation of local customs. Certainly not a democracy, it mirrored as a matter of course the social and economic differences running through peasant society; the statement that "nothing could have been less egalitarian than a French village community" may be accepted as more or less applicable every-

---

[61] L. Stone, *The crisis of the aristocracy*, 380, 214; Everitt, "Farm labourers," 400, 438–40, 460–2.

[62] Stone, *The crisis of the aristocracy*, 259.

[63] M. Bloch, *Les Caractères originaux de l'histoire rurale française*, 2nd ed., Paris, 1952, 175.

where.[64] It was the better-off farmers and peasants who were dominant in its affairs, and the poor and the landless had little or no voice.

Endowed with self-conscious existence, prior organization, and collective values and traditions, the village community could serve as a vehicle for peasant interests and the means to defend surviving forms of communal autonomy against incursion. It was therefore the natural soil for rural protest and resistance. Agrarian rebellion almost invariably began in the mobilization of village communities, their members summoned to rise by the violent ringing of church bells in the parishes and then flowing together in growing crowds fed from all parts of the countryside. The German peasant war was primarily such a movement of *Gemeinde* or communities, whose standpoint and interests were reflected in many rebel demands. French seventeenth-century agrarian rebellions similarly found in the union of communities a rudimentary type of organization. This structural feature was congruent with the inherent properties of agrarian society. For, in the case of peasants and rural people set amidst relatively circumscribed conditions and strongly attached to a locale, the village community contained the main potentiality of joint action. It was the elementary cell from whose coalescence with other similar cells peasant struggles, whether against the state or landlords, developed.

[64] Goubert, *Louis XIV and twenty million Frenchmen*, 40; for further discussion of the village community, see Chapter 7 in this book.

4

Monarchy, absolutism, political system

I

In *Richard II*, Shakespeare puts into the king's mouth this expression of
the mystique of royalty:

> Not all the water in the rough rude sea
> Can wash the balm off from an anointed king;
> The breath of worldly men cannot depose
> The deputy elected by the Lord.

Many other passages of the play are preoccupied with variations on the
same theme. Thus,

> What subject can give sentence on his king?
> . . . .
> And shall the figure of God's majesty,
> His captain, steward, deputy elect,
> Anointed, crowned . . .
> Be judged by subject and inferior breath
> . . . O! forfend it, God . . .

And:

> no hand of blood and bone
> Can gripe the sacred handle of our sceptre
> Unless he do profane, steal, or usurp.[1]

Yet *Richard II* is the true story of a rebellion and the deposition of a king.
And it was to illustrate rebellion that the earl of Essex had this same play
performed in London in February 1601, on the eve of his unsuccessful
coup against Queen Elizabeth that led him to the scaffold; while the queen
herself, prompted by the symbolism of the performance, declared, "I am
Richard II; know ye not that?"[2]

---

[1] *Richard II*, act 3, sc. 2, lines 54–7; act 4, sc. 1, lines 121–9; act 3, sc. 3, lines 79–81.
[2] J. E. Neale, *Queen Elizabeth*, New York, 1957, 386, 398.

These texts provide a fitting introduction to the view of another basic context of our early modern revolutions, the government and political system of the royal states with their exaltation of rulers, on the one hand, and the inherent conflicts, strains, and weaknesses that made them prone to certain types of revolution, on the other.

The renewal and further advance of monarchy in Western Europe from the end of the fifteenth century is a dominant motif of the age, one that has been painstakingly traced out by many historians.[3] In England, France, and the realms of imperial Spain, a similar development of territorial consolidation and expansion, administrative centralization, and political integration ensued that made the kings a greater power than ever before. There is no need to exaggerate the extent of this progress, which involved a lengthy evolution at uneven tempo interrupted by upheavals, halts, and retrogressions and was by no means complete even in the mid-seventeenth century. Still, writ large in all the kingdoms we see rulers and their officials steadily exploiting the older resources and institutions of royal authority and creating new ones as well to strengthen centralized government. In some instances we see them bite deep into their people's purses and acquire armies at their will to chastise refractory subjects and wage foreign war. Their state-building efforts entailed the gradual subjugation of nobilities, the destruction of the independence of church and clergy, the loss or decay of liberties by many corporate groups, the curbing or disappearance of the autonomy and particularism of provinces and towns. When the Protestant Reformation supervened upon this process, it introduced fresh elements and energies making for and against the supremacy of kings, which proved of incalculable political consequence in the life of states. The roots of revolution lay in the gigantic, many-sided confrontation between the weight and will of monarchical regimes aspiring toward undisputed mastery and the disparate forces, old and new, that obstructed their path.

It is sometimes suggested that this forward march of absolutism and state building under early modern kings was itself a "revolution." Thus, the "Tudor revolution in government" is the label one historian has given the political changes carried out in England in the 1530s by Henry VIII and his minister, Thomas Cromwell, which he supposes to mark the transition from a medieval to a modern state. French historians have maintained the same thesis respecting the governmental changes effected in the earlier seventeenth century in France. The real "revolutionaries," asserts Mousnier, "were in fact the king and king's council, who introduced new measures and undermined long-established customs, privileges, franchises, and 'liberties.' " Those who hold that the revolt of the Netherlands

[3] The relevant chapters of the *New Cambridge modern history*, v. 1–5, Cambridge, 1957–64, contain an up-to-date survey of this development.

was an essentially "conservative" movement have similarly argued that the basic revolutionary force in the Low Countries was the centralizing absolutist aspirations of Philip II's government rather than the resistance by its opponents. To such a paradoxical extreme has this notion been carried that it is even contended that the rebellions against the princes of the age were "counterrevolutionary."[4]

Although this line of thought, a variation on the well-known theme of "revolution from above," might seem no more than a harmless use of metaphor, it illustrates anew the boundless confusion that infects the idea of revolution. It extends the prestige of the revolutionary metaphor to governments, hailing their sponsorship of modernizing change as "revolution." This entails, though, an oddly distorted perspective. For if such change is achieved more or less peacefully through consensus and the adaptive devices of the political system, then it is a *reform;* whereas if it is imposed upon a resistant people by the massive application of coercion, it is still change promoted by power holders and incumbents. The latter kind of change, however, is often associated with authoritarian or even despotic regimes. No better example of it could be cited than the so-called revolution from above in Soviet Russia after 1929, the forced collectivization of the land, which helped to give birth to a totalitarian dictatorship. Only the pervasive influence of the revolutionary myth could ever have induced modern historians to speak as though even governments make revolution. The most conclusive refutation of this fallacy and delusion was provided more than a century ago by the anarchist philosopher Proudhon: "To suggest that government can ever be revolutionary implies a contradiction, for the simple reason that it is government."[5]

II

In considering the political context of our early modern revolutions, it is preferable to look first at the monarchies themselves in the particular aspects pertinent to our inquiry.

---

[4]G. R. Elton, *The Tudor revolution in government*, Cambridge, 1953; R. Mousnier, *The assassination of Henry IV*, London, 1973, 211; L. Rogier, "Het karakter van de opstand tegen Philips II," *Bijdragen voor de geschiedenis der Nederlander 10*, 2–4 (1956); M. François, "Revolts in late medieval and early modern Europe: A spiral model," *Journal of interdisciplinary history 5*, 1 (1974).

[5]P. J. Proudhon, *Idée générale de la révolution au XIXe siècle*, 1851, cited in J. Ellul, *Autopsy of revolution*, New York, 1971, 211. For an example of the now frequently expressed view of Stalin's rule as "revolution from above," see S. Cohen, *Bukharin and the Bolshevik revolution*, New York, 1973, ch. 9. B. Moore, *The social origins of dictatorship and democracy*, Boston, 1966, also makes liberal use of the formula to describe the imposition of modernizing change by incumbent elites. An incisive critique of this and other misconceptions of revolution is given by E. Weber, "Revolution? Counter-revolution? What revolution," *Journal of contemporary history 9*, 2 (1974).

Although the crowns of England, France, and Spain were each heir to their own distinctive political and religious traditions, they were all divine-right kingships, a characteristic constantly stressed during this period. This aspect of their position was apparent in the fact that all of them claimed to hold their authority immediately from God as His lieutenant or vice-gerent and to be accountable only to God for its exercise. One of the common corollaries of this belief was the conviction that resistance to divinely appointed sovereigns was sin. Another that was frequently apt to be associated with it was the principle of indefeasible hereditary succession. On the importance of divine right as an essential ingredient of their legitimacy, the English and continental monarchies did not differ from one another; the Tudors were no less kings by divine right, and commonly accepted as such by their subjects, than were the princes of the Valois and Habsburg dynasties.[6]

To give an account of the nature of government in these monarchies is difficult due to their diversity and to the very complex patterns of traditional and more recently acquired powers and attributes of which their authority consisted. Broadly speaking, however, all three were absolute monarchies. Needless to say, this does not mean that they were unlimited. Each of them confronted genuine limitations based on law, custom, and religion; each of them also had to deal with various institutions, including representative assemblies or parliaments in kingdoms and provinces, in which some of the most important of these limits were specifically embodied. Yet, as we survey their career across the sixteenth and first half of the seventeenth centuries, it is clearly absolutism that we see coming into the ascendant without exception and hence in all an ever widening supremacy and competence inherent in the ruler's personal will and decision, together with increasing efficacy in subordinating to the ruler's policy and purposes the rights and privileges of subjects and restraining institutions.

Some writers, it is true, would deny the attribution of absolutism to England on the ground that the limitations that continued to operate upon its government made it different from the kingships of the continental states.[7] Other writers hold that, even in France and Castile, the ruler's

---

[6] I refer to divine right here as a general conception of the basis of legitimacy and obligation rather than as a distinct political theory of monarchy entailing the assertion of specific royal powers and claims. In the latter sense, it was controversial and a product of problems and circumstances of the sixteenth and seventeenth centuries; in the former sense, it was widely accepted. See the discussions in J. N. Figgis, *The divine right of kings*, 2nd ed., Cambridge, 1934; J. W. Allen, *A history of political thought in the sixteenth century*, 3rd ed., London, 1951; and, for England, C. Morris, *Political thought in England: Tyndale to Hooker*, London, 1953; and W. H. Greenleaf, *Order, empiricism and politics*, Oxford, 1964, chs. 2–3.

[7] See G. R. Elton, "The rule of law in sixteenth-century England," in *Studies in Tudor and Stuart politics and government*, 2 v., Cambridge, 1974, v. 1; and J. P. Cooper, "Differences between English and continental governments in the early seventeenth century," in *Britain and the Netherlands*, ed. J. Bromley and E. Kossmann, London, 1960.

acceptance of the obligation to consult representative assemblies prevented absolutism from developing in the sixteenth century.[8]

Like other kinds of government, however, absolutism admits of several degrees and variations and did not present a uniform appearance or conform to a single model.[9] It should be understood as a *relative* absolutism,[10] emerging gradually out of medieval kingship, and certainly not as identical with the untrammeled autocracy characterizing the contemporaneous Russian tsardom or Ottoman sultanate. At no time did any of the monarchs or theorists of absolutism in our early modern states claim that rulers were simply free of limits, that subjects had no rights against them, or that they could seize their people's property or persons in any circumstances at their mere will or pleasure.

Among the crucial criteria of royal absolutism were the ruler's ability to impose taxes and to make laws without consultation or assent of subjects. It seems quite clear that the French kings and the Spanish monarchy in Castile and its Italian realms were possessing themselves of this power in practice and eventually as an acknowledged right, that they made substantial progress toward it in the sixteenth century, and that the institutional obstacles to its exercise were weakening into mere formalisms, falling into desuetude, or disappearing in the course of the period as a whole.[11]

The English case differs in that the crown never gained the authority to legislate or demand subsidies from subjects of its own will; Parliament not only retained its importance but experienced considerable institutional development in the reigns of the Tudor and early Stuart kings. Notwithstanding these facts, though, it is no more than a misleading half-truth to picture the English monarchy simply as limited and under the rule of law.[12] More correctly, one might say that it was somewhat less absolute, or both absolute and limited, with the latter aspect and its sustaining tra-

[8] See R. Major, "The French Renaissance monarchy as seen through the Estates General," in *Government in Reformation Europe 1520–1560*, ed. H. Cohn, London, 1971; and *Representative institutions in Renaissance France 1421–1559*, Madison, 1960; G. Griffiths, "The state: Absolute or limited?" in *Transition and revolution*, ed. R. Kingdon, Minneapolis, 1974.

[9] See F. Hartung and R. Mousnier, "Quelques problèmes concernant la monarchie absolue," *International Congress of Historical Sciences*, Rome, 1955, v. 4, *Relazioni;* and J. Vicens Vives, "The administrative structure of the state in the sixteenth and seventeenth centuries," in Cohn, *Government in Reformation Europe.*

[10] See J. A. Maravall, "The origins of the modern state," *Journal of world history 6*, 4 (1961), 800.

[11] See M. Wolfe, *The fiscal system of Renaissance France*, New Haven, 1972; H. G. Koenigsberger and G. L. Mosse, *Europe in the sixteenth century*, New York, 1968, 228–30; J. G. Shennan, *The origins of the modern European state*, London, 1974, ch. 3; Vicens Vives, "The administrative structure of the state."

[12] Elton, "The rule of law in sixteenth-century England." The suggested formula of "the supremacy or sovereignty of the king-in-parliament" as an analytical description of English government (G. R. Elton, *The Tudor constitution*, Cambridge, 1960, 14, 231) is equally erroneous and misleading, first, because it leaves out of account the absolutist features in the position of the crown itself, second, because it postulates a condition neither wholly appli-

ditions and institutions more strongly entrenched than in the continental states; yet some definite features of absolutism it did indeed possess.

Thus, like the crowns of France and Spain, the English monarchy had no superior in its realm, it was not in any way answerable to its subjects for its policy or actions, and no lawful means or agencies existed to control, correct, or coerce it if it was guilty of excess or wrongdoing. In regard to the church, its powers after the Reformation well exceeded even those of the kings of France or Spain, enjoying as it did independent ecclesiastical supremacy with no relation to papal or other religious authority. Although it could not make laws in Parliament without consent, it nonetheless possessed the quasi-legislative prerogative of issuing commands on a great variety of matters under the name of royal proclamations, which at times approximated or even became in effect a lawmaking power. This quasi-legislative prerogative also included the right to dispense from parliamentary statutes and even to suspend their operation altogether, an attribute that invested the crown with wide freedom from legal restraint.[13]

The clearest evidence of English absolutism, however, was the crown's possession of "absolute power," something very similar to what French and Spanish jurists held to be inherent in their own monarchies.[14] In the English context, absolute power designated that part of the royal prerogative that permitted the king to disregard the common law and normal legal process when in his judgment matters of state and policy, the general welfare and safety of the kingdom, or the *arcana imperii* were at stake.[15]

cable, assured, nor permanent until the successful outcome of the struggle against the absolutism of the Stuarts in the seventeenth century.

[13] See J. J. Greenberg, "Tudor and Stuart theories of kingship: the dispensing power and royal discretionary authority in sixteenth and seventeenth century England," Ph.D. thesis, University of Michigan, 1970, for a helpful discussion.

[14] For similar distinctions in France and Spain between the king's absolute and ordinary power and views concerning the coexistence of absolute power with private rights, see W. F. Church, *Constitutional thought in sixteenth-century France*, 63–4, 68–9, 226, 232; R. Mousnier, "Les concepts d'"ordres,' d'"états' . . . á la fin du XVIIIe siècle," *Revue historique* 247, 502 (1972); J. A. Maravall, *La Philosophie politique espagnole au XVIIe siècle*, Paris, 1955, ch. 5; B. Hamilton, *Political thought in sixteenth-century Spain*, Oxford, 1963, 28, 39–42. The topic is further discussed in later chapters of this book in connection with various revolutions.

[15] See M. Judson, *The crisis of the constitution*, New Brunswick, 1949, ch. 4, and Greenberg, *Tudor and Stuart theories of kingship*, chs. 1–3, for a discussion of the doctrine of the king of England's absolute power. The connection of absolute power with the *arcana imperii* appears in E. Kantorowicz, "Mysteries of state: An absolutist concept and its late medieval origins," in *Selected studies*, Locust Valley, 1965. The background to the Tudor–Stuart doctrine of absolute power is treated by S. B. Chrimes, *English constitutional ideas in the fifteenth century*, Cambridge, 1936, 43, 59–60; and C. H. McIlwain, *The growth of political thought in the west*, New York, 1932, and *Constitutionalism ancient and modern*, rev. ed., Ithaca, 1947, 75–111, 123–35. McIlwain's well-known account of the absolute and limited features of the English monarchy and their respective spheres of authority is flawed by its failure to recognize that these two spheres were not equal and coordinate, but rather absolutism was the superior and controlling, taking priority over limitation at the royal discretion.

This entailed an indefinite range of action subject only to the king's discretion. Absolute power was no new attribute of kingship, but the Tudor sovereigns enlarged it, and their Stuart successors exploited it more strongly still. In consequence, it became the justification or pretext for arbitrary methods and royal invasions of public and private rights, including finally the attempt to tax without Parliament's consent. English judges in the earlier seventeenth century even construed absolute power to mean that the king "had the laws in his own breast" – a formula, ironically, that the popes and Roman emperors once used for their own absolutism.[16]

In spite of the expansion of absolutism and its brutal collisions with rebellious subjects, royal government never became uniform or monolithic, even in the kingdoms where it suffered least limitation. Confusions of jurisdiction and rivalries and conflicts among governmental institutions abounded under its rule. Its actual power was more like an intricate mosaic of particular prerogatives, rights, and powers than a homogeneous, all-inclusive authority. The attributes of sovereignty that were ascribed to absolute kings by royalist lawyers and political philosophers, such as the French thinker Jean Bodin, were more often than not greater in theory than the powers these same kings could dispose of in practice.[17] The monarchies of our early modern states also continued to be in many respects conservative and traditionalistic, as befitted regimes ruling hierarchic societies and of centuries-long growth from ancient origins. Absolutist kings did not quarrel with social privilege, of which their own position was the supreme manifestation: They quarreled only with privileges that resisted their authority or claimed immunity from their government. In building their more centralized states, they did not sweep the stage clean with a new broom, and many older and outmoded political forms and institutions survived the reign of absolutism, like scenery left standing while a new play was performed.

III

Beyond the question of the nature of kingship is the further question of the political system and social foundation of the monarchical regimes. What

---

[16] The phrase was used by Justice Berkeley on behalf of Charles I in 1637, in the ship-money case (S. R. Gardiner, *Constitutional documents of the Puritan revolution*, 3rd rev. ed., Oxford, 1936, 122). Pope Boniface VIII and the Emperors Honorius and Theodosius had made the same claim for themselves; W. Ullmann, *Principles of government and politics in the Middle Ages*, 2nd ed., London, 1966, 75.

[17] Bodin held that sovereignty was inherent in every government and that it consisted of absolute power over citizens and subjects of which the chief mark was the power to make law. In monarchies, sovereignty belonged to the prince. Bodin considered the English monarchy to be absolute, like the French, and advanced a number of arguments to prove that Parliament had no share in the sovereign power (J. Bodin, *The six bookes of a commonweal*, trans. Richard Knolles, ed. K. D. McRae (1606; reprint ed. Cambridge, 1962), bk. 1, ch.8, 96–8).

was the relation of monarchies to the society of orders and from what sources did they draw their strength?

Historically, the conditions favoring the development of absolutism and administrative centralization were the same in England, France, and Spain. Political breakdown, misrule, and the decline of government during periods of the fifteenth century created a widespread desire for order, internal peace, and the restoration of government in the following age. The body politic submitted to reinvigorated kingships that could bring these inestimable gifts. The loyalty of subjects was activated and sustained by a resurgent patriotism and pride in their country's new strength and unity, of which the monarch and ruling dynasty were the embodiment. International rivalry and conflicts strengthened these sentiments, while also necessitating the acquisition of power by the monarchical states to wage and finance wars of unprecedented magnitude. The dissemination of humanistic culture and education caused a higher value than ever before to be set on the active life of the citizen and promoted as a virtue the ideal of service to the prince, state, and commonweal among aristocratic and bourgeois elites. Some of the strongest currents of the time were thus magnetized about the pole of royal greatness and glory.

In a certain sense, the monarchies that emerged in the sixteenth century, those "new Messiahs," as Michelet called them, became a power standing above society, a power that strove to subject all orders, groups, and aspirations to its own superior purpose. The supposition that the crowns were primarily class instrumentalities, that they possessed a special basis of support in the bourgeoisie or another class, or, as the German Marxist scholar, Kautsky, believed, that they served the interest of merchant capitalism with which they were allied in opposition to nobilities, is quite untenable and should be relegated to the rubbish heap.[18] In a famous dunning letter sent in 1523 to Charles V, Jacob Fugger of Augsburg, the greatest capitalist in Europe, declared that only his loans had made possible the emperor's election:

It is well known that your Imperial Majesty could not have gained the Roman Crown save with mine aid . . . For had I left the House of Austria and . . . been minded to further France . . . How grave a disadvantage had in this case accrued

---

[18] K. Kautsky, *Thomas More and his Utopia*, New York, 1959, 17. For a recent reaffirmation of this view of the class basis of absolutism, see A. Lublinskaya, *French absolutism: the crucial phase 1620–1629*, Cambridge, 1968, 26. The Marxist position on this point is not wholly clear or consistent. At times, Marx and Engels held that the absolutist state was relatively independent in relation to nobility and bourgeoisie; see the citations and discussion in P. Anderson, *Lineages of the absolutist state*, London, 1974, 15–16 and ch. 1. This well-informed Marxist work attempts to get beyond dogmatism and recognizes the central importance of the relations between rulers and nobilities. Nevertheless, it remains locked in the stale, misconceived formula that absolutism was "irreducibly feudal" and constituted a "feudal state" (39–42).

to your Majesty and the House of Austria, Your Majesty's Royal Mind well know-eth.[19]

But reflection not merely on this letter but on the relations as a whole between rulers and their bankers, creditors, revenue farmers, and financial agents makes it evident that it was princes who gained the most from dealings with financiers rather than the other way around, drawing heavily on them for loans, defaulting repeatedly, and frequently plunging them into ruin through bankruptcies and failure to repay. If anything is clear, it is that the power of kings in early modern Europe still far exceeded the power of capital and could exploit it, just as it exploited all other social powers, for its own hegemony.

Essentially, the foundation of the monarchies' advance was their success in harnessing to their policy, government, and goals the interests and ambitions of the elites of the society of orders. The political system of the monarchical states normally reflected a symbiosis between crown and elites, in which the first as supreme received loyalty, obedience, and service, bestowing in return material and honorific rewards upon the second. Above all, the political system was a symbiosis between crown and nobilities; and, speaking generally, it was especially nobilities or aristocracies that, under supreme and absolutist kings, constituted the dominant and governing class (I use the term *class* here without any particular Marxist connotations) in the early modern states.

The conflicts between monarchs and nobilities and the struggle of rulers against over-mighty subjects that historians are accustomed to stress in connection with the process of royal state building was just one side of their relationship. Along with this struggle – as manifest, for instance, in the destruction that the Tudor sovereigns meted out to dissident or too powerful magnates, or in Francis I of France's confiscation in 1523 of the duchy of Bourbon after the treason of the duke, or in his successors' bloody strife with the *grands* down to the reign of Louis XIII and the Fronde – there also proceeded the taming and assimilation of nobilities as servants and instruments of kings. And while this was taking place, whether by blandishment or by force, the nobilities of the sixteenth and seventeenth centuries were also being steadily replenished and recruited from families who owed their rise or further eminence to royal favor and offices. So the aristocratic order gradually tended to exhibit in certain respects the characteristic of a nobility of service whose main political orientation lay in-

---

[19] R. Ehrenberg, *Capital and finance in the age of the Renaissance*, London, 1928, 80. The imperial election of 1519, at which Charles V was chosen, cost the emperor "nearly a million gold Gulden, of which nearly half went in bribes to the Electors and their advisers." Most of this money was borrowed by the Habsburg monarch from the firm of Fugger; see K. Brandi, *The Emperor Charles V*, London, 1939, 106.

creasingly toward the governments and courts of royal masters and the political careers of whose more ambitious members were likely to be closely tied to royal interests.

The creation of the political system of absolutist monarchy depending upon a symbiosis between crown and nobilities was the work of the ablest kings. It cannot be repeated too often that, despite the extension of bureaucratic methods of government, the multiplication of royal officials, and in the case of France in the early seventeenth century the monarchy's use of extraordinary agents, outside the regular body of officials, to further its hegemony, the adherence and cooperation of nobilities nevertheless remained indispensable to the functioning of the royal state.[20] In England, the assimilation of the aristocratic order in this way was considerably advanced by Henry VIII in the 1530s and 1540s, and finally completed by his daughter, Queen Elizabeth, under whom the political system took the shape it was to possess until destroyed by the revolution of 1640. In Spain the same achievement was mainly due to two strong rulers, Charles V and Philip II. In France, this symbiosis was the most precarious and vulnerable and had to be constructed and reconstructed through a succession of political crises and revolutionary breakdowns lasting from the civil war of the later sixteenth century down to the rebellion of the Fronde in the middle of the seventeenth century.

The symbiotic relation of monarchy to elites was founded in practical terms on the ruler's position as supreme patron in a patronage-ridden society. In this regard, the political system merely reproduced one of the fundamental traits of the society of orders. Far richer than any of their subjects, the fountain of honors, and increasingly the sole source of public authority in their kingdoms, absolutist rulers were vastly endowed to act as supreme patrons. To nobilities they could dispense titles, great offices, lands, pensions, loans, and many other gifts; to bourgeoisies, a multiplicity of financial and commercial opportunities and social advancement into the aristocratic order. To corporate groups, towns, and trading associations, they could grant or withhold privileges. To lawyers, the most politically important of the professions, they could offer a career in their service. To churchmen they could give benefices and (although this was mainly the case in the Catholic countries) secular offices.

The effective employment of patronage and its denial to those who offended was one of the most important ways by which successful kings secured the obedience and cooperation of the major elites whom they utilized in their rule. Royal government in the sixteenth and seventeenth centuries thus presented at the same time the dual features of a growing

[20] See F. Braudel, *La Méditerranée et le monde méditerranéan à l'époque de Philippe II*, 2nd rev. ed., 2 v., Paris, 1966, v. 2, 54.

bureaucratic apparatus of officials, secretariats, conciliar organs, judicial bodies, and departments of state to correspond with the expanding scope of monarchical activity in peace and war and of patronage operating widely throughout the governmental structure, not only between kings, their chief nobility, favorites, and ministers but also between the latter and their clienteles as well as lower down in central and provincial administration.

As factional contests for favor and influence by elite groups were the regular accompaniments of the patronage-dominated political life of monarchy, it was a common strategy of sovereigns to exploit these rivalries in the interests of their own power. Commenting upon this point in reference to Queen Elizabeth, an English politician of the time noted, "She ruled much by faction, and parties which she her selfe both made, upheld, and weakened, as her owne great judgement advised." And he added, "She was absolute and Soveraigne mistress of her graces," and "all . . . to whom she distributed her favours . . . stood on no better termes than her princely pleasure, and their good behaviour."[21] Similar observations could equally have been made about other kings, like Charles V, who in a political testament instructed his heir, Prince Philip of Spain, how to manage the feuds and factions in his court and government to the best advantage of the crown.[22]

IV

Connected with the monarchy's role as supreme patron was the central importance of office in the political system. Both as an attraction to aristocracies and as one of the chief goals of the ambition of subjects, office exerted a manifold influence upon politics and social structures, although it could be a source of weakness as well as strength to kings, and its effects were not identical in the different states.

The core machinery of the central government in the English, French, and Spanish monarchies was mainly managed by men whose social origins lay in the lesser nobility or gentry, the bourgeoisie, and sometimes even humbler strata. They formed a cadre of secretaries of state, ministers, councillors, legal and financial administrators exemplifying traditions of professional expertise and fidelity to royal interests. Mainstays of monarchical authority, these elites based on office owed their distinction, whether originating in their own or a previous generation, to the immediate service

---

[21] Sir Robert Naunton, *Fragmenta regalia*, London, 1641, 4.

[22] The text of Charles V's so-called political testament of 1543 is printed in Brandi, *The Emperor Charles V*, 485–93, a document offering a profound revelation of kingship; see also the discussion in J. Fernández-Santamaria, *The state, war and peace: Spanish political thought in the Renaissance 1516–1559*, Cambridge, 1977, 237–47. For Charles's later testaments of 1548 and 1555, see the essays by B. Beinert and L. Sánchez Agesta in *Carlos V (1500–1558). Homenaje de la universidad de Granada*, Granada, 1958.

of the crown. The ruler was to them both sovereign and patron. Specimens of the most notable of this kind – although many others could be found in less powerful positions – were the English William and Robert Cecil, father and son, who served Queen Elizabeth and James I in the weightiest offices, gaining peerages and enormous fortunes in the process; the line of Spanish royal secretaries such as Francisco de los Cobos, servant to Charles V, to whom office brought riches and ennoblement and whose daughter married a duke; or the number of French dynasties of officials like the Laubespine, Neufville, Sublet, Bouthillier, Phelypeaux, and other families, high servitors and councillors of the French monarchy over successive generations who reaped nobility and other rewards to match.[23]

Men of this type, stemming from lesser nobilities or below and prominent in the work of state building, were preferred by kings as trusted servants because they were likeliest to be exclusively devoted to the monarchy and its hegemony. But the higher nobility was also increasingly drawn to office. Not only were its ranks being enlarged by the exceptionally successful men who made their careers through office and royal favor, but the greater lords, despite the traditions of independence and separate bases of territorial power that some of them possessed, were desirous of office for the honor, profit, authority, and opportunities of patronage it gave. More and more, office under the crown became a necessary ingredient of high political status and influence. Kings used it to integrate nobilities within their rule, and the latter tried to extort it at times of royal weakness of the kind the French monarchy experienced in the revolutionary civil war of the later sixteenth century. Accordingly, the higher nobility is found entering into many prominent positions in the government of kings: in the viceroyalties of the Spanish monarchy during the sixteenth century and subsequently in some of the chief offices of Spanish central administration as well; in the provincial governorships of France and the Netherlands before the revolt; as ministers, privy councillors, and representatives of royal authority in regional and county government in England; and in great court, household, and military offices in all the kingdoms.[24]

[23] See L. Stone, *The crisis of the aristocracy*, Oxford, 1965, *passim*, and *Family and fortune*, Oxford, 1973, ch. 1; H. Keniston, *Francisco de los Cobos*, Pittsburgh, 1958; N. Sutherland, *The French secretaries of state in the age of Catherine de Medici*, London, 1962; O. Ranum, *Richelieu and the councillors of Louis XIII*, Oxford, 1963; J. Shennan, *Government and society in France 1461–1661*, London, 1969, 43–4, 48–9.

[24] A. Dominguez Ortiz, *Las clases privilegiadas en la España del antiguo régimen*, Madrid, 1973, ch. 4; J. Lynch, *Spain under the Habsburgs*, 2 v., Oxford, 1965–9, v. 2, 133; Shennan, *Government and society in France*, 60–2; R. Mousnier, "Les rapports entre les gouverneurs de province et les intendants dans la première moitié du XVIIᵉ siècle," in *La Plume, la faucille et le marteau*, Paris, 1970; P. Rosenfeld, "The provincial governors from the minority of Charles V to the Revolt," *Standen en landen 17* (1959); Stone, *The crisis of the aristocracy*, 464–70, 259–60.

Office, however, must be seen in yet a wider context than its relation to the phenomenon of patronage if its political ramifications are to be understood. For what gave it its largest impact on the political system of the monarchical states, and consequently also affected some of their revolutions, was its proprietary nature combined with the institutionalizing of the practice of venality. Although this development began at an earlier date, it reached its apogee during the sixteenth and seventeenth centuries, when it came to stand out as one of the main features of royal government.

The fundamental fact about offices was that many if not most were bought and sold, granted for life, or became hereditary and thus were held as a form of private property.[25] The description of the governmental structures of the English, French, and Spanish monarchies as bureaucracies must accordingly be understood in a particular sense: They were bureaucracies wherein royal officials were likely to be owners of their offices and, except at the highest levels, often not removable at the discretion of the ruler. These conditions certainly did not prevent the existence of either professionalism or expertise among officials, but they modified the public aspect of office as a trust by its proprietary aspect as a possession to be exploited for the personal interests of its owner.

The sale of offices was a common practice in all the states, whether by kings, by officeholders themselves, or by ministers and politicians with places to bestow or influence to use for a price. Venality merged easily with patronage because the help of patrons and intermediaries was often indispensable to office seekers. The treatment of office as a private resource was encouraged by the low payment of officials. With crown salaries seldom adequate as a rule and often in arrears, an important part of the income of many officials came not from royal masters but from the fees exacted from users of their services, from perquisites, gratuities, bribes, and other gains their positions threw in their way. Standards of official conduct were correspondingly lower and looser than a later age would demand, and proprietary office created a broad gray zone between the permissible gift or rake-off to an official and outright corruption. It would have been thought unreasonable to expect an officeholder not to profit by his place, an investment for which he had probably paid good money. Nevertheless, the greed, dishonesty, and malversation of officials was a proverbial topic, inciting continual criticism, satire, and denunciation.

Venal offices contributed everywhere to inefficiency in government, encouraged official corruption and vested interests resistant to reform, and tended to weaken the monarchies' control of their bureaucracies. Within these broad characteristics, however, some differences and contrasts appear among the various states.

[25] See K. Swart, *Sale of offices in the seventeenth century*, Hague, 1949, for a general survey of the subject.

In England, the monarchy, although increasingly conferring most offices for life and also permitting venality, did not adopt the latter as a systematic method of raising money. The traffic in offices therefore never became established as a source of royal revenue and was mainly conducted by officeholders and patrons for their own benefit. If the crown itself obtained any pecuniary advantage from the practice, it did so by consenting that officials should use their offices for gain, in effect transferring some of the cost of paying them from its own treasury to the public. Also absent in England was any direct connection between nobility and office. The latter conferred no distinct rank or privileges and was desired more for economic, political, and honorific reasons than as a prerequisite to social advancement. Moreover, offices of county government were never sold and were undertaken by noblemen and gentry as a service to prince and state without pay. These conditions limited the scope and effects of venality. The monarchy, not directly profiting from the system, did not have the same motive to invent needless new offices that operated elsewhere, nor was the passion for offices as widespread or as consequential socially as in other states. And royal officials, despite the existence of graft and corruption, did not develop a separate bureaucratic identity but remained on the whole indistinguishable from the rest of the governing elite whose loyalties they shared until the autocratic actions of the Stuart monarchy provoked the disaffection that culminated in the revolution of 1640.[26]

In Spain, the sale of offices gradually spread to every level of government, municipal, colonial, and central, as the monarchy turned to it for revenue and began the practice of creating offices for no other reason than to sell them. While Philip II kept venality in bounds, his successors extended it, adding offices out of financial necessity and selling positions of responsibility previously excluded from purchase. The pursuit of office thus became an obsession in Spain, sanctioned by its central social values. Office was a haven to noblemen, who enjoyed special means of entry, a profession and dignity to the crowds of law graduates, the *letrados*, who filled such a large place in Spain's government, and an avenue of ennoblement to commoners. Under the weak rulers of the seventeenth century, venality and the increase of officials made Spanish administration steadily more cumbrous and inefficient, a heavy weight upon society capable of being moved, if at all, only by the most determined minister. But the monarchy refrained from alienating high offices or making them hereditary, so that no real equivalent to the French *noblesse de robe* emerged in Spain. Moreover, the bureaucracy, especially in Castile, the focal point of Spanish rule, was so integrated with the monarchy, from whose absolut-

[26] See G. Aylmer, *The king's servants*, London, 1960; and J. Hurstfield, "Office-holding and government mainly in England and France," in *Freedom, corruption and government in Elizabethan England*, London, 1973.

ism it profited, that it never assumed a posture of political independence or played any role in the revolutions that afflicted the Habsburg state in the mid-seventeenth century.[27]

Empleomania and venality of office reached their extreme in France, which as the most populous of early modern kingdoms probably had a greater number of officials relatively and absolutely than any other: About forty thousand in the early seventeenth century is one estimate.[28] Driven by an unremitting need for money, the Valois and Bourbon sovereigns transformed venality into a predominant social and political institution of their regimes. They sold all kinds of offices in their service, continually established new offices to put on the block, and, by assigning personal or hereditary nobility to certain grades of offices, created alongside the traditional sword nobility another nobility of functionaries, the *noblesse de robe*, at the higher levels of the governmental bureaucracy. After 1604, the monarchy, in response to demand, also permitted office to become hereditary or otherwise transferable in return for the payment by officials of the *droit annuel*, a yearly premium based on the value of their charges. With this added hereditary feature, a privilege known as the *paulette*, offices exercised an even stronger attraction, and the interests of their owners in them became even more strongly entrenched. Office was a standard form of investment, a common avenue of social ascent, an ingredient in a marriage settlement, an asset in a family fortune.

Through venality, proprietary officials came to form a vital element in the governing class and administration of the realm to a degree unparalleled elsewhere. And, as the roots of venality sank deeper into French society, it became a ceaseless cause of controversy. Many critics denounced it for encouraging corruption and complained of the oppression due to the superfluity of officials who exploited subjects. Noblemen bitterly resented venality for allowing an upstart bourgeoisie to gain nobility and a preponderant position in the government of the kingdom by means of wealth. Conflicts between the orders over venality of office, such as the quarrel that flared up between the deputies of the nobility and the third estate in the Estates General of 1614 because of a proposal to suppress the *paulette*, militated against their common action and strengthened the independence and absolutism of the monarchy over all its subjects.[29]

[27] J. Parry, *The sale of public office in the Spanish Indies under the Habsburgs, Ibero-Americana*, v. 37, Berkeley, 1953; Lynch, v. 1, 185, v. 2, 133, 268–9; Dominguez Ortiz, *Las clases privilegiadas*, 144–5; R. Kagan, *Students and society in early modern Spain*, Baltimore, 1974, pt. 2.

[28] A. L. Moote, *The revolt of the judges*, Princeton, 1971, 6; see the inconclusive discussion of the number of venal offices in the main treatment of the subject, R. Mousnier, *La Vénalité des offices sous Henri IV et Louis XIII*, 2nd rev. ed., Paris, 1971, 129–49.

[29] See J. M. Hayden, *France and the Estates General of 1614*, Cambridge, 1974, 119–23. The sale of offices was also attacked in previous meetings of the Estates General during the later sixteenth century.

But countering the financial advantages of venality to the crown were its political drawbacks. Although venal officeholders owed the monarchy their position, they were also liable to be victims of its fiscality. When the king of France created new offices on top of old, subdivided existing functions between two, three, or even four incumbents, demanded loans from his officials, or threatened to revoke the privilege of the *paulette* unless paid to confirm it, their incomes and authority suffered. Professionally organized into corporate bodies related to their functions, royal *officiers* evinced a striking political ambivalence, being equally capable of fierce loyalty to the monarch and of tenacious bureaucratic opposition to defend their interests. Nowhere was this more so than in the *parlements*, the crown's sovereign courts, which possessed great judicial and administrative responsibilities, including the duty to register royal edicts, which they could use for obstruction, criticism, and delay. The judges of the *parlements* were a formidable collective power: The guardians of legal principle, claiming to share in public authority, professing the strongest fidelity and obedience to the king, their recalcitrance and independence at times posed serious obstacles to his commands.

On account of the unique position occupied by its officials, French absolutism up to the time of Louis XIV has been described with some justification as "monarchy tempered by venality of offices."[30] Only in France was it possible for high career servants of the crown by their political and legal opposition to have initiated a rebellion, as did the magistrates of the Parlement of Paris in 1648, when their resistance to the government's fiscality and their insistence on reform unleashed the Fronde, the last great revolt against the monarchy before 1789.

Having always to reckon with the possibility of bureaucratic obstruction or insubordination, the monarchy would have abolished the sale of offices if it could, as Cardinal Richelieu, Louis XIII's iron-willed minister, would have liked to do. It was never possible, though, either financially or politically, to carry out so drastic a reform. Thus, to circumvent its bureaucracy of unremovable *officiers* whose charges were their property, the monarchy began to make increasing use of intendants, special agents of the central government who were technically *commissaires* with temporary commissions revocable at will. To them the king gave extraordinary powers that superseded the jurisdiction of his regular officials. In the 1630s and 1640s about 150 intendants were appointed, and they played a crucial role in executing the fiscal edicts in the provinces, which were straining France to the limit and which the regular financial officials were often reluctant or unwilling to enforce.[31] It is not surprising, therefore, that the

---

[30] Mousnier, *La Vénalité des offices*, 666.

[31] R. Mousnier, "Etat et commissaire: Recherches sur la création des intendants des provinces (1634–1648," in *La plume, la faucille, et le marteau*. See R. Bonney, *Political change in*

intendants were included as a principal grievance in the complaints voiced by the Parlement of Paris that led to the Fronde.[32]

V

These attributes of the political system we have been discussing – the symbiotic relation of crown to elites, the role of patronage, the attraction of offices – converged in royal courts, their chief and natural habitat. But the Court, which was at once the prince's residence, the center of his government, and the summit of a hierarchic, ceremonious society, signified more than a place or an institution. It was an archetypal symbol, too. The Court stood for the entire public and social world that absolute monarchy created, for the glamor of its power, the luxury of its pleasures, the vast resources it controlled, the envy and faction that pursuit of its favor excited, the fabulous rewards it gave to some, the calamitous fate it brought to others.

It is easy to see the centrality of the Court from the voluminous literature produced in the early modern states dealing with the character, training, and conduct of the perfect courtier and gentleman. Castiglione's elegant Italian treatise, *The book of the courtier*, a dialogue published in 1528 and set in the ducal court of Urbino, was perhaps the most influential and widely disseminated work of this genre, which included a host of original writings and translations in English, French, Spanish, Italian, and other languages. The preoccupation of politicians, moral philosophers, and literary men with courtiership is convincing testimony to the magnetic attraction exerted by courts upon the imagination and life of the societies they ruled.[33]

What is equally evident, though, are the ambiguities in attitude that the Court evoked. The courtier ideal as Castiglione and others pictured it, displaying a harmony of inward and outward virtues, had its antithesis in a concurrent vein of cynicism, disillusionment, and revulsion toward the Court and the dubious nature of the courtier's success in its polluted air. Anticourtiership was hardly less prevalent than the glamorizing of the courtier; and, although it possessed familiar precedents and sources in Greco–Roman and late medieval literature, the anticourtier theme rose to a crescendo in the sixteenth and seventeenth centuries, an insistent nega-

France under Richelieu and Mazarin, 1624–1661, Oxford, 1978, 30 and ch. 2, for the intendants in the 1630s and 1640s. The latter work contains a comprehensive discussion of the intendants and their activity.

[32] On the financial, social, and political aspects of venality of office in France, Mousnier, *La vénalité des offices*, provides an authoritative synthesis.

[33] See the useful bibliography of contemporary writings and translations on this subject up to 1625 in R. Kelso, *The doctrine of the English gentleman in the sixteenth century*, Urbana, 1929, 169–277.

tive commentary on the gravitational pull of the political system of monarchy and the Court.[34]

The anticourtier tradition could be illustrated by a long, varied anthology containing such tropes as the corruption of courts, the vices of courtiers, and the contrast between a courtly and a country life manifest in the unnatural sophistication of the one and the wholesome simplicity of the other. Not surprisingly, the authors were sometimes disappointed courtiers themselves who had failed in the Court's lottery of fortune or suffered shipwreck in its dangerous waters. More or less contemporaneously with Castiglione's *Courtier*, the Englishman, Sir Thomas Wyatt, composed an indictment of the Tudor court under Henry VIII describing the parasitism and hypocrisy of courtiers who by their falsity make "tyranny to be the right of a prince's reign."[35] Also at about the same time, the Spanish Bishop Antonio de Guevara wrote *The dial of princes*, *The dispraise of the court*, and other treatises subsequently highly popular throughout Western Europe, in which he exposed the moral hazards and degeneration incident to courts.[36]

In France, the vogue of Castiglione did not fail to provoke criticisms of his courtier ideal as inextricably blended with dissimulation and the art of self-advancement whereby adaptability became servility, diplomacy duplicity, and flexibility deviousness.[37] Similar reservations toward courtiership occurred in English discussions, which expressed concern over its dangers to ethical integrity.[38] Gentlemen and authors associated with the Elizabethan and Stuart court frequently voiced their awareness and criticism of the disparity between its ideal and the actuality. Sir Walter Raleigh's poem *The lie* displays a tone of cynical contempt: "Say to the Court it glowes and shines like rotten wood." To the poet Edmund Spenser, the courtier was a man with "a guilefull hollow hart," who practices

[34] See especially Pauline Smith, *The anti-courtier trend in sixteenth century French literature*, Geneva, 1966; and C. Uhlig, *Hofkritik im England des Mittelalters und der Renaissance*, Berlin, 1973, for surveys of the literature of this important subject.

[35] Sir Thomas Wyatt, "Of the courtier's life, written to John Poyntz." Wyatt, one of the finest poets of his time, died in 1542 after a disillusioning and perilous career as a courtier of Henry VIII. This poem, needless to say, was not published in Wyatt's lifetime.

[36] Antonio de Guevara, *El relox de principes* (1529); *Libro llamado menosprecio de la corte, y alabanza de la aldea* (1539). Guevara also wrote an *Aviso de privados y doctrina de cortesanos*, dedicated to Cobos, the secretary of Charles V. His *Menosprecio de la corte* became "dans tous les pays le bréviaire de tous les gentilhommes lassés de la vie de cour" (R. Costes, *Antonio de Guevara, Bibliothèque de l'école des hautes études hispaniques*, 2 pts., 1925–6, pt. 2, 117; see also A. Redondo, *Antonio de Guevara [1480?–1545] et l'Espagne de son temps*, Geneva, 1976, 372–405.)

[37] Smith, *The anti-courtier trend*, 26–8.

[38] See D. Javitch, "*The philosophy of the court*: A French satire misunderstood," *Comparative literature 23*, 2 (1971), 195–7, and *Poetry and courtliness in Renaissance England*, Princeton, 1978, ch. 4.

deceit, malice, slander, and strife, and the Court itself a mercenary market where everything is sold, a place

> To fawne, to crouche, to waite, to ride, to runne,
> To spend, to give, to want, to be undonne.[39]

The prudential counsels contained in the *Essays* by the Englishman Francis Bacon and in *The courtier's manual* by the Spaniard Balthasar Gracián resemble each other in reflecting the same equivocal Court milieu with its pragmatism of moral casuistry, its art of self-concealment, and its cool and unscrupulous calculation.[40] Similarly, the lucid, unillusioned conceptions of human nature in the *Mémoires* of Cardinal de Retz and the *Maximes* of the duke of La Rochefoucauld, both prominent actors in the Fronde, are shaped by the knowledge of courts and courtier society as well as by the experience of rebellion: they depict a world of egoism, ingratitude, and unprincipled ambition, devoid of either generosity or honor.[41]

Honor is certainly one of the keys to anticourtier sentiment.[42] The philosopher Montesquieu in the earlier eighteenth century was to express in connection with honor the kernel of a good deal of previous adverse judgments on the nature of courts. As an opponent of absolutism, he spoke of "le misérable caractère des courtisanes" and described the corruption of honor when it was put into contradiction with honors, so that the courtier could at the same time "be covered with infamy and with dignities."[43]

Expressions of the anti-Court theme, of which innumerable examples might be given, were perennial in the monarchical states, called forth as the dark, the negative side of the power and magnetism of courts. Primarily moral, there was nothing necessarily subversive in them. Nonetheless, criticism, disapproval, and dislike of courts could at times intensify into hatred and condemnation, assume a political character, and be converted to rebellion. Aristocratic conspiracies were sometimes actuated by anti-

---

[39] *The poems of Sir Walter Raleigh*, ed. A. Latham, Cambridge, 1962; E. Spenser, "Colin Clouts come home again," lines 688–702, "Mother Hubberd's tale," lines 905–6.

[40] F. Bacon, *Essays* (1625); B. Gracián, *Oraculo manual y arte de prudencia* (1645). The latter had numerous translations. An English version of 1685 is entitled *The courtiers manual;* the French translation bore the title, *L'Homme de cour.*

[41] See A. Adam, *Grandeur and illusion: French literature and society 1600–1715*, London, 1972, 264–70; and A. Krailsheimer, *Studies in self-interest from Descartes to La Bruyère*, Oxford, 1962, chs. 4–5; for these two noblemen and the Fronde, see Chapter 13 in this book.

[42] In general discussions of honor as a central value of the sixteenth and seventeenth centuries, such as C. L. Barber, *The idea of honour in the English drama, 1591–1700*, Gothenburg, 1957, and C. B. Watson, *Shakespeare and the Renaissance concept of honour*, Princeton, 1960, its relation to courts and courtiership is largely neglected. This latter subject is of considerable significance and deserves systematic investigation. It is also overlooked in J. von Kruedener, *Die Rolle des Hofes im Absolutismus*, Stuttgart, 1973, which is disappointingly brief and superficial, as well as too abstractly sociological in its treatment of the role of the court.

[43] Cited by J. Pitt-Rivers, "Honour and social status," in *Honour and shame: The values of the Mediterranean society*, ed. J. Peristiany, Chicago, 1966, 73, 74.

Court resentments at the domination of a faction or a favorite, and the spirit of resistance among the Huguenots of France and the Calvinists of the Netherlands, as likewise among the English Puritans and Scottish Covenanters, was increased by their conviction of the treachery and irreligion in the courts of Catherine de Medici, Philip II, and Charles I. Hostility to the Court, if strong enough, was always a possible ingredient of revolutionary disaffection in the monarchical states.

VI

Another essential and noteworthy feature in the political context of early modern revolution was the monarchies' relation to subject kingdoms, to provincial particularism, and, in one or two instances, to subject ethnic communities. All of these were part of the same problem of political integration with which the rulers of the sixteenth and seventeenth centuries had to wrestle.

In the case of subject kingdoms, this problem was the result of the union of crowns through marriage, inheritance, and conquest, which created associations of states having little or no common tie or loyalty save the ruler and dynasty. The advent of King James VI of Scotland to the English throne in 1603 as heir to Queen Elizabeth placed both countries thenceforth under the same prince. The Spanish monarchy, although far bigger, was built up in a similar way with momentous political consequences. Marriage united the crowns of Castile and Aragon and perpetuated their common rule through its offspring. The kingdom of Naples and the duchy of Milan were won in war with France, justified in the former case by hereditary claims derived from the crown of Aragon. Most of the Netherlands came to the Spanish monarchy by inheritance from the dukes of Burgundy, although one or two of the provinces were added by purchase and another by conquest. Philip II's annexation of Portugal in 1580 was based on his claim to succeed to the Portuguese crown as legitimate heir upon the extinction of the native line of kings.

The primacy of the principle of hereditary dynastic succession made kingdoms resemble family property that could be legitimately transmitted to strangers and foreigners. When such dynastic unions occurred, the constituent states remained formally separate and independent, however, retaining their indigenous institutions of government. They were to be ruled, according to a Spanish jurist of the time, "as if the king who holds them all . . . were king only of each one of them."[44] Upon his accession in England, James I assumed the additional title of king of Great Britain;

---

[44] J. de Solórzano Pereira, *Politica Indiana*, 1647, cited in J. H. Elliott, *The revolt of the Catalans*, Cambridge, 1963, 8.

nevertheless, his attempt at a closer political union of England and Scotland failed, and the two kingdoms continued to be separately governed, with their own laws, privy councils, administrations, and parliaments.[45] Spain achieved a measure of unity in imperial administration by means of a structure of conciliar bodies centered at Madrid to oversee the monarchy's possessions. The council of state as the principal organ advised the king on the government of all his realms, and particular councils, like those of Aragon, Italy, Portugal, and the Indies, supervised the resident administration in the different states.[46] Even with the development of supraterritorial institutions, though, the Spanish monarchy retained its dual character as an empire composed of independent states merely owing allegiance to the same sovereign. This meant that the king of Spain's power was not uniform throughout his realms but varied according to their respective constitutions, laws, and customs. "Almost an absolute monarch in Castile," so his position in the sixteenth century has been described,

he was a ruler with very limited power in . . . the Netherlands. What he could do in an official capacity in Mexico, governed by the laws of Castile, he could not possibly do in Aragon or Sicily. The ruler of the Spanish empire, the most powerful monarch in the world, was first and foremost king of Castile and king of Aragon, count of Flanders . . . duke of Milan.[47]

The structure of dynastic unions was vulnerable to problems and tensions that were in turn related to some of the conditions of revolution. The prince's absenteeism in most of his states, an inevitable consequence relieved at best by rare visits, was apt to cause resentment among both natives and nobility that they were disregarded or their interests neglected. True, some subjects profited from a union of crowns, as did the Scots who followed their King James to England or the numerous non-Castilians who served the Spanish monarchy. Others, however, felt deprived by their prince's absence of prospects of patronage, rewards, and service. After his return in 1559 from the Netherlands to Spain, Philip II seldom went outside Castile and in almost forty years never left the Iberian peninsula again to visit his other European dominions. Nor did his successors, Philip III or IV, ever set foot in the Spanish Netherlands or their Italian states. James I returned only once to Scotland in twenty-two years, and his son, Charles I, allowed eight years to pass after his accession before traveling there to be crowned. Neither of these two Stuart kings or their Tudor predecessors even laid eyes on their other realm of

[45] But in 1638 Charles I appointed a committee for Scottish affairs in the English privy council to advise him when rebellion was looming up in Scotland.

[46] See the survey of the councils of the Spanish monarchy by J. M. Batista I Roca in the foreword to H. G. Koenigsberger, *The government of Sicily under Philip II*, London, 1951.

[47] Elliott, *The revolt of the Catalans*, 8; see *ibid.*, ch. 1, for an acute discussion of the nature of the union of crowns under the Spanish monarchy.

Ireland, which was governed in their name by a lord deputy or lieutenant. Such neglect had its effects upon the grievances and ill feeling of provincial kingdoms.

Moreover, if the monarch were a stranger, then his government would stir up antiforeign sentiments. The marriage in 1554 of Mary I, Henry VIII's daughter, to the future Philip II of Spain was highly unpopular in England, despite the safeguards provided to ensure English independence of Spanish domination and the rights of natives over foreigners in appointments to offices. Such was the political opposition to the Spanish marriage that it led to rebellion. England did not remain part of the Spanish empire only because Mary died in 1558 without heirs, to be succeeded by her sister, Queen Elizabeth.[48]

In another case, a similar outburst of xenophobia occurred in Castile after the Habsburg prince, Charles I, arrived in Spain in 1517 to assume his inheritance, unable to speak Spanish and bringing with him Flemish advisers who proceeded to appropriate lucrative positions in the kingdom for themselves. Two years later, when Charles was forced to become an absentee because of his election in Germany as emperor, the resentment of the Castilians became even greater, for they cared nothing about an emperor and wanted only a king of Castile. These grievances contributed their share in provoking the great Comunero rebellion.

A fundamental problem of dynastic unions was that, despite the theoretical equality and independence of the constituent states, one of them tended to occupy a predominant position, reducing the others to provincial dependencies. Thus Castile, where the monarchy resided and from which it drew its greatest resources – Spain's overseas possessions belonged to the crown of Castile – became the paramount state of the Spanish empire after the middle of the sixteenth century. This was inevitable, given Castile's overwhelming importance to the military and maritime enterprises of the Spanish government, not to mention the degree of absolutism that the crown achieved in Castile and the fact that imperial administration was based in Madrid. Naturally the Castilianization of the monarchy aroused discontent in its other possessions. Aragonese and Catalans believed that Castilians enjoyed the greatest benefits of office and that Castilian noblemen received preference over those elsewhere. A discourse written by an Aragonese in 1626 on the inutility of the union of Aragon and Castile, complained that the monarchy had fostered Castile's aggrandizement at the expense of its other subjects: "And all this comes from not having a king of their own nation."[49] When the ruler made demands or introduced innovations in his non-Castilian domains, they might be opposed as dictated by alien interests or as contrary to native privileges.

[48] See Chapter 9 in this book.   [49] Cited in Elliott, *The revolt of the Catalans*, 12–13.

Philip II's efforts to establish the Inquisition in the Netherlands were among the actions that contributed in the provinces to a climate of rebellion in the 1560s, and his appointment of a Castilian nobleman in 1590 as viceroy of Aragon, in alleged violation of the latter's privileges or *fueros*, helped to provoke Aragonese resistance.

In particular, the wars the Spanish monarchy maintained became a serious cause of strain in some of its non-Castilian domains. With the unavoidable commitments its imperial position imposed on it in the Mediterranean, the Atlantic, Italy, and Northern Europe, the monarchy was obliged to consider the interests of its separate crowns in light of the overall aims of its policy and strategy. War with the Turks in defense of the Mediterranean, the preservation of its transoceanic possessions, the long rivalry and periodic wars with France, the protection of the communications connecting its European states by land and sea, the struggle against Protestant heresy, and its dynastic relation to the policies of its Habsburg cousins in Germany and the Holy Roman Empire were all pieces in the pattern of Spanish involvement in great-power conflicts. Although Castile bore the biggest share of the burdens of empire, the monarchy expected its other states to aid in its necessities and to contribute to their own defense. Some did little for this purpose, whereas others were quite heavily exploited. The aggravation of military and fiscal pressures upon Spain's realms in the 1630s because of war with France at the most desperate period of the monarchy's history formed an essential part of the background to rebellion in Portugal, Catalonia, Naples, and Sicily.

In a somewhat similar way, Charles I treated Scotland as a dependency subordinate to England and English policy makers, and the crown at the same time ruthlessly exploited Ireland on behalf of the English and Protestant interest. These policies provided fuel for revolt in both kingdoms.

Provincial particularism within kingdoms, if usually a less formidable problem than separatist tendencies and other kinds of opposition connected with dynastic unions, presented analogous obstacles to royal state builders. In spite of the evolution of national sentiment at the end of the Middle Ages and of the widening loyalty fixed upon sovereigns, the tenacity of attachments to smaller, more localized communities remained a basic characteristic of the early modern states. Alongside subjects' acceptance of obligation to the prince ran maybe competing allegiances interwoven with their *pays*, *patrie*, county, *patria chica*, which were rooted in older continuities and closer affections.[50] These provincial allegiances were products too of persisting diversities of cultural and sociopolitical conditions that made for strong insularities under the common rule of kings.

[50] See J. H. Elliott, "Revolution and continuity in early modern history," *Past and present* 42 (1969); A. Everitt, *Change in the provinces in the seventeenth century*, Leicester, 1972, ch. 1; A. Dominguez Ortiz, *The golden age of Spain 1516–1659*, New York, 1971, 15.

Provincial societies in unitary kingdoms were apt to react with hostility and anger when the exercise of authority from the monarchical center threatened traditional structures and values, whether it took the form of unaccustomed exactions, alterations in religion, or suppression of local privileges and liberties. Moreover, provincial fidelities were frequently knit to great territorial families, who were more like petty sovereigns than subjects in their prestige and following. In England it was said of the Percy earls of Northumberland at the time of the northern rebellion of 1569 that "the north knows no prince but a Percy."[51] A similar observation was made to Cardinal Richelieu in 1632 apropos of the duke of Montmorency's role in the Languedoc rebellion: "The character of the house of Montmorency is so impressed in Languedoc that the people regard the name of the king as imaginary."[52] Wherever there existed what an English minister of state called "the old good-will of the people, deep-grafted in their harts, to their nobles and gentlemen,"[53] it could link up with provincial resistance to anointed kings.

Of the states of our early modern revolutions, France, which was not involved like the Spanish kingdoms in a union of crowns, was most susceptible to the disruptive consequences of provincial particularism. The French provinces possessed to a far greater degree than elsewhere a distinctive identity, an identity that was formally recognized in a number of them by the enjoyment of juridical-political privileges and the existence of representative institutions to defend these privileges against the unrestricted sovereignty of the crown.[54] In Brittany, Provence, Burgundy, Languedoc, Normandy, and other provinces, denominated *pays d'états* because of their provincial assemblies of estates, the operation of royal authority and its agents was subject to conditions that retarded the progress of absolutist centralized government. The association of some of the provinces with prepotent noble houses whose members were governors only served to aggravate the problems of provincial insubordination and autonomism. The removal of these provincial barriers to full subjection and wider political integration and concentration of authority proved to be one of the greatest difficulties the French absolute monarchy confronted.

In contrast to France, England, although experiencing provincial rebellion, was least prone to the affliction of provincial particularism as it became in the course of the sixteenth century the most unified of kingdoms.

[51] J. B. Black, *The reign of Queen Elizabeth*, Oxford, 1936, 104.

[52] Cited in J. B. Perkins, *France under Mazarin with a review of the administration of Richelieu*, 2 v., New York, 1886, v. 1, 139.

[53] R. R. Reid, *The king's council in the north*, London, 1921, 20.

[54] See M. Marion, *Dictionnaire des institutions de la France aux XVIIe et XVIIIe siècles*, Paris, 1923, *s.v.*, "Provinces" ; R. Mousnier, "La Participation des gouvernés à l'activité des gouvernantes dans la France des XVIIe et XVIIIe siècles," *La Plume, la faucille et le marteau*, 239–41.

Not only did the Tudor monarchy succeed in harnessing the governing class most effectively to its supremacy, but that class possessed the most fully developed national consciousness of any elite in Europe. The crown established new organs of central authority to control its outlying regions in the north and west, and it gradually weaned its provincial subjects away from any dangerous loyalty to rival magnate powers. The high degree of unity it achieved was aided by the absence in England of any counterpart to the provincial assemblies of estates in France that could offer a hold to particularism and autonomism. Instead, the English and Welsh counties were represented only at meetings of the kingdomwide Parliament, which thus served a vital function in the state-building process.

A third aspect of the problem of integration as it affected the political context of revolution was the existence of ethnically separate communities that resisted assimilation by the dominant monarchical state and its civilization. The main instances of this were the Spanish Moriscos and the Irish, both of them cases of a colonial situation in which conquered peoples lived in their own land as inferiors under oppressive alien rule.

The Moriscos were the Moorish subjects of the Spanish monarchy who had been compelled since the early sixteenth century to renounce Islam for Christianity. The policy of forcible conversion, sanctioned by Charles V and Philip II, was a continuance of the *reconquista* mentality that animated Catholic Spain in its agelong conflict with Islam for possession of the Iberian peninsula and that likewise made it a pillar of orthodoxy in the great religious struggles of the sixteenth century. Settled as minorities in various parts of Castile and Aragon, the Moriscos preserved their cultural identity most completely in Granada, the last surviving Muslim stronghold to fall (in 1492) before the Spanish sovereigns. Although nominally Christian, they retained their Arabic tongue, their distinctive dress and customs, and an indigenous aristocracy and performed occupations as petty traders, artisans, peasants, and cultivators for Old Christian landlords. Unlike the Jews, expelled from Spain in 1492 (as the Moriscos were finally to be in 1609), and many of whom to avoid expulsion became Catholic to bear thenceforth together with their descendants the ambiguous status of *conversos* with all its disabilities, the Moriscos remained a people apart. The hatred, contempt, and periodic persecution visited on them by Spanish Christians was the sign of opposed civilizations, not just of the difference between conqueror and conquered.[55] By the mid-sixteenth century, with the growing menace of the Ottoman Turks in the western Mediterranean and the presence in North Africa of Muslim rulers friendly to the Ottomans, the monarchy also began to regard the Moriscos as an internal

---

[55] See Braudel, *La Méditerranée*, v. 2, 119.

danger to Spain's safety, a concern not unjustified; there was reason to believe that Morisco agents aided Spain's Muslim enemies in the hope of deliverance from oppression.[56] Thus, the antagonism of the dominant Catholic state and society toward a culturally separate subject community in its midst was a cause of continual tension and repressive methods that harbored ample seeds of rebellion.[57]

The Irish case, although even more complex, nonetheless reflected a parallel domination superposed on an opposition of civilizations. Although joined to England by a union of crowns, Ireland was in many ways less an autonomous kingdom than a colony governed by the English privy council, an English viceroy and administration, and English law. Its history under the Tudors was marked by rebellions, and not till James I's time in the earlier seventeenth century did English control, once confined to a small part of Ireland, extend throughout its territory. The native or old Irish of Gaelic origin, who were the most numerous inhabitants, lived in a tribal society disintegrating under English pressure. The other ingredients of the population were the old English, the landowning descendants of Englishmen who had settled in Ireland during the Middle Ages, and the new English and the Scots, who came as immigrants in growing numbers in the reigns of Queen Elizabeth and the early Stuarts. Both native Irish and old English were Catholics, but, following the final triumph of the Reformation in England at the accession of Queen Elizabeth, the state religion imposed on Ireland was Protestant: Therefore the mass of Ireland's people belonged to a prohibited faith. The general English conception of the indigenous Irish and their way of life expressed the contempt of a colonizing power for "natives" as inferiors and savages, mingled with prejudice against and dislike for their Catholicism.

During the sixteenth century, the English monarchy encountered intermittent revolt in Ireland; by the seventeenth, with its rule now far more secure, it was striving vigorously to fasten English institutions of government upon Ireland. To give a sure foundation to English-Protestant ascendancy, it also promoted a policy of plantations, which brought increasing numbers of Protestant colonists, English and Scottish, to settle in Ireland. This policy, effected by large-scale land confiscations and expropriation of its inhabitants, produced deeply disturbing effects in the country. Plantations threatened not only the native Irish but also eventually menaced the old English aristocracy of Catholic faith, who took pride in their English ancestry and connections and wished to remain loyal to the crown. In due course, Charles I's treatment of Ireland aroused all its dis-

[56] A. C. Hess, "The Moriscos: An Ottoman fifth column in sixteenth century Spain," *American historical review 74*, 1 (1968).

[57] See for an account of the Moriscos with references to the literature, Braudel, *La Méditerranée*, v. 2, 118–31; Lynch, *Spain under the Habsburgs*, v. 1, 205–10; and Ch. 9 of this book.

parate interests against his government. But both in the later Tudor and the early Stuart reigns, at the heart of Ireland's problems, intricate as they were, lay the tensions between a colony and a colonizing power, and the resistance of an indigenous society against religious and cultural subjugation by its rulers of alien state and civilization.[58]

VII

To complete our examination of the political context of our early modern revolutions, we must look rapidly at the important role of representative assemblies, which were widespread throughout Europe in the sixteenth and seventeenth centuries. These institutions, variously known as *états*, *stati*, *cortes*, parliament, *parlamento*, *Landstände*, and so forth, had originated during the later Middle Ages, called into existence by rulers as the best means to obtain their subjects' money and advice. During the sixteenth century, among the realms pertaining to our inquiry, they were found in the Spanish monarchy in Castile; in Valencia, Aragon, and Catalonia, the three appendant states of the crown of Aragon, which had both their own particular and a general *cortes*; in Naples and Sicily; and in the Netherlands, which possessed separate provincial estates in a number of provinces and a States General of the Low Countries. The English monarchy had parliaments to deal with in England, in Ireland, and, after 1603, in Scotland. The French monarchy contained more than twenty provincial assemblies of estates and an Estates General of the kingdom. In the German principalities affected by the peasant war, there were numerous assemblies of estates.[59]

Many variations existed in the constitution of these bodies. Commonly they consisted of the three great orders of clergy, nobility, and towns or bourgeoisie. There were frequent exceptions to this rule, however. Here and there the peasant estate was directly represented, as in a few of the provincial assemblies of the Netherlands and in Germany in the assemblies or diets in the Tyrol, the margravate of Baden, and the ecclesiastical principality of Kempten, among others.[60] Sometimes the clergy was ab-

---

[58] See the "Historical Introduction," in R. Dunlop, *Ireland under the Commonwealth*, 2 v., Manchester, 1913, v. 1.

[59] See A. Marongiu, *Medieval parliaments: a comparative study*, London, 1968; and G. Griffiths, *Representative government in Western Europe in the sixteenth century*, Oxford, 1968, for a survey of these assemblies, with a useful selection of documents in the latter work. On German estates, see F. Carsten, *Princes and parliaments in Germany*, Oxford, 1959. The papers collected in D. Gerhard (ed.), *Ständische Vertretungen in Europa im 17. und 18. Jahrhundert*, Göttingen, 1969, contain a good discussion of relevant problems and literature; see especially G. Birtsch's essay, "Die landständische Verfassung als Gegenstand der Forschung."

[60] F. Rachfahl, *Wilhelm von Oranien und der Niederländische Aufstand*, 3 v., Halle, 1906–24, v. 1, 251; P. Blickle, *Landschaften im alten Reich*, Munich, 1973, 28, and the adjacent map showing the representation in upper German estates. Kempten was one of several principalities with only a peasant estate.

sent because the clerical estate met in representative bodies of its own. In one case, the Cortes of Castile, representation was limited to eighteen privileged towns. Occasionally the greater and lesser nobility were present as separate estates. In the English Parliament, on the other hand, the lesser nobility or knights of the shire met in one body with the representatives of the towns as the House of Commons. In Naples, the capital city of Naples, which had its own council or senate of *eletti*, was not represented in the Parlamento of the kingdom.[61] In the Netherlands, the States General was composed of delegates of the separate provincial estates or states.

The nature of representation by these institutions corresponded broadly to the structural characteristics and distinctions of the society of orders. It was not the people, nor the will of the people, nor the prince's subjects as individuals, that were represented. Representation was based on orders, on corporations, and on organized territorial and juridical communities. It was also infused with the prevailing ideas of legal and social inequality. A definition of assemblies of estates in the German context as "a corporate unity of certain privileged classes representing the *Land* over against the ruler"[62] has been criticized as containing anachronistic liberal assumptions of the nineteenth century, and it has been maintained instead that the estates "did not represent, but were the *Land*."[63] Here the emphasis falls on the privileged and superior orders, the *meliores et maiores terrae*, as actually identical with or constituting the community. Another conception combines the latter view with one that sees the estates as "personifying" the community, kingdom, *patria*, or *Land*.[64] In the English case, the contemporary theory of Parliament held that all Englishmen were present at its meetings either personally or by proxy.[65] Nevertheless, it was the realm, consisting of county and borough communities and of peers and commons, that was represented, not the people. Moreover, the persons legally qualified to sit in Parliament or vote for its members were only a small proportion of the king's subjects.

Thus, privilege and inequality were inscribed in the English Parliament, notwithstanding that in the factual sense of its political centrality and relation to constituents it was the most representative body of its kind in Europe. Although a comprehensive definition of assemblies of estates

---

[61] Marongiu, *Medieval parliaments*, 154–5.
[62] This is the definition given by G. von Below, "System und Bedeutung der landständischen Verfassung," cited in Birtsch, "Die landständische Verfassung," 39.
[63] O. Brunner, *Land und Herrschaft*, cited in *ibid.*, 140; see also the discussion in Blickle, 38–47.
[64] Marongiu, *Medieval parliaments*, 223.
[65] P. Zagorin, *The court and the country*, London, 1969, 86; see the general discussion in G. R. Elton, " 'The body of the whole realm': Parliament and representation in medieval and Tudor England," in *Studies in Tudor and Stuart politics and government*, 2 v., Cambridge, 1974, v. 2.

is perhaps impossible to come by,[66] they were always, as has been rightly said, part of a "system of privilege" and of "juridical inequality" of which economic and social inequality formed the foundation.[67]

Representative assemblies existed primarily to give effect to the principle of limitation of rulers' powers by the necessity of the consent of the community or subjects to certain acts of government. This was their raison d'être, despite their innumerable differences in composition and organization, form of elections, type of electors, frequency of meetings, procedure, powers of deputies, relations between the orders, and so on. When princes' financial needs exceeded their ordinary revenue resources, they were obliged to turn for assistance to the estates; or they might summon them to participate in legislation or to advise and concur on weighty matters like the making of treaties or on war and peace. Meetings were an occasion to voice complaints and petition for redress of grievances. As subjects were always reluctant to grant money, some reciprocity was implied between the estates' assent to taxes and the ruler's readiness to redress grievances. In seeking assistance, the latter also had to explain his needs, which in turn involved the estates in discussions of policy, as did their grievances and suggestions for reform.[68]

Derived from the medieval polity, the institutional role of representative assemblies was implanted in a domain of lawful rights and liberties theoretically immune from arbitrary treatment by the ruler. These organs thus formed a limited "populistic" element in the royal states; they embodied what has been called the "ascending theme" of government as an emanation of the community's consent, as against the "descending theme" personified by charismatic monarchs owing their position and authority to divine appointment.[69]

In exercising their functions, representative assemblies were wont to appeal for justification of their position to immemorial custom, prescriptive privileges, and formal pacts and concessions by rulers recognizing subjects' liberties and rights. This mode of argument, which I have earlier called the "ideology of the normative past," looked to antiquity, custom, and rudimentary contractual traditions as a source of authority and a limit upon absolutism and royal power.

Thus, the States General of the Netherlands in its differences with its Habsburg sovereigns invoked the Joyeuse Entrée of Brabant, conceded in 1356 by the duke of Brabant and sworn to thereafter by his successors,

[66] See the allusion to the "Definitionsfeindlichkeit" of assemblies of estates by Birtsch, "Die landständische Verfassung," 41.

[67] G. Oestreich, "Ständestatt und Ständewesen im Werk Otto Hintzes," in Gerhard, *Ständische Vertretungen*, 66.

[68] Griffiths, *Representative government in Western Europe*, xv–xvi.

[69] See Ullmann, *Principles of government and politics*, for a discussion of "ascending" and "descending" themes of government in medieval law, politics, and political theory.

including Charles V and Philip II, a sort of constitutional contract confirming the authority and consent of the estates in various matters of government.[70] The Cortes of Catalonia was the guardian of the Constitucions sworn to by the king at his accession, which formed the basis of the principality's liberties against arbitrary taxation and other abuses.[71] The *fueros* of Aragon served the kingdom's Cortes in the same way as a barrier to absolutism.[72] The Parlamento of Sicily looked to the Capitoli of former rulers for support of its privileges.[73] The Parlamento of Naples relied similarly on capitulations and privileges, confirmed by Charles V in 1540, as the bulwark of the Regno's liberties, one of which was that new taxes could not be imposed "without parliament."[74] The English Parliament in its controversies with Queen Elizabeth and the first two Stuart kings appealed to the precedents of the common law, to the ancient constitution, and to the Magna Carta to safeguard the legal rights of subjects from invasion.[75] French provincial estates could cite royal confirmations of their privileges, made to them when their provinces were united to the domain of the French king or afterward.[76]

Needless to say, the relationship between princes and representative assemblies was not only one of conflict. There was also cooperation and consensus. The faculty of certain of these bodies to survive and grow, most notably in the case of the English Parliament, depended partly on their usefulness to rulers, which made it worthwhile for the latter to summon and consult them frequently. There were, of course, particular historical conditions that help to explain the differing destinies of assemblies of estates, but one of the reasons for this difference was that some were too useful or entrenched to be dispensed with.

Although princes did not necessarily wish to rid themselves of representative assemblies, they did want them to be cooperative and acquiescent, consenting to money grants when asked, offering constructive counsel, and not directing their energies primarily to criticism or obstruction. In the long run, therefore, opposition was inevitable between monarchs and estates standing athwart the path of absolutism. It was inevitable when the estates, as was often the case, served as vehicles of particularist inter-

[70] Griffiths, *Representative government in Western Europe*, 302; and P. Geurts, "Het beroep op de Blijde Inkomste in de pamfletten uit de tachtigjarige oorlog," *Standen en landen 16* (1958).
[71] Elliott, *The revolt of the Catalans*, 45.
[72] *Ibid.*, 7; Lynch, *Spain under the Habsburgs*, v. 1, 197, 330.
[73] Koenigsberger, *The government of Sicily*, 149–60, for an account of the Sicilian parlamento.
[74] R. Villari, *La rivolta antispagnola a Napoli*, 2nd ed., Bari, 1973, 13–15.
[75] For a general discussion, see J. G. Pocock, *The ancient constitution and the feudal law*, Cambridge, 1957, ch. 2; and Judson, *The crisis of the constitution*.
[76] Griffiths, *Representative government in Western Europe*, 214, and the following documents 1–2, referring to the privileges of Provence and Burgundy; Bonney, *Political change in France under Richelieu and Mazarin*, 344–6, cites other French examples.

ests or aristocratic power in provinces or dependent kingdoms that held out against the integrative efforts of centralizing governments. It was equally inevitable when rulers, in order to obtain a free hand in government, tried to constrict the functions of the estates or to win an uncontrolled authority to tax, to legislate, or to make major changes in government or religion.

In the two centuries after 1500, many representative assemblies declined or atrophied, some were reduced to docile instruments or settled into a static pattern devoid of initiative or dynamism, others disappeared. Looking back upon the recent past in his republican tract, *Oceana* (1656), the English political theorist James Harrington observed of princes and parliaments: "Where are the estates, or the power of the people in France? Blown up. Where is that of the people in Aragon, and the rest of the Spanish kingdoms? Blown up." He also noted where estates were in the ascendant on account of revolutions: "On the other side, where is the king of Spain's power in Holland? Blown up . . . Nor shall any show a reason . . . why the people of [England] have blown up their king, but that their kings did not first blow up them."[77]

By the sixteenth century, the French Estates General was already much neglected by the crown. It had only an insignificant role in supplying money – the king could impose the *taille* in large parts of the kingdom of his own will and preferred to have recourse to the separate provincial estates for subsidies. It also failed to develop effective legislative attributes.[78] After its meetings in 1468 and 1484, it was not even convened again till 1560, given a new lease on life by royal weakness and the imminent approach of a revolutionary civil war in France. For the remainder of the century it met intermittently and strove to strengthen itself. Upon the return of peace, however, it was summoned only once more – in 1614 – after which it became extinct. Efforts to revive it in the Fronde came to naught, and it made its brief final appearance as a resurrected ghost at the inception of the French revolution in 1789.

The French provincial estates lasted longer and met more often than the Estates General, but they too gradually underwent a similar fate. Those in the central provinces had mostly ceased to exist before 1600. Those in

---

[77] James Harrington, *The commonwealth of Oceana, Political works*, ed. J. G. Pocock, Cambridge, 1977, 264.
[78] Griffiths, *Representative government in Western Europe*, 121–2; Shennan, *Government and society in France*, 35; and see the important studies by J. R. Major, *Representative institutions in Renaissance France 1421–1559*, and "The loss of royal initiative and the decay of the Estates General in France, 1421–1615," in *Album Helen Cam. Studies . . . International Commission for the history of representative and parliamentary institutions*, v. 23–24, Louvain, 1960–1, v. 24. Despite my inability to agree with several of Professor Major's arguments, his main explanation for the decline of the Estates General – that it was of little usefulness to the crown – is very convincing.

the provinces of the periphery, united later than the former to the royal domain and direct government of the crown, were more important. It was to them that the king mainly went for imposts, and their privileges included the right in some measure of assessing and administering their own taxes. In due course they succumbed to absolutism, as their privileges were whittled away and invaded, some in the sixteenth century, many others by Louis XIII and Richelieu. An assault on the taxing powers of the estates of Burgundy was decreed in 1629. The estates of Provence were abolished and supplanted in 1639 by a differently constituted, smaller body. The assemblies of Poitou, Périgord, Guienne, Dauphiné, Normandy, and other *pays d'états* were simply no longer summoned by the king after various dates in the first or second half of the seventeenth century. Those that survived all came under the crown's administrative tutelage and control.[79]

Other types of traditional representative institutions in France also fell into disuse. Here we need only mention the assembly of notables, a consultative body occasionally convoked by the crown that consisted of designated members of the clergy, nobility, and officials of the *parlements* and other royal courts. Louis XIII summoned it for advice in 1626, when Richelieu found it of little assistance. This was its last meeting, although it too made a ghostly reappearance on the eve of the French revolution.[80]

What alone remained important as a possible basis of institutional opposition to absolutism in France as representative assemblies declined or expired was the Parlement of Paris and other sovereign courts of the crown with their prestige, their entrenched magistracy, and their professional traditions as guardians of the law.[81] The Parlement of Paris possessed a great *ressort* or jurisdiction extending over a third of the kingdom. In discharging its duty to register royal edicts before they became law, it could protest, raise questions of legality, and discuss and criticize the government's policies. Of course, Louis XIII and Richelieu tried to muzzle it and to suppress its intervention in matters of state, but it was to have its hour in the Fronde.

In most of the Spanish kingdoms, representative assemblies underwent a fate similar to France's. During the course of the sixteenth century, the monarchy, by its success in suppressing rebellion, made the Cortes of

[79] See Mousnier, "La Participation des gouvernés à l'activité des gouvernants dans la France des XVIIᵉ et XVIIIᵉ siècles," 239, 249; B. Porchnev, *Les Soulèvements populaires en France de 1623 à 1648*, trans. from the Russian, Paris, 1963, 129; Marion, *Dictionnaire des institutions*, 219 (*s.v.* "Etats provinciaux"); and the discussion of the provincial estates in Bonney, *Political change in France under Richelieu and Mazarin*, ch. 15.

[80] Mousnier, "La Participation des gouvernés à l'activité des gouvernants dans la France des XVIIᵉ et XVIIIᵉ siècles," 235–6; and see the account of the assembly of notables in 1626 by Lublinskaya, *French absolutism*, with its partiality to Richelieu and absolutism as the "progressive" forces of their time.

[81] Shennan, *Government and society in France*, 44–5.

Castile a compliant institution for voting subsidies, and it pared down the privileges of the kingdom and Cortes of Aragon so that they became amenable to royal sovereignty.[82] The Parlamento of Naples, which met biennially in the first forty years of the seventeenth century, was no longer summoned after 1642.[83] That of Sicily remained intact, never having given serious trouble to the crown.[84] The Cortes of Catalonia passed through the chastening experience of the defeat of the rebellion of 1640, which its opposition had helped to inspire.[85]

The States General of the Netherlands and the Parliament of England were the main exceptions to the decline, stagnation, and disappearance of representative institutions at the hands of absolutist sovereigns in the great Western European kingdoms. The first, despite its structural weaknesses and vulnerability to particularist interests, rose to ascendancy as the focus of a federal republic during and because of the provinces' revolt against Spain.[86] The second emerged from the sixteenth century in a stronger position than ever before. The fact that the Tudor kings found Parliament indispensable in establishing the statutory foundations of their own widening supremacy is one of the keys to this development. Although sometimes at odds with the crown, generally it cooperated, thus contributing to make royal government more effective. Thereby its own stature increased even as the monarchy's power grew greater.

Historical circumstances and institutional peculiarities favored the fortunes of the English Parliament. Compared with France, England suffered little from the disruptive forces of provincial particularism. The king of France could and did disregard the Estates General in order to approach his provincial estates for money. The latter in turn had no wider horizon than their own provincial interests. England in contrast was free of rival provincial estates, and the whole kingdom was subject to the authority of one central assembly that was an integral part of the king's government. Unlike the French and some other assemblies, the English Parliament was based only to a limited extent on organization by orders. Instead of the separate orders deliberating apart or presenting their own respective grievances, it consisted of two Houses, an upper House of temporal and spiritual peers, the Lords, and a lower House of county and borough members, the Commons. This structure facilitated cooperation and helped to reduce the conflicts of orders that weakened the Estates General of France and some of the provincial estates. The House of Commons, whose size

---

[82] Lynch, *Spain under the Habsburgs*, v. 1, 43–4, 344–5; and Chapter 9 in this book.

[83] Marongiu, *Medieval parliaments*, 212–13.

[84] Koenigsberger, *The government of Sicily*, 160–1.

[85] Elliott, *The revolt of the Catalans*, chs. 8, 10.

[86] The Estates General before the revolt is described by Koenigsberger, *Estates and revolutions*, Ithaca, 1971, ch. 4. G. Malengreau stresses its proneness to particularism, *L'Esprit particulariste et la révolution des Pays-Bas du XVIe siècle*, Louvain, 1936.

grew steadily in the sixteenth century as the crown enfranchised additional communities, also had a much larger membership than third estates elsewhere, which strengthened its representative capacity.[87] Moreover, the boroughs were coming to be more and more represented by gentry, not townsmen or bourgeois. This made the House of Commons a predominantly aristocratic assembly; in fact, there was probably no more aristocratic representative body of its kind in Western Europe.

The English Parliament also differed from other comparable national representative institutions in its power to make binding decisions. This was not possible for the French Estates General, whose deputies lacked plenary authority to vote money or surrender one privilege to gain another: All they could do was present grievances and bring back recommendations to those who had sent them. Similarly, the States General of the Netherlands, although good at opposition, was composed of deputies with limited powers who had to refer money and other questions back to their principals, the provincial estates.[88] Members of the English House of Commons, on the other hand, enjoyed full power to conclude on behalf of their constituencies. The two Houses could at their discretion vote subsidies and pass bills, which, if they received the royal assent, were then binding on the people and communities of the kingdom. The effect, of course, was to increase Parliament's usefulness as a working institution.[89]

For all these reasons, Parliament served the crown's needs well, as long as it was controllable. By the time the Stuart kings encountered it, it had become the most powerful of central assemblies, a great political forum for the governing class, and a body endowed with privileges, traditions, and a corporate consciousness that made it nearly as hard for the crown to live with as to live without. Its members, moreover, displayed a keen awareness of their representative relation to their constituencies and the kingdom, feeling that they served for the nation and its people, as well as to deal with the needs of the king.[90] It was this spirit that gradually undermined royal domination of Parliament's proceedings in the earlier decades of the seventeenth century.

More often than not, representative assemblies in the sixteenth and seventeenth centuries became weak and enfeebled, busied themselves with small matters, lacked ambition to play a greater role than rulers permitted,

---

[87] See G. R. Elton, " 'The body of the whole realm,' " in *Studies in Tudor and Stuart politics and government*, v. 2, 41–2.

[88] See the account of the powers of deputies by Koenigsberger, *Estates and revolutions*, ch. 7; and J. R. Major, *The Estates General of 1560*, Princeton, 1951, 74–5.

[89] General discussions and comparisons of the divergent histories of the English parliament and other representative assemblies are offered by J. R. Major in *The Estates General of 1560* and other writings; A. R. Myers, "The English parliament and the French Estates General in the Middle Ages," *Album Helen Cam*, v. 24; Elton, " 'The body of the whole realm.' "

[90] Chapter 12 in this book.

and served as organs of aristocratic privilege, vested oligarchic interests, and narrow sectional concerns. Few were fit to take a leading part in struggles against kings. However, when we attempt to see them in their overall relation to the phenomenon of early modern revolution, what matters more than their weakness or inadequacies is what they stood for in the political system of the royal states. They were a symbol, and in some measure an actualization, of traditions of liberty and of the juridical principle of limitation of power by consent of subjects and community.[91] Neither traditions nor principle lost their significance or ceased to exercise their influence in the face of evolving absolutism. Representative institutions therefore fulfilled a variety of functions in both fact and idea within the context of revolution. They provided a platform of political opposition and even became the organizing center of revolt. Rebels invoked their authority to sanction the right of resistance to divinely ordained kings. Theories of popular sovereignty and contractual conceptions of government of wider or narrower import were grafted onto them. Attempts were made to revitalize them and to reproduce them in fresh settings. Revolutionary governments arose out of them or sought legitimacy through them. The unrepresented lower orders turned to them to demand representation themselves. In short, estates and parliaments gave to rebels at once an instrument, a model, and an ideal that could have manifold effects upon their political thought and action.

[91] This might be no less true even when the estates were merely defenders of particularist privileges. As Professor Meuvret has remarked, particularism "n'en a pas moins représenté la forme concrète qu'a prise maintes fois la lutte pour la liberté" ("Comment les français du XVIIe siècle voyaient l'impôt," in *Etudes d'histoire économique*, Paris, 1971, 298.

5

Economy, conjunctural factors, the crisis of the seventeenth century

I

In the two preceding chapters, we have been examining the context of our early modern revolutions primarily from the standpoint of structures – both structures of society and structures of government and politics. In the first, we have considered the form of society in which these revolutions occurred, certain of the larger collectivities of which it consisted as a society of orders, and their pertinent characteristics and interrelations. In the second, we have looked at the monarchical state of the period, its political system and governmental features, and the weaknesses to which it was prone. We are justified in describing these as structures because we are dealing in both cases with durable configurations persisting through time in a dynamic interplay of institutions and conditions, which create at once the arena and limits of possible action by revolutionary actors. There will be a specific determinate relation between every revolutionary event and these structures that enclose them and with whose general characteristics they are in some particular way coordinated.

In the present chapter we have in view a different kind of context, consisting not of structures but of events, contingencies, and trends belonging broadly to the economic domain. These do, of course, interact with structures and may help to modify them in the long run, but they are nevertheless distinct from them. The matters that fall under this head have sometimes been referred to by French scholars as *conjoncture*.[1] They include prices, taxes, rents, subsistence crises, trade cycles, contractions and expansions – in short, singular occurrences and short- and long-term

[1] See the discussion, "Qu'est-ce que la conjoncture," by H. and P. Chaunu (*Seville et l'Atlantique* (1504–1650), *2nd partie: partie interprétative*, v. 8b, pt. 1, 9–14), which ascribes to the domain of *conjoncture* a more systematic and integral character than is perhaps possible. A quantitative, statistical basis for conjunctural factors is generally regarded as indispensable by present-day economic historians.

movements and convergences chiefly of an economic character. Of such phenomena one historian has said, "Many revolts are explicable simply by *'la conjoncture'* . . . without the need to seek the causes in the social structure."[2] Other writers have seen a crisis of the seventeenth century involving conjunctural factors behind the rebellions of the 1640s. We must accordingly consider how far these contingencies may bear upon the context of sixteenth- and seventeenth-century revolutions.

It would be easy to cite examples of opinions during the period that connected some of its rebellions with adverse economic developments. Heinrich Hug, a local official and eyewitness chronicler of the German peasant war around Lake Constance and the Black Forest, blamed the beginning of the revolt upon the crop failure and high grain prices that followed the bad weather of the summer of 1524: In their need and misery, he said, the peasants would no longer yield obedience.[3] Peasant outbreaks by the so-called Croquants in the southwest of France in the 1590s during the civil war were ascribed by officials to taxes and other exactions.[4] In England in 1607, at a time of agrarian disturbances in the midlands, enclosures were cited in the House of Lords as the cause of "domestic commotions."[5] This explanation accorded with a longstanding view of reformers and politicians ascribing such disorders to enclosures by greedy, profit-seeking landlords. Similarly, in 1622, a period of acute trade depression, English clothiers warned the government of the effects of unemployment: "The livelihood of so many thousands being taken from them . . . consider how difficult [it] will be . . . to contain them from mutiny and rebellion."[6]

These comments direct us toward the recognition of certain elemental forces that acted immediately upon the conditions of life of the peoples of the early modern states. The most important, because universal in its impact, was the annual harvest, which affected not only grain prices but the cost of other consumables. "Right up to the time of the French Revolution and beyond in Europe," it has been remarked, "the threat of high prices for food was the commonest and most potent cause of public disorder."[7] We learn from Professor Hoskins' study of English harvest fluctuations between 1480 and 1619 that 35 of the 140 harvests of this period were failures to some extent: in a normal decade, therefore, an average of one

[2] R. Mousnier, *Recherches sur les soulèvements populaires en France de 1485 à 1787: Questionnaire* (Centre de recherches sur la civilisation de l'Europe moderne), Paris, n.d., 13.

[3] Heinrich Hug's *Villinger Chronicle*, in *Quellen zur Geschichte des Bauernkrieges*, ed. G. Franz, Munich, 1963, 89.

[4] J. Loutchitzky, *Documents inédits pour servir à l'histoire de la réforme et de la Ligue*, Paris, 1875, 340–54; for further discussion of the Croquants, see Ch. 7 in this book.

[5] J. Thirsk and J. P. Cooper (eds.), *Seventeenth-century economic documents*, Oxford, 1972, 107.

[6] *Ibid.*, 15.   [7] P. Laslett, *The world we have lost*, 2nd ed., New York, 1971, 118.

harvest in four.[8] This meant that the average price of wheat in those years stood anywhere from 10 percent to 50 percent or more above the norm.[9] The really bad harvests of the same period, when the price was 25 to 50 percent above the norm, totaled twenty-three, slightly more than one in six. There was also a marked tendency for bad and good harvests to run consecutively over several years. For the many Englishmen (probably a half or more of the population) who depended in some degree on wages and were compelled to lay out most of their income in food and drink, the effect of successive bad years was calamitous and spelled hunger and starvation.

The "dreadful fifties," as the same writer has called the middle years of the sixteenth century, opened with three consecutive bad harvests in 1549, 1550, and 1551, followed by several good harvests and then by the disastrous harvests of 1555 and 1556, the last of which was "a year of famine over most of Northern and Western Europe." In England a concurrent monetary debasement also took place, so that the price index constructed by modern scholars shows that consumables between 1545 and 1557 shot up from 191 to 409. Moreover, rack-renting and encroachment on common lands by landlords also intensified during these years.

It is plausible to associate these adverse conjunctural conditions, as Hoskins does, with the acute social tensions of the reign of Edward VI (1547–53) culminating in the Norfolk rebellion of 1549, the biggest English agrarian revolt of the century. Yet we should note as a caution that twenty years earlier, in the years 1522–6, there were five good harvests in succession, of which Hoskins conjectures that they must have aided Henry VIII to raise the unprecedented taxes and loans he needed for his French war. We know, however, that in 1525 the king's exactions, the so-called Amicable Grant, met strong popular opposition, that thousands gathered to protest it who proclaimed that their captains were "poverty" and "necessity," and that Henry had to abandon his demands in the face of such resistance.[10]

Modern historians have associated the drastic deterioration of living standards due to grain shortages and consequent price rises with various revolutionary occurrences. In 1566, the famous "hunger year" of the Netherlands, rebellion began in the epidemic of iconoclastic rioting that swept the provinces. Some of the impetus to this outbreak perhaps stemmed from the subsistence crisis and famine conditions of 1565–6, which hit the impoverished wage earners in the cloth manufacturing towns of the Low

[8] The material in this and the next two paragraphs is derived from W. G. Hoskins, "Harvest fluctuations and English economic history, 1480–1619," *Agricultural history review 12*, 1 (1964). A second article in *ibid. 16*, 1 (1968), deals with the period 1620–1759.

[9] The norm is based upon a thirty-one–year moving average; see *ibid.*, fig. I.

[10] See Edward Hall, *Chronicle*, ed. C. Whibley, 2 v., London, 1904, v. 2, 42–3; A. Fletcher, *Tudor rebellions*, 2nd ed., London, 1973, 17–20.

Countries particularly hard. It is significant nevertheless that the rioters directed their attacks mainly against churches and the ornaments of Catholic worship and hardly at all against wholesale grain merchants, rich burghers, and hoarders.[11]

The Croquant peasant risings in France during the 1590s, which have already been mentioned, coincided with a severe Europe-wide subsistence crisis caused by the cold, wet weather of the coldest decade of the sixteenth century. The worst years of scarcity were the four between 1594 and 1597, when "the rain fell incessantly all over Europe from Ireland to Silesia," bringing successive harvest failures, rocketing grain prices, and famine.[12] Amid these conditions, the peasants and *menu peuple* were driven to revolt by the plundering of troops and the ravages of taxation in the last phase of France's long revolutionary civil war.[13]

As still another case due to causes of the same kind, we have the acute subsistence crisis of 1647–53 in large parts of France "of an intensity and duration hitherto unknown," according to a modern scholar, with its appalling accompaniments in famine, disease, and soaring mortality.[14] Probably the suffering it inflicted, which was naturally cruelest for the poor peasants and artisans, contributed to the conditions out of which the Fronde arose.[15] These same years between 1647 and 1652, which were such hard ones in so many places, also brought a subsistence crisis of ruined harvests, scarcity, and high bread prices to Andalusia. The years 1650 and 1651 were the two worst of the century in this region of Spain, and the period was punctuated by localized urban and rural outbreaks, which were "revolts of hunger."[16]

Conjunctural factors usually operated jointly rather than singly in their

---

[11] See the discussion of the conjunctural aspects of the wave of iconoclasm by C. Verlinden, "Crises économiques et sociales en Belgique á l'époque de Charles-Quint," in *Charles-Quint et son temps*, Paris, 1959; C. Verlinden, J. Craeybeckx, and E. Scholliers, "Prince and wage movements in Belgium in the sixteenth century," in *Economy and society in early modern Europe*, (ed.) P. Burke, New York, 1972; H. Van Der Wee, "The economy as a factor in the start of the revolt in the southern Netherlands," *Acta historiae Neerlandica 5* (1971). The events of 1566 are interpreted from a Marxist economic standpoint by E. Kuttner, *Het hongerjaar 1566*, Amsterdam, 1949.

[12] Hoskins, 38; E. Ladurie, *Times of feast, times of famine: a history of climate since the year 1000*, New York, 1971, 66–7.

[13] E. Ladurie, *Les Paysans de Languedoc*, 2 v., Paris, 1966, v. 1, 401–2; and Ch. 7 in this book.

[14] P. Goubert, "The French peasantry of the seventeenth century: A regional example," in *Crisis in Europe 1560–1660*, ed. T. Aston, New York, 1965, 162.

[15] Ladurie, *Times of feast, times of famine*, 57; R. Mousnier, "The Fronde," in *Preconditions of revolution in early modern Europe*, ed. R. Forster and J. Greene, Baltimore, 1970, 134–6. There were naturally regional variations in the incidence of such crises: that of 1647–53 did not have the same impact on southwest France as in the north, according to Y.-M. Bercé, *Histoires des Croquants: Etude des soulèvements populaires au XVIIe siècle dans la sud-ouest de la France*, 2 v., Geneva, 1974, v. 1, 22. See the discussion of the conjunctural relation of these revolts in the southwest in *ibid.*, v. 1, pt. 1.

[16] A. Dominguez Ortiz, *Alteraciónes Andaluzas*, Madrid, 1973, 18, 22–39.

effects. Another of them besides the annual harvest that could thus affect the context of revolutions was the burden of fiscality, especially when it coincided with other economic adversities. One historian of French taxation has asserted that only religious persecution had an influence comparable to fiscal oppression in arousing men to resistance.[17] Unaccustomed imposts that ran counter to tradition or group privileges and were perceived as irregular or unjust as well as burdensome were particularly resented. In addition, payments to the central royal fisc and its agents may have had a distant impersonality that made them more objectionable to subjects than were customary payments or services to landlords or church.[18]

Royal fiscality figured prominently in the conjunctural background of various revolutions. Imposts by the local authorities that raised food costs at a time of generally unfavorable *conjoncture* helped to precipitate the revolts of Naples and Palermo in 1647.[19] In England, the ship-money tax that Charles I levied in the later 1630s, not to mention other royal fiscal expedients, was one of his most flagrant provocations to revolution; the opposition to it, however, should be seen as influenced not only by strictly conjunctural factors but equally if not more so by the conviction of its illegality as a nonparliamentary exaction.[20]

France was the classic land where the state's exactions played a major role in the conjunctural context of rebellion. The revolt of Guienne in 1548, the largest insurrectionary movement in France in the first half of the sixteenth century, was directed against the excesses of royal fiscality.[21] Similarly, most of the localized revolts of the earlier seventeenth century had a predominantly antifiscal character.[22] French peasants, the unprivileged, and the urban poor suffered not only from the *taille* but from a host of indirect taxes, state monopolies, and the plague of syndicates of tax farmers whose agents aroused violent hostility.[23] Moreover, the fact that rebels usually did not understand the reasons for economic fluctuations, while the depredations of fiscality were clearly visible to them, made it an obvious target for their wrath. The significance of the fiscal aspect in France

[17] G. Ardant, *Histoire de l'impôt*, 2 v., Paris, 1971–, v. 1, 428.

[18] See *ibid.*, v. 1, 431; and the remarks by Bercé, *Histoire des Croquants*, v. 1, 129–30.

[19] M. Schipa, *Masaniello*, Bari, 1925, 65; and see the account of Spanish fiscalism in the kingdom of Naples in R. Villari, *La rivolta antispagnola a Napoli*, 2nd ed., Bari, 1973, ch. 4; and G. Coniglio, *Il viceregno di Napoli nel secolo XVII*, Rome, 1955, 259–76; for Palermo, see H. G. Koenigsberger, "The revolt of Palermo in 1647," in *Estates and revolutions*, Ithaca, 1971, 257–58. See Ch. 8 in this book for further discussion of these revolts.

[20] P. Zagorin, *The court and the country*, London, 1969, 114–15, and Ch. 12 in this book.

[21] See G. Procacci, *Classi sociali e monarchia assoluta nella Francia della prima metà del secolo XVI*, Turin, 1955, 218; and Ch. 7 in this book.

[22] See Ardant, *Histoire de l'impôt*, v. 1, sec. 3, "Les Révoltes fiscales," esp. ch. 4; and Chapters 7–8 in this book.

[23] J. Meuvret, "Comment les français du XVIIe siècle voyaient l'impôt," in *Etudes d'histoire économique*, Paris, 1971, 306.

is clearly seen from a comparison with England. If England experienced far fewer revolts than France of the kind that has been termed *soulèvements populaires*, one of the principal reasons was that the English peasants and lower orders generally were much less victimized by fiscal oppression and were, indeed, either exempt or only lightly subject most of the time to direct taxation by the crown.[24]

It was war above all that aggravated the abuses of fiscality, besides the other burdens it laid on the luckless communities exposed to the horrors of quartering and pillage by the soldiery. During the 1630s and 1640s, when the French and Spanish monarchies were belligerents in the Thirty Years war, the financial strains incident to the conflict caused their ruthless extractiveness to exceed all previous limits. In France, the unprecedented demands of the royal fisc helped to incite the epidemic of localized insurrections already referred to, while also preparing the way for the Fronde. Likewise in some of the possessions of imperial Spain, the heavy taxation the Spanish monarchy extorted, combined with other pressures it inflicted owing to the necessities of the war, was a spur to the revolts against its rule in the 1640s.

Conditions such as periodic harvest failures, subsistence crises, and their attendant hardships, were intermittent, short-term adversities, as were also for the most part the excesses of fiscality. Their presence manifested itself in numerous forms of collective violence, ranging from sporadic food and tax riots, to agrarian and urban revolts whose targets were landlords and the rich or the royal state and its officials, to rebellious movements by inferior strata as incidents within much bigger revolutionary disorders. If we try to estimate the importance of these short-term factors in the conjunctural context of revolution, it is apparent that their effect was greatest upon the unprivileged, the urban plebeians, and the rural laborers and poor peasants, whereas the higher up in the socioeconomic scale we look, the less their impact was likely to be. Thus, if we distinguish generally between elites and masses as the actors in revolution, conjunctural factors of this kind exerted their most direct and strongest influence upon masses, not elites.

It is hardly possible, however, to treat conjunctural circumstances in isolation because they intersected with other conditions as well as with perceptions, expectations, and beliefs. There can accordingly never be a simple, mechanical causality from *conjoncture* to revolution as additional factors invariably intervene between the two. Nevertheless, it seems to have been the case in early modern Europe that the wider the social participation in a revolution, the smaller, as a rule, the importance of short-run conjunctural phenomena in giving rise to it. Hence it can also be said

[24] See C. S. L. Davies, "Les Révoltes populaires en Angleterre (1500–1700)," *Annales E.S.C.* 24, 1 (1969), 53–4.

that in the genesis of the biggest revolutionary civil wars of the sixteenth and seventeenth centuries, all of which without exception were initiated and led by aristocracies and elite groups, conjunctural factors had a comparatively circumscribed role; whereas, conversely, their significance was much larger in rebellions that were dominated by the action of the inferior orders and oppressed, whether in the town or country.

Why this should have been so is not difficult to understand. "For most of the people, most of the time," a scholar has remarked of our period, "political matters scarcely existed."[25] There is considerable truth in this observation, even though certain revolutions provide significant exceptions to it. It serves to make the fact intelligible that the lower orders in the early modern states, who commonly lacked political knowledge or interests, whose lives were spent in a continual struggle for subsistence, and whose participation in the public affairs of kingdoms was slight or nonexistent, should be more readily mobilized by adverse *conjoncture* than by politics.

Of course, there is no inherent reason why peasants or lesser urban folk should not be susceptible also to the influence of political ideas, values, and ideologies; that they *can* be is apparent, for instance, in the role of political goals in the German peasant war, to be considered later. Moreover, even in what are held to be largely spontaneous outbursts of wretchedness and hunger, there are always at least certain rudimentary political beliefs present without which they could not be activated. Yet it remains fairly commonly true, as another writer has pointed out, that "at the base of the awareness of the lower classes of the *ancien régime* is the idea that the level of prices, not the injustice of their condition, rules their destiny."[26] This statement is borne out in the localized disturbances that broke out repeatedly in seventeenth-century France. In these nonelite insurgencies, the explosion of popular violence was usually aimed at those most visibly identifiable as the authors of economic woes or fiscal exploitation: rarely the landlord but mainly the royal tax agents or the sellers or hoarders of grain and consumables. It was *conjoncture* that was most likely to preside over such revolts unless political and ideological programs could gain an entrance and subsume their grievances within a broader vision of reform and change.

II

Of wider import than conjunctural factors of the kind so far mentioned were those reflecting long-term movements with their gradual effects on

---

[25] A. Everitt, *Change in the provinces in the seventeenth century*, Leicester, 1972, 9.

[26] F. Furet, "Pour une définition des classes inférieures à l'époque moderne," *Annales E.S.C.* 18, 3 (1963), 463.

different economic sectors and their possible cumulative impact on the position of entire social groups, occupations, and orders. Two such movements in sequence marked the European economy between the sixteenth and seventeenth centuries, the first till about 1620 a phase of dynamic growth and expansion, the second, which increasingly set in thereafter, a phase of recession and contraction.

The former phase is associated with the aggregate of trends known to historians as the price revolution.[27] Despite an occasional dissent, this term has passed into common use as a comprehensive designation of the prolonged inflation that lasted through the sixteenth century, then slackened, and finally came to an end about the second quarter of the seventeenth. The assessment of its nature and significance, however, depends upon the construction of specific price indexes with all their pitfalls and on the way in which they are interpreted. Thus, an increase of prices that averaged slightly over 2 percent annually in Tuscany and Lombardy in the last half of the sixteenth century, or in the case of England no more than 1.5 percent annually from 1532 to 1580, may hardly seem excessive, judged against the inflationary experience of the twentieth century.[28] From this standpoint a sceptical scholar has rejected the notion of the price revolution altogether as unfounded and serving merely to obscure the finer contours of the economic history of early modern Europe.[29] But beside the overall secular trend that left price levels four and five times higher in 1600 than they had been in 1500, there were also shorter oscillations and violent swings, as well as marked disparities among different categories of prices affecting incomes and living standards. Then, too, the inflation followed an earlier period in the fifteenth century when the price level had remained comparatively stable. It was the combined operation of these multiple factors (evoking from contemporaries a continuing stream of comment and complaint about the unprecedented dearness of all things)

[27] In the following remarks I have made use of a seminar paper on the historiography of the price revolution by my student, Mark N. Friedrich. General discussions containing relevant graphs and data will be found in F. Braudel and F. Spooner, "Prices in Europe from 1450 to 1750," *Cambridge economic history of Europe*, v. 4, Cambridge, 1967; F. Mauro, *Le XVIe siècle européen: Aspects économiques*, Paris, 1966, pt. 2, ch. 3; F. Spooner, "The economy of Europe 1559–1609," *New Cambridge modern history*, v. 3, Cambridge, 1968. On conjunctural developments of the period in the countries of Western Europe, including demography, prices, and wages, the discussion and tables collected in the volume by C. Wilson and G. Parker (eds.), *An introduction to the sources of European economic history 1500–1800*, London, 1977, are extremely helpful.

[28] C. Cipolla, "The so-called 'Price Revolution': Reflections on the Italian situation," in Burke, *Economy and society*, H. Kamen, *The iron century 1560–1660*, London, 1971, 59.

[29] Cipolla, "The so-called 'Price Revolution' "; see also the cautionary comments by J. Gould, "The price revolution reconsidered," in *The price revolution in sixteenth century England*, ed. P. Ramsey, London, 1971.

that justifies the treatment of the sixteenth century as an inflationary era of "exceptional magnitude."[30]

The reasons for this development have been sought equally in both monetary and "real" changes in the European economy and society. The first kind of explanation stresses primarily the massive increase of money supply due to the flood of American silver entering Europe through Spain, coinage debasements, intensified velocity of monetary circulation, and expansion of credit. The second kind cites as chiefly important the well-attested fact of sustained population growth, which it adduces to account not only for a rise in overall demand but also for the decline of money wages, the soaring trend of rents, and the higher movement of prices in the agricultural than in the industrial sector.

Although specialists frequently employ elements of both theories, all the proffered explanations of the price revolution involve gaps and uncertainties in data, methodological hazards, and technical problems of interpretation that perhaps make a definitive solution impossible. It is nonetheless apparent, however, that the sixteenth century was borne forward by a dynamic economy of expanding volume of trade, new and bigger markets, development of various industrial sectors, greater agricultural specialization and improved productivity, and more populous cities owing to demographic increase and rural migration; an economy, too, that was adverse to traditional wage and price patterns, depressing the position of wage earners and creating strains for everyone with inadaptable rents or incomes but offering new opportunities of wealth and prosperity to many others who could profit from the secular trend.

In turn, this long-term *conjoncture* also exercised decidedly stimulating effects on social mobility. Indeed, "not for centuries," it has been suggested, "had European society been as fluid as it became in the sixteenth century."[31]

Yet it is not at all clear how this expansive conjunctural climate might contribute to the context of revolution. The usual opinion is that it could do so by way of social mobility. There are several alternative forms in which such mobility might manifest itself.

One is simply in the gross fact of more families moving up or down within the existing social structure.

Another, and as a possible accompaniment to the first, is by the appearance of marked incongruences in social position, whereby the upwardly mobile are higher on one dimension of stratification, such as wealth, than on other dimensions, such as power or social esteem. These incongruences are sometimes believed to be a consequence of intensified mobility in traditional societies and have been considered by some students a potent

[30] Spooner, "The economy of Europe," 20.   [31] Koenigsberger, *Estates and revolutions*, 5.

source of social tension owing to the supposed tendency of the groups affected "to reequilibrate their status."[32] In addition, it has also been contended that a "fruitful way of linking social and economic change to revolutions is through the theory of status inconsistency, which holds that a society with a relatively large proportion of persons undergoing high mobility is likely to be in an unstable condition."[33]

A third manifestation of mobility is by an alteration in the character of the structure itself, so that some entire strata, groups, occupations, or orders are raised or depressed relative to others.

The most pervasive mobility in sixteenth- and seventeenth-century Europe was of the first kind, a conclusion that seems fairly certain despite the inadequacy of quantitative data to detail its full extent. This was evidenced, as we have previously pointed out, in the expansion of aristocracies and titles in all the early modern states, in the development of a nobility of office in France, in sharper socioeconomic differentiation in city and country, in the large fortunes amassed in finance and international trade by bourgeois elites, and in the wider channels of advancement available to them and others through the service of princes. Conversely, there was probably greater downward mobility than before for families whose incomes and styles of life were threatened or undermined by inflation. The numerous decaying gentlemen sunk by poverty below the position of their ancestors and the takeover of the lands of needy seigneurs by bourgeois buyers and creditors were both familiar features of the time.[34]

The second manifestation of mobility, associated with status incongruence, was also a fact in early modern societies. Perhaps its best-known exemplification was the distinction between *noblesse de robe* and *noblesse d'épée* in France, the former owing its position ultimately to wealth and gaining power in the bureaucratic service of the crown but made nevertheless to feel its inferiority to the nobility boasting ancient origin and military functions. Alongside this distinction, however, a continuous interpenetration between the two branches also went on in the course of the seventeenth century, as family alliances and a mingling of interests eventually eroded

---

[32] G. Germani, "Social and political consequences of mobility," in *Social structure and mobility in development*, ed. N. Smelser and S. Lipset, Chicago, 1966, 371-2. This theory of status incongruency has been formulated by G. Lenski, "Status crystallization: A non-vertical dimension of social status," *American sociological review 19*, 4 (1954).

[33] L. Stone, *The causes of the English revolution 1529-1642*, London, 1972, 54.

[34] The suggestion, however, of the decline of the French nobility between 1560 and 1640 due to economic difficulties and other problems is surely mistaken; see D. Bitton, *The French nobility in crisis 1560-1640*, Stanford, 1969. Rather, what took place in France, as elsewhere, was the replenishment and consolidation of the noble order between older and more recently arrived elements, while its social supremacy persisted. See F. Braudel, *La Méditerranée et le monde méditerranéen à l'époque de Philippe II*, 2nd rev. ed., 2 v., Paris, 1966, v. 2, 49-54, for an emphatic denial that nobilities declined due to the price revolution.

the social frontier between them.[35] Moreover, we should bear in mind that the frictional effects of status incongruences are likely to be checked or mitigated in the society of estates or orders, inasmuch as this society ceaselessly reproduces itself by propagating in its members a mentality and values sanctioning hierarchy, inequality, and acquiescence in the prevailing social scheme.

The third kind of mobility, involving a change in the basic structure of stratification and therefore in the relative positions of the constituent strata, was of least importance in the period. Some modifications did of course take place. Thus, merchants and money men rose in status in England, and they rose even more in the Dutch republic, where the formation of a republican regime during the Netherlands revolution gave preeminence to bourgeois and urban oligarchies, while both the number and importance of the nobility diminished. The status of officials and of the professions, especially of the lawyers, also rose everywhere in Western Europe. Yet, if we look at the sixteenth and seventeenth centuries as a whole, it is impossible to observe any break in social continuity or a major alteration of the social pattern resulting from mobility. Society in general remained a hierarchization with aristocracy as its fundamental principle, landed nobilities in a dominant position and enjoying the highest prestige, and noble rank as the most desired objective of families on the rise.

The foregoing account does less than justice to the manifold aspects and subtler consequences of mobility, a process that can never be reduced to a simple schematism. Given the considerations mentioned, however, we may still wonder whether there was any discernible relationship between the conjunctural environment of secular growth in the early modern era and the latter's revolutions and whether mobility was the middle term between them. Unlike short-range conjunctural factors, whose influence within the context of revolution is frequently easily perceivable, those of the long term evidently present a much more problematic character. To bring the question into closer focus, however, we may look briefly at the main if not the only case in which such a relationship has been strongly emphasized, namely, the English revolution of 1640.

Two opposing views of the problem have been presented, each to be sure also involving noneconomic considerations, but in both of which *conjoncture*, social mobility, and the position of the gentry are among the crucial variables.[36]

The first view holds that the majority of the English gentry, who of

[35] This point is heavily stressed, for example, by G. Roupnel in a study based on Burgundy, *La ville et al campagne au XVIIe siècle: étude sur les populations du pays Dijonnais*, Paris, 1955 (first published 1922), 167–77.

[36] For a selection of the most important writings belonging to this controversy and a survey of the literature, see L. Stone (ed.), *Social change and revolution in England 1540–1640*, London, 1965.

necessity lived wholly or mainly from their landed incomes, suffered economic reverses and decline in the century before 1640 because they did not or could not sufficiently adjust to the inflationary conditions of the age. Downward mobility in turn made them socially embittered and politically resentful toward the court and central authority of the crown and thus led to disaffection and the revolt against Charles I.

This account, sketched out some years ago by H. R. Trevor-Roper,[37] must be dismissed, if only because there is no good reason to believe that long-term conjunctural trends were unfavorable to the gentry as an order or that it underwent decline. On the contrary, the evidence indicates that the opposite was more generally the case.

The second view, which draws explicitly on the theory of status incongruence, maintains that an exceptional mobility in English landed society marked the century up to 1640, of which the principal manifestation was the rise of the gentry in numbers, relative proportion of landed possessions, and political status. Concurrently, the wealth, prestige, and power of the peerage declined relative to the gentry so that the distance between the two ranks narrowed. Owing to these developments, it is argued, the gentry emerged as the political leaders of the nation and were able to mount a revolutionary challenge to the monarchy in Parliament.

This account of the rise of the gentry and its significance, due in its present form to Lawrence Stone (an earlier version was proffered by Professor R. H. Tawney),[38] clearly possesses some substance in that the increasing size, prosperity, and political importance of the gentry has to be recognized as a major feature of early modern English social history. Nevertheless, not only is it most unlikely that the peerage declined, but the specific connections postulated between mobility and the revolution of 1640 have little basis in fact. For instance, it is hard to detect any *social* tensions that can be directly attributed to the rise of the gentry; the strongest, most consequential tensions to make themselves felt in English society were political and religious, and these were not an outgrowth of mobility. Similarly, it is also difficult to find any indication that the rise of the gentry was accompanied by status incongruence; indeed, the more eminent members of the gentry order were high on *all* dimensions of stratification: wealth and power as well as status. Finally, there is no discoverable correlation between the rise of the gentry and the division in which the English revolution began, the same sort of people, as Stone acknowledges, being found on opposite sides, without any distinction of social

[37] See especially H. R. Trevor-Roper, *The gentry 1540–1640*, Cambridge, 1953.

[38] The main argument is stated at length in *The crisis of the aristocracy, 1558–1641*, Oxford, 1965. More summary statements invoking the theory of status incongruence are given by Stone in "Social mobility in England, 1500–1700," *Past and present 33* (1966), 28, 33–6, 50, and *The causes of the English revolution*, 111–12. Tawney's "The rise of the gentry" is extracted in Stone, *Social change and revolution in England*.

status or economic position.[39] Thus, although owing partly to *conjoncture* there may have been an unusual amount of mobility in the eighty or a hundred years preceding 1640, its role in the context of the English revolution, at least as a direct causal factor, was in all probability slight. All that can really be said, I believe, is that, without a gentry of wealth, political influence, and social authority in England and its local communities, and without the predominance of men of this kind in the House of Commons, the revolution could not have taken the form it did as a successful revolt within the governing class against the crown.

III

The long growth phase of the sixteenth century apparently culminated during the 1590s and was then followed after about 1610–20 by a phase of deceleration and recession lasting down into the latter part of the seventeenth century. Like the great inflation, the reasons for this reversal of the secular trend, as well as its extent, are matters of debate, and its timing and incidence can be seen to have varied within the European economy.[40] There is considerable agreement, however, that the long-term conjunctural climate had changed from expansion to contraction; "half a century of slumps, bankruptcies and shocks of war" is one economic historian's summary of these decades.[41]

About the major shifts that occurred there can be little doubt. The demographic upsurge of Western Europe came to a halt, as surplus humanity pressed ever harder upon deficient resources and a too low agricultural productivity, and as recurrent epidemics and subsistence crises took their toll. Spain, which contained about 8.5 million people in 1600, suffered an absolute reduction of 1.5 million in the seventeenth century; by 1650, moreover, the population of Castile itself had fallen by a quarter. Italian population also fell from about 13 million to 11 million in the first half of the century. France, most heavily populated of our early modern kingdoms, with around 19 million in 1600, experienced repeated cycles of high mortality so that its population stood little or no higher at the end of the century than at the beginning. In England and the Dutch republic, population increase either ceased or slowed down markedly in the earlier half of the century.[42]

[39] Stone, *The causes of the English revolution*, 55–6, 143–4.

[40] A concise summary of interpretations of the problem is given by J. P. Cooper, in *New Cambridge modern history*, v. 4, 9–14.

[41] F. Spooner, "The European economy 1609–50," in *New Cambridge modern history*, v. 4, 69. For a more extended view of this period of depression, see J. De Vries, *The economy of Europe in an age of crisis 1600–1750*, Cambridge, 1976.

[42] J. Lynch, *Spain under the Habsburgs*, 2 v., Oxford, 1965–9, v. 2, 126–8; H. Kamen, *The iron century*, 22–3; P. Goubert, *L'Ancien Régime*, v. 1, 35–44; R. Davis, *The rise of the Atlantic economies*, Ithaca, 1973, 90–1; De Vries, *The economy of Europe*, 4–6.

Economic depression also formed an important part of the picture. Slumps in cloth manufacture and exports, lower employment, shrinking markets, and dislocations due to war and to monetary debasements and manipulation were widespread. The most dramatic change was the severe deterioration of the Castilian and Spanish economy, where the heavy demographic loss went hand in hand with a long-term fall of treasure imports, the gradual collapse of the American trade, and industrial decline. France experienced a period of economic reverses from which it only began to recover in the later part of the century. The impact of European depression was smaller in England, which nevertheless suffered a severe industrial and commercial downturn in the 1620s, followed by only a partial revival and then by a renewal of depression coinciding with the mid-century revolution. The Dutch republic, with its newly won independence from Spain, may have been an exception altogether, for the earlier seventeenth century was a time of rapid all-around development that carried it to a prime position of prosperity and power. It has been pointed out, however, that toward 1650 population growth had started to decline, other economic indicators in trade, industry, and agriculture were becoming less favorable, and "the sources of . . . expansion in the Dutch economy showed signs of exhaustion."[43]

The scythe of death and destruction that swept through much of Western and Central Europe in the Thirty Years war made its grisly addition to the adversities of *conjoncture*. Upon the expiration of the eleven-year truce in 1621, Spain renewed its war with the Dutch, assisted Habsburg imperial arms in Germany, and after earlier limited conflicts with France entered into full-scale hostilities with the French monarchy in 1635, which endured for nearly a quarter of a century. Engaged in the Low Countries and Germany, in Italy and the Pyrenees, in the Channel, the Caribbean, and the Pacific, it staggered under a burden that sapped its strength. France also, fighting on external fronts and its own territory invaded, was drained by its ordeal. Only England, although briefly at war with both Spain and France between 1625 and 1630, refrained from active involvement in the continental conflict that inflicted such severe strain upon the French and Spanish monarchies.

Accompanying these changes a new pattern in the structure of Euro-

---

[43] Both De Vries, *The economy of Europe*, and Davis, *The rise of the Atlantic communities*, chs. 6–7, 9, 12–13, contain a conspectus and details on different countries. The key significance of the decline of Spain's American trade and treasure imports for the weakening of the European economy has been lengthily stressed by H. and P. Chaunu, *Seville et l'Atlantique*; a survey and references on the topic are given by Lynch, *Spain under the Habsburgs*, v. 2, 184–93. For the Dutch republic, see J. De Vries, *The Dutch rural economy in the golden age, 1500–1700*, New Haven, 1974, 113–14. A very interesting picture of France's economic and demographic expansion and contraction is given in E. Ladurie's inaugural lecture of 1973 at the Collège de France, "Motionless history," *Social science history 1*, 2 (1977).

pean power also gradually took shape during the first half of the century. Economic disaster and military defeat led to Spain's decline as a great power, apparent by 1660. France, weakened by war and repeated revolts, temporarily regressed. Italy's former economic position was eclipsed as the Atlantic and the Baltic decisively outstripped the Mediterranean in commercial importance. The Dutch republic rose to commercial and industrial supremacy in Western Europe, with England treading at its heels, and both states also emerged as aggressive contenders against the colonial empires of Spain and Portugal.

Some historians have represented the conjunctural turn from expansion to slowdown and malaise as a pervasive crisis of both the European economies and societies. Seen from this perspective, the conditions prevailing after 1620 marked a major break and turning point and, although appearing to be separate and unrelated, were in reality part of a common pathology due to the same causes. This is the alleged "general crisis of the seventeenth century," which has been advanced in recent years as the explanation for disparate developments of the time, including the revolutions of the mid-century.[44]

The crisis has been pictured as at once political, social, and economic, but to consider what light it might shed on the contemporaneous revolutions it is first necessary to ask whether in fact any such crisis occurred. By contrast, for instance, with the Great Depression of the 1930s and its manifold ramifications, the reality of which no one doubts, the crisis of the seventeenth century is affirmed by some scholars but denied by others.[45] There is some difficulty, moreover, in speaking of a *crisis* in reference to a secular trend whose chronology not only remains vague but is held to have lasted forty or fifty years, if not longer.

Perhaps the notion of a general crisis, however, is least open to objection if it is understood essentially in an economic sense as consisting of the particular features in different states and regions associated with the onset of long-term depression, as I have summarized them above. So conceived, it designates a conjunctural environment that economic historians have

[44] References to the literature and theories of the "general crisis of the seventeenth century" may be found in Kamen, *The iron century*, pt. 4; and especially in T. Rabb, *The struggle for stability in early modern Europe*, Oxford, 1975, chs. 1-3. Among the chief contributions are the papers by E. Hobsbawm and H. R. Trevor-Roper which helped to stimulate the entire discussion. Both are reprinted in *Crisis in Europe 1560-1660*, ed. T. Aston, and Trevor-Roper's also in his *Religion, the Reformation, and social change*, 2nd ed., London, 1972.

[45] See *ibid.* for some indications of the literature. Besides Hobsbawm and Trevor-Roper, proponents of the general-crisis thesis include J. Polisensky, "The Thirty Years War and the crisis and revolutions of seventeenth-century Europe," *Past and present 39* (1968). Among the sceptics are A. Lublinskaya, *French absolutism: The crucial phase 1620-1629*, Cambridge, 1968, chs. 1-2, J. H. Elliott, "Revolution and continuity in early modern Europe," *Past and present 42* (1969), and J. Shennan, *Government and society in France, 1461-1661*, London, 1969, 62-70.

recognized as widespread, even if certain exceptions to it may be found, most notably Holland, whose "golden age," according to a Dutch scholar, actually coincided with the period of crisis.[46]

But the thesis of a general crisis becomes altogether improbable when the latter is pictured as an interlocking economic, social, and political crisis, which by reason of its exceptional severity provides the comprehensive origin and explanation of the revolutions in the middle decades of the century.

If these revolutions are to be taken as evidence of a general crisis, we may well wonder why the revolutions that broke out eighty years before, during the 1560s, are not similarly regarded. At that time long revolutionary civil wars began in France and the Netherlands, conflicts that were much larger and more destructive than most of those in the 1640s. In Spain there was the revolt of the Moriscos of Granada, in Scotland a civil war, and rebellions also in England and Ireland. Yet no one has spoken of a general crisis of the sixteenth century in connection with these revolutionary events.[47] A glance at two of the interpretations of the general crisis only confirms our scepticism as to its existence in the all-embracing sense posited by its advocates.

Eric Hobsbawm, one of its first proponents, maintains that the crisis consisted in Europe's failure to overcome the obstacles to the triumph of capitalism. It thus occurred because the preceding economic growth was still set in a feudal matrix from which it was unable to achieve a breakthrough. Persisting forms of older socioeconomic relations prevented sustained economic development, encouraged concentration on unproductive investment and luxury consumption, and militated against expansion of the home market, of industrial production, and of the division of labor. The crisis was accordingly "the last phase of the general transition from a feudal to a capitalist economy." It was resolved in different ways, one of which was the creation of the new colonalism of the later seventeenth and the eighteenth centuries. But its main solution proved to be the English "bourgeois" revolution of 1640, "the most decisive product of the seventeenth-century crisis," which assured the supremacy of capitalism and freed England's economy for indefinite progress.[48]

What is principally apparent in this account is the absence of evidence that could demonstrate the actuality of a general crisis in the terms de-

---

[46] I. Schöffer, "Did Holland's Golden Age coincide with a period of crisis?" *Acta historiae Neerlandica 1* (1967).

[47] See Elliott, "Revolution and continuity."

[48] Hobsbawm, "The crisis of the seventeenth century." The inspiration of Hobsbawm's "stage" interpretation is Marx's treatment of merchant capital in *Capital*, v. 1, where the commercial capitalism of the sixteenth century is analyzed as nonrevolutionary because it lived in the pores of a feudal society that it had no impulsion technologically or otherwise to transform.

scribed. Hobsbawm's Marxian obsession with the problem of economic stages and "the transition from feudalism to capitalism," as if the latter embraced everything significant in European change, has exaggerated a secular phase of depression of varying incidence into a general crisis of a century's duration, a period of time, incidentally, for which the idea of crisis has little meaning. Likewise, the connection seen between the crisis and the English revolution of 1640 is equally groundless and unconvincing; no evidence is supplied to substantiate it, nor is any attempt made to explain how the one gave rise to the other, much less how the English revolution was a "bourgeois" revolution in the sense of securing capitalist supremacy.

Another proponent of the general crisis theme is Trevor-Roper, who has explained it in a different way as a consequence of the tension between the early modern society and state. He pictures the Renaissance monarchies expanding in power through the sixteenth century until their cost and extravagance, their ever-increasing bureaucracies, and their governmental inefficiency became an intolerable burden to the societies they dominated. The post-1620 depression coincided with a widespread reaction against their excesses aimed at royal courts. The animosity was actuated by the resentment of the many who were excluded from the court system and unable to share in its advantages and opportunities. "It was an attitude of hatred: hatred of 'the Court' and its courtiers, hatred of princely follies and bureaucratic corruption, hatred of the Renaissance itself." With these sentiments went a new spiritual climate, a mood of austere moralism and condemnation of luxury and pleasure. These developments were the origin of the revolutionary situation that culminated in the rebellions of the 1640s in the English, French, and Spanish monarchies as the state's pressure upon society reached the breaking point. Trevor-Roper accordingly attributes these rebellions to one and the same crisis and suggests a uniform model for all of them based upon the conflict between "outs" and "ins," subjects and courtiers, Court and Country.[49]

Although this version of the crisis of the seventeenth century abounds in striking and perceptive observations, it is just as untenable in fundamentals as the preceding one. We are asked to believe in a general crisis, but in support we are merely offered the circular argument that the revolutions of the 1640s prove the existence of an antecedent crisis. The latter, however, needs to be demonstrated independently of its supposed consequences before we can even begin to consider whether there was a connection between the two. It might be easier to accept the general crisis if the revolutions of the time all really did conform to a common model. But, as a number of critics have pointed out, they failed to do so, and it

[49] Trevor-Roper, "The general crisis of the seventeenth century," in *Religion, the Reformation, and social change.*

will be shown later that they belong instead to several different types.[50] There is indeed no way in which the revolutions of Scotland, England, and Ireland, of Catalonia, Portugal, Naples, and Palermo, and of the Fronde in France, can all be accommodated to the same explanatory structure or referred to identical origins. As I have made clear elsewhere, not even the English revolution, from which Trevor-Roper extrapolated to formulate the overarching hypothesis of a Court–Country antinomy, fits the model in the way required to make it applicable.[51]

In reality, the mid-century revolutions sprang from diverse origins and reveal only partial interconnection at best. The two most widespread conditions found in conjunction with them have already been emphasized. The Thirty Years war contributed by its fiscal and military oppression to revolts in France and some of the Spanish kingdoms. The English monarchy, though, did not take part in the war, so the revolts against Stuart rule were largely independent of its effects. The advent of lengthy economic depression, attended by subsistence crises, epidemics, and other hardships, aggravated the misery and discontent of subjects and was a factor in some rebellions. Both conditions determined the woeful conjunctural climate, whose role in instigating revolution nevertheless varied from the large in certain cases to the inconsiderable in others.

Correspondingly, we cannot find one general crisis leading to the rebellions of the 1640s but must see instead a number of separate crises that comprised the revolutionary history of the time. Because all these rebellions bore the imprint of the particular vulnerabilities of the monarchies and states to whose history they belonged, no single mode of representing or explaining them will suffice. Only by first recognizing this fact can we profitably explore the parallels and differences in character and causal background that may be discovered among them.

[50] See the contribution of Mousnier and Elliott to the "general crisis" symposium, in Aston, *Crisis in Europe.*
[51] See Zagorin, *The court and the country,* ch. 4.

6

Religion, the Reformation, millenarianism

I

Orléans, December 1560: the meeting (the first in seventy-five years) of the Estates General of France, summoned by the young king, Francis II, to advise a way to allay the strife between Catholic and Protestant that threatened his kingdom with civil war. The chancellor of France, Michel de L'Hôpital, addressed the assembly's opening:

> The division of language is not what makes for the separation of realms. Rather it is the difference of religion . . . that divides one realm into two. Hence the old proverb, one faith, one law, one king, and it is difficult that men of . . . diverse and contrary opinions should refrain from resorting to arms.

There was more love, he lamented, between an Englishman and Frenchman of the same faith than between two Frenchmen of different faiths. In vain L'Hôpital pleaded for moderation, for France was shortly to be plunged into a destructive revolutionary conflict.[1]

Eighty years later, in 1641, the English philosopher, Thomas Hobbes, saw his own country engulfed in similar troubles. The dispute over religion and between the spiritual and civil power, he then wrote, "has of late, more than any other thing in the world, been the cause of civil wars in all parts of Christendome."[2]

Later still, another British philosopher, David Hume, safe in the haven of the eighteenth century from the unimagined upheaval of the French revolution yet to come, looked back in his *History of England* upon the revolution that Hobbes had witnessed. He reflected on the explosive effects when the religious spirit mingles with faction. Their combination,

---

[1] H. Amphoux, *Michel de l'Hôpital et la liberté de conscience au XVIᵉ siècle*, Paris, 1900, 167; J. Mariéjol, *La Réforme et la Ligue*, in *Histoire de France depuis les origines jusqu'à la Révolution*, ed. E. Lavisse, Paris, 1903–11, v. 6, pt. 1, 34–5.

[2] Letter from Hobbes to the earl of Devonshire, August 1641, cited in G. C. Robertson, *Hobbes*, Philadelphia, 1886, 55.

he observed, contains "something supernatural and unaccountable" that baffles ordinary prudence and causes the usual motives of human society to fail. It was this spirit, which Hume and his contemporaries termed enthusiasm, that he believed had united in the Puritans with an attachment to civil liberty. To it he ascribed the contempt for authority and the gloomy and sullen disposition of independence that opposed the Stuarts.[3]

The English Puritans, the Huguenots of France – and to them we must at least join the Huguenots or Calvinists of the Netherlands and the Covenanters of Scotland – all, without exception, were the offspring of the Protestant Reformation. The Reformation, a European movement of manifold aspects that took well over a century to run its course, was not in itself a revolution. In some places where Protestantism became established, it was done by the command and authority of the state, and we have previously given reasons why regime-instituted change of this kind does not belong to the domain of revolution. But revolutions were certainly part of the Reformation's history and were associated with its progress, whether in the attempts of rebels to introduce or impose it, to carry it further than the state permitted, or to resist it. Of the four biggest revolts of early modern Europe, only the Fronde was free of its influence, whereas the French civil war, the Netherlands rebellion or war of liberation from Spain, and the English revolution are unintelligible unless we take into account the seeds of resistance nurtured in an auspicious Protestant soil. The Scottish rebellion of 1638 symbolized by the National Covenant, which began the sequence of revolutions in the Stuart kingdoms, also bore the mark of rebellious Protestantism in its origin. Not that the Reformation and Protestantism should be considered the exclusive cause of these revolutions, for they cooperated with various other forces distinct from themselves. But by their magnitude and character they introduced a novel element into the revolutionary process of early modern Europe, novel, if not in its essence, at least in its scope and power; and the fatal divisions issuing from them, the spiritual energies they released, and the original forms of religious community they created, together combined to establish a further fundamental context for various revolutions in the sixteenth and seventeenth centuries.

II

We find a foreshadowing of the contribution of religion to these early modern revolutions in its role in certain preceding medieval conflicts. One such case was the English agrarian revolt of 1381, which involved towns-

[3] Hume (1711–76) began to publish his *History of England* in 1754. For the passages cited and comments, see L. Bongie, *David Hume, prophet of the counter-revolution*, Oxford, 1965, xii–xiii.

men as well as peasant villagers and was among the biggest movements of its kind in the Middle Ages. Although it is impossible to be sure how much the teachings of the great heresiarch, John Wyclif, helped to incite it, the yeast of a socially subversive religious radicalism was clearly active in its gestation. Thus there was the popular preaching of poor priests like John Ball and John Wrawe, who expounded a simple Biblical egalitarianism in the name of which they condemned both serfdom and the wealth and power of the institutional church. This message was linked with the peasants' grievances. When the rebel leader, Wat Tyler, parleyed with Richard II at Smithfield, he demanded the end of serfdom and "that all men should be free and of one condition," and he also called for the disendowment of the church, whose goods should be divided among the people, and for the retention of only one bishop in England. There may have been, too, a hidden religious inspiration behind the mysterious underground organization, the "great society," of which we hear in connection with the revolt but whose existence is uncertain. One of the watchwords of this rumored *magna societas*, "Now is the time," is pregnant with religious as well as political meaning, hinting as it does at some impending momentous change or *kairos*.[4]

Another medieval revolution in which religion played a dynamic part was the Hussite struggle in Bohemia in the early fifteenth century. This was "*the* revolution of the late Middle Ages," as one of its historians says, and it belongs to the same type of revolutionary movement as do the greatest civil wars of the sixteenth and seventeenth centuries.[5] With the English heretic, Wyclif, among its theological parents and the great Czech preacher and spiritual leader, John Hus, as its inspirer, Hussitism originated as a demand for reform within the church. Soon it came into violent collision with ecclesiastical and political authority, "the reform passing into reformation, the revolt into revolution." Here, prefiguring the later achievements of Luther, Zwingli, Calvin, and other reformers, was the turning point from heresy to Reformation.[6] By revolutionary means, the Hussites discarded the Catholic church and papal rule, waged fierce war

---

[4] See M. Mollat and P. Wolff, *Ongles bleus, Jacques et Ciompi: Les Révolutions populaires en Europe aux XIV*ᵉ *et XV*ᵉ *siècles*, Paris, 1970, 206–9; R. Dobson (ed.), *The peasants' revolt of 1381*, London, 1970, 373, 233, 379–83. Six letters, alleged to have been written by John Ball and others to arouse the commons, were recorded by monastic chroniclers of the revolt. The phrase, "now is the time," which occurs in them may attest to the existence of a revolutionary organization. R. Hilton and H. Fagan accept the letters as authentic and as revealing in Ball the mind of a "mature political thinker" (*The English rising of 1381*, London, 1950, 100–3). For further comments on the possible character of this "great society," see also Hilton's later publication, *Bond men made free*, New York, 1973, 214–15.

[5] H. Kaminsky, *A History of the Hussite revolution*, Berkeley, 1967, 1; see also F. Heymann, *John Zizka and the Hussite revolution*, Princeton, 1955.

[6] Kaminsky, 3; G. Leff, *Heresy in the later Middle Ages*, 2 v., New York, 1967, v. 2, 607.

against the Bohemian king and Holy Roman Emperor, and for a time established the first independent church in Europe, as Protestantism was to do in the next century.

The religiopolitical doctrines of Hussitism, or what perhaps is better called its political theology, brought powerful impetus to the movement. Wyclif's theory of dominion, according to which a right title to lordship derives only from God's grace, so that sin or loss of grace makes a ruler into a tyrant, became a doctrine of armed resistance in Bohemia. It has been justifiably described as an "ideology for revolution" in the Hussite context.[7] The ecclesiology of the radical Prague reformers reinforced this ideology. It conceived the church in exclusive terms as the community of the faithful obedient to Christ's law, of which utraquism – that is, communion in two kinds, and in essence the offering of the chalice to the laity – was the precise criterion, or, even more restrictively, as the small number of the elect warring against antichrist. These beliefs carried apocalyptic and eschatological overtones that suggest the idea of committed participation in the providential drama of history, a conviction that has frequently sustained later revolutionaries.[8]

Among other basic features of the Hussite revolution was the role taken by the Bohemian nobility as patrons and protectors of reformation, a pattern that was later to repeat itself with the Huguenot and Puritan aristocracies. The support of these secular governors of society was vital to the survival of Hussitism, and Professor Kaminsky speaks of their coalition with the religious leaders of the movement in the "programmatic defense of the reform." In September 1415, when the Hussite barons met in Prague to protest John Hus's execution at the council of Constance, they swore to defend Christ's law and its preachers "to the . . . shedding [of] our blood."[9]

Moreover, the Hussite revolution possessed an inner momentum that drove it to the most extreme lengths, giving rise along the way to bitter conflicts between its more conservative and its radical adherents and culminating in the attempt to found a utopian religious society. It passed through a series of divisions leading from Hus to utraquism, to the foundation of the holy city of Tabor practicing distributive communism under its priest governors, to a violent millenarianism, and to the split within Tabor itself between the unbridledly antinomian Pikarts and Adamites, offspring of the heretical Brethren of the Free Spirit, and their opponents. Religion was the energizing force of these developments, which embodied a passionate Czech nationalism and also included acute socioeconomic op-

---

[7] Kaminsky, *A history of the Hussite revolution*, 85–8; and see the same writer's "Wyclifism as the ideology of revolution," *Church history 32*, 1 (1963).
[8] Kaminsky, *A history of the Hussite revolution*, chs. 2–3.   [9] *Ibid.*, 142, 143.

positions reflected in theological controversies over the nature of the sacrament and the relation of the Christian to the world.[10]

III

In spite of its heroic struggle, Hussitism, restricted primarily to a single region, belongs to the prehistory of the Reformation. A century after John Hus's execution, however, the public appearance of Martin Luther in Germany and his success in achieving religious change inaugurated the Protestant era in European civilization. Luther's generation of reformers and the one following it spread Protestant ideas far and wide, shattering forever the spiritual unity of Western Christendom incarnated in the Catholic church. Cutting across the hierarchic structure of early modern society, Protestantism reached all strata in some measure. It won converts in every rank, generated churches and sects, and found adherents even in the Catholic lands from which it was eventually to be eradicated.

To say that Protestantism was primarily a religious phenomenon, whatever its other intricate aspects and effects, would be no more than the truth. Its core belief, justification by faith alone, coupled with its appeal to the Bible as the ultimate arbiter and living word, came as a message of spiritual renewal to many of the sixteenth-century people who heard it – a message bringing release from the pious formalism and external observances of which average late medieval religion too often consisted. Those who first encountered the reformers' preaching and teaching, or who were later called upon to defend the Reformation against its enemies in an age of cruel confessional strife, confronted Protestantism as a personal decision and not merely as a stereotyped inheritance or social convention. To be sure, there were different motives and degrees of commitment on the part of people who accepted Protestantism. We hear, for instance, of Huguenots of state as well as of religion and similarly of the distinction between political and religious Puritans.[11] Nevertheless, the heart of the matter was that Protestant devotees experienced their faith as a deliverance of conscience and conduct from an oppressive clerical institution and from false and burdensome beliefs and ceremonies.

As a religious movement, though, Protestantism was bound to have immeasurable political repercussions. Church and religion were closely interwoven at many points with the regimes of the time; ecclesiastics were

---

[10] *Ibid.*, chs. 6–10; and the same writer's "Chiliasm and the Hussite revolution," *Church history 26*, 1 (1947). I have relied heavily on Kaminsky's work for its perceptive treatment of Hussite ideas and its rich textual citations.

[11] For contemporary illustrations of these distinctions, see P. de la Place, *Commentaires de l'éstat de la réligion et république*, 1565, in *Choix de chroniques et mémoires . . .* , ed. J. Buchon, Paris, 1836, 41; H. Parker, *A discourse concerning Puritans*, London, 1641, 13. I owe the first reference to my colleague, Professor Donald Kelley.

powerholders and superiors over land and men; the church possessed vast influence and wealth; religious teaching sanctioned secular authority; it shaped mentalities and sociocultural values. More than merely inward, any change in religion could not fail to be full of political consequence for a world in which its significance was so pervasive.

Moreover, the Reformation opened with inflammatory slogans on its banner. Luther's famous proclamation of "the liberty of the Christian man" and "the priesthood of all believers," his rejection of papal authority, his denunciation of clerical immunities, and his appeal to Scripture and conscience against the powers of the world seemed to announce an assault upon earthly as well as spiritual tyranny. True, the volcanic reformer never meant his theological gospel to become a declaration of secular liberation. Nevertheless, some of his followers immediately took it in this light. Although he promptly turned in fury to disavow this misinterpretation of reformation, calling down fire and sword on the seditious contemners of God-ordained temporal superiors, the seed had fallen on fertile ground.[12] It is accordingly not surprising that the rebellious German peasants should have invoked Biblical arguments infused with the new religious ideas in 1525 to justify their grievances.[13]

The spread of the Reformation added confessional enmity to the many other reasons for conflicts between states, at the same time rooting religious disunion among their subjects. Whether governments voluntarily accepted a change of religion, as some of the monarchs, princes, and urban regimes of Northern Europe did, or remained faithful to Catholicism, nothing in their political tradition or experience prepared them to deal with creedal diversity among Christians other than by compulsion. Catholic authorities regarded the appearance of such diversity as a menace to obedience, peace, and social subordination. The pest of heresy endangered the state no less than the church. The ruthless persecution that all forms of Protestantism underwent in the sixteenth century in the domains of the French and Spanish crowns, or in England at the hands of Henry VIII and his Catholic daughter Queen Mary Tudor, reflected the determination of rulers to extirpate a soul-destroying infection that sowed subversion through religious disaffection. And this attitude was not merely the result of bigotry. For it was obvious that if subjects were divided from their rulers in so fundamental a matter as religion they might well be led into political opposition or revolt.

Protestant authorities themselves were no less hostile to dissent, which

---

[12] Luther's writings of 1520, *To the Christian nobility of the German nation, On the Babylonian captivity of the church*, and *Concerning Christian liberty*, were manifestos of defiance and emancipation from subjection to pope and church. For these and Luther's subsequent development, see the concise account by G. Rupp in *The new Cambridge modern history*, v. 2, Cambridge, 1958, ch. 3.

[13] See Chapter 7 in this book for further discussion.

they too endeavored to repress. The chief denominations to emerge in the Reformation – the Lutheran or Evangelical, the Calvinist or Reformed, and the Anglican churches – alike claimed an exclusive religious dominion where they held sway. Despite the differences in the way they conceived the church and its relation to secular authority, each rejected toleration and pluralism. Under different modalities they all retained the medieval principle that a Christian society must consist of one church order, creed, and worship coextensive with the secular order. Accordingly, they regarded civil subjection and subordination to the ecclesiastical institution supported by the state as inseparable from one another. That the religion of the subject should differ from the magistrate's once the Reformation had been installed in place of Catholicism seemed to the great Protestant churches an affront to God as well as fraught with evil political consequence. Although practical obstacles sometimes made such uniformity impossible to achieve, the thrust of Protestant governments was generally in that direction.[14]

Luther (d. 1546) and Calvin (d. 1564) were born a generation apart, and in time the latter's effect upon the Reformation far exceeded Luther's. For, although Luther's chief greatness was as theologian and preacher, Calvin was not only both of these but also in the highest degree a legislator and organizer. Lutheranism lacked the determined impulse toward expansion that so vitally infused Calvinism. With its basic locale in Germany and Scandinavia, it reached its widest limit by the mid-sixteenth century. From Geneva, however, where he arrived in 1536 and eventually established an unrivaled personal supremacy, Calvin conducted a universal religious mission, training clergy for service abroad, fostering proselytism, and founding churches. The leadership and teaching radiating from Geneva absorbed and canalized many earlier strivings for reformation. By the 1560s Calvinism and its ecclesiastical system had entrenched themselves far and wide. They had become the backbone of Protestantism in France and the Netherlands, the strongest influence upon the growing Puritan movement within English Protestantism, and an active power in Scotland, not to mention their impact elsewhere in Europe.

A corresponding contrast existed between Lutheranism and Calvinism in their conception of the church's relation to the state and secular power. Having repudiated the spiritual and worldly authority of pope and priests, Luther eventually renounced any independence for the church and con-

---

[14] Still to my mind the most profound and illuminating discussion of the sociology of early Protestantism and of the character of the new denominations shaped by the reformers as belonging to the "church-type" of religious association is the great work of E. Troeltsch, *The social teachings of the Christian churches*, 2 v., London, 1931, v. 2 (trans. from the German original of 1912). This part of Troeltsch's study refers to what subsequent modern scholars have called the "magisterial Reformation," based on state compulsion and the cooperation of governing classes, in contradistinction to the "radical Reformation" of the sects.

sented to its subjection to the prince or magistrate. The idea of the church as an autonomous, juridically fortified, self-governing institution was alien to him. Not that Luther idealized the secular power; on the contrary, he took a strongly pessimistic view of it as the coercive force needed to prevent sinful men from robbing and destroying one another. For the true Christian and his religious life, though, justifying faith was an inward possession indifferent to power. Thus Luther's ultimate attitude toward the political domain was one of resignation, and in the Lutheran states, with the disappearance of the papacy, the government of the church fell to secular rulers.

Calvin, however, conceived the church quite contrariwise as an independent, self-subsistent society vis-à-vis the secular authority. Its relation to the magistrate in a rightly reformed state was to be one of cooperation and mutual aid but in no way based on subservience or the surrender of its autonomy. The duty of the magistrate in religion was to remove superstition and idolatry, encourage the preaching of the word of God, and promote Christ's kingdom by executing the church's judgment on sinful men. The church in turn was to hold the magistrate in honor as one to whom obedience was due. But Calvin endowed the church with initiative, juridical authority, and a self-directing life that prevented it from becoming a tool for the expediencies of rulers.[15]

The Reformation, as the emergence of distinct denominations indicates, was not one but many reformations, which brought multiple schisms in their train. Protestantism harbored numerous tensions and contrary possibilities within itself – toward rebellion and toward submission, toward domination and toward renunciation, toward individualism and toward community, toward the restitution of a primitive Christian ideal of fellowship and toward acceptance of the sinful order of history. From its outset, the movement away from Rome displayed a bewildering variety of forms. Quite as significant as the establishment of Protestant churches, which all in their different ways relied on the state, was the splintering within Protestantism manifest in the appearance of sects. Although a few of the latter may have had some continuities with earlier medieval heresies, they were mostly new creations. These groups – anabaptists, spiritualists, antitrinitarians, and other heterodox bodies – represented the "radical reformation" as opposed to the "magisterial reformation" of the great Protestant denominations. Despite their diversity, they tended to conform to a distinctive pattern of religious association. They were founded on the voluntaristic principle of personal fellowship as small, select communities of

---

[15] See the penetrating treatment by Troeltsch, *The social teachings*, v. 2, and the further discussions by J. W. Allen, *A History of political thought in the sixteenth century*, 3rd ed., London, 1951, pt. 1, chs. 2, 4; G. de Lagarde, *Recherches sur l'esprit politique de la réforme*, Paris, 1926, ch. 5, pts. 2–3; W. Mueller, *Church and state in Luther and Calvin*, New York, 1965.

believers who rejected compulsion and refused any part in an official, state-supported church. The keynote of their religious life was abnegation, holiness, and the suffering of the cross as the true Christian's lot. Standing as many of the sects did for an ethically uncompromising Christianity that took Jesus' teachings in the New Testament as its literal guide, they were persecuted by Catholic and Protestant orthodoxy alike as heretics and enemies of society. Indeed, the sects were opposed to the profane world, whether they tried to detach themselves from it, as they commonly did, or whether, as occasionally happened, they attempted to subject it by violence to the rule of the godly in anticipation of a millennial kingdom.[16]

What historians have long familiarly called the "wars of religion" in early modern Europe is merely another way of describing the revolutions and civil wars that issued from the Reformation. It was the impact of the Reformation upon his century that instructed Francis Bacon to include "innovation in religion" as one of the principal causes of sedition in states.[17] Both in introducing or resisting innovation subjects might turn rebels. Even if they should have conscientious scruples against rebellion, religious persecution could wear them away. Polarization of religious belief among subjects or between rulers and subjects created grave new sources of instability in imperfectly united and integrated kingdoms. When religious divisions supervened on other tensions and oppositions, the political order might not withstand the strain. Enrico Davila, the acute, near contemporary historian of the sixteenth-century French war of religion summed up the calamitous result of this condition upon France. "So by degrees," he commented, in tracing the origin of the civil war,

the discords of great men were confounded with the dissentions of Religion; and the Factions were no more called the discontented Princes and the Guisarts; but more truly and by more significant names, one the Catholic, the other the Hugonot party. Factions, which under the colour of piety, administered pernicious matter to all the following mischiefs and distractions.[18]

This was France in 1560, falling into a revolutionary civil war. But there were numerous other cases during the sixteenth and seventeenth centuries when religion helped give the cue to revolution. The English and Spanish

[16] Early Protestant sectarianism encompassed a considerable range of belief and practice, running from the asceticism and literalism of the anabaptists to the rationalistic tendencies of the Socinians; see G. H. Williams, *The radical reformation*, Philadelphia, 1962, for the history and description of these various groups. Troeltsch, *The social teachings*, remains fundamental for the understanding of the "sect-type" in early Protestantism.

[17] "Of seditions and troubles," *Essays* (1625); another of Bacon's essays, "Of unity in religion," gives a forcible description of the rebellions resulting from the effort to maintain religious unity by the sword.

[18] E. Davila, *The historie of the civil warres of France*, 2 v., London, 1647, v. 1, 93–4. This English translation of Davila's work is dedicated to King Charles I. Davila (1576–1631) published the original Italian edition in 1630.

monarchies were no more immune to the virus of religious differences and were to feel its baneful effects equally in inciting the resistance of subjects.

IV

Religion could be an important component in the motives and ideologies of revolution, and it gave legitimacy and moral strength to rebels. This was as true of Catholicism, where it took a revolutionary road, as of Protestantism. The Pilgrimage of Grace of 1536, the most formidable revolt the Tudor monarchy ever faced, mobilized to resist Henry VIII's break with Rome and other religious changes under banners bearing the device of the Five Wounds of Christ. The Pilgrims' oath included a vow to preserve Christ's church, and their song ran:

> Christ crucified,
> For thy wounds wide,
> Us commons guide,
> That pilgrims be.[19]

In a movement containing many separate grievances and cross-currents, the defense of the Catholic church was the broadest rallying cry. The same concern was evident in the Western rebellion of 1549 against Edward VI's Protestantizing rule.[20] It also animated the Catholic conspirators and exiles of Queen Elizabeth's reign, who realized that only a revolution backed by foreign intervention could restore the Catholic church in England.[21] We find it equally as an aspect of the French civil war in the resistance by the Catholic League activists to the succession of the Protestant Henry of Navarre to the throne of France.[22]

Terms like commitment, conviction, devotion, dedication, and, at the extreme, fanaticism, are unavoidable when we consider the religious context of certain early modern revolutions. The instances cited above pertain to Catholicism, but it is more important to look at the Protestant side, especially as exemplified in the Huguenots and Puritans, where Calvinist influence was strongest, for it was they whose impact on revolution was to be the most profound.

These faithful brought an intense commitment to the service of reformation, of which we can gain an impression in various ways. One angle, for example, is afforded by the martyrological works produced in and for

[19] M. and R. Dodds, *The Pilgrimage of Grace*, 2 v., Cambridge, 1915, v. 1, 129, 175–6, 213; see Ch. 9 in this book for further discussion.

[20] See Ch. 9 in this book.

[21] See G. Mattingly, "William Allen and Catholic propaganda in England," in *Aspects de propagande réligieuse*, Geneva, 1957, 336.

[22] See E. Armstrong, *The French wars of religion*, 2nd ed., New York, 1971, Ch. 2; and Ch. 10 in this book.

the reformed churches. In them was set down the bloody history of self-sacrifice and suffering in the cause of the gospel. Devout authors collected and preserved the record of the victims of Catholic persecution as a testimonial to faith. The martyrologist of French Calvinism, Jean Crespin, a Genevan scholar and printer, published such a chronicle, the first of several successively larger versions, in 1554. It contained accounts of the famous and obscure, from Wyclif and Hus, the heralds of reformation, to the latest martyrs who perished for religion in France. Reporting the ghastly scenes of execution along with touching human details, extracts of letters and conversations, and professions of belief, these narratives communicated the dedicated spirit of the men and women who accepted death for the sake of faith.

Crespin's writings also served the French-speaking adherents of the reform in the Netherlands ruled by the Spanish monarchy, whose churches had close ties with the Calvinist religious organization in France. In the Dutch language, the principal martyrological work composed on the model of Crespin's for the reformed congregations of the Low Countries was the work of Adrian van Haemstede, a Calvinist minister of Antwerp, and first published in 1559.[23]

These histories were frequently revised, reprinted, and translated in the later sixteenth century and beyond.[24] It is noteworthy that their appearance stemmed from the 1550s and 1560s, the decisive years when Calvinism, despite unremitting persecution, was emerging as the dominant form of Protestantism in France and the Netherlands, and when the churches in both countries were becoming increasingly politicized as well.

In England, the great Protestant martyrologist was John Foxe, whose *Book of martyrs* was no less a product of this same period. Foxe was one of the religious exiles who left England to escape the Catholic restoration of Queen Mary Tudor between 1553 and 1558. Some of these exiles on their return home became an active leaven of Puritanism in the English church as a result of their continental experiences and exposure to Calvinist influence. Foxe began his *Acts and monuments* while a refugee in Strasbourg, and it was published in 1563, after the reestablishment of a Protestant

---

[23] I have consulted Crespin's *Acta martyrum*, Geneva, 1556, and the much larger version, *Histoire des martyres*, 1619, ed. J. Benoit, 3 v., Toulouse, 1885–9, the introduction to which contains some details on his life and work. He hailed from Arras in the Netherlands, and, although much of his narrative is devoted to France, he also included martyrs of the Netherlands as well as of England, Italy, and Spain. The comparable work by van Haemstede is *De gheschiedenisse ende den doodt der vromer martelaren*, Antwerp, 1559. For these martyrological writings, including editions and translations, see *Bibliotheca Belgica: Bibliographie génerale des Pays-Bas . . .* , 1st ser., v. 19, *Martyrologes, Liste sommaire*, and *passim*. See also D. Kelley, "Martyrs, myths, and the massacre: The background of St. Bartholomew," *American historical review 77*, 5 (1972), for a discussion of the martyr tradition and Crespin's contribution to it in French Protestantism.

[24] See *ibid.*, for references to these writings.

state church by Queen Mary's successor, Queen Elizabeth. A much expanded version followed in 1570. Foxe's graphic account of the Protestant martyrs executed during the Marian persecution affixed itself permanently in the memory and imagination of English Protestantism. His history was not only crucial in shaping the anti-Catholic mentality within English Protestantism generally but in a more particular sense was one of the informing elements of the militant Puritanism that rose against Charles I.[25]

We cite these examples because it is important to see how a tradition of religious dedication was created and fostered in the continental reformed churches and among the English Puritans, which would be available in due course for the exigencies of political combat. Another illustration is provided by Calvin's attitude toward what is known as Nicodemism. This curious term, apparently invented by the reformer himself, was taken from Nicodemus, the Pharisee mentioned in the gospel of John as a man who believed in Jesus' mission but from fear would only visit him secretly at night.[26] Calvin accordingly used it as a synonym for the conciliators and backsliders who disguised their real convictions behind an outward conformity to Catholic rites. This practice he ascribed especially to people in court and university circles. Although he realized the trials of believers threatened by persecution (his letters to the French churches "under the cross" show his concern and sympathy), he could not condone any concession to idolatry.[27] In several tracts written in the 1540s, he strongly condemned Nicodemism, referring bitingly to people who merely talked Christianity and hoped for reformation instead of bearing witness to their faith. Calvin demanded from converts and church members a firm and unequivocal loyalty.[28]

Yet a further angle on commitment is offered by the dissemination of illegal Protestant literature in Marian England, France, and the Netherlands as the churches lay under persecution. Foxe the martyrologist declared: "God hath opened the Presse to preach, whose voice the Pope is never able to stop with all the puissance of his triple crowne."[29] Neither

---

[25] J. Foxe, *Acts and monuments*, 1563; see C. Garrett, *The Marian exiles*, Cambridge, 1938, 155–6, and W. Haller, *Foxe's Book of martyrs and the elect nation*, London, 1963, for the character and influence of Foxe's work.

[26] John 3:1–2.

[27] For Calvin's letters of guidance and consolation to the French churches suffering persecution, see numerous examples printed in *Letters of John Calvin*, ed. J. Bonnet, 4 v., Philadelphia, 1855–8, *passim*.

[28] On Nicodemism, see D. Cantimori, "Italy and the papacy," *New Cambridge modern history*, v. 2, 267–8, " 'Nicodemismo' e speranze conciliari nel Cinquecento Italiano," in *Studi di storia*, Turin, 1959, and C. Ginzburg, *Il Nicodemismo. Simulazione e dissimulazione religiosa nell' Europa del '500*, Turin, 1970, which contains important new material.

[29] Cited in D. Loades, "The press under the early Tudors," *Transactions of the Cambridge bibliographical society 4*, pt. 1 (1964), 29.

danger nor censorship could prevent the circulation of forbidden writings by reformers in Catholic kingdoms. A regular underground trade in religious propaganda was carried on, fed by secret presses and transmission belts. In the Netherlands and elsewhere, heretical publishers used forged and false imprints on their books to escape detection.[30] From centers on the continent, the English exiles of Mary Tudor's reign infiltrated seditious and anti-Catholic publications into England to sustain the faith. In 1555 in Strasbourg the vitriolic *Warnyng for Englande* appeared, an attack on Mary's marriage to Philip of Spain. Wherever they go, the Venetian ambassador reported of the exiles, "they licentiously disseminate many things against the English government and the present religion."[31] In France the proscribed reformed churches also conducted an active propaganda. Among its agents was Laurent de Normandie, a former French royal official who migrated to Geneva in 1548 after his conversion. There he became a leading printer and publisher, maintaining for over twenty years an extensive traffic in heretical works by Calvin and other Protestant writers, which were smuggled into France. Normandie has been called "one of the great secret forces of French Protestantism in this epoch." Twenty-one people on the list of those whom he supplied with books are known to have been slain for heresy in France.[32] The tenacity shown by the militant Calvinism of the mid-sixteenth century in the work of religious propaganda was to be equally characteristic of Puritanism, whose supporters during the reign of Queen Elizabeth and the early Stuarts made continual use of the press to propagate their demand for further reformation in the Church of England.

As a last illustration of commitment in the cause of religion we should notice the willingness of these adherents of the reform to leave their homes and become exiles and refugees. Religion, it is true, was not necessarily the sole cause of their departure, for economic reasons were often also important, but it was the chief and most general one. The largest exodus took place in the Netherlands. Persecution by the Spanish authorities drove whole communities to England and Germany for refuge, where they established churches on the Calvinist model. In Brussels, the seat of Spanish government, it was reckoned that the emigration from the Low Countries to England had amounted to as many as thirty thousand people by 1566.[33]

---

[30] See M. Kronenberg, "Forged addresses in Low Country books in the period of the Reformation," *The Library*, 5th ser., 2, 2–3 (1947).

[31] Loades; see also J. Loach, "Pamphlets and politics, 1553–8," *Bulletin of the Institute of Historical Research 48*, 117 (1975).

[32] H.-L. Schlaepfer, "Laurent de Normandie," in *Aspects de la propagande religieuse*, 177, 181–2.

[33] See F. Rachfahl, *Wilhelm von Oranien und der Niederländische Aufstand*, 3 v., Halle, 1906–24, v. 2, pt. 2, 538. According to H. Schilling, the most common total accepted in recent research for the sixteenth-century emigration from the Netherlands is fifty thousand (*Niederländische Exulanten im 16. Jahrhundert*, Gütersloh, 1972, 13n).

Other refugees in the Netherlands later fled from the south to Holland and the northern provinces as they came under Calvinist control during the rebellion against Spain. Many French exiles from persecution went to Geneva, some to London and various German cities. During the Marian restoration of Catholicism in England, an elite of Protestant exiles already referred to left their country for Frankfurt, Geneva, and other reformed centers. Invariably, emigration was accompanied by the formation of refugee churches. The same phenomenon repeated itself later among the English Puritans of the earlier seventeenth century, when under the goad of Charles I's religious repression and their dissatisfaction with the condition of England, about twenty thousand people migrated under Puritan auspices to Massachusetts in the decade prior to the revolution of 1640.[34]

Needless to say, a high state of commitment is a characteristic of all vital religions and was by no means the peculiar property of Calvinists and Puritans. What must be stressed, however, is the fervent spirit actuating the two in their struggle for reformation. This spirit was an indispensable preparation should believers take the path of warfare against kings. Faith creates deep loyalties and, when politicized, becomes a powerful source of militancy.

V

Religious zeal and dedication (part of what Hume meant by "enthusiasm") was not the only force that equipped the Huguenots and Puritans for a role in revolution. Two other factors were even more significant: first, the social inclusiveness of these religionists, which made political involvement inevitable; second, their church structure and organization, which was well adapted for political uses. We shall look at each of these in turn.

A parallel development is observable in the growth of the reformed churches in France and the Netherlands and of Puritanism in England. They all were and remained minorities amid an environing Catholicism or Anglicanism; however, in the case of all three, their doctrines and preaching exerted an appeal that attracted people of every status. Coming later on the scene than Lutheranism, Calvinism apparently won most of its early converts among the lower urban and mechanic orders. Soon, however, it began to penetrate the bourgeoisie, the professions, the officials, and eventually the nobility. From all indications, a modern scholar's description of the Protestant forces in Guienne in the southwest of France at the mid-sixteenth century holds more generally as well: "a heteroge-

[34] See Schilling, *Niederländische Exulanten*, which contains a good, up-to-date bibliography; P. Collinson, *The Elizabethan Puritan movement*, London, 1967, 113–14; Garrett, *The Marian exiles*; E. S. Morgan, *The Puritan dilemma: the story of John Winthrop*, Boston, 1958, 66, 79; C. Bridenbaugh, *Vexed and troubled Englishmen*, New York, 1968, ch. 12.

neous and composite social bloc, an amalgam of different ranks and social strata."[35] The makeup of a list of 800-odd participants in Calvinist assemblies at Montpellier in 1560 confirms this picture. The status or occupations of 561 of them is known. Most (some 300) were artisans, mainly textile and leather craftsmen. The rest were professionals such as physicians, lawyers, and apothecaries, merchants and bourgeois, noblemen (13 of them), and a score or so of rural people.[36] In Lyons, also, we see the Calvinist movement taking hold at all levels – among rich and poor, consular families and notables as well as among the *menu peuple*.[37]

For the Calvinist congregations of the Netherlands a similar conclusion holds. Henri Pirenne in his *History of Belgium* spoke of the Calvinist advance as "fatally revolutionary," owing to the success of its religious propaganda among the workers in the industrial areas of Flanders and the south. Economic misery, he thought, drew them to Calvinism in the sixteenth century as it drew their proletarian descendants to socialism in the nineteenth.[38] Some of these workers were perhaps to be in the mobs that sacked the churches in the summer of 1566. But, as another historian of the Netherlands rebellion has emphasized, the reformed churches were broadly based and contained not only workers and artisans but merchants, members of the learned professions, and, above all, *"zahlreiche Magistratspersonen."* Rather than displaying any uniform class character, they drew their adherents from the most varied strata and occupations.[39]

The preceding observations require some qualification with regard to the peasants, or *masse agricole*, who in France and elsewhere were probably as a rule the least receptive to the Calvinist reform. The connection between the dissemination of Protestantism and literacy, which was undoubtedly lower among peasants than urban folk, may partly account for this fact. Ladurie in his regional study of Languedoc has stressed the urban–rural cleft in the spread of French Protestantism. Nevertheless, he has also had to take account of such significant exceptions as the breakthrough of Calvinism among the peasants of the Cevennes, who became firmly attached to its religious teachings. (As a result, they are even pic-

---

[35] G. Procacci, *Classi sociali e monarchia assoluta nella Francia della prima metà del secolo XVI*, Turin, 1955, 203.

[36] See the table and discussion in E. Ladurie, *Les Paysans de Languedoc*, 2 v., Paris, 1966, v. 1, 341–3.

[37] N. Davis, "Strikes and salvation at Lyons," *Archiv für Reformationsgeschichte 56*, 1 (1965). For a similar picture of Calvinism's development in still another region of France, see A. Galpern, *The religions of the people in sixteenth-century Champagne*, Cambridge, 1976, chs. 4–5.

[38] H. Pirenne, *Histoire de Belgique*, 7 v., Brussels, 1922–32, 3rd rev. ed., v. 3, 428, 435, 436.

[39] Rachfahl, *Wilhelm von Oranien*, v. 2, pt. 2, 526–7.

tured on Weberian lines as having become worldly ascetics, a people "triste et libre," who repressed pleasure and practiced thrift.)[40]

The general problem of the social diffusion of reformation Protestantism involves a number of variables and can only be worked out fully through detailed local studies. Yet there is little reason to doubt that Calvinism, despite the different proportions of the elements represented in it, possessed a broad social appeal. Taken as a whole, it was neither plebeian, nor bourgeois, nor aristocratic, but all three at once.

The same was no less true of Puritanism. Over the whole long course of its efforts to carry reformation further in the English church, from Queen Elizabeth's days to the revolt against Charles I, the Puritan movement never lacked for widespread social support. Its clergy received the backing of laymen of all kinds, from the inferior orders and "the industrious, middle sort of people" to substantial bourgeois and noblemen. The breadth of the Puritan appeal, reflected both in its social diversity and the loyalty demonstrated by elites, was what made it such a force in ecclesiastical controversies, one which the monarchy and church authorities found impossible to eradicate.[41]

The adherence of nobilities and aristocracies to reformation was a decisive step in the evolution of Calvinism. To gain converts and patrons in the governing class accorded with Calvin's hopes and intentions. The reformer did not oppose the social hierarchy and its inequalities but wished above all to imbue it with Protestant beliefs and to put elites to the task of realizing a Christian order as the helpmate of the church. He actively tried to enlist the support and sympathy of the great and powerful. Thus he dedicated his *Institute of the Christian religion* to King Francis I of France and carried on an extensive correspondence with princes and great lords on behalf of the reform.[42] Moreover, some of the French Calvinist ministers were noblemen, including Theodore Beza, Calvin's collaborator and successor in Geneva, a man of the greatest authority in all the reformed churches.[43]

In France by 1560, Calvinism had obtained a significant foothold among the nobility. It reached into the highest court and aristocratic circles, including converts in the duke of Montmorency's family and among the house of Bourbon, princes of the blood, and had made strong inroads in the provincial nobility as well. The *noblesse* had become military protectors

[40] Ladurie, *Les Paysans de Languedoc*, v. 1, 348–56; see also the same writer's "Les Paysans français du XVIᵉ siècle," in *Conjoncture économique: structures sociales*, Paris, 1974, 350–1.

[41] See P. Zagorin, *The court and the country*, London, 1969, 170–87.

[42] See Calvin's numerous letters of this kind in Bonnet, *Letters of John Calvin*, passim.

[43] See R. Kingdon, *Geneva and the consolidation of the French Protestant movement 1564–1572*, Madison, 1967, 18–19, and *Geneva and the coming of the wars of religion in France 1555–1563*, Geneva, 1956, 6.

of the reformed congregations, and a kind of seigneurial Protestantism had appeared, particularly in the south and west.[44] In the Netherlands the accession of the nobility as believers and sympathizers was on a smaller scale but still enough to be politically considerable.[45] As for the Puritans, the involvement of eminent aristocratic *dévots* as patrons and partisans of reformation runs like a red thread through the history of the movement. Indeed, a statement about the duty of the Christian nobleman in a treatise on nobility written by a Puritan cleric who had been a Marian exile may be taken as expressing the attitude of Puritanism and Calvinism alike:

> But this is peculyer to noble men, to relieve the cause of the gospell faintinge and fallynge . . . [to] ayde impoveryshed religion, to shield it . . . with theyr patronage . . . Theyr parte it is, to fight for theyr homes and Churches. They be in manner the pastours of the people . . . For great, yea greatest weight, hathe a noble mans judgmente. Wherby, both the Tyranny of Prynces is brideled, and the rage of the commen people repressed.[46]

Once nobilities and elites became affiliated with dissident religious movements, the political activation of these movements was inescapable. Such people – secular leaders of society and part of its governing class – were unlikely to submit tamely to persecution and would counter repression with opposition and resistance. They also had political interests with which the interests of the churches became entwined through their adherence. In this way, a process of politicization brought the Huguenots of France and the Calvinists of the Netherlands into the arena of combat against Catholic kings. In England, although the situation was different, the monarchy itself being Protestant, the extreme antagonism eventually aroused by Charles I's rule in the 1630s forged the alliance between Puritanism and other forms of opposition that overwhelmed the crown.

The path Calvinism followed is most clearly seen in France. In his advice to the French churches, Calvin consistently opposed forcible resistance to persecution or attempts to establish the reform by violence. Only preaching and the word were to be used for the "avancement du royaume de Dieu." But he was contending against an increasingly impatient spirit. As their numbers grew, the reformed believers began to abandon clandestine worship, to hear public sermons, and to commit violent acts of iconoclasm that were a provocation to Catholics. The Huguenot nobility carried its bellicose inclinations into the Protestant congregations, and the restraints upon resistance weakened. The religious division converged with

---

[44] See the general account by L. Romier, *Le Royaume de Catherine de Medicis*, 2 v., Paris, 1922, v. 2, 241–69. For the religious convictions of the high nobility adhering to the reform, see N. Roelker, *Queen of Navarre Jeanne D'Albret 1528–1572*, Cambridge, 1968; A. Whitehead, *Gaspard de Coligny*, London, 1904; and J. Shimizu, *Conflict of loyalties: politics and religion in the career of Gaspard de Coligny*, Geneva, 1970; and Chapter 10 in this book.

[45] Rachfahl, *Wilhelm von Oranien*, v. 2, pt. 2, 531 ff.

[46] Laurence Humphrey, *The nobles*, 1563, bk. 2, sig.m.11–12.

the dangerous competition for power between the two great rival dynasties of Bourbon and Guise, the one linked to the reform, the other the
foremost champion of Catholicism. The monarchy, left after Henry II's
death in 1559 in the ineffectual hands of his young sons, Francis II (1559–
60) and Charles IX (1560–74) and the Queen Mother Catherine de Medici,
was caught amid these explosive tensions. The conspiracy of Amboise in
1560, the unsuccessful attempt by Huguenot noblemen and Bourbon followers to seize Charles IX and expel Guise influence from the royal government, thrust the Protestant reform into the very center of state differences. Even though Calvin disapproved and disavowed the conspiracy,
Geneva naturally extended all possible assistance to the Huguenot leaders
in the conflict that loomed. For Calvinism was bent first on securing tolerance for itself and ultimately on the victory of its own religious system.
The revolution that was the reality of the war of religion arose from Calvinism's fateful coalescence with the dynastic and political forces bent on
controlling and limiting the French monarchy.[47]

In the Netherlands a comparable situation hastened the politicization of
the reform. Here Calvinism was less widely established and had fewer
noble adherents. Nevertheless, in the 1560s, a formidable aristocratic
movement, which the Protestant nobility helped to organize, took shape
against the Spanish administration under Philip II's regent, Margaret of
Parma, its personnel and policies, and its severe persecution of Protestants. Concurrently, the Calvinist congregations became ever bolder and
more aggressive, emerging from the underground to hold open assemblies
in defiance of the heresy laws and Inquisition. The Huguenot party in
France had already set the example of resistance. Thus an amalgamation
of religious and political differences caused Calvinism in the Low Countries to merge into the opposition to the government initiated by the nobility – a nobility by no means predominantly Protestant but containing a
militant Calvinist core.[48]

Five years of protest and agitation in the Netherlands, amid the waning
authority of the regent, culminated in the iconoclastic convulsion of 1566.
The riots began in Flanders on the Feast of the Ascension in mid-August
and within a few weeks had swept the provinces from south to north.
Antwerp, the great emporium of the Low Countries, and many other

[47]For a general discussion of the religious-political fusion in France, see R. Nürnberger,
Die Politisierung des französichen Protestantismus, Tübingen, 1948, which also contains useful
references to Calvin's French correspondence. For the political rivalry between Bourbon and
Guise and the conspiracy of Amboise, see L. Romier, *La Conjuration d'Amboise*, Paris, 1923,
and the discussion by N. Sutherland, "Calvinism and the conspiracy of Amboise," *History*
47, 160 (1962). The latter places the responsibility for violence upon the passing of the
Protestant movement from the control of disciplined evangelists into the hands of "politicians
and extremists," so that "the churches were forced into the struggle that ensued" (*ibid.*, 137–
8).
[48]See Ch. 11 in this book for further discussion.

towns were plunged into disorders. The mobs assaulted priests and religious, plundered churches, and destroyed altars, mass ornaments, pictures, statues, and tombs. The central government was powerless, and local authorities were unable, and sometimes unwilling, to suppress the disturbances. Among the participants were the workers of the textile districts, artisans, port laborers, and guild members. Because the preceding year had been one of subsistence crisis, hunger, and unemployment, economic distress may have aggravated social tensions.[49] The violence, however, displayed a strongly symbolic character, being nearly always aimed at Catholic targets. Fundamentally, it was the product of disaffection and fomentation by Calvinist hot gospelers.[50] It made no difference that Calvin, Beza, and other luminaries of the reform always condemned popular action against Catholic worship unless expressly approved by the magistrate. As in France, where the Huguenots were also frequently guilty of iconoclastic outrages, such cautions could not control the fury of fanatical believers determined to uproot idolatry.[51] The outbreaks, followed shortly by other insurrectionary acts, provoked the terrible repression by the Spanish regime that ensued. The events as a whole were the expression of a simultaneous religious and political crisis that signaled the onset of the first wave of revolution in the Netherlands.

In the case of Puritanism, the involvement of an organized clerical vanguard and aristocratic lay sponsorship gave the movement a political aspect from the beginning. The Elizabethan religious settlement of 1559 established the Protestant national church as it was to remain until the revolution of 1640. The crown's ecclesiastical supremacy was recognized by law, and it appointed the bishops who were immediately responsible for church government. The Puritans, however, criticized the church as insufficiently reformed; its services, according to them, retained popish ceremonies, and its government by bishops, some contended, was contrary to Scripture. To Queen Elizabeth, James I, and Charles I, Puritanism naturally represented a challenge to the crown's power in religion as well as a disobedient spirit in the state. Despite royal disapproval and intermittent repression, the Puritan ministry and its lay sympathizers persisted in their efforts for reformation. Over many years, they tried incessantly to change its liturgy; they also strove either to get rid of bishops in favor of a church order on the Calvinist model or to limit episcopal powers

---

[49] For the possible conjunctural aspect of the outbreaks, see Chapter 5 of this book.

[50] For symbolic violence, see Ch. 1. The iconoclasm of 1566 is discussed further in Ch. 11.

[51] Many examples of Huguenot iconoclasm in France are cited by H. Baird, *The rise of the Huguenots*, 2 v., New York, 1879, *passim*. For official Calvinist disapproval of the unauthorized destruction of images, see Romier, *Le royaume de Catherine de Medicis*, v. 2, 201–6, 225–6; Kingdon, *Geneva and the coming of the wars of religion*, 46, 81; R. Linder, *The political ideas of Pierre Viret*, Geneva, 1964, 119–20.

and functions. In localities where they were strong, they even covertly attempted to introduce the services and forms of church polity they favored. Although they did not achieve the changes they desired, their preaching, moral influence, and persistent nonconformity impressed their presence firmly upon the Anglican establishment. Always they made use of political means. Puritan ministers held conferences and meetings; they and their lay patrons and allies instigated petitions to king and Parliament, promoted bills on religion and discussion of their grievances in the House of Commons, and propagandized for their principles in press and pulpit. They possessed an important forum for their views in Parliament, to which many Puritan gentlemen were elected, especially in the earlier seventeenth century.[52]

As loyal subjects of a Protestant ruler and state, the Puritans did not come to advocate forcible resistance until 1640, by which time Scotland, stirred by its own grievances and Calvinistic sentiments, was already in revolt against the authority of Charles I; but the Puritans were highly adept at political methods in the cause of reformation. It was thus only a comparatively small transition when the severities of Charles's English government finally provoked the wrathful Puritans – the preachers and their flocks, the pious aristocratic and bourgeois pillars of religious nonconformity – into a direct political struggle that was to end in the overthrow of the monarchy itself.

The structure of the Calvinist communities facilitated their adaptation to political activism. Unlike Luther, Calvin placed heavy stress on the visible church as an organ of religious and spiritual control, and he endowed it with a corresponding institutional form. A well-defined pattern, derived with modifications from Geneva, was common to the Calvinist churches. Each local church or congregation was governed by a consistory of ministers and elders; the separate churches were joined through their consistories into wider neighborhood associations (*colloquys*, classes, presbyteries) and further into provincial synods, culminating in the national synod as the supreme ecclesiastical authority. The consistories coopted their members subject to ultimate ratification by the churches. Lower bodies were subordinate to higher ones. The enforcement of orthodox doctrine and good moral conduct was an important part of the churches' function. The consistories maintained a surveillance of church members and had power to admonish and judge the erring and sinful. Offenders were re-

---

[52] On the political activity and organization of the Puritan movement, see J. E. Neale, *Elizabeth I and her parliaments 1559–1581*, London, 1953, and its sequel, *Elizabeth I and her parliaments 1584–1601*, London, 1957; Collinson, *The Elizabethan Puritan movement, passim*; M. Walzer, *The revolution of the saints*, Cambridge, 1965, chs. 4, 7–8; Zagorin, *The court and the country*, chs. 4, 6.

fused the sacrament until penitent, with excommunication as the ultimate religious penalty.[53]

This in briefest outline was the polity of the Reformed church in France and the Netherlands, which many Puritans also wished to see established in England and which was adopted by the Presbyterians and Covenanters in Scotland.[54] Appropriately enough, Calvin and the Huguenots described it generally as discipline, a term equally indicative of its spiritual jurisdiction and its exacting moral regimen. The English Puritans also called it "the discipline," and were sometimes known as the "disciplinarian" party in consequence.[55] It was a polity equally noteworthy for its faculty of self-direction, its institutional independence of the secular power, its joining of laymen with clergy in the administration of church affairs, and its resemblance to a sort of republicanism reflected in church government by a hierarchy of select bodies representing the community of believers.

For purposes of resistance, as more than one modern scholar has pointed out, the Calvinist discipline possessed exceptional advantages.

The congregations, the consistories, the synods – could as they stood be easily converted into political sections. They could form the cadres of a military organization; they were peculiarly adapted to tap or to drain the financial resources of the party. The material strength of Calvinism is proved by the resistance offered in France to an overwhelming Catholic majority, whereas in Bavaria and Austria a nobility and people almost entirely Lutheran succumbed to governments possessed of small resources.[56]

The same observation is broadly true of the churches in the Low Countries, despite the concrete differences between the two rebellions and the greater, earlier development of Calvinist organization in France. In both cases, the Huguenot communities became the religious nuclei of revolutionary parties headed by nobilities. The ecclesiastical organs functioned alongside the political organization brought into existence by rebellion. The network of congregational cells helped to mobilize believers, to instill

[53] Calvin's church constitution for Geneva was delineated in the *Ecclesiastical ordinances* of 1541; see B. Kidd, *Documents illustrative of the continental reformation*, Oxford, 1911, 589 ff. His *Institute of the Christian religion*, bk. 4, also describes the Calvinist church order and its officers.

[54] A general survey of Calvinist church government is given by J. T. McNeill, *The history and character of Calvinism*, New York, 1954. For France, see "The discipline of the reformed churches of France," in *Synodicon in Gallia reformata*, ed. J. Quick, 2 v., London, 1692, v. 1, and the account in Kingdon, *Geneva and the consolidation of the French Protestant movement*, 37–42. For the Netherlands, P. Geyl, *The revolt of the Netherlands*, London, 1958, 80–2; for England and Scotland, Collinson, *The Elizabethan Puritan movement*, pt. 6, ch. 1, and G. Donaldson, *The Scottish reformation*, Cambridge, 1960, ch. 8.

[55] See the references in note 54, and Donaldson, *The Scottish reformation*, 185.

[56] Armstrong, *The French wars of religion*, 3.

militancy, and to sustain the struggle amid defeat and adversity.[57] In the same way afterward in Scotland, the Presbyterian kirk that came into being with the rebellion of 1638 imparted its energy and resources to the maintenance of resistance to Charles I. The English Puritans, by contrast, never achieved a comprehensive level of religious organization even after 1640, although the activation of the clergy and congregations strongly affected the course of the revolution.

There was also an international side to Calvinism's organizational thrust in the sixteenth century due to the unique position of Geneva. Parallels, not entirely fanciful, may be seen between Calvinist Geneva, Jacobin Paris, and Communist Moscow as headquarters of revolution.[58] Richard Hooker, the great Elizabethan theologian and political thinker, in criticizing the Puritans' subjection to Calvin's influence, acidly described the reformer's international authority:

Beza was one whom no man would displease, Calvin one whom no man durst. His dependants both abroad and at home; his intelligence from forrein churches; his correspondence everywhere with the chiefest; his industry in pursuing them which did at any time openly either withstand his proceedings or gainsay his opinions . . . his writing but of three lines in disgrace of any man as forcible as any proscription throughout all reformed churches; his rescripts and answeres of as great authority as decretal epistles.

Two things, Hooker declared, trouble these later times, "one that the Church of Rome cannot, another that Geneva will not erre."[59]

Geneva's authoritarian discipline suggests resemblances to modern Communist party discipline. In 1564, the Geneva consistory charged Merlin, a leading Huguenot pastor in France and Geneva, with schismatic doctrine and ordered him to retract and make a public apology. On refusing, he was deposed from the ministry; it was the end of a "long and distinguished career in the service of the Reformed faith." Another French minister who fell into disgrace at Geneva and was deposed and excommunicated had to acknowledge to the consistory that he was a deserter of the church, a rebel to his oath, and a calumniator before he was restored to communion. Professor Kingdon, who mentions these instances, comments that the acceptance of such humiliation demonstrates the "great power of excommunication as an instrument of social discipline in that age."[60] We may also be inclined, though, to see a certain similarity with

---

[57] See H. G. Koenigsberger, "The organization of revolutionary parties in France and the Netherlands during the sixteenth century," in *Estates and revolutions*, ch. 9; R. Kingdon, "The political resistance of the Calvinists in France and the Low Countries," *Church history 27*, 3 (1958).

[58] As suggested by Kingdon, *Geneva and the coming of the wars of religion*, 128.

[59] R. Hooker, *Ecclesiastical polity*, 2 v., New York, 1873, v. 1, 125, 128.

[60] Kingdon, *Geneva and the consolidation of the French Protestant movement*, 22, 27–8.

the later Communist practice of autocriticism and self-abasement as a means of political-ideological control over party members. We may perhaps also note a certain parallelism between expulsion from the church, with its possible consequences of guilt and isolation, and expulsion from the Communist party – in both cases a fateful separation inflicted upon those who had once made a commitment.

The "international" directed by Calvin and Beza at Geneva helped to coordinate and to unify the forces of reform. The missionaries who were trained there for service in France and the Low Countries absorbed Calvin's teachings and carried them abroad. Nearly all the earlier national synods of the French Reformed church (the first was held in 1559) were presided over by men either sent directly from or closely connected with Geneva.[61] During the later sixteenth century, outstanding personalities in the French and Dutch churches, as well as the chief clerical lights of Puritanism in England and Presbyterianism in Scotland, sojourned in Geneva at one time or another and returned to their countries as defenders of the Calvinist "line" on ecclesiastical discipline.[62] In the same connection, a recent historian of Elizabethan Puritanism has pointed out how in the early 1570s

an urge to confer and to organize possessed all the reformed churches under the influence of the Geneva *oraculum;* it was felt in France, the Netherlands . . . as well as in Scotland and England. National synods were held which adopted or revised confessions of faith and forms of discipline, and which issued instructions for the distribution of local churches . . . There was little local spontaneity in this activity, and yet it owed nothing to the initiative of governments.[63]

Although it should never be forgotten that Calvinism and Puritanism were religious, not political movements and that their primary concern was with the preaching and realization of God's word, not with power, they must be considered among the principal factors in the contexts of the revolutions with which they were associated. The adherents of the reformed churches who took up arms during the later sixteenth century against the Valois and Habsburg monarchs in France and the Netherlands brought moral and ideological passion to these rebellions; they imported into them principles, ideas, and political demands that were consequential in their history and outcome. Likewise, the Elizabethan Puritans and Scottish Presbyterians who were the contemporaries of continental Calvinism in its ordeal of survival shared many of its beliefs and ideals. In both England and Scotland they transmitted to their religious successors of the seventeenth century traditions derived from the experience of an embattled Protestantism that were to help blow up the Stuart monarchy.

[61]*Ibid.*, 73.   [62]*Ibid.*, 127–8.   [63]Collinson, *The Elizabethan Puritan movement,* 111.

VI

Finally, as yet another element in the religious context of some of our early modern revolutions, we must note the role of millenarianism. In recent years a convergence of studies by historians, anthropologists, and sociologists has revealed the wide extent of millenarianism as a transcultural phenomenon. The diversity of its manifestations among both primitive and civilized peoples, from the Sioux Indian ghost dance and Melanesian cargo cults to Mahdism in Islam and recurrent expressions in medieval and modern Christianity, has also been investigated. Convincing suggestions have likewise been advanced pointing to the analogous features and probable historical connections between religious millenarianism and later professedly secular revolutionary movements.[64]

Millenarianism belongs primarily to the ideological domain and is apt to consist of a relatively highly elaborated set of ideas or beliefs. These can be reductively generalized in a transcultural sense divested of their historical particularities or differentia. Thus, in a comparative perspective, millenarianism may be seen as a species of salvationism with the following generic characteristics: first, the salvation awaited is to be collective, embracing the entire community or all the elect or faithful; second, it is to occur in this terrestrial world, before the eye of sense; third, it is expected imminently as a soon-to-be-consummated event; fourth, it is to be total, utterly transforming earthly existence from sin and evil into good; fifth, it will be accomplished through the intervention of supernatural agencies.[65] To this summary one might add further refinements, such as the likelihood that a messiah or prophet will be associated with the millenarian creed and that the latter will posit a catastrophic period of suffering and oppression for the faithful just prior to the longed-for salvation.[66]

When we turn to the presence of millenarianism in early modern Europe, this description has to be supplemented with a more specific historical content. What we find in this case as the ultimate source of millenarian ideology are the Judeo–Christian apocalyptic writings in the Bible, which inspired over many centuries a complex tradition of speculation and

---

[64] See Sylvia Thrupp (ed.), *Millennial dreams in action*, New York, 1970; and Y. Talmon, "Millenarism," in *International encyclopedia of the social sciences*, New York, 1968, v. 10. N. Cohn, *The pursuit of the millennium*, rev. ed., Oxford, 1970, is the main historical treatment. See also G. Lewy, *Religion and revolution*, New York, 1974, pt. 2; and the discussion in P. Zagorin, "Theories of revolution in contemporary historiography," *Political science quarterly 88*, 1 (1973), 37–9.

[65] This is the formulation of N. Cohn, "Medieval millenarism: Its bearing on the comparative study of millennarian movements," in Thrupp, *Millennial dreams*, 31; see also his *The pursuit of the millennium*, 13.

[66] Talmon, "Millenarism," presents an extended summary of the generic features of millenarianism.

prophecy. From these writings millenarianism has also taken its name: for the term, like its Greek-derived synonym, *chiliasm*, refers directly to the thousand-year reign of the saints in an earthly kingdom with Christ as head, as pictured in the Book of Revelation. Both this book in the New Testament and the Book of Daniel in the Old are millenarian manifestoes.[67] They are visions of a complete reversal of the sinful world order, of a victorious war against evil by divine judgment, of the final overthrow of oppressive thrones and profane kingdoms, and of the end of history through the appearance of a new heaven and a new earth ruled by God and his saints. These eschatological projections must be seen in part as the inspired vengeance fantasies of Jewish and Christian victims of history. The two apocalypses were each the product of a period of persecution, national or religious, by Hellenistic and Roman rulers. In common they reflect the burning wish for retribution against diabolical tyrannies to be realized in the last days when the saints rule in power. They are also filled with a rich, mysterious imagery of beasts and monsters, angels and devils, the Ancient of Days, the book of life, the lake of fire, the holy city of the New Jerusalem descending from heaven, all seen against a gigantic canvas of the saved and damned. These images are of vital importance because millenarian beliefs may depend for their effect not only on their ideas but also on the symbol-charged pictures that embody them and resonate in the imagination as emblems of the destruction of the wicked and triumph of the righteous.

During the Middle Ages, a dense accretion of interpretation of the Scriptural apocalypses appeared, along with many other prophecies of a new age tied to various charismatic figures. On the one hand, Catholic orthodoxy, as the theological expression of a world-dominating institution, tried to remove the radical sting from millenarian inspiration with Saint Augustine's doctrine that the millennium was already realized in the church. On the other hand, millenarianism entered into a wider subversive current of antipapal, antinomian, and egalitarian ideas that flowed through medieval and Reformation Europe.[68]

The most significant post-Biblical contribution to the millenarian tradition came from the twelfth-century Italian mystic and exegete, Joachim of Fiore. Joachim advanced a scheme of universal history based on the esoteric meaning of Scripture and the apocalypse. It conceived of mankind's course in three successive ages or stages (*status*) corresponding to the persons of the Trinity. The first was the age of the Father and the Law, the second the age of the Son and the Gospel, the third and culminating age, already begun, according to Joachim, that of the Holy Spirit. This

[67] See especially Daniel 7 and Revelation 20–1.
[68] Cohn, *The pursuit of the millennium*, contains a detailed account.

status was the *consummatio seculi* preceding the Last Judgment: an age of love, joy, and freedom, of a completely spiritualized church, and of men united in praise and contemplation of God.[69]

Joachimism was equally a prophecy, an eschatology, and along with Saint Augustine's *City of God* the greatest religious philosophy of history the Middle Ages possessed.[70] It offered a complete explanation of the meaning and pattern of history, which looked to an approaching spiritual kingdom on earth as the inevitable fulfillment of the divine plan. Its influence was manifold, mingling also in heretical movements and revolts. Its ideas were very likely at work in the Hussite revolution, whose Taborite phase brought medieval millenarianism to its highest pitch. The priest, Martin Huska, most eloquent of the millenarian preachers of Tabor, voiced the Joachimite prophecy that "there will be a new kingdom of the Saints on earth, and that the good will no longer suffer." He also offered a poignant revelation of the motive of his millenarian faith when he said, "If Christians were always to have to suffer so, I would not want to be a servant of God."[71] A century afterward, another revolutionary preacher who carried a burning millenarian message into the German peasant war, Thomas Müntzer, also drew on Joachimism for some of his inspiration.[72]

In explaining the upsurge of millenarian movements at various times, students have generally agreed that they were apt to be a reflex of acute dislocation and breakdown and the product of social or natural calamities that engendered exceptional insecurity and anxiety. War, plague, revolts, rapid economic change, disruption of communal bonds, and drastic deterioration of living standards have all been cited as examples of the predisposing conditions for millenarian movements. It is also commonly held that the latter gain their main following among low-status, politically weak, and exploited groups who are especially defenseless against the effects of humanly inflicted deprivation or natural disasters.[73]

From this standpoint, millenarianism appears primarily as a particular religious expression of social protest. Thus, in Karl Mannheim's judgment, "the chiliastic experience is characteristic of the lowest strata of society. Underlying it is a mental structure peculiar to oppressed peasants, journeymen, an incipient *Lumpenproletariat*, fanatically emotional

---

[69] See M. Reeves, *The influence of prophecy in the later middle ages*, Oxford, 1969, pt. 1, ch. 2, which provides an authoritative treatment of Joachimism.

[70] K. Löwith, *Meaning in history*, Chicago, 1949, ch. 8, discusses Joachimism as a philosophy of history in the context of other philosophic attempts to decipher the design of history.

[71] Kaminsky, *A history of the Hussite revolution*, 351–2, 400, stresses the Joachimite origins of Taborite millenarianism transmitted, it is suggested, probably via the heresy of the Free Spirit.

[72] Reeves, *The influence of prophecy*, 490. Müntzer had studied a pseudo-Joachimite work on Jeremiah.

[73] Cohn, *The pursuit of the millennium*, 59–60, and see also his discussion in Thrupp, *Millennial dreams*; Talmon, "Millenarism"; M. Barkun, *Disaster and the millennium*, New Haven, 1974.

preachers."[74] Although this was often (but by no means universally) true of the millenarianism of the late Middle Ages and early modern era, it is also important not to overlook the additional fascination of millenarian ideology as an unfolding of the design of history. On this account it exerted a strong, independent attraction upon intellectuals; and, correspondingly, a recurrent feature of millenarian movements in Christian Europe was the participation of priests, lay preachers, and intellectuals. Millenarianism accordingly possessed a dual property: On the one hand, it drew on recondite Scriptural and other sources, which required learning for their interpretation; on the other hand, it gave direct expression to elemental desires and wishes. Without straining analogies too far, it may be compared in some respects with revolutionary Marxism in that the latter functions both as a complex theory only intelligible through intensive study (few calling themselves Marxists have read or understood *Capital*) and as a simplified doctrine of hope and confidence in a future ideal society.

Millenarianism, considered in its immediate bearing upon revolution in sixteenth- and seventeenth-century Europe, should not be identified, though, merely with the prediction of Christ's Second Coming or even with the conviction that the last days are close at hand. Such beliefs could be held peacefully, in quiet detachment, or simply speculatively by separate individuals, without arousing any resistance to the established order. Moreover, modern scholars have discovered that these beliefs exercised considerable influence during the period because of the religious upheavals and hatreds produced by the Reformation. The apocalyptic books were searched to forecast the date of the papacy's demise, the conversion of the Jews, the destruction of the fourth world monarchy prophesied in Daniel (which could be identified either with Rome or with great secular states), and the advent of the millennial kingdom. Due to the disasters suffered by the Protestant cause in the Thirty Years war, Protestant thinkers of the earlier seventeenth century were particularly receptive to such eschatological themes, which were taken seriously by theologians, philosophers, and scientists. Later in the century, Sir Isaac Newton carried on the tradition, devoting concentrated effort to the explication of the apocalypse as the key to God's plan.[75] Because of the currency of these ideas, it has been suggested, millenarianism may have signified "not alienation from the spirit of the age but a total involvement with it."[76]

However, millenarianism of this general kind must be distinguished

---

[74] K. Mannheim, *Ideology and utopia*, New York, 1936, 204.

[75] For the currency of millenarian ideas, see H. R. Trevor-Roper, *Religion, the Reformation and social change*, 2nd ed., London, 1972, 173, 247–8; F. Yates, *The Rosicrucian enlightenment*, London, 1972, 48, 57; B. Capp, *The Fifth-Monarchy Men*, London, 1972, 232–7; R. Evans, *Rudolf II and his world*, Oxford, 1973, 276; F. Manuel, *The religion of Isaac Newton*, Oxford, 1974, ch. 4.

[76] W. Lamont, *Godly rule*, London, 1969, 13.

from its specific revolutionary variety. It might be said to resemble in its import the subsequent nineteenth-century idea of progress (to whose development it in fact contributed).[77] Both formed a climate of opinion containing certain assumptions about time and history shared by different people and schools of thought, yet without necessarily giving rise to any revolutionary consequences.

In contrast, the millenarianism that issued in revolt went well beyond the mere prediction of the approaching millennium, just as post-1789 revolutionism went well beyond the mere belief in progress. Apart from the traits already mentioned, it had certain additional peculiarities of its own.

In the first place, it manifested itself with a driving urgency and a call to violence. The revolutionary millenarian conceived himself as an immediate actor in the cosmic drama drawing to its climax. He felt himself chosen to participate both as witness (in the religious sense) and agent in the impending realization of the supernatural events foretold by the Biblical prophecies.

In the second place, he made a clear separation between the elect, of whom he was one, and the ungodly, who were condemned to destruction with the passing of the old dispensation. His eschatological vision was fueled by bitter hatred of the spiritual deformities of the clergy, the tyranny of princes, and the injustice of the lordly, rich, and powerful. All these enemies of the Lord he believed he might deservedly smite, in anticipation of the lifting of the curse from mankind through the earthly rule of Christ and his saints.

In the third place, the supernatural order for which he thirsted was to be one of perfect justice and equality. Its advent would mark the restoration of the pristine government of Christ when the last should be first. It combined themes out of man's Edenic state before the Fall, the Mosaic law, and the New Testament. It could simultaneously authorize the wildest antinomian license and the most rigorous asceticism.

In sum, revolutionary millenarianism was a dynamic synthesis of futuristic consciousness of the new and the myth of the normative past, impelled toward violence by the intensity of its eschatological faith in the imminent reign of Christ and his elect.

Millenarianism of this extreme kind was comparatively rare and appeared infrequently in revolution. As an element of any importance it is found in our period in only three cases: the German peasant war, the anabaptist revolt of Münster in 1534, and the English revolution. Wherever it arose, it was associated with radical Protestant sects – in the early sixteenth century especially with anabaptism, in the mid-seventeenth century with some of the more heterodox offshoots of English Puritanism.

[77] See E. Tuveson, *Millennium and utopia*, new ed., New York, 1964.

These separatist religious bodies, with their members gathered in the main from impoverished lower strata, their spiritual elitism offsetting their worldly inferiority, and their susceptibility to enthusiasm, became at certain moments the vehicle of the ideology of millenarian revolt.[78]

The widest influence of this ideology coincided with the first twenty years of the Reformation. Luther's defiance of Rome opened the way to a growth of sectarianism that broke completely free of any ecclesiastical control. Expectations of religious renewal and freedom inspired an outburst of apocalyptic prophecy. Already in 1521 at Zwickau in Saxony – a town that was one of Thomas Müntzer's way stations on his pilgrimage toward the peasant war four years later – the weaver Nicholas Storch and other prophets were proclaiming the approaching millennium, denouncing noblemen, priests, and landlords, and calling for the annihilation of the godless by the elect.[79] Anabaptist sects provided the most fruitful soil for these beliefs. By its very nature anabaptism was not a single or unified phenomenon but consisted of heterogeneous religious communities who shared the practice of believer's baptism as their most obvious common trait. Although many adhered to pacifist nonviolence as part of their dedication to the principles of the Sermon on the Mount, others responded to inflammatory preachers who held forth bloodthirsty doctrines of the use of the sword in preparation for the imminent millennium. Müntzer influenced some of the early anabaptists in this direction, as he did other groups of covenanted Christians who conceived themselves as elect. Similar ideas were also disseminated by the anabaptist missionaries, Hans Hut and Melchior Hoffmann, in central and northwest Germany and the adjacent northern provinces of the Netherlands. Hoffmann's followers, the Melchiorites, were roused to a white heat of eschatological expectancy by him and his disciples.[80]

Millennial revolt charged with the fervor of apocalyptic prophecy broke out amid the German peasant war and was to reappear again amid analogous circumstances of crisis and hope in the Fifth Monarchy movement of the English revolution. Its high point, however, occurred in the West-

[78] Another small outbreak of millenarian violence, involving maybe three or four thousand people, took place in France at the beginning of the eighteenth century among the Huguenots of the Cevennes in Languedoc, provoked by the persecution inflicted on them after the revocation of the Edict of Nantes in 1685. This movement, the revolt of the Camisards, was inspired by the apocalyptic prophecies and accompanied by manifestations of convulsionary hysteria. At this time the Calvinist communities of the region exhibited some of the same traits as had the more radical Protestant sects of the past; see the accounts in Ladurie, *Les Paysans de Languedoc*, v. 1, 605–29, and S. Mours and D. Robert, *Le Protestantisme en France du XVIIIème siècle à nos jours*, Paris, 1972, pt. 1, ch. 3.

[79] See L. Zuck, *Christianity and revolution*, Philadelphia, 1975, 29–30, for textual illustrations; and G. Rupp, *Patterns of reformation*, Philadelphia, 1969, ch. 6.

[80] See J. Stayer, *Anabaptists and the sword*, Lawrence, 1972, for a full and careful discussion.

phalian city of Münster in 1534, when anabaptist rebellion released the millenarian spirit in its most untrammeled form.

Münster was an ecclesiastical principality. The events that made it notorious followed hard upon the municipal council's acceptance of the Lutheran reform in 1532 in defiance of its prince-bishop. Immediately, the emergence of anabaptism alarmed the city's magistrates and sowed further religious dissension. To Münster in 1533–4 flocked Melchiorites and other anabaptists from the Low Countries and Germany, numbering perhaps seven thousand in a city of about fifteen thousand.[81] These zealots, who were driven by persecution, were drawn to Münster because of prophecies that it was to be the site of the New Jerusalem. Of the Dutch anabaptists who came, most were poverty-stricken work people badly hit by depression and unemployment and therefore, it has been suggested, disposed to unrest and rebellion.[82] The leaders of the apocalyptic in-gathering, the baker Jan Matthys, John of Haarlem, and the journeyman tailor Jan Beukels, John of Leyden, were charismatic prophets given to dreams and revelations. The words and personalities of these two fomenters of eschatological violence exerted an irresistible fascination on their followers. They were supported by some local notables in Münster, including a leading preacher turned anabaptist from Lutheran, Bernhard Rothmann, who expounded a theological justification of the sword in the hands of the elect as the necessary prelude to the Second Coming.

In the first months of 1534 the anabaptists took control of Münster in a conquest facilitated by internal social and economic division. From the city they sent out emissaries to other towns in an unsuccessful attempt to incite them to revolt. Many citizens fled or were expelled; the rest either converted or submitted. In place of the previous order, the anabaptist prophets established a regime of repression and holy war. It was a militant theocracy in which community, church, and state were all one. They abolished money and imposed community of goods in restoration of primitive Christian practice. They instituted forms of government modeled on the Old Testament and made polygamy compulsory after the example of the Jewish patriarchs. The polygamy decree provoked considerable resistance, which was ruthlessly crushed. In the midst of these developments the city was forced to withstand a fifteen-month siege by the bishop's army reinforced by other German princes. After Matthys's death, John of Leyden became the messianic ruler of the movement, his position that of

[81] J. Stayer, "The Münsterite rationalization of Bernhard Rothmann," *Journal of the history of ideas 28*, 2 (1967), 179; Williams, *The radical reformation*, 364.

[82] See C. Verlinden, "Crises économiques et sociales en Belgique à l'époque de Charles-Quint," in *Charles-Quint et son temps*, Paris, 1959, 184–5, who connects the anabaptist revolt at Münster with economic misery due to adverse conjunctural circumstances. He speaks of it as "above all a movement of proletarians."

an omnipotent Davidic king reigning over his court and faithful in the New Jerusalem. No word of protest or opposition to his domination was permitted. Public spectacles, divine revelations, and a reign of terror enforced by executions helped to maintain him in power. Moral antinomianism coexisted with a rigorous surveillance of sins, many of which were punishable by death. Meanwhile, the inhabitants were dying of hunger as the siege tightened and food ran out. Münster became a "nightmare kingdom" (Norman Cohn's phrase) in the grip of an apocalyptic dictatorship actuated by the high-tension belief in the imminent millennium.[83]

The anabaptist revolt ended in June 1535 with the fall of the city and the merciless slaughter of its defenders. The episode left an ineffaceable impression on Protestant memory for at least a century and a half, if not longer. It remained a byword for the dangers of spiritualistic enthusiasm, and the charge of communism and sexual libertinism was thenceforth always available against radical sectarians who departed from the orthodoxy of the churches. As a result of the debacle, continental anabaptism was largely cured of any further proclivity toward violence and reverted to pacific and apolitical detachment as the keynotes of its religious life.

If we ask in light of the foregoing how millenarianism fits into the typology of early modern revolution, I believe, as I have suggested in a previous chapter,[84] that it is better understood as a phenomenon potentially incident to several types of revolution rather than as a distinctive type of its own. The case of Münster may be an exception in that it occurred relatively separate from any larger encompassing revolt. But even here the anabaptist influx and forcible establishment of an eschatological regime could not have happened without acute internal conflicts between Catholics and Lutherans, the city and its prince-bishop, and rich and poor. In other cases in Europe, millenarian revolt always appeared as "a revolution within the revolution"; it was injected or surged up inside prior, bigger revolutions of different kinds. Such was the Taborite phase of the Hussite revolution, and we shall see the same to be true of the millenarian aspect of the German peasant war and the English revolution.

There may, of course, be individual revolutions wholly or largely dominated by millenarian ideology. The anabaptist revolt at Münster is one such case, and an even more important example is the great Taiping rebellion in nineteenth-century China.[85] To recognize, however, that revolutions of different types can harbor the possibility of engendering millenarian movements makes it easier to understand how millenarian themes

[83] For accounts of the anabaptist revolt, see Cohn, *The pursuit of the millennium*, ch. 13; and, with fuller consideration of the theological and religious ideas, Williams, *The radical reformation*, ch. 13, and Stayer, *Anabaptists and the sword*, chs. 11–12. Some documentary illustrations are contained in Zuck, *Christianity and revolution*, pt. 4.

[84] Chapter 2 in this book.

[85] See the review of "millenarian revolts" in Lewy, *Religion and revolution*, pt. 2.

can also be absorbed into modern revolutionism and combine with sophisticated organizational techniques and realistic methods of political struggle. As one writer has rightly commented, "Certain mass movements of modern times, such as revolutionary Marxism and Bolshevism, share many of the characteristics of revolutionary millenarianism."[86] The fact that these movements are professedly secular and antireligious is not decisive. Their ultimate goals possess a similar eschatological content, and some of the fervor they evoke is enlisted in a similar cause of millennial transformation. The belief or disbelief in the intervention of supernatural forces is relatively unimportant in view of this fundamental parallelism.[87] The proclamation by Marx, Engels, Lenin, and Mao Tse-tung of the communist order that lies at the end of the long revolutionary road is unmistakably eschatological in its disregard of historical experience and in its utopian faith in a perfected age. The classless society, the withering away of the state, the new socialist man, from each according to his ability and to each according to his needs, from the government of men to the administration of things, from the kingdom of necessity to the kingdom of freedom – these are all essentially translations in secular disguise of the age-old religious conviction of the revolutionary millenarian that he is an actor in a world-decisive struggle destined to culminate in a new heaven and a new earth.

[86] *Ibid.*, 237; and see the observations in Talmon, "Millenarism."
[87] This parallelism could easily be extended. To point it out is also to realize that millenarianism cannot be considered an exclusively primitive and "preopolitical" phenomenon, the revolutionary precursor of later, higher forms of rebellion of which revolutionary Marxism is the most advanced stage (for this view, see E. Hobsbawm, *Primitive rebels*, Manchester, 1959). On the contrary, as I have remarked in the text, futurist fantasies of transformation and a wholly just world order are quite capable of entering into and influencing modern revolutionary movements in decisive ways.

PART III

Revolutions

7

Agrarian rebellion

I

In this and the following chapters, we pass from the general and contextual considerations of the first two parts of our study to a discussion of the different types and selected cases of early modern revolution. Our aim in this present part is to bring out the distinctive forms and variety of revolutions in the sixteenth and earlier seventeenth centuries and to illuminate by means of some particular examples the range and permutations of revolutionary action that the early modern world engendered.

We begin with agrarian rebellion, the most profound, the fiercest expression of defiance and resistance by the common folk of this society.

Here we enounter, first of all, the peasant. But, like his medieval forebears how rarely did he speak for himself, how difficult it is to know his thoughts and feelings! Although revolt may occasionally throw a strong light on his mind and griefs, he remains obscure, a part of the great inarticulate mass at the base of his society. Yet he is an inescapable figure, as elemental as the great tortoise of Indian mythology, which was said to uphold the world, for it was his obedience and toil that sustained the princes, nobilities, and landlords, his rulers and betters.

In the main we are compelled to see the peasant through eyes remote or different from his own, from the angle of the literate and those who did not share his life. Numerous images of him exist among the wealth of contemporary prints and paintings, most memorably of all, perhaps, in the art of the great Netherlander master, Pieter Brueghel, born around the time of the German peasant war. Brueghel depicted his peasant subjects with a sympathetic objectivity at their work and pleasure, comical, sometimes grotesque beings possessed of a terrible strength and a brutal, overflowing vitality. Seeing how near he was to the event, it is easy to imagine Brueghel's peasants, their thick bodies, powerful limbs, and weather-beaten faces, among the mass of villagers that rose up in 1525 in Germany.[1]

A familiar attitude of the time was contempt for the peasant's coarseness and his base vocation. In England, in a tract written contemporaneously with Kett's agrarian revolt in 1549, the author, one of the sharpest observers of his day, voiced regret at this patronizing view of the lowly cultivator:

What occupation is more necessarie or so profitable for man's life as this is? . . . and how little is it regarded? Yea, how much is it vilified, that [the] nobilitie reputes them but as villaines, pesauntes, or slaves, by whom the proudest of them have their livinges. So that I mervaile muche theare is anie (seeinge a vilitie and contempte of the thinge) will occupie the feate of husbandrie at all.[2]

From France in the first half of the seventeenth century derive the realistic scenes of peasant life painted by Louis Le Nain, the finest contemporary native artist of this genre, whose career (circa 1593–1648) spanned the climactic period of French peasant outbreaks. The peasant families of his pictures, perhaps taken from his own Picard region, afflicted by war and successive pillaging, live in poverty and want, but they are endowed with dignity and humanity.[3] Far grimmer is the impression conveyed in the famous literary portrait of the peasant by the moralist La Bruyère:

One sees certain fierce animals, male and female, spread over the fields, black, livid, and burnt by the sun, fixed to the earth which they dig and turn with an unconquerable obstinacy. They seem to be able to speak, and when they raise themselves to their feet, they reveal a human face; and in effect, they are men. At night they withdraw to their dens, where they live on black bread, water, and roots. They spare others the pain of sowing, labouring, and harvesting in order to live, and therefore they deserve not to be in want themselves of the bread which they have sown.

This description was composed at the height of Louis XIV's reign and resembles the account that modern scholars have given of the French peas-

---

[1] Brueghel, circa 1525/30–69. His earliest biographer, Carel van Mander, stressed Brueghel's delight in peasant subjects, remarking that he represented them as "they really were, betraying their boorishness in the way they walked, danced, stood still or moved . . . The peasants' faces and limbs, where they are bare, are yellow and brown, sunburnt; their skins are ugly, different from those of town dwellers" (*Schilderboek*, 1604, cited by F. Grossman, *Brueghel: the paintings*, London, n.d., 7–8). A. Bartels, *Der Bauer in der deutschen Vergangenheit: Monographien zur deutschen Kulturgeschichte*, Leipzig, 1900, contains an excellent selection of prints of German peasants of the sixteenth and seventeenth centuries. See also R. W. Scribner, "Images of the peasant, 1514–1525," *Journal of peasant studies 3*, 1 (1975).

[2] *A discourse of the commonweal of this realm of England*, ed. E. Lamond, Cambridge, 1893, xi–xiv, 123. I have altered the text slightly. First printed in 1581, the editor ascribes this work to John Hales, a leading mid-century social reformer. More recently, though, it has been attributed to Sir Thomas Smith, a Tudor official and intellectual; see M. Dewar, "The authorship of 'The discourse of the commonweal,' " *Economic history review*, 2nd ser., *19*, 2 (1966).

[3] On Le Nain, see A. Blunt, *Art and architecture in France 1500–1700*, London, 1953, 179–80. *Les Frères Le Nain*, the catalog of the 1978 Paris Le Nain exhibition at the Grand-Palais, discusses questions of attribution and subject matter.

ants' destitution and suffering in bad times. It may serve equally to high-
light the distress that underlay some of the French agrarian revolts earlier
in the century.[4]

To approach these revolts, whether in France or elsewhere, we first
need to distinguish them analytically from the background of recurring
low-level rural protest to be found in the peasant-based states of the age.
The early modern society was turbulent anyway, and its people turned
swiftly to self-help and violence. There is no reason to doubt the frequency of disorder flaring up in one community or another due to anger
over some immediate grievance. Quite limited in scale, taking the form of
brief, isolated threats or perhaps a riot, these minor incidents or micro-
seditions were likely to fade away or be repressed almost as quickly as
they arose. The number of participants in them also tended to be correspondingly small. In the English county of Kent, for instance, no popular
disturbance between 1558 and 1640 seems to have involved more than a
hundred people. Likewise in the French province of Provence, we are
told, the disturbances of the seventeenth century were most often narrowly local and of very brief duration.[5] Occurrences of this sort might
cause a slight concern to the authorities, but in a comparative sense they
are below the threshold of revolt. Similarly, we may question whether a
duration of longer than a single day is sufficient, as one writer has prem-
ised in the case of France, to demarcate a revolt from a riot or other mo-
mentary disturbance.[6] Admittedly, we have no precise, agreed-on formula to resolve this problem, which must therefore be left to the historian's
informed judgment. Nevertheless, I believe we may at any rate recognize
that most of the episodes of peasant and rural disorder we come across
represent merely the comparatively unimportant, repetitive murmur of
discontent or protest endemic to the society, which are thus to be differentiated from the bigger, more protracted, and altogether more formidable outbreaks that rise above them to signal the undeniable reality of agrarian rebellion.

A further distinction needs to be observed between agrarian rebellion
as the main and central point of action and its presence as a subordinate

---

[4] J. de La Bruyère, *Les Caractères ou les moeurs de ce siècle*, (1688), cited from 4th ed., 1689,
ch. 11. See the account by P. Goubert, "The French peasantry in the seventeenth century:
A regional example," in *Crisis in Europe 1560–1660*, ed. T. Aston, New York, 1965, for
certain similarities, although La Bruyère's picture is even darker and more extreme.

[5] P. Clark, "Popular protest and disturbance in Kent, 1558–1640," *Economic history review*,
2nd ser., *29*, 3 (1976), a study that includes both town and country and illustrates the influence of conjunctural factors on such disturbances; for Provence, R. Pillorget, *Les Mouvements
insurrectionnels de Provence entre 1596 et 1715*, Paris, 1975, 987.

[6] See Y.-M. Bercé, *Histoire des Croquants: étude des soulèvements populaire au XVII⁰ siècle dans
la sud-ouest de la France*, 2 v., Geneva, 1974, v. 2, 674, for the specification of a popular revolt
as the formation of an armed crowd from several different communities that maintains itself
longer than a day.

aspect within other encompassing types of revolution. Agrarian grievances and peasant insurgency could manifest themselves in several different kinds of movements. They could be a part, for example, of some provincial revolts and revolutionary civil wars. From a typological standpoint,
however, the examination of agrarian rebellion presupposes for it a predominant and focal role within the domain constituted by the revolutionary event.

If we attempt to chart the highlights of agrarian resistance in the lands
and time span that concern us, a number of striking differences appear.
The realms of peninsular Spain did not experience any rebellions, and
certainly none of any significance, that were predominantly peasant and
agrarian in character. We do, of course, find occasional peasant involvement in other types of movement, such as the Castilian revolt of the Comuneros in 1520, a great urban rebellion, and the revolt of Catalonia in
1640, a provincial rebellion. We also find a few outbreaks in seigneurial
villages accompanying the disturbances of 1647–52 in Andalusia, reac-
tions due to hard times and whose main sites were the cities of Seville,
Granada, and Cordoba.[7] What we do not see in Spain, however, is any
major rebellion based on the rural countryside and its inhabitants. The
last insurrection of this kind that we can observe had taken place during
the later fifteenth century in Catalonia – the war of the *remensas*, in which
the peasants freed themselves from servitude and the heaviest seigneurial
obligations. Thereafter, the peasant masses of rural Spain remained largely
immune to agrarian revolt.[8] The same seems also to have been true in this
period of the Spanish monarchy's possessions elsewhere in Europe, although there was a peasant side to the Naples revolt of 1647, essentially
an urban rebellion.[9]

In the case of England, we find peasant grievances as a strand in certain
wider movements like the Pilgrimage of Grace of 1536 and the great revolution of the 1640s. We also see small, intermittent rural disorders
throughout the period, frequently coinciding with depressed economic
conditions and apt to be aimed against enclosures, high prices, hoarders,
and forestallers.[10] The first and biggest agrarian insurrection of the sixteenth century was Kett's rebellion of 1549, centered in Norfolk. Some
forty-five years later, we note scattered rioting and attempts upon enclo-

[7] Gutiérrez Nieto, *Las comunidades como movimiento anti-señorial*, Barcelona, 1973; J. H.
Elliott, *The revolt of the Catalans*, Cambridge, 1963, 421–2; A. Dominguez Ortiz, *Alteraciónes
Andaluzas*, Madrid, 1973, 22–39, 48–53.

[8] See R. Hilton, *Bond men made free*, New York, 1973, 112, 117–18; J. H. Elliott, *Imperial
Spain*, London, 1963, 26, 29, 69.

[9] R. Villari alludes to a *"guerra contadina"* in connection with the Neapolitan revolt, "Mov-
imenti antifeudali dal 1647 al 1799," in *Mezzogiorno e contadini nell' età moderna*, Bari, 1961,
118–41; see also Chapter 9 in this book.

[10] See J. Thirsk, "Enclosing and engrossing," in *The agrarian history of England and Wales
1500–1640*, ed. J. Thirsk, Cambridge, 1967.

sures and grain supplies, a product of the poor harvests and hard times of the 1590s.[11] Again, in 1607, a series of risings broke out against enclosures in several of the midland counties, which lasted about a month and involved crowds as large as five thousand people. The insurgents called themselves levellers and diggers, names afterward famous when borne by radical groups in the English revolution.[12] Two decades later, between 1628 and 1631, the crown's enclosure of royal forests in several western counties led to resistance by communities and tenants of the region. Finally, during the 1630s we meet with occasional disturbances in the Fens, the marshy areas of the east coast, where villagers opposed the drainage reclamation projects of the crown and entrepreneurial landlords, which threatened their livelihood and communal rights.[13] In the other possessions of the English monarchy, Ireland, and, after 1603, Scotland, we find no movement that can be categorized as an agrarian revolt. In England itself, Kett's rebellion exceeded all other demonstrations of peasant resistance and was the only one of its kind to present a serious danger to authority.

It was on the soil of the French monarchy that the highest incidence of agrarian rebellions occurred, besides countless lesser manifestations of peasant and other disorders. The first and biggest such revolt in the sixteenth century was that of 1548 in Guienne and other southwestern provinces, a conflict that continued for about five months and roused tens of thousands to action.[14] Peasant revolts also erupted as subsidiary episodes in the long revolutionary civil war that wracked France from 1562 to al-

---

[11] *Ibid.*, 229; E. Lipson, *The economic history of England*, 3 v., London, 1929–43, v. 2, 400–1; see also Ch. 5 in this book.

[12] Thirsk, "Enclosing and engrossing," 232–5; Lipson, *The economic history of England*, v. 2, 403.

[13] D. G. C. Allan, "The rising in the west," *Economic history review*, 2nd ser., 5, 1 (1952); Thirsk, "The farming regions of England," *The Agrarian history of England and Wales*, 38–40; Lipson, *The economic history of England*, v. 2, 374–6.

[14] For the revolt of 1548 in Guienne, see G. Procacci, *Classi sociali e monarchia assoluta nella Francia della prima metà del secolo XVI*, Turin, 1955; Y.-M. Bercé, *Croquants et Nu-pieds*, Paris, 1974, ch. 1; and J. H. M. Salmon, *Society in crisis: France in the sixteenth century*, New York, 1975, 35–7. Bercé's regional work of synthesis on revolts in the southwest does not discuss this event in detail but stresses its scale and archetypal character (*Histoire des Croquants*, v. 2, 674–5). The latter contains a table of dates and locales of the main southwest revolts from 1548 to 1707, as well as maps indicating their distribution; *ibid.*, 674–5 and end. It also lists the different kinds of outbreaks (*ibid.*, v. 2, 855–63) but fails to explain this enumeration or its basis, thus making it all but impossible to understand. Bercé estimates a total of 450–500 revolts in the southwest (Aquitaine) from 1590 to 1715 (v. 2, 681–2); this figure, however, is far too large and needs indefinite scaling down, inasmuch as it includes many very small events and is also based on counting outbreaks or "*éclats*," into which the individual movements are subdivided. For revolts in Provence between 1596 and 1715, the similar work of synthesis by Pillorget, *Les Mouvements insurrectionnels*, contains data on the number and kinds of movements (379–80, 386–9, 988). This study proposes no criterion of revolt and conflates all disturbances or occurrences of collective violence, whatever their size, nature, or object, under the general head of "insurrectional movements." Its figures also present unexplained

most the end of the century. There were such outbreaks in the late 1570s in Dauphiné, others in Normandy and Brittany in the 1590s, and in the period 1592–5 the southwestern provinces were the site of the Croquant revolts, a name that was to reappear in succeeding peasant movements of the earlier seventeenth century.[15] After these last we see, again in the southwest, an agrarian revolt in 1624 in Quercy. Then we reach the 1630s and 1640s, the period immediately preceding the Fronde, when France was overwhelmed by a paroxysm of agrarian uprisings, along with other kinds of revolution sometimes difficult to separate from one another. Nearly every year of this strife-torn time brought one, two, or more revolts in the rural countryside extending over numerous provinces from south to center to north, although the main sites were in the southwest.[16] These chronic convulsions mobilized insurgents by the scores of thousands. Porchnev has even suggested that the Croquant revolts of 1636–7, affecting more than a quarter of France in the territory between the Loire and the Garonne, constituted the greatest peasant rebellion in French history.[17] Another serious outbreak with peasant involvement was the Normandy revolt of the Nu-pieds in 1639, which is better considered, however, as a provincial rebellion. Because of the insurrectionary epidemic and other troubles of these calamitous years, the realm of Louis XIII and Richelieu was reduced to a condition of *"dérèglement,"*[18] autocratic monarchy contending against sedition and resistance as a fitting prelude to the Fronde.

Finally, we come to Germany and the peasant war, which we have included in order to widen our comparative base. When Mousnier made his study of French peasant revolts in the seventeenth century, he picked contemporary Russian and Chinese peasant struggles for comparison.[19] This was an unfortunate choice, notwithstanding the manifest interest of the ensuing account. If we want to understand the possibilities and nature of peasant action in early modern Europe, we need particularly to consider agrarian rebellion in France alongside its counterparts within states of the same society. In a broad sense, English, French, and German peasants (and, as far as the last are concerned, we are dealing primarily with southern and western Germany) belonged to a similarly structured social

discrepancies: for example, the number of movements between 1596 and 1635 is stated as 103 in one place and 108 in another (380, 933).

[15] For the term *Croquant*, and the peasant insurrections connected with the civil war, see the discussion of French agrarian rebellions in the present Chapter 7 below.

[16] Besides the works of a regional focus cited above, n. 14, see B. Porchnev, *Les Soulèvements populaires en France de 1623 à 1648*, trans. from the Russian, Paris, 1963, for a survey of revolts in the earlier seventeenth century containing chronological tables and accompanying maps.

[17] *Ibid.*, 60.　　[18] V. L. Tapié, *La France de Louis XIII et de Richelieu*, Paris, 1967, 205.

[19] R. Mousnier, *Fureurs paysannes: Les Paysannes dans les révoltes de XVIIe siècle*, Paris, 1968; for a critical discussion, see M. Gately, A. L. Moote, and J. Wills, "Seventeenth-century peasant 'furies': some problems of comparative history," *Past and present 51* (1971).

organism and felt the effects of parallel political and economic changes that dominated the transition from the later Middle Ages to the early modern epoch. Politically, the regimes in which they were subjects also resembled one another more than they did the Russian tsardom or the Chinese empire. Despite their differences, these peasants accordingly had more in common with each other than with either Russian or Chinese peasants. Thus, even the distinctive features of peasant revolts in France are likely to stand out most clearly when seen in relation to movements of the same type elsewhere within the Western Europe of the sixteenth and seventeenth centuries.

In Germany, the peasant war was preceded by a number of agrarian rebellions usually regarded as forerunners.[20] Germany, of course, was neither a unitary kingdom like England or France nor a dynastic association like the states of the Spanish monarchy. It consisted, rather, of hundreds of separate, independent political entities weakly joined together in the federal structure of the "Holy Roman Empire of the German Nation" under the emperor as its elective head. The empire was a vast conglomeration of territorial principalities big and little, secular and ecclesiastical lordships, imperial knights, and free imperial cities, among whom particularist interests held sway; it contained many overlapping jurisdictions and states with discontinuous domains; it still nominally included the Swiss confederation, Italian fiefs, and several of the Netherlandish provinces.[21] Of the empire's many ruling families, the Habsburgs, the house of Austria, were preeminent, their hereditary lands and acquired possessions running east to west from the borders of Hungary to the Rhineland.

In the late fifteenth and first years of the sixteenth century, repeated peasant insurrections took place in southern Germany. Directed against both secular and clerical authorities, they appear in the southwest and in eastern Switzerland; in Austria; in Württemberg, site of the "Poor Conrad" revolt of 1514; and on the upper Rhine in the successive "Bundschuh" revolts, the last in 1517, where the rebels proclaimed their plebeian defiance of superiors by displaying the rude peasant's shoe as their emblem.[22] These recurrent struggles culminated in the peasant war, which embraced nearly all the previous areas of revolt and also extended far beyond over west, southwest, and central Germany, besides including diverse

---

[20] G. Franz, *Der deutsche Bauernkrieg*, 9th ed., Darmstadt, 1972, bk. 1, discusses these earlier revolts as "*Vorläufer.*" The maps at the end indicate their location and also the regions affected by the peasant war.

[21] G. Benecke, *Society and politics in Germany 1500–1750*, London, 1974, chs. 1–2, contains a useful description of the Empire and its components.

[22] Franz, *Bauernkrieg*, bk. 1; A. Laube, "Precursors of the peasant war: *Bundschuh* and *Armer Konrad*," *Journal of peasant studies 3*, 1 (1975).

Austrian lands.[23] Although it remained a cluster of separate outbreaks rather than a single integrated movement, it stands out as not only the greatest mass uprising in German history but as probably the biggest agrarian rebellion ever to take place in Western Europe.[24] At its height in the spring of 1525, as many as 300,000 peasants were said to be up in arms.[25] This figure may well be exaggerated, given the notorious unreliability of sixteenth-century estimates of this kind, but of the unprecedented magnitude of the German peasant revolt there can scarcely be any doubt.

II

Shorn of its empirical diversities, agrarian rebellion in its basic typological features may be summarized as follows, using the criteria suggested in an earlier chapter.[26]

First, its socioeconomic participation is primarily peasant in character and is accordingly dominated by low-status cultivators, tenants, and workers of the land subject to nobilities and landlords.

Second, its geographic and political space remains more or less restricted so that it only expands and aggregates over a limited extent.

Third, its aims express preeminently the grievances and desires of peasant communities, which range from a call for the removal of elementary economic burdens to demands for personal freedom, communal autonomy, and political reforms. The targets of threat and violence, corresponding to the aims, may be immediate political authorities, the lives and property of landlords, or agents of the central government.

Fourth, rebel mobilization and organization always build upon and utilize existent community structures and networks of the agrarian socioeconomic order.

[23] The peasant war actually extended as far as East Prussia where, after repression had succeeded nearly everywhere, a final salvo of rebellion broke out in September 1525; see F. Carsten, "Der Bauernkrieg in Ostpreussen 1525," *International review of social history 3* (1938). Maps of the peasant war in Franz, (*Bauernkrieg*), Putzger (*Historischer Weltatlas*, 84th ed., Berlin, 1963), and the *Cambridge modern history atlas*, Cambridge, 1912, leave much to be desired in the way of detail and clarity.

[24] See F. von Bezold, *Geschichte der deutschen Reformation*, Berlin, 1890, 449.

[25] This figure is often cited; see *ibid.*, 486, and H. Holborn, *A history of modern Germany: the Reformation*, New York, 1959, 173.

[26] For these criteria, see Chapter 2 in this book. The remarks that follow are directed to early modern agrarian revolts. General discussions and reviews of the literature and problems of peasant and agrarian revolutionary movements appear with increasing frequency. For some specimens, see E. Wolf, *Peasant wars of the twentieth century*, New York, 1969, and "On peasant rebellions," in *Peasants and peasant societies*, ed. T. Shanin, Baltimore, 1972; H. Landsberger (ed.), *Rural protest: peasant movements and social change*, London, 1974; see also the useful paper written for my seminar by D. Deal and published as "Peasant revolts and resistance in the modern world: a comparative view," *Journal of contemporary Asia 6*, 2 (1976). Hilton, *Bond men made free*, deals generally with the characteristics of medieval peasant movements.

Fifth and last, rebel mentality, justificatory belief, or ideology draw their strength from custom, religion, or both.

These can be seen as the irreducible traits or core elements constituting agrarian rebellion as a form of early modern revolution. Around them, however, additional characteristics and complications may gather as we look at the concrete reality of certain of these movements.

Such revolts, if predominantly peasant conflicts, seldom consist entirely of peasants.[27] As Hilton has observed, there were few "pure" peasant movements "in the sense that the participants and leaders were exclusively of peasant origin."[28] Likely to be commingled in them, too, were craftsmen, tradesmen, and other miscellaneous common folk who, as we have previously pointed out, belonged by occupation and habitation to the rural and village world.[29] On occasion we also find lower clergy and bourgeois elements among the rebels, and sometimes we see noblemen or other elites giving leadership, assistance, or complicity.

A further feature often noticeable in agrarian revolts – especially the larger movements – is their influence upon the town. The spark of rebellion that breaks out in the country spreads to adjacent towns, or to the principal town of the region, igniting parallel revolts that may either remain independent or combine with rural and peasant rebels. The English peasant revolt of 1381 provides an earlier example in the support it received from Londoners as the insurgent forces approached the capital. The 1548 rebellion in Guienne included a revolt in Bordeaux, the chief city of the province and seat of the provincial government. In the Norfolk revolt of 1549, the movement coalesced around Norwich, the economic and political center of East Anglia, which first cooperated with the rebels and then was seized by them.[30] The involvement of towns and townsmen was especially widespread in the German peasant war and also occurred in some of the French seventeenth-century agrarian rebellions.

This phenomenon of town involvement was a result of the internal social, economic, and other tensions existing in early modern towns with

[27] I have previously referred (see Chapter 3) to differences among anthropologists and other students concerning the meaning of *peasant*. In our present context, the description offered by Barrington Moore is satisfactory, if not exhaustive: "A . . . history of subordination to a landed upper class recognized and enforced by the laws . . . sharp cultural distinctions, and a considerable degree of de facto possession of the land, constitute the main distinguishing features of a peasantry" (*Social origins of dictatorship and democracy*, Boston, 1966, 111n.).

[28] Hilton, *Bond men made free*, 122, and 35–7, 112–13, 125–8, for other comments on the mixed composition of peasant movements.

[29] See Chapter 3 in this book.

[30] On London in 1381, see Hilton, *Bond men made free*, 186 ff. The involvement of Bordeaux (and other towns) in the revolt of 1548 is discussed by Procacci, *Classi sociali*, 220–1, and Bercé, *Croquants et Nu-pieds*, 20 ff. For the support of Kett's rebellion in Norwich, see A. Fletcher, *Tudor rebellions*, 2nd ed., London, 1973, 65–6. Several of these cases are discussed in Chapter 8 of this book.

their heavy inequalities, upon which the rural outbreak acted as a catalyst. In the German case particularly, there had been numerous specifically urban insurrections prior to the great agrarian revolution of 1525.[31] But the reason for the urban accompaniment to such conflicts is also to be seen in the overlap and interdependence of town and country. Everywhere, some towns performed essential market functions for their rural areas; peasants inhabited town suburbs; wine growers, market gardeners, and other small agriculturalists were part of town populations; municipal governments, like those of German imperial cities, had peasant subjects of the surrounding rural zone under their political jurisdiction; the urban well-to-do owned lands or seigneuries with peasant tenants; and citizens like the German *Ackerbürger*, a status found in numerous towns, held and cultivated land as their occupation. The diverse ties that thus linked rural folk with urban, together with the possible congruence of interests among plebeian strata, facilitated alliances and the diffusion of revolt from one to the other.

In recognition of the fact that agrarian and peasant rebellion might be associated with urban risings and lead to wide plebeian participation in its area of action, some historians prefer to view it within the vaguer, more inclusive category of popular revolts. This is the description frequently applied to French seventeenth-century insurrections, which one recent writer has defined as movements "in which peasants or artisans constitute the dominant clientele and where the insurrectional theme presents a specifically popular ideology." (Noble resistance, conspiracies, and religious wars are thereby held to be excluded, even though they may carry the popular masses in their train.)[32] For similar reasons, it has been pointed out that the German peasant war was fundamentally a revolt of the "common man," of nonprivileged townsmen, citizens, and even miners, and not only of peasants. The same observation has likewise been made about the Norfolk revolt of 1549, which has been called a "rising of the common man, the man in the street as well as the man in the field."[33]

To clarify these "popular revolts," certain typological refinements have

[31] See K. Kaser, *Politische und soziale Bewegungen im deutsche Bürgertum zu Beginn des 16. Jahrhunderts*, Stuttgart, 1899; and R. Endres, "Zünfte und Unterschichten als Elemente der Instabilität in den Städten," *Historische Zeitschrift*, Beiheft 4, *Revolte und Revolution in Europa*, 1975.

[32] See the titles of Porchnev, *Les Soulèvements populaires*, and Bercé, *Histoire des Croquants*, which speak of their subjects as "soulèvements populaires." The definition is from the latter, v. 1, 2. Note, however, that Bercé's shorter work, *Croquants et Nu-pieds*, which covers the same ground, refers in its subtitle to "peasant revolts" ("soulèvements paysans").

[33] See P. Blickle, "Thesen zum Thema-der Bauernkrieg als Revolution des 'gemeinen Mannes,' " in *Historische Zeitschrift*, Beiheft 4, 129–30, and *Die Revolution von 1525*, Munich, 1975, pt. 2, ch. 2. The German peasant rebels often referred to themselves as the "common man"; see the citations in *ibid.*, 177–9. For the Norfolk revolt of 1549, S. T. Bindoff, *Ket's rebellion*, London, 1949, 20.

been suggested for the French cases. Bercé, whose definition of them we have just quoted, has employed a "typologie des émeutes du XVIIᵉ siècle" of four classes, representing their immediate causes, occasion, and objective. According to this schema, there are revolts of or arising from (1) the high price of bread; (2) the quartering of troops; (3) the collection of *tailles;* (4) the activities of tax farmers.[34]

Another historian of French revolts in a provincial setting considers them generically as "insurrectional movements," which fall into three types: (1) conflicts within the same village or town over material issues, power, or prestige; (2) conflicts between a village or town and an external enemy, whether seigneur, bishop, tax farmer, soldiers, or other, in defense of property or community privileges; (3) conflicts between the province, as represented by particular groups or corporate bodies, and the central royal power.[35]

What the foregoing instances demonstrate, the German, English, and French alike, is that revolutions are often apt to be composite, polyvalent phenomena not easily reduced to a single type or model. They display, as would be expected, properties susceptible to typological description in several alternative ways. We must remember, however, that the type is an abstract construct based on criteria that represent a selection, accentuation, and assemblage of certain relevant characteristics from the multifold reality. The several types proposed for French revolts are both too restrictive in themselves and too exclusively related to the French cases to be adaptable to wider comparative study in the early modern context; moreover, some "insurrectional movements" are merely expressions of collective violence, which do not qualify as revolts at all. On the other hand, the description of the German peasant war as more than a peasant struggle, as a "revolution of the common man," has slight value for typological purposes, pertinent as it is to the particular case.

Thus, I believe that agrarian rebellion provides the best and most appropriate category for getting a purchase on the numerous movements in which peasant action constitutes the center of gravity of the revolutionary event. It is the peasant who stands at the heart of agrarian revolts, no matter which other elements are present. We also require agrarian rebellion as a type in order to distinguish peasant-dominated conflicts from urban revolts; for the latter, too, will constitute a type whenever urban rebels are the main actors on the revolutionary scene, whether appearing

[34] See Bercé, *Histoire des Croquants*, v. 2, 537–8; the same writer's *Croquants et Nu-pieds*, 82 ff., also contains a typological treatment of these revolts.
[35] Pillorget, *Les Mouvements insurrectionnels*, 151–3. The author declares that he will not classify movements according to social groups such as peasants or artisans because in specific cases "it is not always possible . . . to discern in an *émeute* a majority participation – in particular in those towns where peasants, artisans, merchants, and lawyers all live within the walls, alongside one another" (*ibid.*, 150).

alone or as the focal point of a more diverse involvement. Furthermore, there is no need to multiply the types of revolution by an overly elaborate differentiation. Parsimony is preferable, and the single category of agrarian rebellion will accommodate the several variations that are observable in its concrete, individual manifestations.

III

THE GERMAN PEASANT WAR

Of the agrarian rebellions of early modern Europe, the German peasant war was the most complex and many-sided. It contained the broadest social participation, the greatest variety of revolutionary projects pursued by rebels, the most highly developed ideology, and the fullest vision of reform. Its history disproves the conventional assumption that peasant movements are condemned to be narrowly apolitical, dedicated only to redressing specific injustices, and unable to strive for basic change.[36]

Whereas most French agrarian revolts were elicited by hatred of the state's oppressive tax exactions, and Kett's Norfolk revolt by grievances against landlords, the peasant war took on both rulers and landlords at once, partly because in the peculiar conditions of Germany the two were often identical. These same conditions also made it impossible for the revolt to have a primary center. Fragmented like the German political structure itself, with its myriad units, the peasant war broke out and spread in scattered nuclei, pitted against many independent authorities who exercised power over peasants and town lower orders – territorial princes, bishops and cathedral chapters, abbots and monastic houses, counts and other possessors of little statelets, and city councils.

In spite of its regional differentiation and dispersion and a consequent diversity of conditions, the main origins of the peasant war lay in similar long-term causes. In the socioeconomic domain, the conjunctural trends of the century prior to 1525 tended to be advantageous for many peasants, while at the same time imposing new strains upon agrarian communities. Accelerated population growth in the later fifteenth century increased the

---

[36] See Deal, "Peasant revolts and resistance," 433. Robert Redfield, an anthropologist of peasant societies, expresses a common opinion in remarking how "in European history . . . no peasant revolt had revolution as its goal" and that peasants were only concerned with abuses of power and the failure of gentry and elites to perform their traditional role (*Peasant society and culture*, Chicago, 1956, 35, cited in M. Gluckman, *Order and rebellion in tribal Africa*, New York, 1963, 12). As regards the literature devoted to the German peasant war, it is increasing very rapidly due in part to the observance in 1975 of the revolt's 450th anniversary, which has stimulated a flood of publications. Some of the latter are cited in the following notes. For an extensive survey of writings on the subject, see T. Scott, "The peasants' war: A historiographical review" (2 pts.) *Historical journal* 22, 3–4 (1979). V. Thomas (ed.), *Bibliographie zum deutschen Bauernkrieg und seiner Zeit*, Stuttgart, 1976, is a bibliography of publications since 1974, containing 373 titles.

competition for land, stimulated the partition of tenancies, and made it harder for peasant offspring to obtain holdings. Pressure on the communal resources of villages and manors – the common fields, woods, and so forth – intensified. Lords sought to extract higher rents for land and higher fines for entry to tenancies. As economic differentiation grew more pronounced within peasant communities, so did the frictions between peasants and the lords of land and serfs.

Serfdom, which, although declining, was still apparently widespread in the southwest and west on secular and ecclesiastical estates alike, neither prevented peasant well-being nor necessarily made for a depressed position within the agrarian community.[37] Its disabilities, however, were a hardship in several different ways. For one, a deceased servile tenant was obliged to pay a heriot or death duty (*Todfall*) to his lord or *Leibherr*, which could amount to as much as a third or more of the value of his goods. For another, the effects of serfdom upon marriage and the descent of holdings were particularly troublesome. Inheritance lay through the mother, so that marriage between serfs of different lords, which frequently did occur in areas of intermingled lordships, led to serious complications because the heir of a father belonging to one lord could not succeed to the paternal tenancy if the mother belonged to another. Confusion of obligations also resulted, as well as possible conflicts of rights between lords and succession disputes among peasants. Lords accordingly tried to prevent intermarriage and sometimes exchanged serfs. Then, finally, serfdom strengthened the lords' ability to control their peasants, to demand more services, payments, or new obligations, and to assert their economic and political interests against the peasant community.

In the political-juridical domain, the decisive factor behind the peasant war was the thrust of rulers and lords to gain new forms of power over their subjects and peasants. This was manifest in their attempts to set aside custom, to decree new law, to demand fresh exactions, to extend the competence of their courts and officials, and to encroach on the self-governing attributes of agrarian communities. The process was highly complicated due to the dismemberment of Germany and the existence of different overlapping authorities to which peasants might be subject: they might simultaneously be under the high justice of the territorial ruler, the low justice of a nearer jurisdiction, and subordinate as well to immediate lords either as free or servile tenants. The greater territorial princes, engaged in state building by ways analogous to the slow development of absolutism in the Western European monarchies, wished to remove the barriers of feudal custom and intermediate powers hindering their sovereignty to tax and legislate. Their reception of Roman law in place of cus-

---

[37] See the discussion of the peasant order in Chapter 3 in this book.

tomary codes was bound up with this need. To reduce their peasants to deeper subjection was one of their goals, as was another to subjugate the towns of their principalities. In the petty states, the ruler was also the landlord, so that here governmental and seigneurial authority were completely enmeshed.

Peasant communities, however, possessed their own autonomous sphere of activity and traditional forms of cooperation in villages and manors. Apart from their role in social and religious life, communities were concerned with the operations of the agricultural economy, the access of members to communal resources under specified restrictions, and the supervision in these and other matters of the rights and duties of tenants and inhabitants according to custom. They exercised their collective functions through their own officials chosen either by themselves alone or in conjunction with their lords. Of course, only peasants with land were full members of the community, which was by no means either democratic or egalitarian. The village community, or *Gemeinde*, with its attributes of autonomy was a protection to the peasant and an obstacle to the exclusive legal order, tighter political domination, and heavier economic demands that princes, lords, and masters wanted to impose on him. Through their communities, peasants preserved a degree of independence against superiors. In numerous cases prior to 1525, complaining or rebellious communities of villagers and tenants negotiated with their ruler or higher authority about grievances, sometimes with third parties as arbitrators.[38] Hence, it is understandable that the defense and self-assertion of the *Gemeinde* should have become one of the fundamental issues of the peasant war.[39]

In assessing the overall situation and the effects of *conjoncture* during the late fifteenth and early sixteenth centuries, it seems safe to say that the peasant order was not ground down by wretchedness and want. On the contrary, many peasants were well off and intent on preserving or bettering their condition. Rather than increasing exploitation or immiseration

[38] For some examples, including subjects of the prince-abbot of Kempten, the cloister of Ochsenhausen, and the duke of Württemberg, see the documents printed in G. Franz, *Quellen zur Geschichte des Bauernkrieges*, Munich, 1963, pt. 1, sec. A, and *Der deutsche Bauernkrieg, Aktenband*, Darmstadt, 1972 pt. A.

[39] For a discussion of socioeconomic and juridical-political conditions, see D. Sabean, "The social background to the Peasants' War of 1525 in southern upper Swabia," Ph.D. thesis, University of Wisconsin, 1969; P. Blickle, *Die Revolution von 1525*, Munich, 1975, pt. 1, secs. 1–3; and the account in J. Stalnaker, "Auf dem Weg zu einer sozialgeschichtlichen Interpretation des deutschen Bauernkriegs," in *Der deutsche Bauernkrieg 1524–1526*, ed. H.-U. Wehler, Göttingen, 1975; see also H. Buszello, *Der deutsche Bauernkrieg von 1525 als politische Bewegung*, Berlin, 1969, 8–9. I haven't been convinced by the argument of Blickle and of Marxist writers attempting to trace the peasant war to a "crisis of feudalism." For some regional diversity in the economic background, see the picture given of Alsace by F. Rapp, "Die soziale und wirtschaftliche, Vorgeschichte des Bauernkrieges im Unterelsass," in *Bauernkriegstudien*, ed. B. Moeller, Gütersloh, 1975.

driving them to revolt, it was both the need to defend established positions and the wish to gain improvements and throw off older burdens and obligations, which were now more acutely felt as oppressive. Even serfdom was probably much less important on its economic side than as a fetter upon marriage, physical mobility, and personal and communal independence. If we may distinguish the economic from the sociojuridical consequences of serfdom, then the latter bulked larger as a grievance than the former.[40]

Besides the long-term structural and conjunctural developments that underlay the peasant war, equally essential to its outbreak, as well as to its scale and timing was the increasing public ferment and questioning of authority that gripped Germany in those days. We shall see a similar climate surrounding Kett's rebellion and the seventeenth-century French revolts; Germany's condition, however, was far more volatile and grave.

Many voices critical of the existing order in church and empire proclaimed themselves before the peasant war.[41] Reformers both moderate and radical joined in the chorus. Among the latter, the famous *Reformation of Kaiser Sigismund*, "the first revolutionary pamphlet in the German language,"[42] was a call for a thorough religious and political renewal and the purification of society and went through at least eight editions between 1476 and 1522. Even more extreme in its perspective was the *Book of one hundred chapters*, written sometime between 1502 and 1513 by the so-called revolutionary of the upper Rhine, a plea for political and economic freedom that expressed a hatred of the governing powers and a glorification of the peasant whose labor enabled all to live.[43] The air was filled with a virulent anticlericalism reflecting widespread hostility to ecclesiastical wealth and power. Hussite beliefs, too, diffused through various channels, mingled in the rising tide of protest, hope, and desire for reform in

[40] See A. Waas, *Die grosse Wendung im deutschen Bauernkrieg*, Munich, 1939, 43–4; and W. Müller, "Freiheit und Leibeigenschaft-soziale Ziele des deutschen Bauernkrieges?" in *Historische Zeitschrift*, Beiheft 4, 270–1. Contemporary German historiography on the peasant war is strongly preoccupied with differences and disagreements of interpretation between "bourgeois" West German (DBR) and "Marxist" East German (DDR) scholarship. This issue crops up continually throughout the recent literature. For a list of divergent theses with regard to serfdom and the economic background to the rebellion, see R. Endres, "Zur sozialökonomischen Lage und sozialpsychischen Einstellung des 'Gemeinen Mannes,' " in Wehler, *Der deutsche Bauernkrieg*, 61–2. A useful survey of Western and Marxist and Soviet interpretations of the peasant war is given by T. Nipperdey and P. Melcher, *s.v.* "Bauernkrieg," *Sowjetsystem und demokratische Gesellschaft: eine vergleichende Enzyklopädie*, v. 1, Freiburg, 1966.
[41] See G. Strauss (ed.), *Manifestations of discontent in Germany on the eve of the Reformation*, Bloomington, 1971, for a good selection of illustrative texts.
[42] J. Janssen, *History of the German people at the close of the Middle Ages*, 16 v., London, 1905–10, v. 4, 132n.
[43] See Franz, *Bauernkrieg*, 65–6, 68–70. These two works are also discussed in their millenarian aspect as expressions of the hope for a future messianic emperor by Cohn, *The pursuit of the millennium*, 118–26. The *book of one hundred chapters* was not printed and circulated only in manuscript.

every sphere that spread over Germany on the eve of the Reformation. Many prophecies and astrological forecasts predicted some impending calamity or epochal event. The frequency of localized urban and agrarian insurrections testified to the refractory spirit stirring the inferior orders. The Bundschuh revolts of the early sixteenth century offered a fertile ground to some of the more radical ideas then current. Their conspiratorial leader, Joss Fritz, once a serf of the bishop of Speyer, built up an underground revolutionary organization in the belief that divine justice demanded the violent overthrow of the servitudes that rulers and lords laid upon the exploited people. Along with the peasant shoe (a symbol as eloquent as the later *sans-culotte* of revolutionary France), the Bundschuh rebels displayed the crucified Christ on their banner with a kneeling peasant beside him, proclaiming as their slogan, "God's justice only" ("Nichts denn die Gerechtigkeit Gottes").[44]

When Martin Luther presently appeared as a public figure, his resolute rejection of Rome and ecclesiastical authority infused the grievances and expectations in German society with a new intensity. Generations of Reformation scholars, however, who have concentrated on Luther's personal relation to the peasant war, have usually conceived the problem wrongly as a result. Undoubtedly, evangelical beliefs bred of the Reformation had a dynamic effect upon the revolution. But to view the latter primarily through the prism of Luther's history, or to consider it primarily in the light of his or even Protestant influence, is to narrow and distort it.[45] That his teaching may have helped encourage it is true, just as it is likely that his ferocious condemnation of the revolt helped inspire the princes to their bloody repression. Nevertheless, the peasant war was independent of and bigger than Luther. Not only did its fundamental causes long antedate his reformation activity, but it possessed a mighty life of its own that demands examination in its own right. What seems clear, though, is that his sensational defiance of pope and emperor, together with the turmoil it aroused, served as a signal to all the disruptive forces of the age.

[44] Franz, *Bauernkrieg*, 65–74.

[45] A typical example of this distorted perspective is K. Sessions (ed.), *The Reformation and authority: The meaning of the peasants' revolt*, Lexington, 1968, a collection of papers by various writers that is almost entirely concerned with the peasant war's relation to Luther and the Reformation and hardly at all with its characteristics as a revolutionary movement. Equally misconceived for the same reason was the very inadequate session devoted to the peasant war on its 45oth anniversary at the 1975 meeting of the American Historical Association. Or again, we might suppose that a volume of essays entitled *The social history of the Reformation* (ed. L. Buck and J. Zophy, Columbus, 1972) would find room for the peasant war as a significant movement in its own right. Instead, it is discussed by H. Hillerbrand in a paper devoted primarily to Luther, "The Reformation and the German peasants' war," in which the author is eager to exonerate Luther and the Reformation from responsibility for the revolt but takes little or no interest in the latter itself.

The peasants and common folk witnessed the challenge to the traditional order by the burgeoning reform. They were affected by the seething public controversies, the new preaching and countless outbreaks of religious strife, the refusal to pay tithes. They saw the overthrow of the old church by some of the princes and imperial towns, the Emperor Charles V unable to repress heresy, and the revolt of the imperial knights, led in 1522 by Franz von Sickingen in a futile attack against the archbishop of Trier, an electoral prince of the empire.[46] The Reformation plunged Germany into a great crisis of authority, bigger than it had ever known before. It was from this crisis, and from the climate of disobedience it created, that the peasant war received its immediate impetus.

The revolution started in the summer of 1524 with risings in the southwest corner of Germany on the domain of the abbey of Saint Blasius and at Stuhlingen by peasants of the count of Lupfen. Fading and then flaring again, the movement extended by year's end through the Black Forest and the entire region around Lake Constance. Thence gathering momentum, it flamed out of control like a prairie fire, throwing sparks in all directions. During the first months of 1525, the series of revolts spread all over Swabia, into Württemberg, through Alsace and north along the Rhine, into the Palatinate, Franconia, and Thuringia. In May, new outbreaks of revolt engulfed Tyrol and Salzburg and penetrated Styria and Carinthia. In the south, only Bavaria, where the ducal government crushed any agitation before it could expand, remained largely free of the conflagration.

The movement swept up a strange assortment of supporters in its chaotic course. Duke Ulrich of Württemberg, who had previously been deprived of his principality by the Habsburgs, joined the rebellion, calling himself Utz the Peasant, and tried to exploit it to effect his restoration. Mercenary imperial knights, members of an order ground between the upper and nether millstones of the princes and imperial cities, offered their services to the peasants. Some noblemen gave their adherence, and numerous clergy were sympathizers.

The revolution's startling advance was assisted by the lack of adequate power to resist it. When it began, most of the army of the Swabian League, the only effective military force in southern Germany, was absent in Italy, fighting with the troops of the Emperor Charles V against Francis I of France for supremacy in the peninsula. Imperial, territorial, and civic officials stood surprised and fear-stricken as they watched the peasants and common folk rise by the thousands. They could do little to stem the growing insurgency, and there was much temporizing and many local negotiations by authorities with rebel groups. On February 24, 1525, the em-

---

[46] See W. R. Hitchcock, *The background of the Knight's revolt 1522–1523*, Berkeley, 1958.

peror won his decisive victory over the French at Pavia. This event freed the Swabian League veterans to return across the Alps for the repression that ensued.

The main targets of peasant action throughout the revolt were monasteries and castles. Many were attacked and plundered, and their inmates seized or driven away. If anything, peasant hostility was even fiercer against ecclesiastical than secular lords. Captive noblemen were made to swear allegiance to the peasant cause, and some were killed. The most notorious incident happened at Weinsberg, where the count of Helfenstein, with a dozen other lords, was forced to run the gauntlet and speared to death in the presence of his wife and children. Peasant bands also threatened and occupied towns, from which they demanded supplies and aid. Town uprisings and their fusion with rebel peasants led to attacks on the rich, pillaging, and the desecration of churches. Anti-Semitism was a tragic part of the rebellion, as it was of earlier German revolts and the whole German Reformation. Rebels turned their hatred upon Jews, demanding their banishment as usurers and the confiscation of their property. Authorities in some places protected Jews against the threat of rebel violence.

Militarily, the peasants were no match for their rulers and masters. Here and there they had experienced commanders like the imperial knights, Goetz von Berlichingen and Florian Geyer, in Franconia, although Goetz deserted in due course. At times they were armed with artillery, and on occasion some of the Swabian League *Landsknechts*, sons of peasants themselves, refused to fight against them and went over to their side. All told, however, peasant troops, despite attempts at military efficiency, were too ill-disciplined, untrained, and poorly led to withstand noblemen and professional soldiers. With few exceptions, they were regularly defeated and slain by numerically weaker forces. (The biggest peasant success was the victory of the Salzburg insurgents at Schladming in July 1525 against an army captained by the territorial commander, Siegfried von Dietrichstein.)

Furthermore, the separate rebellions did not help each other or coordinate their strategy. Engels lamented the peasants' failure to unite for "concerted national action" and condemned "the appalling narrow-mindedness and the stubborn provincialism which ruined the peasant war."[47] Although true enough, these charges are beside the point. The provincialism of a decentralized Germany was then inevitable (indeed, we shall find some degree of provincialism in every revolution of early modern Europe), and no revolution can be expected to transcend the social and political conditions that determine it.

With the late spring of 1525, repression got under way in earnest as the

[47] F. Engels, *The peasant war in Germany*, 2nd ed., New York, 1926, 119, 130, 151.

German princes mobilized to stamp out the revolt. In Franconia and Swabia, Georg von Waldburg, general of the Swabian League, crushed the peasants in scattered engagements. The Thuringian movement was broken by the united power of the dukes of Saxony and Brunswick and the landgrave of Hesse. Elsewhere the margrave of Brandenburg, the duke of Lorraine, and other rulers joined against rebel towns and peasants. Nearly everywhere the revolution was bloodily liquidated or had flickered out by mid-summer, except for Salzburg and especially the Tyrol, one of the possessions of the emperor's brother, Archduke Ferdinand, where it smoldered on till the summer of the following year. Death, destruction, and horrible reprisals accompanied the peasants' defeat. At Zabern, the duke of Lorraine in battle against the Alsatian insurgents killed twenty thousand men. Whole communities were massacred and villages burned. Leaders and militants were tortured, beheaded, and roasted to death. Scores of rebels were blinded; others had their fingers chopped off. Countless numbers were summarily executed. Fines and confiscations were a routine punishment. With a few exceptions, the powers of Germany acted with insensate fury against the peasants and subjects who had dared to challenge their domination.[48]

IV

The peasant war at its height lasted some three months, from about March through May 1525. Its main participants, as we know, were a mass of peasants and villagers, seconded by the populace in different towns. To grasp its internal structure, we shall look summarily at its organizational features, its leadership, its urban as well as agrarian side, and its ideas, programs, and goals.

Organizationally, rebels had several models available to them. Leagues of princes, imperial knights, and free cities were a traditional part of German political life and very likely afforded some example. The use of oaths of association was also common to the time. The burgher oath in cities was a solemn expression of civic membership and corporate unity; and peasants themselves were obliged to swear oaths of obedience and fidelity to their *Herrschaft* or *Obrigkeit*.[49] Hence, the adaptation of oaths and covenants to the purposes of rebel association is not surprising. Most impor-

---

[48] The preceding summary is based mainly on the chief modern history of the peasant war by G. Franz, *Der deutsche Bauernkrieg*, 1933 and later editions, which is still unsuperseded. Despite his blatant prejudices, Janssen, *History of the German people*, v. 4, bk. 7, "The social revolution," provides vivid details drawn from a wealth of contemporary documentation. Engels, *The peasant war in Germany*, contains a concise narrative.

[49] See B. Moeller, *Imperial cities and the Reformation*, Philadelphia, 1972, 44–5; F. Rapp, "Les Paysans de la vallée du Rhin et le problème l'autorité civile (1493–1525)," *Recherches germaniques 4* (1974), 163–5.

tant as a model was the village community, the social cellule of the peasant world, which could be transposed to various circumstances and on a wider field.

A conspiratorial model also existed in the Bundschuh and its organizer, Joss Fritz.[50] There is no evidence, though, of any prior conspiracy in the origin of the peasant war. Traditions of underground activity may well have lingered in the Rhenish region of the Bundschuh, and Fritz himself, a man continually hunted by the authorities, may perhaps have just lived long enough to see the events of 1525; however, the great agrarian rebellion started without any advance preparation as a localized outbreak. The repeated spread of further risings was due to example and contagion in the disturbed atmosphere of the early Reformation, helped by rumor and propaganda, by the continual appearance of spokesmen and agitators, and by the physical movement of rebel bands and emissaries.

Mobilization followed communal lines as crowds of peasants belonging to a particular lordship, district, or jurisdiction streamed together carrying arms. Communities seem sometimes to have decided as a body to rebel. They then formed bands, or *Haufen*, which were organized and chose leaders paralleling the familiar *Dorf*, or village organization. The opening of revolt included acts of violence, refusal to render services and payments, and threats against lords and superiors. Presentation of grievances, parleys, and negotiations also took place between rebel communities and their lords.

At a further stage these peasant formations began to coalesce into much larger numbers drawn from a broader area. What then emerged as the mobilization process continued were organized bands, troops, or companies of thousands of peasants also called *Haufen*. Thus were created in upper Swabia the *Seehaufe* about Lake Constance, the Allgaüer *Haufe* further to the east, and the Baltringen *Haufe* further to the north, a fusion of villages and communities of different lords in their respective regions. At least five such *Haufen* came into being in Alsace, and others appeared on the right bank of the Rhine, in the Palatinate, Franconia, and elsewhere. These bands evolved a similar organization based on elected leaders and captains, councils of advisers, a clerk for correspondence, and perhaps supervisors of booty. They adopted ordinances to regulate their activities and collected lists of grievances from their constituent communities. The leaders had to deal with military tactics, provisioning, requisitioning of contributions, and other administrative problems resulting from mass re-

---

[50] On Joss Fritz, see Franz, *Bauernkrieg*, 66–79. Engels has an interesting account of Fritz's conspiratorial organization and the *Bundschuh* (78–85). H. Gerlach suggests that there were similar conspiratorial features between Fritz and "the great society" in the English peasant revolt of 1381 (*Die englische Bauernaufstand von 1381 und der deutsche Bauernkrieg; ein Vergleich*, Mersenheim, 1969, 173).

volt. They also communicated with lords and authorities over rebel demands.[51]

Fundamentally, the revolution of 1525 remained fissioned into disparate conflicts that showed no inclination to merge. As Germany was splintered, so was the peasant war. Insurrectionary peasants certainly demonstrated a strong sense of common identity as an order, but always in a bounded context and never to the extent of imagining a general union of revolt.[52] Some revolts, however, bore a particularist stamp and thus remained confined to a single territory and ruler, whereas others acquired a supraterritorial character. The former was the case in the bigger territorial states, notably Württemberg, Salzburg, and Tyrol, as also in such ecclesiastical principalities as Bamberg, Fulda, and Würzburg; the latter, in regions of political fragmentation like upper Swabia, the upper Rhine, and Franconia, with their many small rulers and authorities. In the former category, rebels limited their operations within territorial boundaries, sought to exclude outside *Haufen*, and negotiated directly with their prince; in the latter, on the other hand, the revolts as they unfolded spilled over onto wider fronts.[53]

Most significant was the development of the revolt in upper Swabia. There in early March representatives of the three *Haufen* previously formed out of scattered risings came together in a sort of "peasant parliament" at Memmingen to create a joint alliance. Reflecting the new evangelical ideas that had penetrated the peasant movement, they established a "Christian Union of Upper Swabia," with its aim the furtherance of God's law and justice. The union framed ordinances for itself, issued regulations for preaching, and prescribed an oath of association invoking God's word, law, and brotherly love as its justification. In one version of the oath, the peasants were to swear to have no other ruler but the emperor. According to its constitution, the union consisted of the three *Haufen*, each to be governed by a chief and four councillors, who were to consult and cooperate together. This arrangement contained the imprint of village experience: The peasant villages were commonly administered by a bailiff or mayor and four or more councillors. No community was to make an agreement with its lord without the union's foreknowledge and assent. The rules contained provisions for military discipline and relations with

---

[51] The organizational process can be followed in Franz, *Bauernkrieg, passim;* see also for upper Swabia, Sabean, *The social background of the peasants' war,* ch. 2; and, for Alsace, Rapp, "Les Paysans de la vallée du Rhin." For this and several other topics I have also used a seminar paper by my former student, Scott Garretson, "*Landschaft* and rebellion: The structure and politics of agrarian revolutionary movements in the German peasant war."

[52] See Franz's observations, *Bauernkrieg,* 134.

[53] See Buszello, *Der deutsche Bauernkrieg,* 19–21, 34. This work analyzes the peasant war and its political programs on the basis of the difference between supra- and intraterritorial movements.

outside groups. They also included pledges of mutual aid and obedience to leaders. Even a banner was specified, a red and white flag with a cross.[54]

Under the inspiration of the principle of godly justice, a Christian Union was also formed in April among the Black Forest insurgents. In Alsace, too, it spurred the fusion of a number of *Haufen*, who assembled in May at Molsheim, agreed on oaths and articles of association, and chose one of their leaders as their chief captain.[55] Defeat of the rebellion quickly ended these experiments, but they attest to the unprecedented initiatives the peasant war aroused. The highest level of organization was achieved in the Christian Union of Upper Swabia, which had no parallel elsewhere. Although created to meet immediate needs of defense and mutual aid, it also incorporated a wider political design. Its articles referred to the peasants as a *Landschaft*, or estate, and seemed to envisage their integration within a new reformed order based on God's word and law.

One other version of rebel organization also appeared, the work of the revolutionary millenarian, Thomas Müntzer. Müntzer's preaching prior to 1525 looked increasingly to the existence of an eschatological community of believers in readiness for the last days. He was preoccupied with "the elect friends of God," prophesying that through them God would shortly do marvelous things, "especially in this land."[56] In 1524, in the Saxon town of Allstedt, near the Thuringian locale where he was soon to die in the peasant war, he was organizing his followers into leagues of elect. We hear of two hundred members in the town and another three hundred outside, consisting mostly of copper miners at Mansfeld. They were small, sworn associations united by a covenant to uphold the gospel against the ungodly.[57] To his disciples in the nearby town of Sangershausen, he wrote, "More than thirty Leagues of covenanted elect have been formed – the game is on in all lands."[58] It was with this militant vanguard in mind, groups of elect determined purely by spiritual qualifications, that Müntzer embarked on his millenarian mission in the peasant war.

Who and what sort were the leaders of the revolution? We may gain a certain impression from some of the principal names that emerge. In the Black Forest, the soul of the revolt was its elected chief, Hans Müller of Bulgenbach, an ex-soldier or *Landsknecht* who moved about, it was re-

[54] This description of the Christian Union of Upper Swabia is derived from the relevant documents printed in Franz, *Quellen*, nos. 47–54, which include a "Bundesordnung," "Predigtordnung," and "Landesordnung." For accounts and comments, see Franz, *Bauernkrieg*, 127–30; and Buszello, *Der deutsche Bauernkrieg*, 53–5.

[55] See Franz, *Bauernkrieg*, 135–6; Rapp, "Les Paysans de la vallée du Rhin"; and the documents in Franz, *Quellen*, nos. 68, 76.

[56] From Müntzer's *Prague manifesto* (1521), in T. Müntzer, *Schriften und Briefe*, ed. G. Franz and P. Kirn, Gütersloh, 1968, 494.

[57] G. Rupp, *Patterns of reformation*, Philadelphia, 1969, 196, 198.

[58] Müntzer, *Schriften und Briefe*, 408.

ported, in almost princely state, clad in a red cloak and plumed hat, a peasant herald preceding, proclaiming the Christian Union. In upper Swabia, the leader of the Baltringen *Haufe* was Ulrich Schmid of Sulmingen, a pious, highly respected blacksmith. In Alsace, the foremost captain was Erasmus Gerber, an illiterate Molsheim tanner. Among the Franconian *Haufen*, several prominent figures appeared. There was the incendiary Jäcklein Rohrbach of Böckingen, a well-off serf of quarrelsome reputation, perhaps once connected with the Bundschuh; another was Wendel Hipler, educated and on the fringes of the lesser nobility, a chancery official of the counts of Hohenlohe who was at odds with his noble master; a third was Friedrich Weigandt of Miltenberg, tavern owner in Mainz. In Württemberg, one of the leaders was the prosperous, devout Matern Feuerbacher, innkeeper of Bottwar, a notable in his community, who tried to guide the revolt on a moderate course. In Tyrol, the outstanding personality was Michael Gaismair, a secretary in the Tyrolean government and then clerk to the bishop of Brixen, offspring of a peasant and miner's family.[59]

Considering these men and others who came to notice, it seems that hardly any of the leaders in the peasant war were peasants themselves. To be sure, several belonged to or had roots in peasant society, but by occupation they were apt to be clerks, artisans, and local tradesmen, some of whom, as we know, had also become converts to evangelical beliefs. In addition, there were the Protestant clergy who took part in the revolution as preachers and ideologues, among them Thomas Müntzer in Thuringia, the most famous, Balthasar Hubmayer in the Black Forest, Andreas Carlstadt, Luther's old colleague and adversary, in Franconia, and Christoph Schappeler in upper Swabia. There was a sprinkling of noblemen as well in positions of importance, Stephan von Menzingen, Goetz von Berlichingen, and Florian Geyer, all of them active in the Franconian revolt.

Finally, there came the lower leadership of rank-and-file cadres who formed the backbone of the peasant movement. From all accounts they were not the village poor or underlings. They included the richer peasants, mayors, bailiffs, and village officials, members of the *Dorfehrbarkeit*, innkeepers, and like worthies. The agrarian rebellion was not borne by the downtrodden dispossessed but by the more prosperous and substantial part of the rural common folk.[60]

In its urban aspect also, the peasant war revealed its amplitude and power. Sufficient inner tensions existed to propel many towns into disorder, tensions of long growth which can be read in the diverse urban revolts

---

[59] These descriptions are based on the biographical information in Franz, *Bauernkrieg*, 103, 135, 117, 142, 189, 191–2, 187–8, 196, 198, 217, 157.

[60] See *ibid.*, 285; and Sabean, *The social background of the peasants' war*, 173–5.

preceding 1525: everywhere restricted civic governments monopolized by patriciates and the wealthiest bourgeoisie; town commonalties and lesser guildsmen resentful at unequal taxation that spared the rich; antagonism toward town councils for their financial maladministration and lack of accountability. Added to these were the ever-present anticlerical grievances: dislike of the clergy's immunities and privileges, which exempted them from civic obligations; opposition to tithes; complaint of the commercial activity of clerical corporations, which made for unfair competition with urban traders. On top of all came the Reformation after 1520, underscoring old and creating new dissensions as religious supervened on socioeconomic frictions.[61]

The peasant war multiplied all these conflicts, threatening cities with a revolutionary situation. In the free imperial cities, constitutionally subject solely to the empire, town councils and commonalties stood generally opposed to each other. In the territorial towns, besides internal stresses, there was also the desire for autonomy against the territorial princely power. The pattern of events elicited in the epochal year 1525 therefore varied in accord with the different constellations of forces within and without that acted upon towns.[62] It must be stressed, though, that revolt came in the first place from the country to the town; the prior mobilization of the peasants was required to give rise to answering urban disturbance or revolt.[63]

Some towns actually united with the peasants. Heilbronn, Rothenburg, and several other imperial cities of Franconia admitted the peasants at the insistence of the populace and entered into fraternal relation with them. Similarly in Thuringia, due to Thomas Müntzer's influence, who was based in the imperial city of Mühlhausen, the revolt combined peasants and town lower orders in a single front.[64]

Elsewhere, imperial city authorities averted complete polarization of their communities or absorption in the peasant camp by appeasement, concessions, and benevolent neutrality toward the rebellious peasants.

[61] On urban tensions and conflicts and the civic Reformation, see Kaser, *Politische und soziale Bewegungen*, pt. 1; Endres, "Zünfte und Unterschichten"; Moeller, *Imperial cities*, 52, 54–5, 60; and S. Ozment, *The Reformation in the cities*, New Haven, 1975. T. Brady's study (*Ruling class, regime and Reformation at Strasbourg*, Leiden, 1978) contains an interesting discussion of the Protestant Reformation and the cities, as well as an illuminating treatment of Strasbourg, with full bibliographical references.

[62] The following remarks on the urban side of the peasant war are based on Kaser, *Politische und soziale Bewegungen*, pt. 2; Franz, *Bauernkrieg*, pt. E, *passim;* Buszello, *Der deutsche Bauernkrieg*, pt. 3; and Blickle, *Die Revolution von 1525*, pt. 2, ch. 2. See also O. Rammstedt, "Stadtunruhen 1525," in Wehler, *Der deutsche Bauernkrieg*.

[63] See the comments of Franz, *Bauernkrieg*, 227–8; and Blickle, *Die Revolution von 1525*, 171.

[64] See M. Bensing, *Thomas Müntzer und der Thüringer Aufstand, 1525*, Berlin, 1966, 143–4.

Pressures from below or the external threat from the peasants themselves dictated this course. Memmingen gave the lead to other Swabian imperial cities by opening its gates and receiving the peasants with sympathy. At the same time, it strove to mediate among the peasants, their lords, and the Swabian League. It was at Memmingen that the upper Swabian *Haufen* formed their Christian Union and adopted the Twelve Articles of the Peasants, the chief programmatic declaration of the revolution. In Alsace, the senate of the imperial city of Strasbourg followed a similar policy of conciliation, compromise, and mediation toward the insurgent peasants, while excluding and remaining quite dissociated from them. Internally, the civic government and ruling oligarchy kept firm control, in spite of the agitation among a population that contained viniculturists and other agricultural occupations as well as many discontented artisans. Both Strasbourg and other Alsatian towns granted citizenship to surrounding monasteries to protect them from the peasants.[65] In Frankfurt am Main, the city council bent to an insurrectionary movement of Protestants and guildsmen and negotiated over grievances expressed in a collection of articles that were widely circulated in the region.

In the towns ruled by territorial princes, the peasant war also evoked a significant response. Most of the administrative centers in the duchy of Württemberg rose. Salzburg's revolt against its prince archbishop brought together the city and the country, uniting peasants, townsfolk, and miners. In Tyrol, the towns joined the revolt, which was hardly less a bourgeois than a peasant movement, as well as including some communities of miners. Insurrection struck the towns in episcopal principalities such as Würzburg, Bamberg, Speyer, Worms, and the Archbishopric of Mainz. The further north the peasant war extended into the ecclesiastical states along the Rhine, the "priests' avenue" of the empire, the more it lost its peasant character and became a purely urban movement.[66]

The German peasant war was unique among agrarian rebellions in our period, as well as those before or after, in the magnitude of its urban involvement; it was also unique in the extent of its cooperation between peasants and townsmen. The active element in urban revolt and support for the peasants came from the middle and lower segments of town populations, from the lesser guilds, from the impassioned preachers of evangelical beliefs, and from the newly formed circles of Protestant townsfolk who embraced these beliefs. The breadth of the urban response was by no means due only to material grievances that may have lain ripe for ex-

---

[65] See J. Rott, "Artisanat et mouvements sociaux à Strasbourg autour de 1525," *Artisans et ouvriers d'Alsace 9* (1965); and the account by Brady, *Ruling class, regime and Reformation*, 199–208.

[66] Franz, *Bauernkrieg*, 228.

plosion. It was equally due to the effect of the idea of God's word and justice, a dynamic moral imperative that helped to generalize the movement.

Where the peasant and burgher revolts formed the closest ties, it was because they shared a common territorial attachment or *Landespatriotismus*.[67] This was most noticeable in the movements that remained territorially limited and probably reached its highest level in Tyrol. In this Habsburg principality, peasantry and towns enjoyed a long tradition of participation in the *Landtag*, or diet, which facilitated their accord in support of the demands made to the territorial ruler. Other factors that forged bonds between peasants and burghers in certain areas of the revolution were a common desire for emancipation from temporal or spiritual misgovernment, the perception of common enemies, and, again, the influence of evangelical teachings.[68] The claim to a justice based on God's word possessed a power transcending immediate situations and distinctions. Its influence undoubtedly served to draw peasant and urban rebels closer, as well as to create sympathy among town commonalties for the peasants' grievances.

This brings us, finally, to the ideology, programs, and goals of the peasant war. Dispersed as it was, the revolution could hardly have had a single, all-embracing goal. Instead, rebels pursued a number of aims related to the different revolts. Throughout, however, we see a general thrust toward freedom and the frequent linkage of immediate grievances with political objectives. Far from being exclusively an economic or social protest, the great agrarian rebellion was also, and perhaps even most of all, a conscious political struggle.

Preceding German peasant insurrections had usually sought their justification in older law and custom. Their appeal to what I have termed the normative past was certainly not devoid of religious meaning, but its main strength depended on the sanctity of what had been. It expressed the belief in an idealized ancient order, hallowed by use, which must be restored or preserved as the right relation between peasants and their particular superiors. Only in the Bundschuh did the germ of a further type of justification apart from custom appear, invoking God's law as the authorization for abolishing peasant servitudes.

There need, of course, be no polar opposition between these two conceptions: customary law, or *das alte Recht*, on the one hand; and God's justice, or *das göttliche Recht*, on the other. Both could incorporate a complex texture of themes, and each could also take something from the other. What finally separates them, however, is that the theological-religious jus-

[67] Buszello, *Der deutsche Bauernkrieg*, 141–2.
[68] See Kaser, *Politische und soziale Bewegungen*, 238, 258–9; and Blickle, *Die Revolution von 1525*, 171, 172–4.

tification is full of universalistic and ethical implications, which the appeal to custom lacks. Hence, historians have emphasized this difference as the cause of a significant contrast between the peasant war and its forerunners. For, owing to the Reformation, the affirmation of Scripture, God's word and law, as the necessary standard in human affairs received a vast new amplification. It thereby became the strongest ideological determinant in the peasant war and the main legitimation of revolt. As Günther Franz has noted, the evangelical interpretation of godly justice was the bridge on which the peasants, who had hitherto known only the old law, passed over onto the road of revolution.[69] But this theological-religious justification did not exclude the claims originating in custom. Rather, it took them up and embraced them within its own comprehensive Biblical principle. Of course, the demand for a justice consonant with God's word could also display a varying content and work in several ways, either less or more extreme. At one end, it could serve hopes of change of a relatively moderate kind; at the other, it could give rise to visions of millennial transformation. However, even though its uses differed, it was decisive in fueling the revolution and imbuing rebels with the consciousness of a new order.

The hundreds of articles of grievances put forward in the course of the revolt, along with the numerous proposals that emerged looking to freedom, reform, and reconstruction, faithfully reflected the extraordinary political ferment the peasant war aroused. Brief as it was, it stimulated an outburst of ideas and aspirations, a variety of programs, and a hope in new possibilities that were unparalleled in other agrarian rebellions. In its effect on the popular mind it can only be compared with some of the revolutionary civil wars of the early modern age. If unwillingness to be ruled in the old way is one of the hallmarks of a great revolution, as Lenin held, then the peasant war gave ample evidence of this characteristic.

Prominent amid the welter of demands were personal freedom for the serf and autonomy for village and urban communities. The insistence on autonomy, it has been rightly said, runs like a red thread through all the grievances and programs.[70] Peasants desired both emancipation from serfdom and social respect and a recognition of worth from their superiors as the necessary basis for any future cooperation. The will to direct participation in political life through corporative and estate organization was another basic theme in peasant programs. Common, too, in many rebellions was communities' insistence on popular election of their parish clergy. In some ecclesiastical principalities, demands were made for the secularization of the state with the transformation of the bishop into secular ruler.

[69] Franz, *Bauernkrieg*, 90.

[70] Buszello, "Gemeinde, Territorium, und Reich in den politischen Programmen des deutschen Bauernkrieges 1525/26," in Wehler, *Der deutsche Bauernkrieg*, 106.

Episcopal cities witnessed a call for the overthrow of the bishop's and chapter's power, the elimination of clerical privileges, and the reduction of both clergy and noble inhabitants to the same level as other citizens. Among the revolts that remained territorially confined, the chief aim was the limitation of the prince's power by the rights and autonomy of the territorial community as expressed through the diet or assembly of estates. In the supraterritorial movements, a frequent goal was the elimination of petty rulers and the absorption of their domains into some larger political structure by a still-to-be-determined reform. Along the same lines, the peasants' articles in some areas expressed the wish to be freed of subjection to their ruler and become immediate subjects of the emperor. Schemes also appeared to strengthen the empire and its institutions in order to make them more representative and curb obstructive particularism.[71]

Because of its wide dissemination and effect, the most important manifesto of the peasant war was the Twelve Articles of the upper Swabian peasantry, produced in March 1525 at Memmingen in the course of the formation of the Christian Union by the upper Swabian *Haufen*. Its draftsmen were two Memmingen Protestants, Christoph Schappeler, a clergyman, and Sebastian Lotzer, a fur dealer, who reduced more than three hundred grievance articles of peasant villages to a concise and representative statement. The Twelve Articles combined a list of practical demands with an ideological justification of the peasant struggle. Replete with Biblical references, they gave eloquent formulation to the conviction of godly justice, which had fused with the revolution and on which the peasants based their case. Despite the fact that the document was composed by religious intellectuals rather than peasants, it was nonetheless an authentic expression of peasant desires and aspirations.[72]

Addressed to the "Christian reader," the Twelve Articles began with a preamble denying that violence was the fruit of the gospel and that the peasants were rebels or against authority. Rather, they wished to live in obedience to Christ and God's word, whereas those who opposed their requests were antichrists and enemies of the gospel. The articles that fol-

[71] See the excellent survey of aims and programs in Buszello, *Der deutsche Bauernkrieg.*
[72] The text of the Twelve Articles with their full title is printed in Franz, *Quellen*, 174–9. Schappeler apparently wrote the preface while Lotzer compiled the list of demands. Every English translation I have seen omits the Biblical references. For detailed treatment of their background, content, and significance, see G. Franz, "Die Entstehung der Zwölf Artikel," *Archiv für Reformationsgeschichte 36*, 3 (1939); E. Walder, "Die politische Gehalt der Zwölf Artikel," *Schweizer Beiträge zur allgemeinen Geschichte 12* (1954); M. Brecht, "Der Theologische Hintergrund der Zwölf Artikel," *Zeitschrift für Kirchengeschichte 85*, 2, (1974); Blickle, *Die Revolution von 1525*, esp. pt. 1, sec. 2, and "The economic, social, and political background of the Twelve Articles," *Journal of peasant studies 3*, 1 (1975). Blickle's useful account includes a quantitative analysis of local grievance articles showing the considerable extent to which the Twelve Articles incorporated demands that the peasants regarded as of the greatest importance.

lowed strongly condemned the oppressions of lords, for which redress was sought. They demanded the election of parish clergy, the reduction of tithes, and their administration by the community. The detestable custom of serfdom was to be abolished because Christ's sacrifice has redeemed all men, and "therefore it is proven from Scripture that we are and wish to be free." Other articles required the restoration to the community of wrongfully appropriated common lands and rights to hunt, fish, and cut wood; the reduction of the grievous burden of labor services; the equitable regulation of rents and dues; the removal of arbitrary criminal jurisdiction and evil new laws contrary to custom; and the abolition of the heriot as an intolerable robbery of widows and orphans. In the conclusion, the peasants submitted their claims to the test of God's word; whatever could be shown not in accord with it they promised to make null and void.

The Twelve Articles dealt with fundamental questions of peasant economy, legal and social condition, and independence. Although they did not envisage the overturn of landlordship or rulership, they did project a significant strengthening of the peasant order by ending serfdom and restricting the powers of landlords and seigneurial and ruler jurisdiction. If the Bible and divine justice was their immanent principle, their keynote was the self-assertion of the organized peasant community, the *Gemeinde*, as the voice and vehicle of peasant interests. They captured and condensed to a high degree the essential character of the agrarian rebellion as a *Gemeinde* movement.

For these reasons, the Twelve Articles achieved exceptional influence. Printed first in March 1525, they were reprinted over twenty times in two months and became known throughout the empire and the entire area of the peasant war. They were imitated or adopted by other revolts and served as a model for additional demands. There is evidence, too, that they were read aloud and discussed in large crowds. Not only did they help to spread the rebellion, they gave currency to the revolutionary doctrine of a justice rooted in God's word.[73]

Throughout the peasant war, ideas of common good and common use recurred in demands and grievances. Even though most programs did not conceive of leveling social differences or abolishing landlordship and property, they looked to more fraternal relations, the curbing of privileges, and equitable government. The article-letter of the Black Forest peasants sketched the vague outline of a reformed society, a Christian brotherhood, to relieve the common man in town and country of his oppression. In the name of godly justice, it called upon noblemen, priests, and monks to

[73] For the range and effect of the Twelve Articles, see Blickle's discussion in *Die Revolution von 1525* and "The economic, social, and political background of the *Twelve Articles*," and G. Vogler, "Der revolutionäre Gehalt und die räumliche Verbreitung der oberschwabischen Zwölf Artikel," in *Historische Zeitschrift*, Beiheft 4.

enter into the brotherhood and live like other folk on penalty of the worldly ban – that is, complete exclusion from all social and economic intercourse.[74] The articles of the Franconian peasantry, imbued with the populist spirit, decreed that all privileged men, spiritual and temporal, shall henceforth possess no greater rights than the ordinary burgher or peasant.[75] The articles of the city of Frankfurt, which were also taken over by other towns, voiced the commonalty's demand for election of pastors, democratization of city government, and economic reforms for the welfare of the lower orders.[76]

Reliance on the estates as the organ of the community was a basic presupposition in the programs of intraterritorial revolts. It probably received its strongest expression in Tyrol in the comprehensive reform plan drawn up at a revolutionary meeting of peasant and town representatives at Meran in May 1525. The Meran articles invoked love of Christ, love of one's neighbor, and the common good as justification to create a "new *Landesordnung*," or territorial constitution. Here peasants and burghers drew on their previous experience of representation in the Tyrolean diet to redefine the territorial community as consisting of their own two orders in a new relation of power to the prince. Although assuming the continuance of Archduke Ferdinand's rule as count of Tyrol, the Meran articles laid down conditions for securing the freedom and autonomy of the common man and territorial community. They took away noble privileges and jurisdiction, abolished the church hierarchy and ecclesiastical property and immunities, provided for the election and dismissal of clergy by towns and villages, and ordained a broad range of political, judicial, and economic reforms as the foundation of a new order.[77]

Elsewhere, rebel programs moved beyond the territorial horizon to seek the political strengthening of the empire. Peasant demands in the southwest to have no other ruler than the emperor reflected this ideal as well as the longing of the peasantry for a place in political life. The fullest statement of the imperial theme appeared in the Franconian revolt in the reform proposals, the work of Friedrich Weigandt, which were probably prepared for a peasant meeting at Heilbronn. Like other programs, this one also proclaimed as its inspiration a Christian brotherhood and the common good. It would have realized imperial unity by such measures as uniform laws, coinage, weights, and measures, an extensive structure of imperial courts, and the prohibition of particularist leagues of princes, noblemen, and towns. It contained many provisions for religious and economic reformation, which were directed against ecclesiastical privileges

---

[74] Printed in Franz, *Quellen*, 235–6. In all probability, the author was the evangelical preacher Balthasar Hubmayer.
[75] *Ibid.*, 368–9.   [76] *Ibid.*, 455–61.   [77] *Ibid.*, 272–85.

and the power of the great financial companies like the Fugger. The highest obedience was to go to the emperor, the protector of peace and concord, under whom all estates were to live in fraternal relation.[78]

The peasant war also brought forth some expressions of republicanism which drew their strength from proximity to the Swiss confederation with its self-governing mountain communities and towns. The Christian Union of Upper Swabia contained certain resemblances to a peasant commonwealth probably derived from the Swiss example. A remarkable pamphlet addressed to the "assembled peasantry" explicitly raised the republican question. The anonymous Protestant author shared some of his ideas with the great Zurich reformer, Zwingli. An advocate of Christian egalitarianism, he offered the peasants a Biblical justification of the community's right to resist evil rulers, and, with the Swiss in mind, argued for a republic as the best form of government. (This pamphlet, incidentally, in direct opposition to Luther, was one of the first formulations of Protestant resistance theory.)[79]

Surpassing all of these ideas and programs in their transcendence of the existing order were those of a purely utopian and visionary character. Such was the reform ordinance for the Tyrol that Michael Gaismair composed in 1526 after the revolution had been suppressed nearly everywhere. Although he had previously led the movement that produced the Meran articles, Gaismair's personal convictions went much further in their radicalism. A Protestant and also somewhat influenced by Zwingli, his design envisaged a state entirely dedicated to God's word with a vital concern for equality and the poor. The godless who persecuted the poor common man were to be exterminated. All privileges were to be taken away as contrary to Scripture and right. Castles and town walls were to be demolished, cities to cease, and everyone to live in villages where no person would be better than another. The government was to be seated at Brixen and to consist of elected representatives from all parts of the land, including the miners. Judges and clergy were to be elected and paid by the community. Cloisters were to be converted into hospitals for the sick and aged. Beggary was to be ended through tithes and public charity. A university was to be established to teach the pure word of God. Gaismair also banned merchants and usury and devoted special attention to the

---

[78] *Ibid.*, 374–81.

[79] The influence of the Swiss example in peasant programs is brought out by Buszello (*Der deutsche Bauernkrieg*, 61–4, 67, 83–90), who also reprints the anonymous pamphlet *An die versamlung gemayner Pawerschaft . . . in hochteütscher Nation und vil anderer Ort, 1525;* for the latter, see also Brecht, "Der Theologische Hintergrund." The republican convictions of Zwingli (1481–1531), a dominant force in the Reformation in southwestern Germany, probably also helped to introduce a republican strain into the radical evangelical ideas of the peasant war; see Moeller, *Imperial cities,* 85 and 85n.

mines of Tyrol, which were no longer to be monopolies of the great financial houses like the Fugger and Hochstetter but pass into common ownership.[80]

This outline of a protosocialist Christian commonwealth was the product of both sincere religious idealism and bitter social hatred of the rich and the oppressor. Even more so was this the case of Thomas Müntzer's millenarian vision. Müntzer was a seminal figure in the sectarian reformation, a religious revolutionary who, in breaking with Luther, expressed his repudiation of Lutheran Protestantism's compromises with the world and its prefigured "bourgeoisification" of Christianity. Marxist historiography from Engels on, however, has consistently grossly exaggerated his modernity as well as his importance in the events of 1525.[81] The impression it seeks to convey that he was the outstanding leader in the peasant war must be rejected as groundless and misleading. It does remain true, nevertheless, that he was the most original religious mind and the strongest personality of the prophetic type who took part in it.[82] For a time he was present among the Black Forest rebels, but the main site of his activity was in Thuringia. There in the spring of 1525, after a previous failure, he was able with the help of another radical preacher, Henrich Pfeiffer, to gain control of the imperial city of Mühlhausen, which was split by religious and social discord. He propagated revolt among the towns and peasants of the surrounding area and tried to rouse the Mansfeld miners. In the middle of May the Thuringian rebellion was crushed at the battle of Frankenhausen. Müntzer himself, who had prophesied that the peasants would win with supernatural aid, was captured, tortured, and beheaded after being forced to recant. He was thirty-seven or thirty-eight years of age.

For Müntzer the peasant war signified the fullest confirmation of the

---

[80] Franz, *Quellen*, 285–90; see J. Macek, *Der Tiroler Bauernkrieg und Michael Gaismair*, Berlin, 1965, for a full account of Gaismair's history and ideas. The latter work, learned but also doctrinaire and sometimes anachronistic because of its Marxist rigidities, should be supplemented by W. Klaassen, *Michael Gaismair revolutionary and reformer*, Leiden, 1978, a discussion of Gaismair's religious and political beliefs.

[81] Such is the image of Müntzer in modern Soviet and DDR scholarship; for examples, see M. Smirin, *Die Volksreformation des Thomas Müntzer und der grosse Bauernkrieg*, 2nd ed., Berlin, 1956; M. Steinmetz, "Die frühburgerlichen Revolution in Deutschland (1476–1535). Thesen," in G. Brendler (ed.), *Die frühbürgerliche Revolution in Deutschland*, Berlin, 1961; and Bensing, *Thomas Müntzer*.

[82] Of the numerous recent studies of Müntzer's life and thought, I have found particularly helpful T. Nipperdey, "Theologie und Revolution bei Thomas Müntzer," *Archiv für Reformationsgeschichte 54*, 1–2 (1963); G. Rupp, *Patterns of reformation*, Philadelphia, 1969, pt. 3; G. H. Williams, *The radical reformation*, Philadelphia, 1962, 44–58. Some of the complexities in interpreting the development and character of Müntzer's ideas may be seen in comparing the differences between Nipperdey's account and H.-J. Goertz, *Innere und äussere Ordnung in der Theologie Thomas Müntzers*, Leiden, 1967. See also J. Stayer, "Thomas Müntzer's theology and revolution in recent non-Marxist interpretation," *Mennonite quarterly review 43*, 2 (1969).

imminent breakthrough of God's earthly kingdom as foretold in the Apocalypse. In his previous writings, hatred of oppression and acceptance of suffering and renunciation mingled with intense expectations of the destruction of the wicked and the triumph of the eschatological community of elect. As already pointed out, he was forming such leagues of covenanted believers while at Allstedt in 1524. There he also delivered one of his most violent utterances, a sermon on the Book of Daniel preached before the two Saxon princes, Duke John and his son, on account of which he had to leave the town. He prophesied the impending fall of thrones and kingdoms and defended the killing of the godless when they stand in the way of the godly. The rulers, he warned, would be overthrown unless they used their sword on behalf of the holy people.[83]

Müntzer thus injected into the peasant war his doctrine of millenarian revolution. In his thinking, the theme of godly justice, which ran all through the rebellion, acquired a unique eschatological meaning. Possessed by the spirit, he spoke as a religious witness and prophet who saw in the peasants' revolt the prelude to the decisive world transformation. It was with this hope that he tried to animate his covenanted brotherhoods. His final letters to them expressed an electric urgency. "Now is the time," (a watchword that had also appeared in the English peasant revolt of 1381) was his repeated refrain, as he summoned them to action in a universal struggle.

The whole German, French, and Italian land is awake, the Master wants to have his game, the wicked must go down . . . The Klettgau, Hegau, Black Forest peasants are up thrice three-thousand strong and their band is growing bigger . . . Even if you are only three who throw yourselves on God and seek his name and honor, you needn't fear a hundred thousand . . . Up, up, up! Have no pity . . . don't listen to the wailing of the godless . . . Rouse the villages and towns and especially the miners . . . You must up, up, it is time . . . on to the dance! . . . The fire is hot. Don't let your swords get cold . . . Cling-clang on Nimrod's anvil, throw his tower to earth! . . . God goes before you, follow, follow! . . . You will see the Lord's help over you.

This was signed, "Thomas Müntzer, a slave of God against the godless."[84]

But noticeably absent from Müntzer's exhortations was any mention of specific demands or outline of a political or social program. Under torture he confessed that he had incited revolt so that Christians should become equal and that princes and lords who opposed the Gospel should be overthrown and killed. He also acknowledged that he believed all things should

[83] Müntzer, *Schriften und Briefe*, 241 ff. The sermon is translated in G. Williams (ed.), *Spiritual and anabaptist writers*, Philadelphia, 1957.

[84] Müntzer, *Schriften und Briefe*, 454–6. Müntzer wrote this letter at the end of April 1525 from Mühlhausen to his Allstedt followers. The meaning of the references to the Italian or Latin (*welsche*) land is unclear.

be in common and given to each according to his need.[85] Yet, with all the fervor of his revolutionary activism, he never described the new order he expected, nor is it possible to deduce from his writings what its nature was to be. This failure was the direct result of his millenarian faith. In his apocalyptic vision of deliverance, he had no need to address himself to actual problems of reform or to spell out the institutions of the new world to come. Along with Gaismair, who would have abolished cities, the prophet Müntzer was one of those "terrible simplifiers," as the great Swiss historian, Jacob Burckhardt, called them, who have frequently arisen in the Western revolutionary tradition.[86]

It is impossible to reflect on Müntzer's melancholy end or the peasant war itself without a sense of tragedy. Revolution may destroy many things of value with its cruelty and violence, but it may also give expression to the unquenchable spirit of freedom in man. The revolution of 1525 did not arise from despair or misery. Borne forward on the same surge of religious revival as the Reformation, it was filled with hope, and in a variety of ways rebels fought to achieve a better world for themselves. How well individual peasants could have understood the religious and political ideas of justice and God's law or how closely in their minds their practical desires and social ideals were connected we cannot, of course, say. But it is inconceivable that rebellion could have expanded on such a scale without some personal identification with and belief in its goals by many of those who took part in it. The peasants' defeat was therefore also the defeat of the ideals that had inspired the revolution. It marked the parting of the way between the German Reformation and the great popular movement that accompanied it, assuring that the Reformation would be directed and exploited to the profit of the princes and governing powers. It strengthened the exclusion of the peasants from the active participation in political life toward which their revolt had aspired.[87] It contributed to the creation of the blight of conformity and subservience in politics and religion alike that was to lie so heavily upon Germany in its post-Reformation history.

V

KETT'S REBELLION

In England, Kett's rebellion of 1549, as we have already said, was the greatest agrarian uprising of the period. Viewed alongside the German peasant war it was, of course, far smaller, less complex, and lacking in a

[85] *Ibid.*, 548.   [86] J. Burckhardt, *Force and freedom*, ed. J. Nichols, New York, 1943, 43.
[87] P. Blickle (*Die Revolution von 1525*, pt. 3) advances a modification of this view, suggesting that in the post-1525 period the peasant estate became gradually more integrated into the political order of some of the territorial states.

political horizon. Nonetheless, it possessed some interesting resemblances to the peasant war, as well as instructive points of difference that further illuminate the structure and limits of peasant struggles.

Enclosure was the main target of agrarian protest in Tudor England. What enclosure signified – or what it did that excited anger and opposition – was explained with admirable brevity by one of the most knowledgeable contemporaries of Kett's revolt. "It is not," he said, "where a man doth enclose and hedge in his own proper ground, where no man hath commons . . . but it is meant thereby, when any man hath taken away and enclosed any other mens commons, or hath pulled down houses of husbandry, and converted the lands from tillage to pasture."[88]

In its offending form, then, enclosure resulted in the landlord dispossessing the peasant community of its communal resources or evicting tenants in order to lay their lands together and turn arable into grass. This might be done legally, depending on the terms and nature of tenancies, or by chicanery and force. Similarly, communities sometimes fought enclosure by litigation, or they tried to resist it forcibly. The usual kind of enclosure riot involved tearing up hedges and invading the enclosed ground. Because enclosure caused disorder and rural depopulation, Tudor policy condemned it. Successive statutes tried to prohibit it, and royal commissions were appointed to enforce these laws. Such measures, however, had little effect against the ability of landlords to frustrate their operation or the pressure of economic imperatives.

Kett's revolt originated in an enclosure riot, just as the peasant war began in a localized outbreak. That riot expanded into an agrarian rebellion was not due to sheer chance, any more than it had been in Germany, but to the predisposing religiopolitical and conjunctural climate. After the powerful, overbearing rule of Henry VIII, his child heir, Edward VI, was on the throne. The regency government headed by the king's uncle, the duke of Somerset, as protector, was weakened by faction and lacked authority. Moreover, in a realm still strongly Catholic, the government had become Protestant, its will set on establishing the Reformation. Besides these problems of political instability and religious discord, both long- and short-term *conjoncture* made the 1540s a period of exceptional difficulty. The effects of population growth on land and rents, repeated coinage debasements, price oscillations and inflation, and the impact of enclosures for sheep provoked a flood of economic complaint and social criticism. Preachers and reformers vied in denouncing the greedy landlords, who placed their private profit above the commonweal. In response

---

[88] This was the description given by John Hales in his 1548 charge to the juries empaneled to present enclosures. Hales was one of the best-informed men of his time on economic and agrarian problems; see R. H. Tawney and E. Power (eds.), *Tudor economic documents*, 3 v., London, 1924, v. 1, 41.

to this agitation, Somerset appointed an enclosure commission in 1548, which was at work at the time of Kett's rebellion. The protector's well-known sympathy with peasant grievances undoubtedly helped to raise expectations that something would be done about them. As in Germany, where a major crisis of authority set off the peasant war, so in Edward VI's England, convergent political, religious, and social conflict precipitated an outburst of revolt.[89] In the summer of 1549, Devon and Cornwall became the scene of a sizable provincial insurrection in defense of Catholicism. The same year also saw agrarian disturbances reach the highest level of the entire century. In Norfolk they blew up into a full-scale rebellion, although numerous disorders erupted in many countries of southern England, Somerset, Gloucester, Wiltshire, Hampshire, Sussex, Surrey, Essex, Hertfordshire, and others.[90]

The revolt in Norfolk lasted around six weeks, from the initial disorders in July to its suppression in late August. It started with enclosure riots scattered over several south Norfolk villages. In one of these incidents at Wymondham, Robert Kett, who held land there, took over as leader. He headed the insurgents as they marched to Norwich less than ten miles away, gathering followers and breaking down enclosures en route. At Norwich on July 12, Kett set up a camp outside the city walls at Mousehold Heath, which the rebels held till their overthrow. With new supporters coming in daily, their number reached about 16,000. The Norfolk gentry, in the face of fear, threat, and ineffective leadership, did little to repress the insurrection. Considerable support for the rebels also appeared in Norwich, and the mayor and other officials cooperated under threat, although after ten days Kett's forces seized the city. The first troops sent against the revolt at the end of July, 1,400 men under the marquis of Northampton, were defeated and withdrew. Then a second army of 12,000 reinforced by 1,200 German mercenaries, under the earl of Warwick's command, fought its way into Norwich on August 23. Four days later, Warwick engaged and crushed the rebels at Dussindale, cutting down over 3,000 of them. Kett and his brother were later captured, tried, and hung as traitors. At least 49 others were also executed. As happened so often in such struggles, repression apparently claimed a far higher toll than did revolt itself.

This is the barest summary of Kett's rebellion, but we can draw on supplementary details to bring out its salient features.[91]

---

[89] See the account of the background in W. K. Jordan, *Edward VI: The young King*, London, 1968, ch. 14.

[90] *Ibid.*, 439–53. See Hales's remark about "general Insurrection" and his list of the affected counties, in Lamond, *A discourse of the commonweal*, lviii.

[91] For description and comments on Kett's revolt, see F. Russell, *Kett's rebellion in Norfolk*, London, 1859; Bindoff, *Ket's rebellion*, and Fletcher, *Tudor rebellions*, 64–77, 142–4. Interesting supplementary details are contained in the fuller recent studies of J. Cornwall, *Revolt of*

As in Germany, the village community and the socioeconomic network in which it was embedded played a central role in the mobilization and spread of revolt. Thus, Wymondham, the site of the enclosure riots of early July, was a market town and meeting place of communities because it stood along a main north–south road and also contained a popular chapel dedicated to Saint Thomas à Becket. The event that brought the rioters together was a local religious festival. The rebel camp at Norwich was recruited not only from people of south Norfolk but from several other parts of the country and adjacent Suffolk as well, where outbreaks also took place. The tocsin of parish churches and the firing of beacons across the county helped to raise the villages, and Kett sent out emissaries to increase his numbers. We can see the imprint of communities on the rebel council, which was based on the traditional county division, the hundred: it consisted of two "governors" or representatives each of twenty-four of Norfolk's thirty-two hundreds and one Suffolk hundred, plus several magistrates of Norwich.[92]

Even though its grievances were nearly all agrarian, the rebellion was a great popular demonstration that swept up peasants, rural artisans, and townfolk. One list of forty-seven participants mentions seventeen husbandmen plus assorted other occupations like butcher, tailor, laborer, miller, cooper, innkeeper, and mason. In Norwich, one of the main English manufacturing and textile centers containing great contrasts between rich and poor, many "vagrand persons," we are told, "were easily assenting to that rebellion." An unsuccessful attempt by insurgents to take King's Lynn and Yarmouth also brought many within and around those towns to the rebel camp.[93] Kett himself was a well-to-do farmer and tanner, his brother a mercer. It is hard to be sure about the economic situation of the peasant rebels. They have been called "a prosperous race," and Norfolk and Suffolk were said to have a higher proportion of tenants with legal security than anywhere else in England. Holdings were small, however, the competition for land keen, and the common fields vital to the peasant economy.[94]

Unlike the German peasant war, no clergy seem to have joined the revolt, yet it had a definite Protestant stamp. Protestant services were held

---

the peasantry 1549, London, 1977; and S. Land, *Kett's rebellion*, Totowa, 1977. The main contemporary account by Nicholas Sotherton has been published by B. Beer, "The commoyson in Norfolk, 1549," *Journal of medieval and renaissance studies 6*, 1 (1976). I have also used an unpublished seminar paper by a former student, J. T. Bennett of the University of California at Los Angeles.

[92] Bindoff, *Ket's rebellion*, 3, 10, 19; Beer, "The commoyson in Norfolk," 84, 88; Fletcher, *Tudor rebellions*, 75, 142.

[93] Bindoff, *Ket's rebellion*, 20; Beer, "The commoyson in Norfolk," 81; J. F. Pound, "The social and trade structure of Norwich 1525–1575," *Past and present 34* (1966).

[94] Bindoff, *Ket's rebellion*, 7–8; Thirsk, "Enclosing and engrossing," 224.

in the rebel camp under an oak called the "tree of Reformation." The few religious grievances also bore a Protestant character. They included demands for a resident clergy to instruct the people in the laws of God and the removal of priests unable to preach, to be replaced by fit men chosen by the parishioners or lord of the town.[95] Probably the explanation of the absence of reformed clergy in the rebellion was the extreme emphasis that contemporary English Protestantism placed on the religious duty of nonresistance to superiors. Even the strongest sympathizers with peasant grievances held to this belief.[96]

The principal targets of rebel anger were landlords and gentlemen. The economic strains of the 1540s created acute conflicts over rents and rights between landlords and peasant communities, undermining the vertical solidarities and paternalistic deference ingrained in the society of orders. All contemporaries regarded the rebellion as a bitter attack on the gentry. A leading writer in 1549 said of the rebels, "Ye pretende a common welthe, howe amende ye it? by killyinge of Gentilmen? by spoylynge of Gentilmen? by imprisonynge of Gentilmen? . . . Is this your true dutie . . . to disobey your betters, and to obeye your tanners, to change your obedience from a kynge to a Kett?"[97] Kett sent out parties to pull down gentry enclosures. The rebels forced gentlemen to abandon their houses and seized their livestock to supply the camp at Mousehold Heath. Captured gentlemen were imprisoned or shown to the crowd, which was asked what to do with them, whereupon "some cryide hang him, and some kill him."[98]

Kett and his followers would not admit to being rebels. Offered a royal pardon if they submitted, they refused, replying that they were not offenders or in need of pardon. In contrast to the German peasant war, the revolt had no political goals. Rebels looked to the crown for redress, and Kett even issued his orders in the king's name and claimed to be defending the king's laws. The rebel appeal was to the crown to compel sheriffs, justices, and other officials to carry out the laws that were to the benefit of the "poor commons."[99]

Apparently the rebel council drew up only one set of grievances, a petition to the king with twenty-nine articles. It shows plainly that the movement lacked an ideology and depended on what I have previously termed mentality or traditional belief. With one exception, the demands, very miscellaneous in character, were based on older law and custom, like the German peasants' *"alte Recht,"* often calling for a return to conditions

[95] Fletcher, *Tudor rebellions*, 72–3, 142–43, (art. 8, 15).
[96] See the views of the reformer, John Hales, in Lamond, lx; and the preachers, Thomas Lever and Robert Crowley, in Tawney and Power, *Tudor economic documents*, v. *i*, 47–50, 57–60.
[97] John Cheke, *The hurt of sedition* (1549), Menston, 1971, sig. Aiiii.
[98] Beer, "The commoyson in Norfolk," 83–4.
[99] *Ibid.*, 83, 85; Fletcher, *Tudor rebellions*, 74–5, 144 (art. 27).

in the first year of King Henry VII (1485). The exception was the famous demand for emancipation from serfdom with its poignant echo of the German peasant war: "We pray that all bonde men may be made free for god made all free with his precious blode sheddying."[100] Here alone the implicit justification was the Bible and God's law. The inclusion of this grievance is puzzling, however; not only was serfdom quite rare by then, but there is no indication of the involvement of any bondmen in the revolt. I am inclined to believe that the article may have come by some unknown process of transmission directly from the Twelve Articles of the German peasants and may have been inserted by the Norfolk rebels without any particular relevance as a faint reflection of the influence of the revolution of 1525 upon their thinking.

Other grievances dealt mostly with the economic needs and interests of small tenants. They did not embody any vision of social change or egalitarian spirit but aimed only to set bounds to the exactions and usurpations of landlords. Some would have reduced rents and other payments to the level of 1485. Tithes to the church would also have been reduced and set at a fixed amount. The problem of land scarcity was reflected both in a provision to limit the purchase of lands by lords of manors and in another prohibiting priests from buying land and requiring them to lease their lands to "temporal men." Although the problem of enclosure was not addressed directly, several articles dealt with the vital subject of rights of common: Lords of manors were not to "common upon the Commons" or profit from them; the common lands and their profits were to be available only for the freeholders and copyholders. This was apparently intended to stop landlords from overstocking or otherwise exploiting the common lands of villages and manors to the community's damage and contrary to custom. Because of the booming demand for wool, which was rising to a peak in the 1540s, Norfolk, besides its cattle, had become a county of great sheep flocks, the biggest in England, and overgrazing by landlords on common lands, whether on pasture and waste or on the arable after harvest, was a prevalent abuse. It was sometimes also a prelude to enclosure. The same grievance underlay another article that no lord, knight, or esquire worth over forty pounds yearly in land should graze sheep or cattle except to supply his own household.[101]

Kett's rebellion was a sad resistance of common folk caught up in the turmoil of economic change, to which the landed governing class was also responding. It bore inscribed in it, like the German peasant war, the reality of village communities and their problems. It was rooted above all in recent conjunctural trends, which were threatening peasant well-being and causing severe strains in landlord–tenant relationships. Although no other

---

[100] Fletcher, *Tudor rebellions*, 143 (art. 16).   [101] *Ibid.*, 142–4, *passim*.

English agrarian insurrection of the period expressed a similar animosity toward gentlemen and landlord superiors, the movement lacked a social or political perspective. In the scale of goals, it limited itself largely to demands for a change of policy and laws to be effected and enforced by the crown. Despite its will to justice and its consciousness of right, it failed to articulate principles and possessed no ideology. The time had apparently not yet come in England when a revolt of the lower orders could develop broad ideas or programs to counter the hegemonic, all-pervasive principles of hierarchy and subordination that maintained the Tudor state and society.

VI
FRENCH AGRARIAN REBELLIONS

French agrarian rebellions provide us with a final example of peasant resistance in early modern Europe. As we have noted earlier, these movements were far more numerous in France than elsewhere. Again and again the rural countryside was convulsed by spasms of violence, which often amalgamated with or accompanied plebeian outbreaks in towns. This tragic history of insurrection and repression, of communal reaction to grievances and oppression, was profoundly revelatory of the condition of French society and the burdens borne by the monarchy's peasant subjects.

In looking at French peasant revolts as modern scholarship has revealed them to us, we observe that none of them occupied a central or culminating position analogous to the German peasant war or Kett's rebellion. Larger or smaller, one followed another, attaining epidemic proportions in the twenty-year period before the Fronde, a dispersed succession of eruptions that in several instances may have achieved a few concessions but were essentially repetitive in character. Even the revolts of 1636–7, described by Porchnev as the biggest peasant rebellion in French history, were not one massive rising but a series of sporadic manifestations scattered over various areas that did not remotely approach the ideological or political level of the German peasant war, splintered as the latter was. There is accordingly no reason to concentrate upon any one particular case as especially important or exemplary in examining the French peasant movements of the time. Instead, despite their confusing multiplicity, it is preferable to try to grasp them briefly more or less in general in order to perceive some of their common and persistent features. We shall direct our view mostly to the revolts of the earlier seventeenth century, with an occasional glance backward to the century before.

These rebellions resembled those of Reformation Germany and Edwardian England in being the product of a climate of disobedience and recalcitrance to authority. Peasants did not rise in isolation but along with or in the wake of other groups.[102] The French monarchy in its stride toward absolutism repeatedly confronted the insubordination and defiance of its aristocratic and privileged subjects who set peasant rebels an example. Reduced to the lowest state of weakness by the later sixteenth-century civil war, the crown barely began to recover its strength in the earlier seventeenth century and was continually forced to contend against the obstructionism and resistance of the high nobility, *parlements*, officials, and others. The reign of Henry IV (1589–1610) brought a return to relative order as the monarchy resumed the path to absolute rule. But the reign of his son and successor, Louis XIII (1610–43), saw incessant conflicts, disaffection, and disorders. During this time, and especially in the ministry of Cardinal Richelieu (1625–42), the government was straining every nerve to master internal opposition and prosecute its state-building efforts, while simultaneously waging a costly international struggle for preponderance against Spain. Its relentless measures aroused a proportionate reaction among its subjects. One of the ministers, Marillac, lamented in 1630:

France is full of seditions, the *parlements* don't punish anyone. The king appoints judges for trial, and the Parlement [of Paris] prevents the execution of their judgments, so that seditions are authorized. I don't know what to hope or apprehend, considering the frequency of revolts, of which we receive fresh news every day.[103]

This condition was acute in the 1630s and 1640s, although only the intensification of an older, recurrent problem. It formed a political climate that, with its numerous challenges to authority, was also favorable to outbreaks of peasant resistance.

In the final analysis, the underlying cause of agrarian rebellion, with hardly any exceptions, lay in the monarchy's construction of its absolutist rule and the grievances incident thereto: in its thrust toward administrative centralization, in its attack upon surviving forms of autonomism, in its determination to quell intermediate powers, in its ruthless disregard of limits to its authority founded in custom and privilege, and in its unrestrained fiscal demands, enforced by violent military methods of collection. Most of all did peasants feel the royal state's assault in its expanding financial requirements. *Tailles*, the ensemble of direct taxes, were the peasant impost par excellence, and indirect taxes of many kinds also depressed peasant livelihood. The ever-growing weight of both added a redoubtable dynamic to explosions of peasant resistance in the seventeenth century.[104]

[102] See Mousnier, *Fureurs paysannes*, 43 ff.

[103] Cited in V. L. Tapié, *La France de Louis XIII et de Richelieu*, Paris, 1967, 205. Tapié observes that for the government to carry on war, repress revolt, and subdue the opposition of local and provincial interests to its general policy, Richelieu had to establish a regime of "public safety" (*ibid.*, 206).

[104] See A. Lublinskaya (*French absolutism: The crucial phase 1620–1629*, Cambridge, 1968, 329, 331) for "the unbearable growth of taxation" after 1629 and especially its connection

All this was visible against the gloomy conjunctural background of the decades after 1620. The time, as we have seen, was one of worsening depression. The classic Malthusian situation of growing pauperism amid excess population, peasant poverty accentuated by too many people and too small landholdings, intermittent subsistence crises, and periodic pestilence, afflicted France more severely than before.[105] They aggravated peasant burdens and increased the resentment against government exactions. With France's entry into its long war with Spain in 1635, government pressures multiplied, adding to the adversities of *conjoncture*. It is, of course, necessary to recognize the variations in the impact of the latter, which hit some regions more than others; and similarly, we are not obliged to postulate a direct temporal correlation or causal link between conjunctural reverses and particular revolts.[106] But there can be no doubt that this long-term conjunctural environment, the combined result of depression and of natural and social hardship and calamities crowned by the miseries of war, created a breeding ground for revolt by arousing the aggressive response of peasant communities and other subjects to the royal state's demands.

Accordingly, an important difference between the French and other early modern agrarian rebellions was the predominance of the antifiscal motif among the former. About this fact there can be little dispute. As the recent chronicler of Provençal insurrections has commented regarding their genesis, "One problem appears very frequently, to the point of giving the great majority of these movements a kind of apparent unity, [the problem] of fiscality."[107] It was this characteristic that has also made it so convenient in the case of France to speak generally of "popular revolts"; for antifiscalism was just as strong a motive of protest by the town poor and lower orders as by peasants, while it was scarcely less a contributory factor in other types of revolution as well.

The corollary to this circumstance was that agrarian revolts were seldom aimed against the landlord or the seigneurial system and its obliga-

---

with external war; on *tailles* and peasant resistance, see Bercé, *Croquants et Nu-pieds*, 94–5. R. Bonney (*Political change in France under Richelieu and Mazarin 1624–1661*, Oxford, 1978, 173–4 and ch. 10) gives a description and quantitative account of the *taille*'s increase, borne mainly by the peasants, and an overview of "tax rebellions."

[105] See the comments of E. L. Ladurie, *Les Paysans de Languedoc*, 2 v., Paris, 1966, v. 1, 502.

[106] In his *Histoire des Croquants*, v. 1, pt. 1, Bercé provides a lengthy review of *conjoncture* in relation to revolts in the southwest. He notes some regional differences and finds no temporal correlation between such events as subsistence crises and the rhythm of revolts but points out how conjunctural factors like food shortages, epidemics, and monetary scarcity "composed the catastrophic landscape in which the demand for imposts became odious and provocative" (v. 1, 42).

[107] Pillorget, *Les Mouvements insurrectionnels*, 153.

tions. It was not the landlord but the fiscal agent of the central government whom the peasant usually regarded as his greatest enemy. Of the peasant movements of the seventeenth century only one, an event beyond the chronological limits of our study, exhibited a distinct antiseigneurial side; this was the "stamped-paper" rebellion of 1675 in Brittany, which was nevertheless occasioned, like so many preceding revolts, by the introduction of a new tax.[108] Within our period itself, the sole peasant protest that included an antiseigneurial aspect was the Croquant risings of 1592–5 in Périgord, Limousin, Saintonge, and several other parts of the southwest. These commotions, however, were merely incidents in the great civil war embracing the kingdom, a product of its anarchy, depredations, and misery, which finally caused the long-suffering peasants to revolt in self-defense. Commonly called Croquants, their name may have derived from Crocq, a town in Auvergne, and *croquant* thenceforth become a synonym for the rebel peasant as well as the root of related terms like *croquandage* and *croquantisme* to describe his nefarious activities.[109]

These first Croquants armed themselves to resist the lawless gentlemen and soldiery who preyed on the helpless villages in this time of anarchy. They were said to be hostile to the nobility and simultaneously refused to pay tithes, *tailles*, and seigneurial dues. Sometimes calling themselves the "third estate," they seemed to hope for a peasant utopia in which the *menu peuple* would be free from all exactions. A decree of their main leader, a notary called La Saigne, even urged the reconciliation of divisive religious quarrels and that "each should live according to his own mind" ("chacun vivroit a sa fantaisie"). The Parlement of Toulouse accused the Croquants of licensing disorder and undermining the "obedience due to magistrates and superiors." During the two or three years of their existence, they held a score or more of assemblies in different provinces, which brought together thousands of people. The Croquant movement was put down by troops without difficulty in 1595 and dissolved with Henry IV's pacification of the provinces at the end of the civil war.[110] None of the later peasant revolts that bore the name repeated the antiseigneurial theme of the first.

The main historical disagreement that has arisen concerning these seventeenth-century revolts centers upon whether they were essentially

---

[108] For an account, see Mousnier, *Fureurs paysannes*, pt. 1, ch. 6.

[109] See Bercé, *Histoire des Croquants*, v. 2, 639–43, for a discussion of the name and its origins. Apparently it fell out of use after the middle of the seventeenth century.

[110] See the texts pertaining to the first Croquant uprisings in J. Loutchitzky, *Documents inédits pour servir à l'histoire de la réforme et de la Ligue*, Paris, 1875, 334–5, 340–54; and Bercé, *Histoire des Croquants*, v. 2, 701–10. The latter gives the best account (v. 1, pt. 2, ch. 1). There are also recent discussions of these risings in Ladurie, *Les Paysans de Languedoc*, v. 1, 399–402; and Salmon, *Society in crisis*, ch. 11.

spontaneous outbreaks and expressions of class conflict or were instigated, rather, by nobility and officials who made common cause with peasants against royal fiscality and centralism.

The former of these views has been propounded by the Soviet scholar Porchnev, the author of the first detailed study devoted to the French peasant risings. Although he did not deny their antifiscal motive, he nevertheless tried to account for them in Marxist terms as spontaneous class demonstrations set in the context of a feudalo-absolutist order. The latter view has been advanced by Mousnier, the leading present-day French historian of the period. Rejecting the Marxian class explanation as well as the idea that the France of the earlier seventeenth century was still a feudal society, he has emphasized the importance of elites in inspiring and abetting peasant seditions.[111]

Of these two conflicting positions, Mousnier's comes much closer to the truth.[112] As the evidence indicates – evidence amply referred to in Porchnev's work itself – the complicity or support of elites was a recurrent feature of peasant insurrections. Had the latter been class conflicts against a surviving feudalism, this could hardly have been the case. Similarly, the absence of any genuine antiseigneurial movement in all these agrarian rebellions shows that peasants did not act as a class but in concert with other social groups opposed to the central state's offensive. They shared with these groups a localism or provincialism that in France was even more formidable in its effects than in other national kingdoms. Local solidarities created paternalistic bonds between peasants and seigneurs, who were impelled to protect as well as to exploit their peasant subjects and who had their own interests in resisting fiscality. For in its exactions the crown also eroded the nobility's privileges, even to the extent of making noblemen liable to certain forms of *taille*, besides the indirect taxes that affected them in common with others. Moreover, when the peasant was forced to submit to the demands of the royal fisc, he might have little or nothing left wherewith to meet his seigneurial obligations. As for the peasant, if he

[111] Porchnev, *Les Soulèvements populaires*. Porchnev, although not the first to discuss the French peasant revolts of the earlier seventeenth century, was the first to make them a center of historical attention and to stress their significance in French history. It is worth noting that as far back as 1886, the American historian J. B. Perkins took account of these movements in his *France under Mazarin with a review of the administration of Richelieu*, 2 v., New York, 1886. He considered them a product of the misery caused by taxation and "to some extent successors to the Jacquerie" (v. 1, 304–7). For Mousnier, see his "Recherches sur les soulèvements populaires en France avant la Fronde," in *La Plume, la faucille, et le marteau*, Paris, 1970, a direct critique of Porchnev's thesis. Mousnier his given his own general interpretation of the peasant revolts in *Fureurs paysannes*. His views and the criticism of Porchnev are adopted in the monographic studies by his students Foisil, *La Révolte des Nu-pieds*, Bercé, *Histoire des Croquants*, and Pillorget, *Les Mouvements insurrectionnels*.

[112] For a helpful review of the controversy with adequate references to the literature, see J. Salmon, "Venality of office and popular sedition in seventeenth-century France," *Past and present 37* (1967).

felt seigneurial rents as a hardship, he nonetheless regarded them as customary payments whose legitimacy he did not challenge, whereas the ever-mounting imposts and oppressions of tax farmers were innovations from without and accordingly to be resisted. Such resistance was considered the more justifiable when noblemen and officials encouraged or tolerated it.[113]

But let us leave this debate for a closer look at the structure of agrarian rebellions in France.

Although these movements naturally arose out of different particular contingencies, what commonly precipitated them was some event related to fiscality: the establishment of a new impost; the extension of a tax to a hitherto exempt area; the introduction of *élus*, royal functionaries assigned to supersede local control of the assessment and levying of taxes; rumors of some fresh oppression with regard to exactions; the appearance of fiscal agents and collectors, the hated *gabeleurs* and *voleurs*. A whole antifiscal mythology acted upon the peasant mind: myths of the king's ignorance of the pressures on his subjects or that he was deceived or robbed by his own financial servants, the cause of the kingdom's miseries; myths that the king out of love for his people would remit or abolish taxes or that the latter would end with the king's death or at the making of peace. There were other myths that exaggerated the terrors of fiscalism, like the rumor that a tax would be placed on births, on marriages, or on deaths. The image of the tax farmer was itself surrounded by myths that pictured him as a cannibal, a vampire, rapacious and unscrupulous, a man who impoverished all estates to enrich himself.[114]

Anything that excited the hatred or intensified the threat of fiscal exactions could light the spark. The revolt of 1548 in Guienne and neighboring provinces, which became the biggest agrarian rebellion of the century, began after Francis I introduced a *gabelle*, a new tax on salt, into the region.[115] The immediate cause of the revolt of the Croquants in Quercy in 1624 was the institution of *élections* or *élus*, whereby royal representatives were to take over from the provincial estates the assessment and collection of *tailles*.[116] The revolt in the towns of Guienne in 1635, which spread to the peasants of the hinterland, started with a new tax on wine and taverns.[117] The precipitant of the Croquant revolts in 1636–7, with their

---

[113] See P. Deyon, "Apropos des rapport entre la noblesse française et la monarchie absolue pendant la première moitié du XVIIᵉ siècle," *Revue historique 231* (1964); and Bercé, *Histoire des Croquants*, v. 1, 127–35.

[114] See Bercé, *Histoire des Croquants*, 607 ff., "La mythologie antifiscale," for a perceptive discussion of this subject, on which I have drawn.

[115] See the account in Bercé, *Croquants et Nu-pieds*, 20–1.

[116] Porchnev, *Les Soulèvements populaires*, 49–50.

[117] Mousnier, *Fureurs paysannes*, 54–5; Bercé (*Histoire des Croquants*, v. 1, pt. 2, ch. 2) provides a long, interesting account.

multiple insurgencies in Saintonge, Angoumois, Poitou, Périgord, and beyond, was a regular onslaught of fiscal demands upon these provinces: the near doubling of *tailles*, rigorous measures to compel payment of tax arrears, and further indirect charges on wine and other consumables.[118] Nearly always it was some manifestation of the crown's exorbitant extractiveness – blamed not on the king but on the corrupt army of fiscal agents and denounced by its victims as an insupportable injustice – that kindled an explosion.

Beneath the infinite complication of incidents comprising these revolts, the same underlying pattern repeated itself. Invariably, just as in the typologically related German and English peasant movements, rebellion was a defense of the community, and the community in village and parish became the institutional cellule of revolt.

Typically, insurrection started with the surge of rumors, the flare-up of resentment at some new excess of fiscality, an act of resistance to soldiers or tax gatherers, and the angry talk of country people in taverns, markets, and fairs. Church bells summoned the parish, whose inhabitants came together in arms. Letters and emissaries were sent around, distant parishes roused, and joint meetings of parishes appointed on a Sunday or a feast day. As the revolt widened, the parishes elected captains; the men marched to meetings with other parishes in military order, perhaps accompanied by their priests. Very soon assemblies of scores of parishes, with thousands of people present, were being held. Thus appeared the "commune," meaning the union or association of parishes, as the widest degree of organization achieved by the revolt. French revolutionary tradition has always identified the commune with militant Paris in 1792–3 and 1871. Here, in the agrarian rebellions of an earlier time, the commune was the insurrectionary assembly of communities with its elected officers and head, to represent the peasants and villagers of a district or province, the *petit peuple* or common folk of the *plat pays*, against the grievances that had called forth their resistance.[119]

This is a compressed sketch or abstract of the revolutionary process that tended to reproduce itself, amid an endless diversity of circumstance, from one peasant revolt to another, as if by a genetic continuity. It is what we see in the revolt of Guienne in 1548, in the first Croquant risings of the 1590s, and in the later Croquant revolts of the 1630s and 1640s. In all of them the union of communities gave rise to the characteristic institution of revolt, the commune, with its deliberative assemblies, speechmakers, agitators, chosen leaders, and military actions.

The higher orders were naturally expected by the crown to aid in put-

---

[118] Mousnier, *Fureurs paysannes*, 66.

[119] The most illuminating discussion of these movements both through particular narratives and overall delineation is the brilliant treatment by Bercé, *Histoire des Croquants, passim.*

ting down revolt but were often guilty of neutrality or of passive or active complicity with antifiscal protest. In the central government's view, they were behind the outbreaks of peasant violence in the countryside. This was the usual explanation contained in the reports sent to Paris in the 1630s and 1640s by the royal intendants in the provinces. The latter, although well aware of the distress wrought by economic hardships, the war, and exactions, did not believe the peasants were capable of acting on their own initiative and held noblemen and *parlements* responsible for inciting, encouraging, or tolerating rebellion. The local nobility and magistrates, on the other hand, placed the blame upon the unbearable weight of taxation and the brutal methods of the tax collectors.[120]

Here and there, seigneurs and gentlemen took a direct part in insurrection. The elected leader of the Croquants of Périgord in 1637 was a nobleman of a certain eminence, the sieur de la Mothe-La Forest, and several other noblemen of standing were also actively involved.[121] Petty, poor seigneurs would sometimes march with their rebel peasants or else would do nothing to stop them. The antifiscalism of seigneurs encouraged the spirit of refusal among their peasants, who felt authorized by their example or protection to resist the agents of the fisc.[122] The Croquants of Poitou in 1636 ordered all gentlemen in the parishes to join them in arms on pain of having their houses burned and nonpayment of rents and dues.[123] (This phenomenon of the impressment of elites into rebellion by the lower orders recurred in early modern revolutions; peasants compelled gentry to join or lead them, a proceeding that also provided the latter with an excuse for their participation when called to account.) Porchnev pointed to the complicity or approval of the seigneurs and "their support of the antifiscal slogans of the popular movements" as noticeable traits of the peasant revolts but nevertheless failed to draw the necessary systematic conclusion from these facts.[124] They make it evident that the French agrarian rebellions of the time were not class conflicts with class aims but one social response among others in a disturbed society to the growth of absolutism and the state's exactions.

Similarly, local officials set an example of disobedience by their tactics of legal opposition and revealed their culpability by their reluctance and

---

[120] See O. Ranum, *Paris in the age of absolutism*, New York, 1968, 203. Many expressions of the opinions of the royal intendants and ministers are contained in the extracts and texts in Porchnev, *passim;* see also Mousnier, *Fureurs paysannes*, 49.

[121] Porchnev, *Les Soulèvements populaires*, 76–7; Mousnier, *Fureurs paysannes*, 88.

[122] Bercé, *Croquants et Nu-pieds*, 109–10, *Histoire des Croquants*, v. 1, 143; Mousnier, *Fureurs paysannes*, 340–1.

[123] See the text of the order, Bercé, *Histoire des Croquants*, v. 2, 738.

[124] Porchnev, *Les Soulèvements populaires*, 95. In the integrity of his researches, Porchnev made available an abundance of evidence and documentation that contradicts his own Marxist prepossessions and explanatory schema.

inefficiency in putting down revolts.[125] In 1548, after the suppression of the rebellion in Guienne, Henry II abolished the privileges of the city of Bordeaux because of the failure of its officials and notables to act against the rebels, who had murdered the lieutenant-general of the province.[126] Although Bordeaux's privileges were restored two years later, the problem of officials condoning or tolerating popular resistance to exactions remained perennial. It reappeared continually during the 1630s and 1640s before the Fronde, when the *parlements* tried to use their legal powers to block the crown's fiscal edicts. In 1640, Louis XIII severely curtailed the privileges of the Parlement of Rouen and sacked some of the judges as a punishment for their inactivity in suppressing the Nu-pieds revolt in Normandy, a movement unleashed by fiscal grievances that we shall notice again in connection with provincial rebellion.[127] In 1643, the actions of the *parlements* of Bordeaux and Toulouse helped to encourage the peasant rebellions that had again broken out in Rouergue and other provinces.[128] Such cases of indirect approval or toleration of popular sedition on the part of officials were frequent. There were understandable reasons for this conduct. The magistrates of the *parlements* and other officials were strongly hostile to the crown's increasing resort to the use of intendants, which undermined provincial privileges and threatened to supersede them in their own functions; in addition, as proprietary officeholders, they too were subject to fiscal exploitation and condemned the barrage of financial expedients that included them among its targets.[129]

The bigger agrarian rebellions like those in the southwest were apt to break out in the spring or summer and go on for maybe four or five months at the most. They were usually limited to the province, and if they spread beyond it was not by expansion and inclusion but by the addition of separate revolts that failed to merge or unite their forces.[130] The numbers at rebel assemblies could be considerable, as some random figures illustrate. In the Guienne revolt of 1548, about fifteen thousand peasants were present at some of the meetings. Ten thousand came together in an assembly of Périgord Croquants in May 1594. We hear of a meeting of ten thousand people held by the Croquants of Angoumois in June 1636, and another of thirty thousand by those of Périgord in May 1637.[131]

The communes of parishes existed to discuss, to fight, and to present

---

[125] See Bercé (*Histoire des Croquants*, v. 1, pt. 1, ch. 5) for a discussion of the relation of venal officeholders to these revolts.

[126] Bercé, *Croquants et Nu-pieds*, 21; Salmon, *Society in crisis*, 37.

[127] See Foisil, *La Révolte des Nu-pieds*, pt. 3, ch. 4; and Ch. 9 in this book.

[128] Porchnev, *Les Soulèvements populaires*, 99, 110.

[129] See W. Beik ("Magistrates and popular risings in France before the Fronde: The case of Toulouse," *Journal of modern history 46*, 4 [1974]) for a suggestive and nuanced discussion of this subject; and Ch. 13 in this book.

[130] Bercé, *Histoire des Croquants*, v. 2, 676.   [131] *Ibid.*, v. 2, 677.

grievances. The Croquants of Quercy in 1624 formed an army of sixteen thousand men out of their assemblies. The peasants came provided with some muskets and lances but were mostly armed with scythes, poles, and clubs. They brought food for three days and money to buy more if needed, a fact suggesting that they were hardly destitute.[132] The commune of Croquants of Angoumois met in June 1636 at the fair in the market town of La Couronne, where ten thousand or more from thirty-odd surrounding parishes assembled, armed with muskets, pikes, scythes, and pitchforks. They were organized into battalions and blockaded the roads to the town. At another Croquant meeting held at Baignes the following month, over six hundred deputies of parishes in Angoumois and Saintonge were present to discuss grievances and the result of their supplications to the king and his representatives in the province.[133] The Périgord Croquants who rose in May 1637 were militarily organized by their elected leader, the nobleman La Mothe-La Forest, who styled himself "general of the communes of Périgord" and was given absolute command over the assemblies. He formed the peasants into detachments under their captains; the men were to supply their own food and weapons, and, while some were kept for action, the rest were sent home to be ready to return for service if called. The general and captains were authorized to judge the "enemies of the liberty of the people" who had approved illegitimate and extraordinary imposts.[134]

Agrarian rebellion was thus sustained by the structure, action, and values of the peasant community. Many of the rebels must not have been among the very poorest peasants; otherwise they would have been unable to equip and maintain themselves at their own cost, as they were expected to do. Mingled with the agricultural folk were other ranks and occupations, such as the numerous village artisans, the scattering of country attorneys and notaries, the petty squires and gentlemen, whom we find in the commune of Périgord in 1637. Even the parish priests, rooted as they were in the community's life, threw themselves into the movement. Four priests were members of the Périgord commune, and more than once the priests joined with their people, as they did in the Angoumois revolt of 1636, when four thousand peasants, armed and organized into a dozen or so companies, were led by their *curés* marching at the head.[135]

The violence in these revolts did not assume a concentrated, systematic

[132] Porchnev, *Les Soulèvements populaires*, 50.

[133] Mousnier, *Fureurs paysannes*, 75–7. A report of the meeting at Baignes, written for his parish by a priest who was present as its representative, is printed in Bercé, *Histoire des Croquants*, v. 2, 740–2.

[134] See Porchnev, *Les Soulèvements populaires*, 77; Mousnier, *Fureurs paysannes*, 88–91; and the text of the Périgord assemblies' regulations, Bercé, *Histoire des Croquants*, v. 2, 751–2.

[135] Bercé, *Histoire des Croquants*, v. 1, 413–14, v. 2, 665–6; Porchnev, *Les Soulèvements populaires*, 62.

character but occurred sporadically against its usual targets: the visible instruments of fiscal administration. The insurgent peasants burned the revenue officials' houses, pillaged their property, and threatened their lives. Collectors, process servers, clerks, employees of the tax farmers, and any who protected them were all fair game of popular anger. The Poitou Croquants named the *élus* as the enemy, declaring that there were two, three, or even six rich ones in every parish who extracted great sums to be sent to Paris while paying almost nothing themselves. The commune ordered such people to be seized, given the justice they deserved, and forced to make restitution for their thievery.[136] Often the peasants marched upon the city where the tax offices were located or agents of the fisc resided or had taken refuge. The Quercy Croquants besieged Cahors, demanding that the *élus* be handed over to them; on the way, they burned and plundered fiscal officials' houses and laid waste their vineyards. The Croquants of Angoumois tried unsuccessfully to occupy Angoulême during the fair of May 1636 in order to massacre the tax agents.[137] There were recurrent incidents in these revolts when the enraged insurgents would seize suspected *gabeleurs*, interrogate and parade them amid blows and insults, and then kill them and mutilate their bodies.[138]

The urban affiliation of agrarian rebellion was due to the antifiscal hatred that townfolk shared with peasants. Thus, peasant and urban revolts might overlap, peasants becoming involved in urban outbreaks, the plebeian population of the towns in peasant movements. Porchnev noted the interconnection of the two types of revolt that sometimes makes it difficult to isolate them.[139] Revolts of the country enveloped the town. The insurrection of 1548 in the southwest spread to Bordeaux and a number of other towns where it received support.[140] The Périgord Croquants occupied Bergerac in 1637, and town insurgencies frequently accompanied the Croquant risings. Conversely, peasants acted as auxiliaries in town revolts.[141] In 1630, Aix-en-Provence was the scene of a considerable urban insurrection precipitated by the threat that *élus* would be introduced into Provence, during which great numbers of peasants from the surrounding villages entered the city to unite with urban *petit peuple* in revolt.[142] Similar episodes took place in Bordeaux and Agen in 1635, when the peasants of the neighboring countryside joined the town outbreaks against the *gabeleurs*.[143]

---

[136] See the text in Bercé, *Histoire des Croquants*, v. 2, 638–9.
[137] Porchnev, *Les Soulèvements populaires*, 50–1; Mousnier, *Fureurs paysannes*, 67.
[138] See Bercé, *Histoire des Croquants*, v. 1, 371–3, for some examples.
[139] Porchnev, *Les Soulèvements populaires*, 132.   [140] Salmon, *Society in crisis*, 36.
[141] Mousnier, *Fureurs paysannes*, 89, 92, 57.
[142] Pillorget, *Les Mouvements insurrectionnels*, 332–4; and Ch. 8 in this book.
[143] Mousnier, *Fureurs paysannes*, 54–7.

The demands and justificatory beliefs of agrarian rebellion were concentrated upon the removal or relief of fiscal burdens as the central goal. Revolt did not engender political programs or produce an elaboration of ideological principles because the peasant movements operated largely within a world of received conventional assumptions respecting the right relation between the king and his people. It was to the king that they addressed their appeal for justice and redress of grievances. Although on occasion their expressions could be bold and sharp, their language toward the sovereign himself was always one of profound respect and loyalty. They did not blame him for their oppression but his servants, the ministers of state, corrupt officials, Parisians, and tax farmers. Hence the slogans often heard in these revolts, like "Long live the king without the *taille*," "Long live the king without the *gabelle*," and "Long live the king, death to the *gabeleurs*."[144] Correspondingly, the strategy of rebels was to lay their grievances before the king and his principal representatives, such as the provincial governor. The Croquants of Angoumois and of Périgord both sent deputations composed of noblemen and others to Paris to see the king and Richelieu, while also negotiating locally with royal authorities.[145]

The revolts were richer in hated than enthusiasm and actuated more by misery and condemnation than by hope. Rebel statements contained a bitter indictment of the fiscal regime with its accompaniments of distress and injustice. They denounced the oppression of the royal ministers, financiers, and Parisian tax farmers as "tyranny" and justified resistance as the only way to reach the king's ears. The Croquants of Angoumois and Saintonge declared that heavy imposts and new charges had forced them to abandon their inheritances, leave their lands uncultivated, and beg their bread. They complained that they had been forced to pay more taxes in two years of the present reign than in the entire reign of the king's father or indeed of all his predecessors since the commencement of the monarchy. "Messieurs of Paris" and the king's council, they affirmed, mock their sufferings while continually increasing exactions "under the pretext of necessities of state." The "insurrectionary communes of Périgord," as the rebels described themselves, attacked the thousand new charges "unknown to our fathers." They condemned the conduct of the troops sent to enforce collections, who treated the peasants with utmost cruelty and acted as if the province "were a conquered country." Despite their many appeals to the king's officials and council, they declared, "we are still under the same tyranny." They warned that God will never permit the de-

144 See Ladurie, *Les Paysans de Languedoc*, v. 1, 495; and Bercé, *Histoire des Croquants*, v. 2. 590.
145 Mousnier, *Fureurs paysannes*, 68, 92.

signs of the king to flourish if maintained "with the blood and sweat of the people."[146]

Occasionally, political suggestions appeared beyond the regular demands for abolishing or lightening imposts and reforming fiscal administration. The Croquants of Angoumois and Saintonge asserted that the ministers had no power to impose new taxes at will, extraordinary charges being reserved only for emergencies with the assent of the Estates General, as anciently practiced. There is no indication however that this idea, a passing allusion, was ever followed up with a specific demand.[147] The Périgord Croquants asked the king to make their province a *"pays d'états."*[148] The Croquants of Poitou actually ordered the reduction of *tailles* and of payments for the support of royal garrisons and further provided, in the interests of equity and the poor, that the parishes themselves should apportion their taxes and administer clerical tithes.[149]

Always in the end, rebellion was crushed, or the insurgents, faced by superior force, submitted and dispersed after presenting and parleying over their grievances. The king would send troops to the affected region to aid the royal governor in putting down the movement; the nobility and other authorities would be commanded to lend their help; meanwhile, royal representatives were conducting discussions with the rebels and attempting to conciliate them by promising sympathetic reception of their grievances. In due course, the rebels would either submit and seek pardon or would be defeated if they continued their resistance. The Angoumois Croquants renounced their revolt on the understanding brought from Paris that they would be pardoned and their complaints considered. The Périgord Croquants were pardoned after first being beaten in a bloody engagement that dealt the death blow to their rising. In this way, by force, negotiation, or a combination of the two, revolt concluded. Perhaps some pockets of resistance, of lawless violence, survived in the area of disturbance, but order was provisionally restored, only to be followed there or elsewhere by another outbreak due to similar kinds of grievances.[150]

Nevertheless, these rebellions were not entirely or invariably futile because they sometimes resulted in the remission of taxes and other concessions. If the king chastised his disobedient subjects, he also wished to appease them. In 1549, the king revoked "forever" in Guienne and the neighboring provinces the *gabelle* that had incited the revolt of the preceding year. The crown's attempt to appoint *élus* in Burgundy in 1629 and Provence in 1630 was given up after the resistance it provoked. The cycle of revolts in the southwest in 1635–7 and the grievances the rebels sub-

---

[146] For the contemporary documents, see Bercé, *Histoire des Croquants*, v. 2, 736–7, 752–4.
[147] *Ibid.*, v. 2, 737. [148] *Ibid.*, v. 2, 753. [149] *Ibid.*, v. 2, 738.
[150] *Ibid.*, v. 1, 366–7, 425–30.

mitted led to the cancellation of several smaller charges, and the taxes withheld during these movements were never paid.[151] Moreover, revolt even went unpunished on occasion if the government thought it politic to act with moderation. Apropos of a revolt in Bayonne in the war year 1641, Cardinal Richelieu wrote, "I don't doubt that the people are guilty and deserve punishment, but the times don't allow us to consider it . . . this has its negative side, [because] one unpunished insurrection facilitates the outbreak of another."[152]

In France, with its pronounced social and political inequalities, where the monarchy operated amidst unparalleled confusion of powers and administrative disorder, with a fiscal system that was exceptionally inefficient, inequitable, and exploitative, peasant revolt almost became an institutionalized form of protest. Peasant and plebeian subjects did not have any recognized avenues of political expression or participation; victimized by oppression, it was only through resistance and violence that they could communicate to the king and central government their distress and anger. Especially was this the case in the earlier seventeenth century, when the forward stride of absolutism went parallel to recurrent outbreaks.

Agrarian rebellion was repetitive. One revolt resembled another, following a similar pattern and aiming at similar goals. Peasant rebels lacked either a political program or an ideological inspiration to direct their eyes beyond immediate grievances toward basic reform or institutional change. They did not reject the seigneurial regime or monarchy, to neither of which did it occur to them to conceive an alternative. They launched their struggle against the evils they felt most strongly and at the people most evidently responsible for the injustices of which they complained. Their resistance was fundamentally a defense of communities against the misgovernment of the royal state in its centralizing and absolutist advance. It was the community, too, that formed the framework for their mobilization, organization, and action, as well as by whose limited horizon their desires and aims were enclosed.

---

[151] *Ibid.*, v. 2, 680; Bercé, *Croquants et Nu-pieds*, 21; Mousnier, *Fureurs paysannes*, 51, 52, 81; Porchnev, *Les Soulèvements populaires*, 296.

[152] Porchnev, *Les Soulèvements populaires*, 297.

8

Urban rebellion

I

Urban rebellion, extinct in the present world of centralized sovereign states, was a regular phenomenon in the former world of less centralized, weakly integrated, early modern states. Look into the well-known treatise, *The greatness of cities*, published in 1588 by the Piedmontese Giovanni Botero to explain the causes that make cities populous and rich. Few of the famous towns of Western Europe that Botero mentioned were immune to urban revolutions in their medieval past, the early modern era, or both. The rich towns of Flanders, most merchantable and frequented for traffic in all Europe because of their light custom duties; Paris, to which the Seine brings an incredible burden of shipping, a city exceeding all others in people and abundance of things; Florence, sovereign over a region of fertile plains and goodly valleys containing many towns and castles; Naples, Milan, and Ghent, formerly residences of princes but now ruled by the king of Spain; Palermo, also under Spain's rule, with its splendid churches and palaces, its lately built pier worthy even of the Romans, and its great new thoroughfare across the city, which has not its like for beauty in the rest of Italy; Spanish towns of honor and reputation – Toledo, Valladolid, Burgos, Barcelona, and Valencia – there was not one that did not at some time or another know the violence and passions of an urban revolt.[1]

Shakespeare, among his innumerable images of life, offers us a picture of one sort of urban revolt that could be transposed to many towns. It is in *Coriolanus*, set in ancient Rome, where the plebeians have risen against the patricians. Driven by hunger and dearth, they are resolved to die rather than starve and charge that the patricians "suffer us to famish, and their storehouses crammed with grain; make edicts for usury, to support usu-

---

[1] G. Botero, *The reason of state*, New Haven, 1956, which also contains his treatise, "The greatness of cities"; see 255, 240, 259, 271, 273, 256, 272, for the allusions in the text.

rers; repeal daily any wholesome act established against the rich, and provide more piercing statutes daily to chain up and restrain the poor."

Here we see one of those recurrent outbreaks, enclosed within the bounds of the urban community, of the poor against the rich and of the inferior commonalty against its privileged superiors. Conjunctural circumstances, too, have their part in causing the grain shortage and famine prices that precipitate revolt in the city. And it is further representative that the demands of the insurgent plebeians are met with a version of the dominant ideology that sanctioned hierarchic subordination and political inequality in medieval and early modern Europe. The patrician, Menenius Agrippa, tells the plebeians the famous fable of the human body whose members senselessly rebel against the belly from which each individual part derives its nourishment. Thus, they are meant to understand by the allegory that

> The senators of Rome are this good belly,
> And you the mutinous members; for examine
> Their counsels and their cares, digest things rightly
> Touching the weal o' the common, you shall find
> No public benefit which you receive
> But it proceeds or comes from them to you,
> And no way from yourselves.[2]

As Shakespeare's realistic fiction illustrates, the urban scene might harbor explosive social and political antagonisms. In this particular instance, there is also a manifest connection between food supply and the preservation of civic order, a matter never far from the mind of municipal and royal authorities. In 1529, amid a season of bad times, Lyon, the second largest city in France, was shaken by a serious riot (a *rebeine*, in local parlance), in which a crowd of two thousand people denounced hoarders, broke open the municipal granary, and attacked some rich men's houses.[3] It is probable that the food or grain riot was the commonest form of urban disorder, episodes of this sort being inevitable in a society of heavy inequality regularly plagued by scarcity. Even though cities may have contained gardens, fields, and livestock, they were divorced from agriculture and forced to depend on external supplies. The need was all the greater in the large towns with their low-paid artisans, their hordes of poor, and their floating population of casual laborers, vagrants, and beggars.

It is in this light that we may understand the aspect of municipal and royal policy that historians of mercantilism have termed the "policy of provision." What this signified in part was the recognition by early modern governments of the necessity to assure a sufficient supply of food to

[2] *Coriolanus*, I, I.
[3] N. Davis, *Society and culture in early modern France*, Stanford, 1975, 27–8, 161.

the populace, grain above all, cheaply.[4] State purchases and stocking of granaries, price fixing, export prohibitions, and regulations forcing rural sellers to frequent urban markets were some of the means used to achieve this end. An inquiry concerning London's food supply that Queen Elizabeth's privy council directed to the city authorities in 1574 shows the concern rulers devoted to this problem. The mayor and aldermen were commanded to report on the quantities and kinds of grain stored in the capital, the prospect and date of arrival of future supplies, the prices fixed on grains for bread and beer, the number of bakers and brewers, and other pertinent details. In the same way, the magistrates of Valladolid in Castile were permanently obsessed with grain provision for their city and stocked the municipal-owned granary after every harvest.[5] To be sure, measures adopted by governments were sometimes ineffective against scarcity, private profiteering, or the contradictions of a fiscal policy that might tax consumables. Nevertheless, apart from any charitable motives, there was a general assumption that the poor must have food, and fear of the poor was a part of contemporary statecraft.

II

In considering urban rebellion, we need be little concerned with the town as it was juridically defined in the states of the time. What we must primarily look to, rather, is the town as a genuine urban place, a concentration of people and activities differentiated socially and economically from its adjacent rural zone of villages and peasantry. The town was likely to be walled. It contained churches and, if it were an episcopal seat, a cathedral. It had quarters and suburbs, perhaps associated with particular occupations. It might serve extensive marketing functions and constitute a focus of commercial or industrial enterprise. It possessed its own governing body of magistrates. If it was a capital or important administrative center, it contained government offices, law courts, noblemen's residences, and palaces. In short, the town was a distinctive environment with its own institutions, a community organism separated from the rural order, the site of a type of existence conscious of itself as apart from the countryside.

We may think, then, of urban rebellions under two distinct aspects: those directed primarily outward against external authority; and those springing from acute internal divisions between upper and lower groups. The latter were much more common in the Middle Ages than in the sixteenth and seventeenth centuries; they reached their greatest intensity

[4] See E. Heckscher, *Mercantilism*, rev. ed., 2 v., London, 1955, v. 1, 128, v. 2, 88, 91.
[5] R. H. Tawney and E. Power (eds.), *Tudor economic documents*, 3 v., London, 1924, v. i, 156–61; B. Bennassar, *Valladolid au siècle d'or*, Paris, 1967, 65.

during the fourteenth century, a time when fierce conflicts between patrician or bourgeois oligarchies and town commonalties, between guild masters and work people, and between rich and poor led to big revolutionary disturbances in many towns.

At the beginning of the fourteenth century, Flanders, the most developed manufacturing region in northwest Europe, was swept by insurrections in Bruges, Ghent, and other cities, protests against patrician domination by the cloth artisans and lower orders. "In all the towns," writes Pirenne, "the commons, directed by the weavers and fullers, overthrew the magistrates, organized themselves, and hastily set up revolutionary governments." The revolt became entwined with Flemish resistance to the king of France; and, when Philip the Fair of France sent an army to crush it, the rebel common folk defeated the gleaming host of French chivalry at Courtrai in July 1302. Seven hundred golden spurs were taken from the vanquished knights and hung as trophies of victory in the church of Notre Dame de Courtrai. "The Flemish artisans," writes Pirenne again, "fought that day as the soldiers of the French republic were to fight centuries later."[6]

Under their prince, the count of Flanders, the Flemish towns, virtually independent city-states at this period, continued to be the scene of violent struggles in which the textile crafts played a predominant role. New revolts broke out in the 1320s, the 1340s, and again at the close of the 1370s. The first of these risings had some interconnection with the simultaneous peasant insurrection in maritime Flanders; the two subsequent movements were directed respectively by the famous popular leaders Jacques van Artevelde and his son, Philip, both of whom perished in them as victims. Ghent, their native city, embodied a long revolutionary tradition that was far from being extinguished in the fourteenth century. These rebellions were not simply embryonic proletarian class conflicts, as Pirenne, under the influence of his vision of modern industrial society, tended to see them. Pervading them also were intense intercraft and interurban differences, as well as resistance to central princely authority. In addition, because of Flanders' location and commercial importance, its urban revolts inevitably had international repercussions and became embroiled in the conflict between the French and English monarchies in the Hundred Years war.[7]

Like Flanders, France in the fourteenth century was subject to frequent

---

[6] H. Pirenne, *Belgian democracy: its early history*, Manchester, 1915, 147, 148, and the entire account in ch. 6; M. Mollat and P. Wolff, *Ongles bleus, Jacques et Ciompi: les révolutions populaires en Europe aux XIVe et XVe siècles*, Paris, 1970, 58–9.

[7] Pirenne, *Belgian democracy*, 152–5; Mollat and Wolff, *Ongles bleus*, 86–90, 60–2, 163–71; see also the detailed discussion in D. Nicholas, *Town and countryside: social, economic and political tensions in fourteenth-century Flanders*, Bruges, 1971.

eruptions of urban rebellion, sometimes directly influenced by the Flemish example. Most significant was the revolt of 1358 in Paris led by Etienne Marcel, provost of the merchants, a position corresponding to head of the city government. A *grand bourgeois* himself, as indeed were also the two van Arteveldes, Marcel aroused the *menu peuple* and the crafts, who were seething with resentment at royal misgovernment and the capital's rich. Grievances born of unfavorable *conjoncture* and wretched conditions underlay the popular upsurge, whereas Marcel himself was a revolutionary reformer who wanted to build an alliance of towns, strengthen the Estates General, and fasten political limitations on the monarchy. His movement also established some slight ties with the Jacquerie, the big peasant revolt that had broken out at the same time in the Ile-de-France and surrounding region. He, too, fell a victim of the rebellion, killed by his own supporters.[8]

Twenty years later, in the summer of 1378, Florence, Italy's prime financial and manufacturing metropolis, which had known many internal upheavals, experienced the revolt of the Ciompi, the fiercest outbreak of social conflict in its history. *Ciompi* was the name given to the lowest stratum of laborers in the Florentine cloth workshops, exploited workers denied even the right to form associations either for religious or economic purposes. The revolt mobilized these disenfranchised men, the members of the lesser guilds, and many of the *populo minuto* or commonalty generally, in an attempt to break the hold of patrician families and the mercantile elite over the city and to enlarge the civic and guild order into a more representative and democratic regime. The struggle achieved some significant concessions and reforms, yet they hardly lasted more than three years before most of them were revoked by a counterrevolutionary revolution.[9] Neither in Florence nor elsewhere did insurrections of the lower orders in the late Middle Ages succeed in reversing for long the trend toward urban domination by oligarchies of one kind or another.

Countless more were the manifestations of tumult and disorder in the medieval towns, with their exclusionist spirit toward outsiders and their perennial internecine quarrels. Factional strife between elites, anti-Semitic pogroms, xenophobic outbursts, strikes, intercraft jealousies, and clashes between corporate groups all contributed their share to the chronicle of urban violence.[10] Such incidents did not cease with the close of the Middle Ages; nor did rebellions cease like the ones we have sketched above, a product of the bitter dissensions between urban elites and populace.

[8] Mollat and Wolff, *Ongles bleus*, 116, 131.

[9] *Ibid.*, 142–62; G. Brucker, *The civic world of early Renaissance Florence*, Princeton, 1977, ch. 1.

[10] See F. Graus, *Struktur und Geschichte drei Volksaufstände im mittelalterlichen Prag*, Sigmaringen, 1971, ch. 1, for a discussion of some general questions relating to the examination of medieval urban revolts and violence.

Nevertheless, the latter conflicts, which had occupied so prominent a place in the revolutionary history of the fourteenth century, not only diminished in number but became of considerably smaller consequence in the sixteenth century and after. By that time the cities had succumbed or were succumbing to princes and royal states who undermined their autonomy or independence and gradually subjected them to their own wider policy and aims.

The Florentine republic fell under the dominion of the Medici, who destroyed its liberty and then formed the territorial state that became the Grand Duchy of Tuscany. The independent traditions of the cities of Flanders had gradually to submit to the centralizing authority of the dukes of Burgundy as rulers of the Netherlands, whose sixteenth-century Habsburg successors also sat upon the thrones of Spain. The Spanish monarchy brought the towns of Castile under closer control through crown-appointed chief magistrates. With the beginning of France's recovery from the Hundred Years war, its kings pressed forward with the disciplining of their towns to make them better serve royal needs and interests.

This was the momentous change confronting so many of the cities in the postmedieval phase of their political and economic existence, a change that entailed a new or stricter subordination to the imperatives and structures of central power. The outward forms of urban self-government could and might persist, but compliance with the policy and financial requirements of rulers was nonetheless expected. Undoubtedly, the expanding grip of central authority brought new opportunities and profitable rewards to the bourgeois sectors that could benefit from the advance of royal absolutism. Yet it also generated tensions and ran counter to traditions of autonomy that died hard in urban communities. In the long run, of course, the cities were forced to bow to kings nearly everywhere. Some of them, however, did not do so without resistance. It was this reluctance to accept the yoke, to surrender communal liberties, and to yield to the will of royal state builders and architects of absolutism that provided the essential background to the majority of urban rebellions in the sixteenth and seventeenth centuries.

III

We are obliged to include urban rebellion as one of the basic types of early modern revolution because of those recurrent situations in which the revolt of the town appears either as the sole presence or as the hegemonical center in the field created by the revolutionary event. Empirically, however, it will be found as subsidiary to several other types of revolution as well. We have already seen, for example, how agrarian revolts could inspire urban revolts, which either remained separate or overlapped with

the peasant movement. Provincial rebellions might also contain urban revolt, as in the case of Catalonia's rebellion in 1640, of which the insurgency of Barcelona was an essential part. Revolutionary civil war was
another type of revolution that invariably subsumed urban rebellion among
its aspects. The revolt of the Netherlands against Spanish rule entailed
numerous urban insurrections, and one of the more significant events of
the Fronde was the revolt in Bordeaux known as the Ormée. Sometimes
the great capital cities themselves caught the contagion of insurrection in
these statewide conflicts. One of the critical developments of the French
civil war was the famous "day of the barricades" in 1588, when Paris
revolted against Henry III and was taken over by the radical adherents of
the Catholic League. In 1648, a repetition of the day of the barricades in
Paris marked the beginning of the Fronde. In 1641–2, the opening phase
of the English revolution, rebel citizens captured the government of London and aligned the capital with the opponents of Charles I. It is noteworthy, incidentally, that in each of these episodes the urban mob played
a decisive role.

Typologically, urban rebellion reflected a distillation of traits widely
characteristic of towns in the early modern states: their reproduction in a
civic context of the hierarchic status structure of the society to which they
belonged; the profound disparities of rights, privileges, and economic condition among their inhabitants; their intense civic patriotism; and their
still incomplete assimilation to the policies and will of national or imperial
governments. Accordingly, the most obvious typological feature of urban
rebellion was its political space, which, even if extending beyond, had the
town as its center. Similarly, the revolutionary actors were town inferior
orders, elite groups, or combinations of both. The aims of revolt were
redress of urban grievances or securing of reforms and liberties in the
interests either of lower orders against elites or of the independence of the
urban community as a whole; and, depending on which of these aims was
uppermost, the targets of attack were urban elites and governing bodies
or external authorities. Rebel action utilized preexistent urban institutions
and communal forms and solidarities. Finally, the beliefs and mentality of
rebels bore the stamp of urban identity and status; demands, correspondingly, were usually rooted in conceptions of prescription, laws, and liberties pertaining to the town and its people.

Of the English, French, and Spanish monarchies, it was the first that
had to reckon least with urban rebellion. In fact, we cannot say that there
was a single instance in England during the entire period of our study. A
book written in 1584 on the laws and customs of London was able to
reflect with satisfaction on the city's loyalty to the monarchy and its "pol-
iticke regiment" by merchant mayors, in contrast to Spanish Naples and
Milan, their government headed by "cruel viceroys," or to sundry cities

in France governed by "insolent Lieutenantes or presidentes."[11] The absence of urban revolts under Tudor and Stuart rule is probably sufficiently explained by some special historical circumstances. First, unlike many cities of the continent, English towns possessed no strong traditions of independence or revolutionary history to inspire them. Second, even before the sixteenth century, the medieval monarchy had already considerably succeeded in integrating the towns and their economies in a body politic more unified than that of other kingdoms. Third, London, the capital, which towered far above all the rest of the towns in its size and economic preeminence (in 1600, London contained about 200,000 people, whereas Norwich, the next largest city, numbered about 12,000), had long stood in close dependence on the crown. Finally, as for internal conflicts in urban communities, they never became so acute as to result in insurrection. Indeed, the sixteenth century was a time when the power of civic oligarchies, despite occasional quarrels in guilds and urban government, was at its highest.[12]

Thus, English urban historians have been obliged to note the rarity of serious disturbances in the towns of early modern England.[13] Probably the worst civic disorder that took place between the reign of Henry VIII and 1640 was the great London riot of 1517 known as evil Mayday, when mobs of apprentices, shopkeepers, artisans, and women attacked the Italian, French, and other foreign craftsmen and merchants in their midst. Coinciding with the hardships of a plague visitation, the outbreak was due to the Londoners' economic resentment of the resident strangers, whose number, it was said, was so great "that the pore English artificers could skarce get any living." Troops mustered by the nobility quelled the disturbance with the help of the municipal authorities. Before quiet was restored, however, over three hundred rioters had been arrested, and thirteen were afterward executed on gallows set up all over the city as an example.[14]

France, afflicted by so many other disorders, was also the most heavily subject to urban rebellions. There were at least two in the earlier sixteenth century, both in the southwest, at Agen in 1514 and La Rochelle in 1542. We have also previously seen that a number of towns took part in the

---

[11]Cited in F. Thompson, *Magna Carta: Its role in the making of the English constitution 1300–1629*, Minneapolis, 1948, 195.

[12]P. Clark and P. Slack, *English towns in transition 1500–1700*, Oxford, 1976, 83, chs. 5, 8, 9. An excellent picture of London government, its personnel, and its close cooperation with the monarchy at this period is given by F. Foster, *The politics of stability: a portrait of the rulers of Elizabethan London*, London, 1977.

[13]P. Clark and P. Slack (eds.), *Crisis and order in English towns 1500–1700*, London, 1972, 19.

[14]The "evil Mayday" riot is described by Edward Hall (*Chronicle*, ed. C. Whibley, 2 v., London, 1904, v. 1, 153–64) and by J. S. Brewer (*The reign of Henry VIII*, 2 v., London, 1889, v. 1, 243–9).

agrarian rebellion of 1548 in Guienne.[15] Not an urban revolt but a manifestation of labor conflict was the strike of journeymen printers in Lyon and Paris between 1539 and 1541. Actuated by grievances over wages and other conditions, the strikers were so well organized and determined that it took the intervention of the crown itself on behalf of the master printers to suppress the movement.[16]

The revolutionary civil war that spanned the last forty years of the sixteenth century in France swallowed up every sort of political violence in itself. Then, after its end, there came on the terrible decades of the earlier seventeenth century already referred to, with their miseries caused by depression, subsistence crises, war, and the relentless demands and pressures of Louis XIII's government. During this period of turmoil, urban rebellion turned into a chronic phenomenon, occurring both by itself and in association with other types of revolution. The cycle of urban seditions started in the 1620s, at the same time as the wave of peasant insurrections, and was finally absorbed in the culminating revolution of the Fronde.

We may gain an impression of the cycle's scope from a chronological list compiled by Porchnev of urban revolts from 1623 to 1647, the eve of the Fronde. It includes 118 altogether for this quarter-century, with 20 revolts in the year 1635 alone. The next highest year was 1639, which had 9; other years saw as many as 8 (1630), 7 (1643), 6 (1628, 1631, 1633), and 5 (1629, 1637, 1640, 1641, 1644). Although this list probably contains some omissions, some events below the threshold of revolt, and others belonging to a different type of revolution (the urban revolts of 1639 in Normandy were part of the provincial rebellion of the Nu-pieds), it is unlikely to be very far wrong. It offers striking evidence of the epidemic of disobedience and resistance that the grievances of this unhappy time provoked in many towns over widespread parts of the kingdom.[17]

---

[15] Chapter 7 in this book.

[16] See the account of H. Lemonnier in *Histoire de France depuis les origines jusqu'à la Révolution*, ed. E. Lavisse, Paris, 1903–11, v. 5, pt. 1, 272–4; and P. Chauvet, *Les Ouvriers du livre en France: des origines à la révolution de 1789*, Paris, 1959, 20–45. (I owe this latter reference to my student, Timothy Miller, and his discussion of the strike in an unpublished seminar paper.)

[17] B. Porchnev, *Les Soulèvements populaires en France de 1623 à 1648*, trans. from the Russian, Paris, 1963, 133–4. This list is described as including revolts "of a certain importance." As it contains no figures, I have compiled the totals myself. At the end of his volume, Porchnev gives a fuller chronological list of urban revolts from 1616 to 1647, totaling 203. Some of the events recorded by Porchnev were quite brief and look more like riots than revolts; for example, the sedition in Lyon in 1632 lasted three days, in Rennes in 1636 three days, at Périgeux and at Agen in 1635 three days, and at Bayonne in 1641 three or four days (*ibid.*, 152–3, 188, 215); Y.-M. Bercé, *Histoire des Croquants: Etude des soulèvements populaires au XVIIe siècle dans la sud-ouest de la France*, 2 v., Geneva, 1974, v. 1, 317, 323. Neither of Porchnev's lists mentions the revolt of La Rochelle of 1627–8. Apparently he did not regard it as a "popular revolt" because of its connection with religion as a resistance by the Huguenots.

The Spanish monarchy had to deal with urban rebellions in several of its states, although on a far smaller scale than in France. Yet it was in the kingdom of Castile in 1520 that the greatest urban rebellion of early modern Europe took place: the revolt of the Comuneros. Contemporaneous with the latter but not connected with it was the Germania of Valencia, an urban revolt centered on one of the principal cities of the crown of Aragon. There were no other urban rebellions in peninsular Spain in the sixteenth century, although the provincial revolt of Aragon in 1591 included a few town disturbances. In the first half of the seventeenth century in Spain itself, we find only some sporadic outbreaks in Andalusian cities between 1648 and 1652, the product of the depressed conditions prevailing in these years.

Outside Spain, in the monarchy's other European possessions, there was the revolt of Ghent in 1539, the only urban rebellion in the Netherlands during the reign of the Emperor Charles V. Lastly, in Italy, both Naples, capital of the Neapolitan kingdom, and Palermo, capital of the kingdom of Sicily, were the scene of several urban insurrections: Naples in 1547 and 1647; Palermo in 1516 and 1647. (There was one more urban revolt in Sicily during the seventeenth century, Messina's in 1674, which falls beyond the boundaries of our study.)[18]

We shall attempt to look more closely at some of the revolts mentioned in the preceding survey in order to ascertain both their structural characteristics and their variations. Here, as previously in the case of peasants, there is the difficulty of penetrating the thoughts and action of urban rebels, nameless as nearly all of them are and speaking so rarely in their own person. Even in the tumult of insurrection we may hear their voices only faintly across the distance that separates them from us. By considering them, however, within their own familiar world and its imperatives, we may perhaps be able to gain an insight into the nature and diversity of these movements and their revolutionary actors.

IV

FRENCH URBAN REBELLIONS

Let us glance first at the earliest urban rebellion of our period to be encountered in France, that at Agen in July 1514. It was provoked by an impost on wine and other consumption articles, which the town consuls had levied in order to raise revenue to repay a municipal debt. After the preliminary murmuring and petty incidents, the revolt began with the tocsin summoning the crowd, which massed in the main square and besieged the town hall; the revolt expired within two weeks, suppressed at

---

[18] For the revolt of Messina, see D. Mack Smith, *A history of Sicily . . . 800–1713*, London, 1968, ch. 22.

royal command backed by the authority of the Parlement of Bordeaux. The uprising was a protest against the growing weight of taxes and was aimed at the local oligarchy of magisterial and rich families, the *plus apparens*, who monopolized offices, ran town affairs in their own interest, and benefited by the unequal distribution of fiscal burdens. The rebels were described as the *menu populaire*. They consisted mostly of artisan strata of different occupations, tradesmen, and some of the poor, as well as of peasants of the rural periphery who came into the town to join the insurrection. Especially noteworthy was the insurgents' proclamation of the "commune" as their watchword, a clamor for a voice in the town government, whose popular organ, the general assembly of inhabitants, had fallen into complete disuse. One of the rebels declared that "the only king is the commune"; the crowd, however, shouted, "Long live the king and the commune!" We have already seen that the commune figured as a recurrent theme in French peasant revolts. Here, in an urban context, it appeared as an expression of the commonalty's desire for a more inclusive civic regime to serve the popular interest.[19]

In France, opposition to fiscality was nearly always the strongest driving force of urban rebellions. Although at Agen its target was the municipal authorities, usually it was directed outward against the exactions and agents of the monarchical state. Hatred of new and unaccustomed taxes, reinforced by a deep-rooted civic and provincial autonomism, combined to stamp the revolts of towns with their predominant anticentralist motif. It was these that also imbued them, amid all their variety of circumstance, with their repetitive character and that facilitated their interaction with agrarian insurrections incited by similar antifiscal causes.

Thus, the revolt of La Rochelle in August 1542 followed an edict by Francis I introducing a *gabelle* on salt into previously exempt provinces of the southwest. There was a rising in the town against the impost, and the main target was the royal governor. The inferior populace provided the active element in the urban revolt, but the movement also spread over the surrounding coastal region, where as many as ten thousand people – noblemen, the owners of salt marshes, and various other elements – resisted the agents of the new tax. The La Rochelle revolt was suppressed by royal troops without difficulty, and at the end of the year the king himself came to the town. The community feared punishment, but the monarch, engaged at the time in war with the Emperor Charles V, thought it more politic to be lenient. He made a speech to the citizens declaring that he would not follow the example of the emperor, whose hands were bloody from punishing the rebellion of Ghent three years before. As Jean Bodin

[19] I have taken these particulars of the revolt in Agen from the account of G. Procacci (*Classi sociali e monarchia assoluta nella Francia della prima metà del secolo XVI*, Turin, 1955, 161–73), who has made use of the sources.

relates the story, Francis I, "with the majestie of his speech terrified them of Rochell and fined them, but yet put no man to death." Moreover, he also "left unto the citie the liberties . . . thereof."[20]

It was this same salt tax that provoked the great agrarian rebellion of 1548 in Guienne and neighboring provinces, with its accompanying urban participation.[21] Encouraged by the presence of peasant bands, whose hatred of the *gabelle* they shared, a number of towns joined the revolt. Bordeaux was the most important place affected. In August, with insurgent peasants nearby, the *menu peuple* of Bordeaux rose, and, among other acts of violence against reputed *gabeleurs*, they slaughtered the king's lieutenant-general, de Monneins, chief representative of royal authority in the province, who was in the town hall. Civic officials, members of the provincial *parlement*, and other notables refrained at first from taking measures against the revolt, as they doubtless endorsed its antifiscal aim. Then, alarmed by the popular disorders, the bourgeois militia acted to repress the outbreak. Near the end of the month, the duke of Montmorency, constable of France, entered the city with several thousand troops and inflicted a harsh revenge in the king's name. He executed almost 150 people, imposed a heavy fine, and abolished Bordeaux's privileges. Two years later, however, Henry II restored the city's privileges; even more important, he had already revoked the objectionable *gabelle*, having promised for himself and his successors in perpetuity never to levy it upon the *"pays."*[22]

Royal paternalism and royal chastisement were the twin poles between which such uprisings revolved, a condition that prevented them from offering any ideological challenge to the regime. The king was father, giver, and punisher; to him his unhappy subjects appealed both for justice and for mercy. Although rebellion relieved popular anger, rebels had no real political alternatives to advance against absolutism and its excesses. They remained fixed to traditionalist premises, which sanctioned opposition to new and unaccustomed exactions and relied on local immunities and privileges as a bar to the demands of an invasive centralism.

The urban rebellions of the earlier seventeenth century were likewise caused by hostility to fiscal oppression.[23] The one great exception was the revolt in 1627–8 of the militant Huguenot stronghold, La Rochelle, which Louis XIII and Richelieu were able to suppress only after a long, grueling siege. But La Rochelle's revolt belonged to a wider movement of a differ-

---

[20] H. Lemonnier in Lavisse, *Histoire de France*, v. 5, pt. 2, 119–20; Procacci, *Classi sociali*, 176; J. Bodin, *The six bookes of a commonweal* (1576), trans. Richard Knolles, ed. K. McRae (1606; reprint ed., Cambridge, 1962), 378–9.

[21] Chapter 7 in this book.

[22] See Y.-M. Bercé, *Croquants et Nu-pieds*, Paris, 1974, 20–43, which contains an account and documents of the revolt of 1548; J. H. M. Salmon, *Society in crisis: France in the sixteenth century*, New York, 1975, 36–7; Bodin, *The six bookes*, 378.

[23] See Porchnev's comments, *Les Soulèvements populaires*, 133–4.

ent type: It was part of the regionally based resistance of the Huguenots in their last-ditch struggle to preserve what remained of the political powers granted them as concessions in the Edict of Nantes at the end of the sixteenth-century civil war. Accordingly, this conflict is better categorized with provincial rebellions, and we shall allude to it again in that connection. As for other urban rebellions in the years prior to the Fronde, it is needless to look at more than a few because all of them tended to display the same recurrent pattern, whatever the events that comprised their separate and individual histories.

In February 1630, a week-long insurrection engulfed Dijon, the capital of Burgundy, a city of twenty thousand people, seat of the provincial *parlement*, and principal center of an extensive wine-producing region. It was the sequel to a royal edict suppressing the Estates of Burgundy and instituting *élections* in the province. Agitated by the loss of fiscal privileges, the Dijonnais feared an onslaught of new exactions – and worst of all a tax on wine. A rumor of the imminent installation of *élus* in the city lit the spark. Into the streets poured a mob of hundreds of people, while civic authorities and elites revealed their sympathy or approval by their inaction. The nucleus of the movement lay in two of the city's seven quarters, the parishes of Saint-Philibert and Saint-Nicolas, occupied by vineyard workers and artisans. Within these overcrowded neighborhoods of dark, narrow streets, mean wooden dwellings, workshops, little stores, and taverns, the communal life of the *menu peuple* flowed. From the suburbs as well, where lived other miscellaneous poor, supporters arrived.

Led by a *vigneron* dubbed King Machas, the mob filled the area around the city hall, marching in a carnival atmosphere to the sound of drums and singing a popular tune, the "Lanturelu," from which the revolt took its name. The insurgents threatened finance officials, plundered houses, and even burned pictures of Louis XIII and Richelieu. After several days of turmoil, the magistrates finally took fright and ordered the bourgeois militia, which had thus far not interfered, to suppress the revolt. The ensuing fighting left a dozen rebels killed, and two more were subsequently executed.

The dilatory conduct of Dijon's magistrates incurred Louis XIII's anger, and, on a visit to the city a few weeks later, he reprimanded them for not preventing the outbreak as was their duty and responsibility. Nevertheless, he refrained from inflicting any punishment on the civic corporation; furthermore, he gave up the plan to establish *élus*. [24]

The Lanturelu revolt in Dijon was exceeded in scale and length by the

---

[24] For the Lanturelu revolt in Dijon, see *ibid.*, 135–43; and R. Mousnier, *Fureurs paysannes: Les paysannes dans les révoltes du XVIIᵉ siècle*, Paris, 1968, 51. Dijon and its poor quarters in the seventeenth century are described by G. Roupnel, *La Ville et la campagne au XVIIᵉ siècle*, Paris, 1955, pt. 2, chs. 1–3.

more serious revolt of the Cascavéoux in Aix-en-Provence between September and December 1630, which was infused by the same interplay of conditions and collective response that formed the underlying structure of so many other French urban rebellions of the period.

In the immediate background loomed the adversities of *conjoncture*. The double curse of poor harvests and the ravages of plague afflicted Aix and its province in the later 1620s. Scarcity combined with disease created untold suffering among the *menu peuple*. So many beggars infested the city that guards had to be posted at the gates to keep them out. Besides these misfortunes due to an inscrutable providence were the increasing demands of the state. Royal troops were quartered on the province. The crown's creation of new offices, ever a cause of fresh exactions, and higher prices on salt, a royal monopoly, aroused protest that these actions had been authorized without the assent of the Estates of Provence. To add to other grievances came the king's decision in 1629 to establish *élus* in the province, an innovation that would undermine at a stroke the privileges serving as a defensive barrier to the royal fisc. Aix was then a city of about twenty-five thousand, Provence's capital and residence of the provincial *parlement*. The prospect of *élus* meant the aggravation of oppression upon an already overburdened and irritated population; it likewise threatened the vested interests and authority of existing officeholders. No wonder that, in the usual way French revolts were catalyzed by fiscal grievances, this new threat caused a rebellion in Aix.[25]

A typical incident kindled the revolt: the arrival in mid-September 1630 of one of those hated special emissaries of central authority, a royal intendant. His fiscal mission was known. At once bells called out the mob, who forced the intendant to flee for his life. For a time the movement was a nearly unanimous front of elites and *petit peuple*. Indeed, the intendant blamed the rising on the former; he did not believe the headless multitude could do anything without the guidance of its superiors. And it was certainly true that provincial noblemen, members of the Parlement of Aix, bourgeois Aixois, and others of the *plus apparens* were all fiercely opposed to *élus* as a new abuse of fiscality that spelled the destruction of local liberties. Not only did they sanction and support popular resistance, they actively incited it.

Laurent Coriolis, president of the Parlement of Aix, became the chief of the insurgents, who formed a sort of party, the Cascavéoux, identified by an emblem of white ribbon and a tiny bell, after which the revolt was named. With the help of his relatives and other *parlementaires*, Coriolis encouraged a mass following of artisans and plebeian inhabitants to attack

---

[25] See C. Fairchilds, *Poverty and charity in Aix-en-Provence 1640–1789*, Baltimore, 1976, 23; R. Pillorget, *Les Mouvements insurrectionnels de Provence entre 1596 et 1715*, Paris, 1975, 313–25.

the property and persons of those associated with the fiscal regime. Leaflets were distributed, and Richelieu's portrait burned in the streets. The dominant slogans were "Long live the king and away with *élus!*" and "*Elus* traitors to the *pays!*"

Of course, the insurrection soon got out of hand. Threats were made against the rich, and Coriolis, an unscrupulous politician, used the popular violence to pursue his personal vendetta against rival clans. At the beginning of November, a great throng of peasants from the neighboring rural zone entered Aix to join with the insurgents. Before they left, there was a night of riot and pillage that terrified the propertied Aixois. It brought the inevitable reaction. The civic authorities mobilized a bourgeois guard to preserve order. The Parlement prohibited all assemblies on pain of death. Vagabonds and other dangerous elements were driven out. Another faction of Cascavéoux with its own emblem was organized to oppose Coriolis's domination in the city. It was at this time that an anonymous pamphleteer condemned the expulsion of the poorest as contrary to the laws of God and nature. "In what way is the city less the *patrie* of the poor than of yours, Messieurs rich men?" the writer demanded. He denounced the wealthy citizens and fiscal officials "who drink the people's sweat and fatten on its flesh."[26]

Although further disorders took place in December, the rebellion subsided through repression and the cessation of elite support. The proximity of the royal general, the prince of Condé, with 5,500 troops, also had its effect. Coriolis fled and was later deprived of his office and imprisoned for life. Considering the outbreak's magnitude, the king did not punish it with great severity. Apparently there were hardly any executions. The Parlement was exiled for a time, and several of its judges were forbidden to exercise their functions and summoned to Paris. The city's right to elect its consuls was abolished for several years, and it was also obliged to indemnify the victims of the previous disturbances. Worst of all, Condé's soldiers were quartered in Aix for a couple of months and allowed to pillage in the area. With all this, however, the crown abandoned its scheme of appointing *élus*, a concession for which it obtained in return a contribution of 1.5 million livres payable over four years. Perhaps, then, the verdict of the recent chronicler of the rebellion of Aix is not inappropriate: "From a certain point of view the insurrection was not useless: The customs and privileges of the province were safe and the '*plus apparens*' satisfied."[27] As for the lesser folk who brought their numbers and militancy to the antifiscal resistance, we have no way of knowing what they thought.[28]

[26] Cited in Pillorget, *Les Mouvements insurrectionnels*, 337.   [27] *Ibid.*, 348.

[28] For accounts of the revolt of Aix, see *ibid.*, bk. 1, ch. 3; Porchnev, *Les Soulèvements populaires*, 143–7; Mousnier, *Fureurs paysannes*, 51–2; and the detailed description with in-

To conclude our view of French urban rebellions, we shall glance briefly at a final example, the insurrections in the towns of Guienne between May and July 1635, and chiefly in Bordeaux, the provincial capital, Agen, and Périgeux. Sharing the same general characteristics, we need not particularize their events. Multiple and separate resistances, each organically rooted in its own urban community, all were nonetheless the product of identical situations and manifested a common repertoire of action and reaction.

In every case, some new exorbitancy of royal finance, a tax on taverns, for instance, or the abolition of an exemption from certain imposts, sparked the outbreak. Then the residential quarters of the poor erupted, mobs of three, five, and even ten thousand took to the streets, and the pursuit of *gabeleurs* became the order of the day. Riot and exultation, violence coupled with aspects of a popular festival and its drunken indulgence, dominated these outbreaks, as the lower orders dropped their workaday routine for the collective action that demonstrated their anger and made them feel their strength. The militant base was always the urban plebs: not made up entirely, perhaps, of what the president of the Parlement of Bordeaux called "the lowest part of the people,"[29] but consisting of a mixture of artisans, journeymen, day laborers, small shopkeepers, and sometimes womenfolk, too, who participated with their men. At Bordeaux a boatman and a tavernkeeper, at Agen a master glover, a pack-saddle maker, and again a tavernkeeper, at Périgeux a physician, stood out as leaders and haranguers of the crowd. Peasants swarmed in from the outskirts to unite briefly with the revolt, as happened in Bordeaux. At Agen six thousand peasants who tried to enter were kept out by the bourgeois militia and burned the property of *gabeleurs* in the vicinity.

Insurrection plunged the towns into repeated disorders. Town halls were besieged, jails broken open, and prisoners released. The violence, though, was not indiscriminate but tended to concentrate upon agents of financial administration, who were hunted down if they could be found and their houses pillaged or burned. Seven perished at Bordeaux, the first victim being the petty functionary who brought the edict to implement the tax on taverns. At Agen, the rebels killed fifteen in two days at the height of the revolt, all identified as finance officials, collectors and farmers of taxes. At Périgeux they massacred a clerk and threatened the royal intendant, who saved himself by flight. "Kill the *gabeleurs!*" and "Long live the king without the *gabelle!*" were the rallying cries. In their fury, the crowds

teresting observations by S. Kettering, *Judicial politics and urban revolt in seventeenth-century France: The Parlement of Aix, 1629–1659*, Princeton, 1978, ch. 5.

[29] Cited in Porchnev, *Les Soulèvements populaires*, 161.

committed bloody atrocities, beating victims to death and mutilating their bodies. Occasionally, they allowed a prisoner to confess or say his prayers. Innocent suspects suffered with the guilty: "Some honest bourgeois of prosperous condition," observers noted, "were considered to be accomplices of the *gabelle*."[30] Obviously, hatred of the tax functionaries could easily flow over into violence against the wealthy.

Nevertheless, passivity, neutral or ambiguous behavior, and even partial support were discernible among the notables and well-to-do. The bourgeois militia of Bordeaux showed little will to act, and the duke of Epernon, governor of the province, reported that "most people consider these mutineers as their liberators."[31] At Périgeux the bourgeois guard was similarly slack. Only at Agen, where the violence was particularly intense and accompanied by a definite social antagonism, did elites and authorities take concerted steps against the outbreak.

These revolts in Guienne, with their peak incidents and intermittent renewals of violence, lasted altogether a couple of months. They were put down at the crown's orders by local and royal forces with the duke of Epernon and his son at their head. Although a few unfortunates were hung, no wholesale reprisals followed. Any such measures would have been highly impolitic considering the inflamed spirit of the population. In September, the king issued a general pardon to the rebels. The disruption they created was such that to appease them the government had to suspend the offending fiscal edicts and to resign itself to a heavy loss of tax collections, which the prevailing circumstances made it impossible to enforce.[32]

Taken as a whole, French urban rebellions were devoid of programs or ideas. In the same way as the concurrent agrarian revolts, they seemed to reflect a stasis in French society despite its exceptional amount of violence and insubordination, an inability by insurgent forces to transcend the existing state of things with any informing vision of an alternative. Although again and again the centralist offensive of the crown led to resistance, the latter failed to give rise to demands for political change. The monarchy's rule and its paternalistic authority were never threatened. This was probably one reason why the king often moderated his punishment of rebels and made concessions to their grievances.

Urban rebellion was essentially a defensive response by the whole community. To the plebeian populace, the punishment of *gabeleurs* was a deserved act of communal justice. If such people took the largest, most active part in these insurrections, that was because they were most sensible of fiscal oppression. But elites usually shared responsibility in some measure.

---

[30] Cited in Bercé, *Histoire des Croquants*, v. 1, 330.   [31] Cited in *ibid.*, v. 1, 306.

[32] The best account of these revolts is in *ibid.*, v. 1, pt. 2, ch. 2; and see also Porchnev, *Les Soulèvements populaires*, 156–86, for some illuminating details.

Their own opposition to exactions helped to legitimize resistance, and they encouraged revolt, whether by actual instigation, covert approval and sympathy, or inaction, when disorder broke out. The involvement of elites was especially evident in Aix in 1630, where the role played by *parlementaires* resembled a miniature dress rehearsal for the Fronde eighteen years later, initiated and led by the judges of the Parlement of Paris.[33]

In the end, of course, such revolts were largely sterile. True, they sometimes extracted concessions, the suspension or revocation of a new exaction, the redress of some grievance. But they were helpless to hold back the advance of absolutism and its centralizing grip because they had no political reforms to propose and conceived of no new institutional limits on the power of the royal state.

V

THE SPANISH MONARCHY

Urban rebellions in the possessions of imperial Spain, as I have pointed out, were less frequent than in France. All told, there were about ten instances, their incidence falling within two separate periods: the first, the earlier years of the sixteenth century in the reign of Charles V; the second, the 1640s during the reign of Philip IV. We need hardly take more than passing notice of the majority of these rebellions for the purposes of our inquiry. It will suffice to select two that stand out both in their contrasts and in their representative significance – the revolt of the Castilian cities in 1520 and of Naples in 1647. In considering them, we shall reverse the usual chronological order: It makes sense here to proceed backward from the *ignis fatuus* of Naples's revolt in the ill-starred 1640s to the monumental rebellion of the Comuneros coinciding with the moment when the Habsburg monarchy of Spain was on the threshold of its European preponderance.

The Naples rebellion of 1647

During the century and a half of our period, Spain's Italian states saw their societies and governing classes increasingly subdued and assimilated into the structure of imperial rule and their resources ever more strongly exploited in the monarchy's dynastic and political interests. The saying became current that "in Sicily the Spanish nibble, in Naples they eat, and in Milan they devour." Despite their formal autonomy under viceroys, these states were essentially dependencies coordinated to priorities determined by Castilian and Spanish masters.

To be sure, there were the occasional outbreaks of resistance, but they

---

[33] This point is made by Porchnev, *Les Soulèvements populaires*, 145.

were rare and more a reflection of particular complaints than of opposition to Spanish domination. Palermo's revolt in 1516–17 was of this kind: a diffuse protest against taxes and other grievances, blamed on two successive viceroys and fueled by mob violence.[34] The city of Naples experienced a similar rebellion in the summer of 1547 over the attempt of the Castilian viceroy to introduce the Inquisition. In both instances, repression triumphed, although concessions were also made.[35] Such movements did not challenge the legitimacy of the regime and quickly lost their élan in the face of its weight and authority. The revolt of 1547 was termed by the philosopher-scholar Croce, one of Naples's most illustrious sons, "the last evidence of Neapolitan independence and political vitality."[36] It is doubtful, however, that this vitality could ever have transcended its persistently anarchic character to focus upon coherent goals. In any event, both the kingdoms of Naples and Sicily remained among the most loyal provinces of the Spanish empire, although briefly stirred to rebellion once again by the dismal circumstances of the 1640s.

The 1640s were a time of disastrous reverses, of staggering burdens the monarchy could sustain only by exhausting effort and new, exorbitant pressures on its subjects, altogether a far cry from the hegemonic position it had occupied in the preceding century. To economic contraction and malaise in Castile were conjoined the huge costs of the lengthy, wide-fronted war with rival powers, the French monarchy and the Dutch republic, that went steadily against Spain. All this was part of Spain's "crisis of the seventeenth century" and decline, of which we have spoken in Chapter 5. The government of Philip IV and his minister, the count-duke of Olivares, in Madrid had not only these problems to contend with: After 1640 it was further weighed down by the provincial rebellions in Catalonia and Portugal, which worsened its war difficulties and threatened the entire imperial system of union of crowns.

Both of these revolts, as well as the typologically different rebellions of Palermo and Naples in 1647, were the common product of the Spanish monarchy's time of troubles.[37] In this sense, but in hardly any other, they were related; the heavier exactions and contributions ordered from Ma-

[34] For a description of this episode see Smith, A history of Sicily, 110–11. The account by E. Armstrong (The Emperor Charles V, 2 v., London, 1902, v. 1, 105–11) likens the revolt of Palermo, which spread to other towns, to the Comuneros of Castile and refers to its "national character," but there is no basis for this view.

[35] For the 1547 revolt of Naples, see G. D'Agostino's treatment in Storia di Napoli, 10 v., Naples, 1967–74, v. 5, pt. 1, 64–8.

[36] B. Croce, History of the kingdom of Naples, trans. F. Frenaye, Chicago, 1970, 113. The original appeared in 1925.

[37] An overview of Spain's condition and the revolts of the 1640s is presented by J. H. Elliott, "The decline of Spain," in Crisis in Europe 1560–1660, ed. T. Aston, London, 1965, and "Revolts in the Spanish monarchy," in Preconditions of revolution in early modern Europe, ed. R. Forster and J. Greene, Baltimore, 1970.

drid affected all of the monarchy's dominions in varying proportions. Apart from this fact, however, each revolt ran its separate course indifferent to the rest. If there was a revolutionary crisis in the Spanish empire during the 1640s, it was actually four crises, not one, joined together only at the center.

Palermo and Naples were two of the biggest cities in Europe, each filled with a volatile mass of plebeian humanity. The first contained about 130,000 people in the mid-seventeenth century, the second over 300,000.[38] In May 1647, revolt broke out in Palermo; in July, Naples followed, probably slightly influenced by the former's example. The immediate origin of both revolts lay visible on the surface. Each was an insurrection of the inferior populace, devoid of elite participation, and due to conjunctural adversities and antifiscal hostility. In Sicily, a harvest failure in 1646, scarcity, price rises, plague, bad weather in the sowing season, which evoked public penances and prayers for relief, and excises falling heavily on grain comprised the climate of revolt. The first demand of the insurgents was the elimination of taxes on grain, wine, oil, meat, and cheese. In Naples, a duty on fruit was the immediate provocation to a resistance in which the Amalfitan fish peddler, Masaniello, emerged from the ruck of the city poor as mob leader and chief.

After spreading to some other Sicilian towns – but not to Messina, its traditional rival – Palermo's revolt came to an end in September, defeated by its own chaotic dissensions and repression. It did not reject Spanish rule but vainly tried to obtain fiscal and political reforms to benefit the guilds and populace at the expense of the higher orders.[39] The revolt of Naples – "the cycle of utopia and disorder," a Neapolitan historian has called it, "which passes in history as the revolution of Masaniello"[40] – was a longer, more spectacular conflict, which went through several phases before its expiration in the spring of 1648.

The period leading up to the revolt was a case history in the pathology of Spanish administration. The intensification of fiscalism in the 1630s and 1640s was associated, paradoxically, with the steady deterioration of state authority. On the one hand, the government levied heavier exactions toward the war, sending large sums as well as soldiers outside the kingdom and, after 1642, no longer summoning the Neapolitan parliament to grant contributions. On the other hand, its financial exigencies placed it more and more at the mercy of rapacious bourgeois creditors and specu-

---

[38] For these figures, see H. Koenigsberger, "The revolt of Palermo in 1647," in *Estates and revolutions*, Ithaca, 1971, 256; and R. Mols, *Introduction à la démographie historique des villes d'Europe*, 3 v., Louvain, 1954–6, v. 2, 506.

[39] See the accounts by H. Koenigsberger, "The revolt of Palermo," and Smith, *A history of Sicily*, ch. 21.

[40] M. Schipa, *Masaniello*, Bari, 1925, 177.

lators, who enriched and ennobled themselves through the needs of the state. The crown was forced to mortgage revenues to tax farmers and to sell monopolies, rights, and offices. In the country, it alienated royal lands and demesnial towns to both the older and new nobility, who extended their sway over peasants and rural communities.[41] Overall, the situation was one of unprecedented administrative and financial confusion, official corruption, economic regression, and subordination of the state's authority to private interests. The absorption of financiers and contractors into the nobility and the vulnerability of the government strengthened aristocratic power in both the city and the kingdom of Naples. Instead of standing over and controlling the nobility, as had been its traditional role, the crown found itself in its time of troubles more indebted and compelled to make concessions to the aristocratic order. Such was the price the Spanish monarchy had to pay if it was to continue to extract wealth from Naples for its imperial policy.[42]

In consequence, what was most apparent was the fracturing and disunion of Neapolitan society under Spain's government. There was at once a lack of any common interest, a resentment of oppression by the lower orders, and an absence of ability or disposition by elites to unite in defense of "justice" or the kingdom's autonomous liberties.

These conditions were inscribed upon the revolution of 1647 and determined its character. The urban rebellion surged up from the lower depths, from the rancor of a population inspired by hatred of exactions, officials, and the abuses of the powerful. On July 7, 1647, an incident of protest against the odious fruit tax started a riot and aroused the mob. Led by the youthful fish vendor Tommaso Aniello, nicknamed Masaniello, thousands collected and rampaged through the city to the viceregal palace. The Spanish viceroy, the duke of Arcos, in danger of his life, fled for refuge to a fortress.

Masaniello came to the fore as a combination of people's tribune, gang boss, and demagogue who orchestrated the violence of his followers. Behind him as advisor stood the aged lawyer, Giulio Genoino, well known

[41] See Chapter 3 in this book.

[42] For the condition and development of Naples in the earlier seventeenth century, see above all R. Villari, *La rivolta antispagnola a Napoli: le origini (1585–1647)*, 2nd ed., Bari, 1973. V. Comparato, *Uffici e società a Napoli (1600–1647)*, Florence, 1974; and F. Caracciolo, *Il regno de Napoli nei secoli XVI e XVII: Economia e società*, Rome, 1966, also contain much valuable information and observations. There is a helpful general survey by R. Colapietra, "Il governo spagnolo nell'Italia meridionale (Napoli dal 1580 al 1648)," in *Storia di Napoli*, v. 5, pt. 1. A number of writers have followed Villari's lead in advancing the questionable thesis of "refeudalization" and a "new feudality" during this period. The sole merit in this view is its conformity to the Marxist schema of the stages of social evolution. Comparato can even refer to the revolt of 1647 as a "failed revolution" (27), thus presupposing an ideal trajectory of historical change prescribed by Marxist theory to which the actual circumstances and revolutionary actors, however, obstinately refuse to submit.

to the Neapolitans for his long effort to restrict aristocratic influence and reform the structure of city government in the bourgeois and popular interest. For ten days Masaniello, acclaimed to the post of captain-general of the people, was dictator of Naples. The crowd had armed itself, whereas the viceroy had no soldiers at the time to suppress the revolt. At this stage, the dominant cry was "Long live the king of Spain, down with the bad government!" There ensued a burst of executions and the plundering and destruction of palaces and houses of tax farmers, officials, and similar targets of the insurgents' wrath. A contemporary chronicler of these events commented: "The Neapolitan people were so heated in their desires, and ˈ animated . . . to the destroying of the houses of public Ministers and artizans of the Royal Court, and also of Lawyers and Farmers of the Gabels, that no bounds were sufficient to stop their arrogance and fury."[43]

The rebels demanded the abolition of taxes and reinstatement of the *capitoli*, or privileges, supposedly conceded to the city of Naples in 1540 by Charles V. These privileges were more imaginary than real. They embodied, nevertheless, the ideal of a return to a normative past that was so compelling to revolutionary actors at this period. They entailed various reforms: popular election of magistrates; equality of vote and power between the one nonnoble and the five noble *sedili* or sections into which the citizens of Naples were divided and on which the city government was based;[44] annulment of imposts decreed since 1540; and submission of requests for taxes to popular ratification. These and other provisions were to be inscribed on marble monuments erected in the public market and elsewhere. Altogether, they would have set limits on viceregal government and weakened the nobility's power in civic administration.

The viceroy was forced to accept all the rebel demands. The cardinal archbishop of Naples, Filomarino, an elusive mediating presence in these events, gave his blessing. But Masaniello's power had completely turned his head, arousing the envy and hatred of his supporters. "He began to govern by himself," wrote a Neapolitan diarist, "without any other counsellors, to change his ways, and became proud and vainglorious."[45] On July 17, he was murdered and his body insulted by the crowd that had hailed him as a deliverer. The next day a revulsion of feeling took place, and, lamented as a saint and a martyr, he was taken by weeping multitudes for burial in the church of the Carmine.

In the lengthy epilogue following Masaniello's death, the revolution floun-

---

[43] A. Giraffi, *An exact historie of the late revolutions in Naples*, London, 1650, 59. First published in 1647 at Venice, this work was translated from the Italian by James Howell and dedicated to the governor and members of the Levant Company.

[44] For the *sedili*, see *Storia di Napoli*, v. 5, pt. 1, 693. One of their main tasks was administering the provision of grain and oil for the city.

[45] Cited in *ibid.*, 237.

dered on amid intermittent violence and without coordinated leadership or goal. Another captain-general was elected who tried to moderate the conflict with the Spanish authorities. The French government, which was now directed by Cardinal Mazarin, Richelieu's successor as chief minister, sponsored intrigues with the aim of detaching Naples from Spain's rule.

In October, a Spanish fleet carrying five thousand troops reached Naples. The viceroy was determined to crush the revolt, and the Spanish forces attacked the capital. They were driven off by the furious defenders, who killed their own captain-general on suspicion of treachery, and the movement in reaction took an anti-Spanish, separatist direction. At the end of the month, a third generalissimo of the people, a blacksmith, Gennaro Annese, proclaimed the city and kingdom of Naples a republic under the protection of the king of France. Through Annese's influence, an exiled French nobleman living in Rome, the duke of Guise, was named head of "the most serene Neapolitan republic."

The remaining phase of the rebellion was marked by wide confusion among contending aims and interests in which the only constant factor was the volatility of the mob. Although the republic issued proclamations and even coinage,[46] Naples provided no soil on which the ideal or practice or republicanism could take root. The duke of Guise tried to exploit his position to acquire a principality of his own, but his efforts came to nothing. Nor was he able to defeat the Spanish forces that were occupying fortresses around the city. A French fleet appeared and then withdrew without a fight because Mazarin would neither support the ambitions of Guise nor stand patron to a republic. The city was divided among the partisans of Spanish government, advocates of French or papal sovereignty, and supporters of an independent republic or monarchy.

Denied French assistance, the republic soon collapsed. In April 1648, after the replacement of the duke of Arcos by a new viceroy and a promise of amnesty and the removal of taxes on food, the insurgent capital admitted Spanish troops and accepted the reestablishment of Spanish authority.[47]

Although the Naples revolution of 1647 is usually, and correctly, regarded as an urban movement, it was also attended by agrarian insurrections. This aspect has been heavily emphasized by Rosario Villari, who exaggerates, however, when he maintains that the conflict had its deepest matrix in the country and that what happened in 1647-8 was "a peasant

---

[46] See the illustrations of proclamations and coins of the Neapolitan republic in *ibid.*, plates 88-9, 92-3.

[47] This description of the rebellion in Naples is based on the narrative in Schipa, *Masaniello*, and the account of R. Colapietra in *Storia di Napoli*, v. 5, pt. 1, 229-51. A summary is given by R. Quazza, *Preponderanza spagnuola (1559-1700)*, Storia politica d'Italia, 2nd ed., Milan, 1950, 166-8, 505-10. R. B. Merriman, *Six contemporaneous revolutions*, Oxford, 1938, 17-27, also discusses it briefly.

war, the most vast and impetuous known to Western Europe in the seventeenth century."[48] The scale and frequency of French peasant revolts in the same period alone suffice to disprove this assertion. In any case, it cannot be convincingly denied that the city of Naples, because of its overwhelming importance in the realm, played the predominant and decisive part throughout the rebellion. Villari's treatment, however, helps to illuminate the neglected rural side of the revolt.

The outbreak in the capital was swiftly followed by local outbreaks in the provinces of Salerno, Basilicata, and elsewhere. Peasants and rural communities rose against baronial government, demanding immediate subjection to the crown. Popular assemblies met to formulate grievances, and there was widespread resistance to seigneurial usurpation on the administrative autonomy and functions of communities. As in other agrarian insurrections we have encountered, these struggles were a communal response of the rural lower orders, in this case to the extension of noble landlord power that had taken place in preceding years. The movement apparently attained considerable scope but could not survive the end of the rebellion in the capital. With the latter's demise, these revolts either subsided through exhaustion or were crushed by the nobility with the help of Spanish troops.[49]

It is difficult to see through to the foundation of the revolution of Naples. At its most elemental level, it was a reaction by the plebeian poor and *lumpen* population against Spanish fiscalism and maladministration. What these masses did and thought, how they were directed or activated, remains obscure. Their violence, however, was the dynamic ingredient that kept the revolt in being. Their symbol was Masaniello, who suddenly rose from nothing to supreme power. In life, he was commemorated by artists and chroniclers. After his death, he survived in memory and legend. Contemporaries associated him, too, with other rebels of the time. A Dutch medal portrayed him as "king of Naples" and placed him in company with the great English revolutionary, Oliver Cromwell.[50]

Besides the plebs, the revolt also derived some involvement from petty bourgeois and intermediate strata in Naples who favored a legal and loyalist solution in the reforms demanded by Masaniello under Genoino's guidance. On the other hand, popular violence and plunder threatened all the rich and propertied, bourgeois and noble alike. Moreover, and most important, the movement failed to gain any support or leadership within the governing class. The nobility of the capital and the kingdom, whose interests tied it to Spanish rule, remained loyal to the monarchy. Popular

---

[48] Villari, *La rivolta antispagnola a Napoli*, 241.

[49] R. Villari, *Mezzogiorno e contadini nell' età moderna*, Bari, 1961, 118–41.

[50] See contemporary drawings and prints of Masaniello and an illustration of the Dutch medal in *Storia di Napoli*, v. 5, pt. 1, plates 81–2, 86–7, 90.

grievances and demands therefore found no sanction or legitimacy in the adherence of the politically dominant groups.

The case of Naples was illustrative of the strains and weaknesses besetting Spanish imperial government in the period of the Thirty Years war and of hostilities with France and the Dutch. It also shows that urban rebellion could lead to such a far-reaching attempt at change as a republic and separation from Spain. The republican and separatist stage of the revolt, however, was largely a superficial development with no organic relation to the movement's underlying forces. As far as can be seen, neither republicanism nor separatism had any real political ideas, inspiration, or commitment to sustain them. Naples seems to have been very weak in both the desire for self-government and the sentiment of a common *patria*. Further evidence of this fact was the absence during the revolt of any demand for the convocation of the kingdom's parliament. The nobility's refusal of support and its solidarity with the Spanish monarchy condemned to impotence any aspiration toward separation or independence.

A significant feature of the rebellion was the French government's attempt to profit from it. Great-power subversion and external interference in revolutionary conflicts were not at all uncommon in early modern Europe, and they were exemplified in France's policy toward Naples. In the 1640s, the French government disseminated anti-Spanish propaganda and supported futile conspiracies in Naples in the hope of bringing it over to French rule. Before the event, moreover, Cardinal Mazarin's agents informed him that the city was ripe for revolution. Following the Neapolitan republic's repudiation of Spanish allegiance, he waited to see if the nobility would turn to France. It didn't, of course, nor was he able to control the duke of Guise's actions as head of the republic. Unless Naples sought affiliation with the French crown, Mazarin was unwilling to intervene directly in the conflict. In the end, therefore, his strategy of exploiting the rebellion failed for lack of any party capable of making French interests prevail.[51]

In the final analysis, what stood out clearest in the events of 1647–8 were the polarization in Neapolitan society and the feebleness of its public spirit. Nothing else could account for the dictatorial power achieved by someone like Masaniello. By turns melodrama, tragedy, and farce, the rebellion of Naples was an explosion of the urban plebs in which every attempt to impose a direction or a goal was in vain. Its reality has been summed up by a distinguished Neapolitan scholar in a hard, although probably justified, judgment: "A society morally and materially, internally and externally, so disintegrated and unfitted to create itself by its own

[51] For French policy, attempts at subversion, and the limits of its intervention, see Merriman (*Six contemporaneous revolutions*, 127–35) and Villari (*La rivolta antispagnola a Napoli*, 200–16).

efforts, can have no other state but what is conceded to or imposed upon it."[52]

The Comuneros of Castile

Pursuing our reverse chronological journey, we turn back from the 1640s to the earlier sixteenth century and the reign of the Habsburg sovereign, Charles I and V (1516–56), Spanish king and Holy Roman emperor, in whose time Spain's destinies became firmly linked to the other European possessions of the House of Austria.

As the ruler of the Low Countries, Charles confronted an urban rebellion in 1539 in Ghent, his natal city. The town had not lost its insurrectionary spirit after the fourteenth century, and it rose up several times together with other Flemish towns during the next century against the emperor's ancestors, Philip the Good and Charles the Bold, dukes of Burgundy. The historian Commines, once the latter's counsellor, observed in his *Memoirs* that the people of Ghent "made no other use of their privileges but as a cause of quarrel with their prince, and their chief inclination was to encroach upon and weaken him." Opposed to a new tax, the artisans and others rose once more in 1539 against princely power. The city went so far as to appeal to the protection of Francis I of France but were refused help. Charles hastened from Spain across France to Flanders and, backed by five thousand troops, inflicted a bloody punishment on the municipality. He executed thirty of the rebels, confiscated civic and guild property, and abolished the city's constitution in favor of the "Caroline concession," which took away its remaining autonomy.[53]

But the revolt of Ghent was only of minor consequence compared with the rebellion of the Castilian cities, the Comuneros or *comunidades*, which broke out in 1520, soon after the beginning of Charles's reign. The latter ran its course at the same time as the entirely separate Germania of Valencia, an insurrection of the guilds, middle strata, and populace provoked by animosity against the Aragonese nobility and its Moorish tenants and laborers. As a radical communal movement (*germanía* was a sworn brotherhood) that inspired kindred struggles in other towns, this revolt in the kingdom of Aragon is of considerable interest.[54] It was overshadowed,

[52] Schipa, *Masaniello*, 177.

[53] P. de Commines, *Memoirs*, ed. A. Scoble, 2 v., London, 1880, 1:365–6. Ghent's revolts in the fifteenth century are described in R. Vaughan, *Philip the Good*, New York, 1970, ch. 10, and *Charles the Bold*, London, 1973, ch. 1. H. Pirenne, *Histoire de Belgique*, 3rd ed., Brussels, 1923, v. 3, 117–28, contains an account of the revolt of 1539 against Charles V; see also the comments of Botero, 112, and Bodin, *Six bookes of a commonweal*, 378.

[54] For discussions of the Germania, see R. B. Merriman, *The rise of the Spanish empire*, 4 v., New York, 1918–34, v. 3, 106–16; Armstrong, *The Emperor Charles V*, v. 1, 97–8, 101–2; and R. García Carcel, *Las Germanías de Valencia*, Barcelona, 1975. L. Bonilla, *Las revoluciones es-*

however, by the Castilian revolution, which presented a far greater danger to royal authority and was also much more significant in its extent, ideas, and political character. Hence, there is good reason to concentrate entirely on the latter.

Few other than specialists in Spanish history have taken much notice of the revolution of the Comuneros. Yet, the insurgency that burst across Castile in 1520 was the biggest urban rebellion of early modern Europe. Not only that, it was the biggest Spanish revolution between the sixteenth and the end of the eighteenth century. An event of such importance demands a place in wider studies devoted to the investigation of the revolutionary phenomenon.

Several generations of historians of Spain have debated the nature of this revolution, arguing chiefly whether it was medieval or modern. To the great scholar, Menéndez Pelayo, it was to be understood "not as the awakening of modern liberty but as the last protest of the spirit of the Middle Ages against the principle of central unity." The same interpretation was even more forcibly expressed by Gregorio Marañon, who described it as xenophobic, reactionary, and opposed to the "universalization of Spain." Its defeat meant "the triumph of progress" over "the final attempt of feudal, medieval Castile to maintain its privileges against royal absolute power, the unifier of the country."[55]

Other Hispanicists have expressed strong disagreement with these views. Menéndez Pidal spoke of the rebellion's republican strain and its "profound desire to innovate in the political institutions of the country."[56] More imposingly and comprehensively still, Maravall has summed up the Comuneros as "the first revolution of modern character in Spain and probably in Europe."[57] Leaving aside the matter of Europe, this opinion of its modernity is held by nearly all the recent historians of the revolt.[58]

I have no wish to enter into a debate whose terms imply a preoccupation with stages and a progressive conception of the history of revolution that I do not share. Similar controversy also obscures understanding of the

---

pañoles en el siglo XVI, Madrid, 1973, a work devoted largely to the Comunero revolt, deals with the Germania in chs. 8–9.

[55] Cited in J. Gutiérrez Nieto, Las comunidades como movimiento antiseñorial, Barcelona, 1973, 77, 98–9. Part 1 of this work contains a review of the historical interpretations of the Comuneros. Another useful survey of the literature is given by J. Perez, "Pour une nouvelle interprétation des Comunidades de Castille," Bulletin hispanique 65, 3–4 (1963).

[56] Cited in Gutiérrez Nieto, Las comunidades, 109–10.

[57] J. A. Maravall, Las comunidades de Castilla, 2nd ed., Madrid, 1970, 16.

[58] This is true of Gutiérrez Nieto, Las comunidades, and also of the most important and comprehensive modern study, J. Perez, La Révolution des "comunidades" de Castille, Bordeaux, 1970. Disagreeing with the interpretation of modernity is the treatment of the Comuneros by P. Chaunu (L'Espagne de Charles Quint, 2 v., Paris, 1973, v. 1, chs. 3–4), who, although depending heavily on Perez's work, rejects his view of the movement.

Netherlands revolution against Spain, which has likewise been regarded as either reactionary or progressive, medieval or modern. Such dualisms are too inflexible to help in making proper sense of the phenomenon. Abandoning preconceptions, what is required is to look at the revolution of the Comuneros as the creation of its time and place. Regardless of whether it is called medieval or modern, we need to see what, in the context, was innovative in its ideas or aims. We have also to explain why it exceeded every other urban rebellion of the age in its political horizon and objectives, to the extent not only of causing a civil war but also of creating a de facto sovereignty rivaling the crown's. In general, we should bear in mind that past-looking and future-looking attitudes are often found in indissoluble conjunction, a fact contributing to the inevitable complexity of revolution.

In coming to a delineation of the Comunero revolution, we might briefly note two points first in order to leave them behind for the central features of the struggle.

The first pertains to a millenarian aspect that has been discerned in it. Religious preaching by monks and clergy figured in the incitement to resistance. Popular beliefs were also apparently in circulation identifying Charles V with the antichrist and investing Juan de Padilla, the revolutionary leader of Toledo, with a messianic mission.[59] Nonetheless, the goals and character of the rebellion were overwhelmingly realistic and political. If the visionary themes of messianic anticipation and an egalitarian millennium appeared at all, they were a very minor strand in the conflict.

The second and more significant point concerns the rural and agrarian accompaniment of the revolt. As we have observed often enough, urban rebellion might elicit agrarian insurrection and vice versa, and the two could either run parallel or interact with one another. The Comunero revolution, no exception, inspired some incidents of resistance by rural communities, peasants, and towns against seigneurial authority. As in the case of the similar uprisings we have just noted in Naples, the usual aim of such rebels was to escape the domination of their lord and achieve autonomy under the immediate government of the crown. In September 1520, the little community of Dueñas, near the Comunero city of Valladolid, rose up and expelled its *señor*, the count of Buendía. Further northeast, the people of Nájera, subjects of the duke of Nájera, also rose, giving as their reason that "they were tyrannized," and were brutally repressed.

---

[59] For the millenarian side as a "forgotten aspect" of the Comuneros, see R. Alba, *Acerca de algunas particularidades de las Comunidades de Castilla tal vez relacionadas con el supuesto acaecer Terreno del Milenio igualitario*, Madrid, 1975.

Palencia, an episcopal town whose lord was the bishop, broke into revolt, demanding autonomy, or *libertad*.[60]

These and similar episodes serve to illustrate the breadth of the Comunero revolution, but antiseigneurial resistance was merely of marginal importance in the movement as a whole. The latter was very strongly urban; its main thrust focused on the question of royal authority and the respective powers of crown and subjects. For the most part, moreover, the rebellious cities refrained from interfering with seigneurial jurisdiction. Probably the only significant result of peasant and small-town protest against seigneurial domination was to contribute in bringing the great nobility into the royalist, anti-Comunero camp.

From what we have previously seen of revolutions, we might perhaps postulate that, the greater the revolution, the more acute the preceding crisis of authority. We know that the German peasant war broke out on the crest of an unprecedented challenge to authority precipitated by the Lutheran reform. We have also seen in France how the aggressions of the royal state provoked a proportional reaction from subjects that plunged the kingdom into epidemic revolt during the 1630s and 1640s. Similarly in Castile, the Comunero revolution germinated in a soil of political instability and crisis, which reached their acute stage after 1516 and the arrival of a foreign king.

This crisis ensued from the death in 1504 of the great Castilian sovereign, Isabella the Catholic. Castile was left to her daughter and son-in-law, Juana and Archduke Philip of Austria. Philip died suddenly two years later, survived by his grief-stricken wife, who was insane and incompetent to rule. Their eldest son, Archduke Charles, the future Charles I and V, was still a child. Castile was therefore governed by regents, by Isabella's husband, Ferdinand of Aragon, then by Cardinal Ximénez de Cisneros, who did his best to defend the interests of the crown. Political stability, based on a balance between nobility and towns under firm royal supremacy, was undermined. A sort of interregnum prevailed, with a vacuum of power at the center, and accompanied by factional division, an uncertain succession, and resurgence of noble independence and disorder.

At Ferdinand's death in 1516, his grandson Charles succeeded to the crowns of both Aragon and Castile, with his mother, Queen Juana, as his nominal cosovereign. He was sixteen, reared in the Netherlands, and ignorant of Spain and its language. The following year he came to Spain to receive his inheritance. We have noted in an earlier chapter the reaction

---

[60] These and similar events are described by Gutiérrez Nieto, pt. 2, in a work that stresses and exaggerates the antiseigneurial direction of the revolt. The same subject is treated briefly by Perez (*La Révolution des "comunidades,"* 464–73). Maravall dismisses the rural and agrarian aspect, contending that the Comuneros represented an urban movement in which the countryside and peasants generally played a minimal and passive role (*Las comunidades,* 45–7).

that was produced in Castile by this foreign ruler accompanied by Flemish ministers, who seemed to consider the kingdom's highest offices and wealth as prey for the taking.[61] The Castilian sense of grievance ran high, and rumbles of revolt were clearly audible. Charles and his advisers, however, were determined to restore royal power and gave no heed to native protest. With his election in June 1519 as emperor, which obliged him to go to Germany and leave Castile to absentee kingship under a governor, events hastened to a climax. When Charles embarked from Coruña in May 1520, the Comunero revolution had already begun.

Thus, a crisis of authority, going back for over a decade, formed the political prelude to rebellion.[62] But the latter sprang specifically from the cities, and what brought it to a head after the advent of the new king was the crown's quarrel with the cities in the Cortes over taxes. In a sense we might say that the Comuneros started as an antifiscal revolt, except that the issue of taxes was only the symbol of much wider, clearly voiced differences.

The Cortes consisted of eighteen privileged towns, each of which sent two *procuradores* or deputies. As nobility and clergy were almost never summoned any longer, Castile was represented by an assembly entirely urban in constitution.[63] In February 1518, Charles met his first Cortes at Valladolid, and it was there, wrote the sixteenth-century chronicler Sandoval, that "the house of Austria began to reign in Spain."[64] The Cortes acknowledged him as king and voted him a *servicio* of 600,000 ducats for three years, accompanied by a lengthy petition of requests and grievances. Upon his election the following year as emperor and the expenses incident thereto, Charles needed more money and summoned another Cortes in March 1520 at Santiago, even though the previous grant was still in effect. This added further fuel to mounting protest and opposition. The crown commanded that the deputies come to the Cortes provided with plenary

[61] See Ch. 4 in this book.

[62] See Perez, *La Révolution des "comunidades,"* pt. 1, ch. 3, for a general treatment.

[63] See G. Griffiths, *Representative government in Western Europe in the sixteenth century*, Oxford, 1968, 1 ff., for discussion and documents relative to the Cortes of Castile. The represented towns were Avila, Burgos, Cordoba, Cuenca, Guadalajara, Granada, Jaen, Leon, Madrid, Murcia, Salamanca, Segovia, Seville, Soria, Toledo, Toro, Valladolid, and Zamora.

[64] P. de Sandoval (c. 1551–1621), *Historia de la vida y hechos del Emperador Carlos V, Biblioteca de autores españoles*, 3 v., Madrid, 1955, v. 1, 126 (bk. 3, ch. 9). This work was first published at Valladolid, 1604–6. Sandoval was historiographer royal of Philip III and a Benedictine who became bishop of Pamplona. The portion of his history dealing with the Comunero rebellion was translated into English during the English revolution; see *The civil wars of Spain*, London, 1652. The translator, James Wadsworth, dedicated his work to three members of Parliament. In a preface, "To the Reader," he commented that so great was the similarity between the revolt against Charles V and "divers late passages in this our Nation, that had not those in Castilla had the privilege of many years before us, wee might have been said to have been their pattern."

power to grant money; the towns, however, wanted to bind them with instructions and oaths so that they would have to refer back to their principals.[65] Toledo and Salamanca refused to attend at all, other towns present balked and spoke of grievances, and the Cortes was removed to Coruña, where the king was preparing to depart. He had annulled binding restrictions upon the deputies by invoking his "absolute royal power" to absolve them from any accountability or promises to their communities.[66] Yet, despite these pressures, only eight towns voted for the *servicio*. Meanwhile, riots had erupted in some of the towns as the signal for rebellion.[67]

The revolution that the Habsburg monarch provoked and the Cortes cities unleashed in the spring of 1520 was able to survive for about a year. It extended over all of Old and New Castile, failing to find a hold only farther south in the cities of Andalusia.[68] It was brought to an end after the decisive defeat of the Comuneros by a royalist army at Villalar in April 1521. This reverse spelled the death of the revolt, although Toledo maintained a lone resistance for a few months longer. In the king's absence (Charles did not return to Spain until July 1522), he was represented by a governor, Adrian of Utrecht, cardinal of Tortosa, his old tutor and future pope, who had to cope with the rebellion and with whom were later joined in office two grandees, the constable and the admiral of Castile. In most of the Castilian cities royal authority was overthrown, and insurrectionary regimes established themselves. The rebel urban communities allied themselves and created a *junta* as an organ of dual power opposed to the king's. Despite the nominal respect and loyalty they expressed for the Castilian monarchy, they posed a formidable threat to its supremacy and evolving absolutism.

We will not attempt to summarize the further details of the Comunero revolution but will look instead at some of the political, social, ideological, and organizational aspects that help to clarify the movement.

That the Castilian cities found it possible to initiate in concert a major rebellion against the crown was partly due to their wide political horizon and comparatively advanced degree of integration within the realm. Nothing like the Comunero movement could have arisen in France, whose urban revolts, as we have seen, were factionalized by particularism and

[65] See H. Koenigsberger, "The powers of deputies in sixteenth century assemblies," in *Estates and revolutions*, Ithaca, 1971, 180–7, for an analysis of this issue and its history.

[66] The formula used was "poderío Real absoluto"; M. Danvila, *Historia crítica y documentada de las Comunidades de Castilla, Memorial histórica español*, 6 v., Madrid, 1897–9, v. 1, 320. This work contains the main collection of printed sources for the Comunero revolution.

[67] See H. Seaver's account of these events, *The great revolt in Castile*, Boston, 1928, chs. 8–14. This work presents a detailed narrative, as does even more fully Perez, *La Révolution des "comunidades,"* which is also indispensable for its extensive analytic treatment. Alba, *Acerca de las comunidades*, 21–44, provides a month-by-month chronology of the revolution.

[68] For the geography of the Comuneros, see Perez, *La Révolution des "comunidades,"* pt. 2, ch. 5.

devoid of political aims. The cities of Castile possessed experience of joint action and weighty political responsibilities. Effectively subordinated by Ferdinand and Isabella, who extended the appointment of a *corregidor* to every important town as its highest official and link with the central government, the cities had at the same time rendered indispensable support to the rule of the Catholic sovereigns. In 1476, the latter created the Santa Hermandad, an association of cities modeled on earlier urban brotherhoods that was given considerable authority in restoring public order and other tasks. The crown looked to the cities for some of its military forces and for money. The cities were incorporated in the Cortes, the kingdom's assembly, as the most important and eventually the sole element. Maravall has referred to "the proto-national policy" of the Catholic monarchs, in which the Castilian cities took an active part. This undoubtedly helps to explain how they were able to build an alliance of communities when they became polarized against the crown, as well as why they could claim to speak for the kingdom.[69]

It was further significant that the towns of Castile at the period of the Comuneros were not split by severe internal discord between commonalties or guild members and elites. Political and social ascendancy lay in patriciates of *caballeros* and *hidalgos*, the aristocratic, privileged sectors of urban society. To such belonged the life oligarchies of *regidores* on the town councils, who, together with the royally appointed *corregidor*, governed the towns. The deputies of the Cortes cities, however chosen, were part of the same upper groups. Officials and lawyers (*letrados*), who played a leading part in municipal life, were similarly affiliated with these elites. Only after and below them came the bourgeoisie proper of commercial and manufacturing interests. And beneath them were the petty bourgeois and artisanal strata, and the unprivileged and lower orders generally.[70] The Comunero revolution involved a heterogeneous formation of all of these elements, embracing elites and commonalty in a resistance that, although it saw political differences and tensions, radical and moderate tendencies, within the rebel camp, nonetheless reflected the entire urban society.

The claims and complaints voiced by the cities before the revolution throw essential light on its origin and subsequent aims. Strong anger had been aroused by the king's appointment of Flemings to the highest offices, more tax projects, and the announcement of the impending royal depar-

---

[69] Maravall, *Las comunidades*, 35–6; on the cities and their relation to the Catholic monarchs, see also J. H. Elliott, *Imperial Spain*, London, 1963, 75–6, 81–4, and S. Haliczer, "The Castilian urban patriciate and the Jewish expulsions of 1480–92," *American historical review* 78, 1 (1973).

[70] See Chapter 3 in this book; Maravall, *Las comunidades*, 44; Perez, *La Révolution des "comunidades,"* 64–71.

ture for Germany. Toledo took the lead in protesting to Charles, and in
the fall of 1519, after its own petitioners had been rebuffed, it proposed
to the other Cortes cities consultation and common action on the following
matters: that the king should not leave Spain; that no money be permitted
to be taken from the kingdom; and that no offices be given to foreigners.
"Since the injury touches us all," Toledo wrote, "we should all join to find
the remedy," a sentiment reminiscent of the great traditional formula associated with European representative assemblies: "Quod tangit omnes
debet approbari omnibus," "What affects everyone should be approved
by everyone." The Toledans also declared that, in the event of Charles's
departure from Spain, he should be asked "to give the cities the part that
the law grants them in providing for the form of government."[71]

The correspondence that passed between Toledo and the other cities
produced a broadly favorable response among the latter. With the summons of the Cortes for March 1520, protest intensified. There was universal indignation that the meeting was to be held in Santiago in faraway
Galicia rather than in Castile. Over the opposition of its *corregidor*, Toledo
adopted a petition that included among its various demands the reform of
the Inquisition and prohibition of the sale of offices. It declared that the
king should not depart the realm and that, if he were determined to do so,
he ought not to have a *servicio*.[72] In a similarly militant action, Salamanca
circulated an outspoken letter drawn up by a group of Augustinian, Dominican, and Franciscan friars in consultation with the city's *regidores*. It
went over the general grievances and urged that the king be refused money
unless he heeded them. Pervaded by a powerful sentiment of both civic
consciousness and Castilian patriotism, this remarkable document called
on the "communities of the realm" to act for "the common good" and
"the conservation of the kingdom" against "so many enslaving and great
evils."[73]

The publicity and agitation accompanying these intercity communications encouraged an insurrectionary disposition and also assured the rejection of royal demands by the Cortes of Santiago–Coruña when it met in
the spring of 1520. They were the ideological forerunners of revolution.
What was notable was their political character. They were anything but a
mere expression of xenophobia. If they voiced anger at the threat of foreign domination, they also touched on issues of internal reform and were
impregnated with ideas of the common good, of limits to ruler power set

---

[71] For this letter from Toledo of November 1519, see Sandoval, *Historia del Emperador
Carlos V*, v. 1, 194 (bk. 5, ch. 3), and Danvila, *Historia de las Comunidades*, v. 1, 247.

[72] Summarized in Sandoval, *Historia del Emperador Carlos V*, v. 1, 199 (bk. 5, ch. 7).

[73] Text in Danvila, *Historia de las Comunidades*, v. 1, 272–4; see also Perez, *La Révolution des
"comunidades,"* 149–51.

by the communities of cities, and of representation and consent as embodied in the Cortes.

From these preliminaries, rebellion emerged with irresistible momentum. First to rise was Toledo, where popular power took over and expelled the *corregidor* and other royalists. In June, many cities followed suit, as mobs attacked representatives of royal authority in an outburst of rioting. Although some towns entered the rebel camp more decidedly than others, few remained under royal control in the course of the summer of 1520. The regent, Cardinal Adrian, confined in Valladolid, which sympathized with the revolt, was powerless to contain it. Royal military forces, despite a few attempts, were too feeble to offer much resistance. For a time all that the crown's supporters and defenders seemed able to do was to bow their heads before the storm.

The sign under whose inspiration rebellion grew was the *comunidad*, the idea of the community. Why *comunidad* and why Comuneros? What singular aspiration was revealed in these words that designate the revolution in Castile?

We have already seen in other revolutions how communalism and the community could serve rebels as an activating bond, a model, and an ideal. Thus, to recall several instances, the German peasant war, coming only five years after the revolt in Castile, was fundamentally a *Gemeinde* movement, or revolution of communities, dedicated to the formation of *new* communities reflecting the common good. Similarly in France, agrarian revolt attained its highest organizational level in the commune as a self-directed association of communities exercising various delegated powers. Probably it is no exaggeration to say that the communitarian image and ideal provided the most potent and widespread symbol to the rebels of the age. It filled the sky as a presiding hope and presence in many early modern revolutions.

So it was in the case of the Comuneros. Internally, in Toledo, Segovia, Salamanca, Valladolid, Madrid, and other cities where the revolt took root, *comunidad* meant in part the establishment of popular power and the urban community's active participation in its government. If municipal democracy is too strong a description, nevertheless a genuine change occurred. In place of oligarchy, governing bodies were approved by and became accountable to popular municipal assemblies. Royal *corregidores* were driven out and others named to serve with councillors as the responsible agents of the community. Parishes or quarters elected their own deputies to represent them in city assemblies, which in turn debated and undertook responsibilities for government and even sometimes for military operations. As a recent analyst of the movement has pointed out, "In the contemporary texts, a city's rallying to the *Comunidad* is always presented as a transfer of powers from the *corregidor* and traditional regime to the deputies."[74] The deputies took an oath; they could be dismissed by their electors; they summoned meetings of the parish or quarter by bell or crier, where discussion and voting also took place. One result of the revolt was therefore the intervention and involvement of commonalties and the populace alongside elite groups in the political life of the city.

Externally, *comunidad* signified the union of the revolutionary communities and their creation of a confederation of cities or *Junta* armed with governmental powers. This was unquestionably the most novel and significant development prompted by the revolution. It occurred in several steps during the late summer of 1520.

Upon Toledo's persistent urging that the cities hold a Cortes "for the good of the commonwealth"[75] – this, of course, without any royal authority – four of them sent deputies to a Junta that met in August in Avila. Other cities at first held back. Then a royalist attempt the same month against Medina del Campo ended in the firing of the city and caused a profound reaction throughout Castile, which accelerated the tempo of rebellion. In addition, at the end of August, Comunero militia under Toledan leadership occupied Tordesillas, the town where the king's mother, Queen Juana, was kept in custody. Although the poor queen's mind was sick, the rebels associated themselves with her and claimed to act in her name as a sanction for their own legitimacy. The Junta accordingly transferred its sessions to Tordesillas, where during September all but five of the eighteen Cortes cities came to be represented. The absentees were Seville, Cordoba, Granada, Jaen, and Murcia.[76]

Despite the fact that the Junta was never free of differences between its more moderate and more radical members, it took on, as an American historian of the Comunero revolution has written, "all the organization of a state, together with the consequent dispossession of the Royal Viceroys and Council."[77] It was formally inaugurated on September 25 by a solemn oath of "union and perpetual brotherhood" among the constituent cities, which they justified in a manifesto as necessary for the good of the realm and to relieve its oppression. By this act the *comunidad* as a covenanted confederation of communities was writ large.[78] (Here we

[74] Perez, *La Révolution des "comunidades,"* 417–18; see the discussion in *ibid.*, 515–28, for an analysis of this development based on the sources.

[75] "Por utilidad de la República" were the words of Toledo's appeal, according to the regent, Cardinal Adrian, in a letter to the king (Danvila, *Historia de las Comunidades*, v. 1, 415).

[76] See the account of the formation and expansion of the Junta in Perez, *La Révolution des "comunidades,"* 173–92.

[77] Seaver, *The great revolt in Castile*, 164.

[78] The text of the oath of brotherhood sworn by the cities and the Junta's accompanying manifesto are printed in Danvila, *Historia de las Comunidades*, v. 2, 76–81, 82–5.

should recall in passing how frequently in other revolutions we have seen rebels unite themselves in oaths and covenants; this was a repeated feature of the revolutionary movements of the time.) The confederation's official title was Junta General, although it was often also called the Santa Junta in token of the elevated and even sacred character of its mission.[79] It was predicated basically on the representative principle, conceiving itself as the Cortes and accordingly entitled to speak for the kingdom and its rulers, referring to itself by such formulae as "the Cortes and Junta General of the Kingdom," and "the deputies of the Cortes and Junta General of the Kingdom in the name of the Queen and King our lords and of the Kingdom which we represent."[80]

Among its early actions the Junta began to organize an army and to exercise authority in other ways. It corresponded with individual cities and sent them orders and suggestions. It recommended *corregidores* and other officials and issued military directives. It had its own secretariat and clerks. Besides its regular sittings as an assembly of *comunidades*, it functioned through committees that dealt with war, political and administrative problems, justice, and finance. The Junta did not recognize the authority of the regents or the royal council of Castile. Nor did it recognize Charles V as emperor, regarding him solely as king of Castile in association with his mother. While avowing loyalty to his person and addressing him with deference, it gradually assumed the functions of an executive government exercising power in right of the kingdom and *comunidades*.

In October, the Junta sent Charles a declaration and petition that embodied the basic program of the rebellion. The demands covered a vast range of topics. Some dealt with the preservation of the realm from foreign domination by barring and removing foreigners from office and through additional protections. Others concerned reform and economy in the royal household and the prevention of judicial corruption, sale of offices, and administrative abuses. Indian slaves were not to be given as gifts. Religion was also included: Bishops were to reside in their sees, and no bull or indulgences (*cruzadas*) were to be published without Cortes approval. A number of provisions referred to the reduction and reform of sales and other taxes. An inquiry was called for into royal finances since 1516 and into the conduct of the king's council. The *servicio* demanded at the Cortes of Santiago–Coruña was to be abandoned.

In addition to these articles, which amounted to a sweeping condemnation of recent government and its attendant grievances, the Junta called for substantial political change. If a governor were appointed, he must be a native and approved by the realm. Royal *corregidores* were not to be ap-

[79] See Perez, *La Révolution des "comunidades,"* 189.
[80] For examples, see Danvila, *Historia de las Comunidades,* v. 2, 86, 87; Sandoval, *Historia del Emperador Carlos V,* v. 1, 300 (bk. 7, ch. 1); see Maravall, *Las comunidades,* 113–14.

pointed unless requested by a city. The demands regarding the Cortes were no less than a declaration of independence on its behalf. It was to meet every three years without royal summons and even in the king's absence. Cities were to follow their own customs in electing deputies without royal interference. The document apparently also looked to increasing the deputies per town from two to three, to be chosen on the basis of estate: one from the clergy, one from the gentlemen (*caballeros y escuderos*), and one from the commonalty (*comunidad*), the latter two to be paid by the city, the former by the cathedral chapter. Deputies were not to be subject to any royal pressure, instruction, or payment. They were to be free to use their powers for the good of the commonwealth (*república*); they were to think only of the service of God, the king, and the public good and of performing the duties committed to them by their cities. Should they or their families take gifts or bribes from the king, they could be punished by death and loss of property. Within forty days of a meeting of the Cortes, deputies would be obliged to render a personal account to their communities of their activity in the assembly.[81]

These *capitulos* caused a contemporary historian of Charles V's reign to write in horror, "Blasphemy and notorious treason . . . a perpetual Commune and destruction of royal power."[82] This last is surely an exaggeration; however, the Comunero aims would clearly have placed the crown under the supervision and partial control of the communities and Cortes. Not even an English parliament could have conceived at this time of such a position for itself in relation to the ruler. This October petition and other Junta statements demonstrated an exceptional breadth of vision informed by a strong political consciousness and set of ideas. They outlined, at least in intention, a constructive series of reforms affecting many problems and grievances so as to secure administrative order and better, more just government. Politically, the rebel cities, although concerned for their autonomy, not only fought for local privileges but claimed to speak for and to the entire realm. References to the common good, to liberty, and to resistance to tyranny and unjust rule were frequent in their declarations. They coupled these statements with repeated professions of fidelity to the interests of the sovereign. Thus, there was no question of suppressing the monarchy but rather of counterposing to it the authority and participation of the communities in the government of the realm. If eighteen Cortes cities could be said to represent the kingdom and its opinion, then the Comuneros demanded for them collectively a continual oversight of royal ad-

[81] The petition's text is in Sandoval, *Historia del Emperador Carlos V*, v. 1, 294–317 (bk. 7, ch. 1); see Danvila's comment that the *capitulos* or demands were "the most faithful and exact expression of the political, economic, and administrative thought" of the Comunero revolution (v. 2, 349).

[82] Pedro Mexía, *Historia de Carlos Quinto* (c. 1551), cited by Seaver, *The great revolt in Castile*, 168.

ministration through an institutional system of public inquest. Raw power and basic political norms were both at issue here, for the Comunero idea of liberty would have made Castile into a limited monarchy with a king responsible to the representative assembly of the realm.[83]

This program had no hope of consideration from Charles V, a prince of absolutist traditions who scorned to deal with rebels. The hard-pressed regents, in regular correspondence with the distant sovereign, implored him for concessions, assuring him that promises made under compulsion need not be kept. The king disregarded their advice: He required submission and would grant only the barest minimum, such as a pardon with exceptions and the remission of the recent *servicio*, being otherwise largely deaf to Comunero grievances.[84] From the fall of 1520, negotiations went on intermittently between the Junta and the regents, but with no result. In the end, the issue was settled by the defeat and suppression of the revolt.

Meanwhile, internal divisions weakened the Comunero cause. The advocates of moderation, although no less desirous of redress of grievances than their opponents, shrank from the Junta's radical proposals. They wanted "liberties" in a limited, traditional sense, meaning royal recognition of rights and privileges with regard to taxes, native independence, and the Cortes, not "liberty" in the broader political meaning projected by the Junta for the realm. Burgos, one of the moderate cities, commercial capital of the north, abandoned the struggle in protest against the Junta's platform and determination to impose its will upon the king. It charged the Junta with sponsoring "innovations" and "a new way of governing."[85] It urged the cities to stick to grievances and leave government to the king. Opposed by the more radical majority, during the fall it went over to the royalist camp.

Similarly, in Valladolid dissensions raged between moderates and Junta partisans. The municipal administration had embraced the *comunidad* less from enthusiasm than from pressure of events and to halt disorders. It would have liked to follow Burgos's path and tried to replace the city's representatives at Tordesillas because they were too favorable to the Junta's position. The militancy of the deputies of the quarters frustrated these

---

[83] Maravall, *Las comunidades*, chs. 3–4, contains the best examination of Comunero political ideas, despite some anachronistic comments and excessive attributions of modernity; see also Seaver, *The great revolt in Castile*, 167, 168. J. Perez carries the thesis of modernity to an altogether unjustified extreme by misleadingly translating *reino* as *nation*, thus reaching the erroneous conclusion that the Comuneros would have replaced the will of the king by the "sovereignty of the nation" (*La Révolution des "comunidades*," 564–5). There was doubtless a considerable admixture of medieval populist doctrine in the Comunero idea that the king was for the community, not the community for the king.

[84] See Seaver, *The great revolt in Castile*, 215–16, 281–2.

[85] Danvila, *Historia de las Comunidades*, v. 2, 88–9; see Maravall, *Las comunidades*, 183–4.

moves, forcing a reconstitution of the city government that aligned Valladolid decisively with the Junta.[86]

What was the leadership and composition of the Comunero movement? Primarily, its character was markedly urban, but almost every part of the social hierarchy and diverse degrees, professions, and occupations were represented in it.

The chiefs were noblemen, gentlemen, and members of the urban patriciate. Juan de Padilla, most popular of the political and military leaders (at Villalar, where they met defeat, the Comunero troops shouted, "Padilla, Padilla, Liberty!"),[87] came of an illustrious Toledo family. His remarkable wife, Doña Maria Pacheco, who courageously continued the struggle after her husband's death, was the sister of the royalist marquis of Mondéjar, count of Tendilla. Don Pedro Girón, an initiator of revolt and for a time captain-general of the Comunero army, sprang from the highest nobility and was a nephew of the constable of Castile, Don Iñigo Fernández de Velasco, one of the regents. Don Pero Laso of Toledo was another of the leaders of eminent noble origin. Antonio de Acuña, related to the great nobility and a Comunero firebrand, was bishop of the Cortes city of Zamora. Francisco Maldonado of Salamanca belonged to a distinguished noble house, and Juan Bravo of Segovia, Alonso de Saravia of Valladolid, and Juan Zapata of Madrid, were *regidores* and members of the elite of their communities.[88]

Within the rebel cities and the Junta, men of intermediate status predominated – urban gentlemen, municipal officials, lawyers and other members of the liberal professions, and merchants. Artisans formed an active force in the assemblies and political affairs of the *comunidad*.[89] When Antonio Guevara, a writer whom we cited earlier in discussing courts, wanted to underline the scandalous effects of the revolt, he pointed to the harness makers, leather sellers, cloth shearers, wool dressers, locksmiths, and the like who exercised authority in Comunero cities.[90]

Many clergy, especially Franciscans and Dominicans, were also outspokenly Comunero. Together with the lawyers and university graduates, they gave the movement its ideological fervor and convictions. Here, too, in the leading role such men played as agitators and propagandists, the

---

[86] See the account of developments in Burgos and Valladolid and their relations to the Junta in Perez, *La Révolution des "comunidades,"* 208–31.

[87] Maravall, *Las comunidades,* 183.

[88] For these and other leading Comuneros, see Seaver, *The great revolt in Castile,* and Perez, *La Révolution des "comunidades," passim*. The concluding volume of Danvila, *Historia de las Comunidades,* v. 6, contains biographical information on many Comuneros, royalists, and other actors along with interesting reproductions of autographs, letters, and other materials.

[89] For discussion of the social composition of the revolt, see Perez, *La Révolution des "comunidades,"* pt. 2, ch. 6; and Maravall, *Las comunidades,* ch. 5.

[90] Cited in Perez, *La Révolution des "comunidades,"* 455–6.

Comunero revolution differed strikingly from other urban rebellions of the sixteenth and seventeenth centuries. The subversive preaching and writing of monks in Salamanca, Toledo, Valladolid, and elsewhere not only contributed to incite revolt but also lent a passionate voice to Castilian grievances and disseminated ideas of justice and liberty. A friar of Burgos told his fellow citizens that a king who acted like Charles V could be disobeyed with just cause; he called on the city, its gentlemen and native-born good men, to defend laws and liberties for the service of God and *patria*. In Valladolid, the radical Dominican Fray Alonso de Medina, strove to keep the *comunidad* firmly on the Junta's side.[91] Ecclesiastics of the cathedral chapters in some cities were ardent adherents of the movement. The Comunero revolution revealed that numerous clergy at this juncture were imbued with principles wholly contrary to the absolutist rule that the Habsburg monarchy subsequently created in Castile.[92]

In connection with religion, it has been suggested that among other elements, *conversos*, that is, new Christians of Jewish origin, also took a part of major consequence in the revolt. Criticism of the Inquisition and proposals for ecclesiastical reforms in Comunero statements have been ascribed to *converso* influence. Royalists of the time made accusations of Jewish instigation as a way of discrediting the Comuneros. The admiral of Castile, one of the regents, told Charles V that "all the evil has come from *conversos*," and the inquisitors of Seville said that "the main cause of the insurrections of Castile have been the *conversos* and persons threatened by the office of the Inquisition."[93]

Because *conversos* permeated urban society, there were many of them in Comunero cities like Toledo and Segovia; but they were also numerous in Burgos, which retreated from the rebellion, and in Seville, which never joined and where the Comunero sympathizers were in fact enemies of *conversos*. Despite the disabilities they suffered, there is no reason or evidence to suppose that *conversos* all thought or acted alike. Scepticism is in order on this question, in which the balance of judgment would seem to favor the conclusion that they had no distinctive or exceptional effect upon the Comunero movement.[94]

Conversos aside, what has been said above about Comunero support is

---

[91] The letter by an anonymous Burgos friar is printed in Sandoval, *Historia del Emperador Carlos V*, v. 1, 229–33 (bk. 5, ch. 38). For Fray Alonso de Medina, see Perez, *La Révolution des "comunidades,"* 195, 219–25.

[92] For the clergy's role in the Comunero movement, see J. Perez, "Moines frondeurs et sermons subversifs en Castille pendant le premier séjour de Charles-Quint en Espagne," *Bulletin hispanique 67*, 1–2 (1965), and *La Révolution des "comunidades,"* 499–505.

[93] Cited in Perez, *La Révolution des "comunidades,"* 509.

[94] The question of *converso* influence is discussed negatively in *ibid.*, 507–14; see also J. Gutiérrez Nieto, "Los conversos y el movimiento comunero," in *Collected studies in honour of Americo Castro's eightieth year*, ed. M. Hornik, Oxford, 1965, for a more positive view. The subject is also considered in Maravall, *Las comunidades*, ch. 5.

confirmed by the exceptions to the general pardon of the rebellion that Charles V granted in 1522. Excepted from pardon were 293 persons, whose collective profile illustrates the participation in the revolt. Nearly the whole social pyramid was involved, with the largest proportion of named insurgents belonging to the intermediate urban strata. As mirrored in the list of the excepted, the revolution was carried on by noblemen, urban gentlemen, merchants and petty tradesmen, professionals, clergy, university intellectuals, artisans – not a unity in a social or economic sense but recruited predominantly from the urban society and, in addition, sharing a similar political outlook.[95]

Opposing the Comuneros was a coalition of some of the cities and the bulk of the great Castilian nobility. Among the Cortes cities, the split between those that did and did not become Comunero was partially reflected in their location and differing economic focus. The most militant of the *comunidades*, Toledo, Segovia, Valladolid, for instance, were in the center and interior of the kingdom; in contrast, the principal cities that resisted the revolution, like Seville in the south and Burgos in the north, were situated on the periphery. Indeed, in January 1521, Seville, Cordoba, Jaen, and eight other towns of Andalusia held a congress at La Rambla and established a royalist league against the Junta.[96] The revolutionary cities of the interior were primarily manufacturing and artisanal centers, devoted to the production of textiles and other goods. The antirevolutionary cities of the periphery were much more involved in foreign trade, the export market, and the international commercial currents of the time; their merchants, especially those of Seville and Burgos, enjoyed monopolistic and other economic privileges from the crown and stood to benefit most from the prospects opened by Spain's discoveries, the Atlantic trade, and Castile's connection with the Netherlands, one of the possessions of Charles V. The industrial cities, on the other hand, were threatened by foreign competition from Flemish cloth and disliked the grip of the exporters (Burgos, for example, had a near monopoly over the export of wool, the product of the immense flocks controlled by the Mesta, the famous guild of sheep owners). Thus, two Castiles seemed to oppose each other in the urban alignment resulting from the Comunero conflict: on the one side, the Castile of the manufacturing cities and producer interests of the interior; on the other, the Castile of the commercial cities and exporter interests of the periphery.[97] Of course, this was just part of the story. Urban and regional rivalries had their effect, too. The southern cities were unwilling to submit to the leadership of Toledo and the cities of the Castilian center who dominated the Junta.

---

[95] For a social analysis of those excepted from pardon, see Perez, *La Révolution des "comunidades,"* 478–88.

[96] *Ibid.,* 403 ff.   [97] For this interpretation, see *ibid.,* 97–107, 453–4.

The decisive factor in saving Charles V was that the nobility threw its weight onto the scale on the royalist side. With all too few exceptions, like the German peasant war, early modern revolutions did not get very far without strong elite support. The leadership and participation of the no-bilities and aristocracies of the kingdom were crucial in the origin and development of nearly all the bigger revolutionary conflicts. In the case of the Comuneros, the great nobility decided in due course to come to the crown's support and thereby sealed the rebellion's fate.

At first, the titled lords of large domains, peasants, and seigneurial towns remained neutral and did nothing, or even sympathized with the revolt. Besides sharing the grievances of other Castilians and agreeing with a number of the Cortes's complaints, they were resentful at being thrust aside by the foreigners who enjoyed the new king's favor. As we have seen, some eminent noblemen, notably Don Pedro Girón, the constable of Castile's nephew and brother-in-law of the duke of Medina Sidonia, figured in the leadership of the revolt. (He was discredited and had to resign as Comunero captain-general after he failed to hold Tordesillas, the Junta headquarters, against the royalists in December.) In some of the early outbreaks of the summer of 1520, insurgents even pressed office in the *comunidad* upon high noblemen, who cooperated to prevent distur-bances, curb extremism, or save their lives and property.[98]

As the rebellion intensified, though, the nobility, whatever its resent-ments, began to rally to the king out of disapproval for the movement's direction and its possible dangers. This attitude was underlined when the constable and admiral of Castile, two magnates, were named coregents with Cardinal Adrian in September.

With urban elites in their own ranks, the Comuneros did not, of course, wage a social war; yet, to a certain extent, the revolution became a con-frontation between the rebel cities and the nobility as royalist supporters. It was only the cities that cherished the political aspirations of the Junta and conducted the struggle against absolutism based on the principle of representation and the claims of the Cortes. When the regents repri-manded the cities and cited the loyalty of the nobility, the commune of Valladolid replied with an indictment of the latter. The great noblemen (*grandes*), it said, have always been disloyal to the kings of Castile and have deposed them, despoiled them, and taken advantage of their necessities. But the cities have always been faithful; and it is they alone who enrich the crown and royal estate with their taxes, who seek not their own inter-ests but the common good of the king and realm, and who are now waging a just war for the liberty of king and *patria*.[99]

[98] For examples, *ibid.*, 461; and Seaver, *The great revolt in Castile*, 98, 100.
[99] This very interesting letter from Valladolid to the regents, dated January 31, 1521, is partially quoted by Seaver, *The great revolt in Castile*, (304–5) and printed in Danvila, *Historia*

It was certainly true, as Valladolid charged, that the grandees looked closely to their private interests. Their selfishness was a regular refrain in Cardinal Adrian's letters to Charles V. "Each one," he wrote,

wants only to preserve his own and . . . to protect his lands, and there are few who sincerely have a purpose and entire zeal to serve Your Majesty and the public good of the kingdom . . . if they did not fear to lose their lands, few would declare for Your Majesty's service . . . the grandees . . . fear lest their lands rise against them. They want to serve Your Majesty, and together with this to secure their houses, and if they cannot do all, they would rather . . . protect their lands than put them in danger by serving Your Highness.[100]

But even if with hesitation or ambiguity, the nobility came to the monarchy's rescue, motivated as much by dislike of the Junta's usurpations and by alarm at the revolutionary contagion as by loyalty. Doubtless the antiseigneurial risings of the fall of 1520 helped to catalyze nobility opposition to the Comuneros.[101] Clearly, the rebellion propagated a dangerous spirit of defiance by subjects. The count of Tendilla, captain-general of Granada, wrote the greater noblemen of Andalusia on behalf of the king and against the Junta, warning of the threat of insurrections on their lands: "The lords of Castile for the most part have only small possessions and don't run as much danger as those of Andalusia who hold many villages (*pueblos grandes*), if these risings of the *comunidad* aren't remedied in time."[102] The marquis of Villena likely expressed the typical noble view of the thrust of the Comunero revolution: "Although the beginning was against the king, the middle, the end, and all the damage was against the grandees and lords and gentlemen of the kingdom, to bring them into subjection and equality to those with whom they ought not to be so."[103]

The mobilization of the nobility ended royalist helplessness and turned the tide of the conflict. The royal forces were made up of the military manpower and resources contributed by the greater nobility, which was promised pay and compensation for damages incurred in the king's service. The Comunero army consisted mostly of levies of municipal militia, plus troops raised in his diocese by the bishop of Zamora, with which he conducted forays all over the north of Castile.

de las Comunidades, (v. 3, 91–4). It was subscribed as coming from the "deputies of the quarters of the very noble and very loyal town of Valladolid."

[100] Cited in Perez, *La Révolution des "comunidades,"* 288; see Seaver, *The great revolt in Castile*, 295, 297–8.

[101] See the previous discussion in the present Chapter 8 in this book, and Gutiérrez Nieto, *Las comunidades como movimiento antiseñorial*, 269. The latter contains an interesting treatment of the nobility's posture during the revolution, as does Perez, *La Révolution des "comunidades,"* 473–8.

[102] Printed in Danvila, *Historia de las Comunidades*, v. 2, 457–9. Tendilla was also worried that the revolt would spread to the newly converted Moorish population of Granada. His letter of October 13, 1520, was addressed to "los grandes cavalleros del Andaluzia."

[103] Cited in Maravall, *Las comunidades*, 260.

The revolution entered its concluding phase after the royalist capture of the Junta city, Tordesillas, early in December. A serious blow, it cost the Comuneros their possession of Queen Juana; thirteen deputies were taken prisoner, and the rest had to flee. The Junta then reestablished itself in Valladolid, its third and last capital. There eleven of the original thirteen cities continued to be represented, some much less committed to the *comunidad* than others. The loss of Tordesillas aggravated disunity among the Comuneros and prompted defections. Moderates, believing victory impossible, wanted peace; militants were even more determined to fight to the end.

Don Pedro Girón, responsible for the loss of Tordesillas and suspected of treachery, gave up his command as Comunero captain-general. In his place, the Junta appointed the popular idol, Juan de Padilla, who received a rapturous public welcome in Valladolid. At the end of February 1521, Padilla took the strategically placed royalist stronghold of Torrelobatón, a noteworthy success. The Junta continued its governmental activity, exerting itself to strengthen the Comunero forces and provide money. It also continued fruitless negotiations with royal representatives and mediators. The temper of the *comunidad* of Valladolid, with its militant deputies of the city quarters, was hostile to all compromise, and the regents could not in any event persuade the king to ratify the needful concessions. Along with Valladolid, the cities of Toledo, Segovia, Avila, and Salamanca remained solid bastions of Comunero strength. Cardinal Adrian commented to the king on the rebels' readiness for sacrifice: "It is a marvel to see so much devotion and the miseries they undergo on behalf of the liberty they hope for. And to sustain themselves in this, they accept many new exactions and excises and other things which they would refuse to pay . . . for Your Majesty's service."[104]

The end came, nevertheless, on April 23, 1521, on the fields of Villalar, a village near Toro and Tordesillas and not far from Valladolid. There Padilla's Comunero army of about six thousand men was defeated by a stronger, more heavily armed body of over eight thousand troops brought together by the regents and led by the Castilian nobility. The three revolutionary leaders captured in the battle, Padilla, Juan Bravo, and Francisco Maldonado, were beheaded the next day. In the immediate aftermath, the revolutionary cities submitted one by one, accepted royal authorities, and received pardon, various individuals excepted. Toledo, headed by Padilla's widow, resisted till October, then also yielded, and obtained pardon for its offenses.

The repression following Villalar was mild on the whole, considering that the revolution was a frontal challenge to the absolutist royal state.

---

[104] Letter of Jan. 26, 1521, printed in Danvila, *Historia de las Comunidades*, v. 3, 82. For the period after the fall of Tordesillas, see Perez, *La Révolution des "comunidades,"* pt. 2, ch. 3.

The mutinous, unhappy feeling of Castile could not be dealt with by a campaign of reprisals, death, and terror, which the regents, in any case, had neither the desire nor the means to carry out. Moreover, the Comuneros themselves had not resorted to exceptionally brutal methods or killed their political opponents when they were in power. In Charles V's general pardon of 1522, 293 persons were excepted. Only 22 of them were executed; about 20 more died in prison before trial; others suffered fines. Subsequent amnesties in 1525 and 1527 extended pardon to some of those who had been previously excepted. Thus, a total of perhaps 100 Comuneros, whether prominent or obscure, had to pay a high price for their participation in the revolt after its defeat. The remainder were apparently able to preserve their lives, most if not all of their property, and their liberty.[105]

The Comunero revolution was a very complex movement, and the foregoing account has only sought to discern some essential general features of its development and structure. Its complexity was due in part to the dualism and interplay between the individual Comunero cities and the Junta. Each of the former was a separate theater of rebellion, while the Junta was the center. A full and adequate understanding would require, among other things, a close examination of the revolutionary history and internal configuration in each *comunidad*, of the relation of each one to the Junta and to some of the others, as well as of the differences and tendencies contained in the Junta itself.

Explanations of the revolution as fundamentally either antiforeign or oriented toward an outmoded Castilian past can only obscure its nature and import. The passionate Castilian pride and patriotism voiced by the Comuneros was a sentiment no less shared by their opponents; the grandees of the kingdom felt it just as strongly. But the Comunero insistence that the realm be preserved from the domination of foreigners was the occasion for further, very significant demands in no way explicable as the product of xenophobia. In the Comunero political attitude there was simultaneously a looking back and a looking forward. The great reign of Isabella and Ferdinand was already becoming a glorious golden age in the eyes of Charles V's subjects, in the same way that it was afterward to be enshrined in memory and history. Comunero statements sometimes treated it as normative, calling, for instance, for the restoration of certain conditions to what they had been under the famous Catholic monarchs.[106] Yet

---

[105] For full details, see *ibid.*, pt. 3, ch. 1, and the summing up, 633.

[106] The Junta program of October 1520 contained a number of references to "los Catolicos Reyes don Fernando y doña Isabel, tan excelentes y tan poderosos"; see Sandoval, *Historia del Emperador Carlos V*, v. 1, 301 (bk. 7, ch. 1) and elsewhere.

the Comuneros, as their adversaries well recognized, also stood for innovations in their claims for the kingdom, cities, and Cortes that had no precedent in the time of Queen Isabella and her consort.

The ideas and program of the revolution implied a rich background of political values, assumptions, and beliefs that came to be articulated as an ideology in Junta statements and other Comunero documents. Ideologically speaking, the rebellion achieved a fuller development than did the majority of revolutions of the sixteenth and seventeenth centuries. Doubtless, many of its ideas were rooted in medieval populist principles and urban experience, from which the conception of the commune as a sworn association in defense of municipal liberties probably derived. But the Comunero program and movement went beyond preceding conceptions and practice in two ways: first, in requiring popular participation in the government of the individual city as a *comunidad;* second, and most important, in demanding for the whole realm a political order of participation and liberty based upon a continuous Cortes as the *comunidad* representing the realm and its communities. The intention, of course, was that there should be an organic and harmonious relation among king, Cortes, and communities; but royal authority and its prerogatives in fiscal and many other matters were nonetheless to be limited by and accountable to the consent of the Cortes on behalf of the realm. Charles V's historiographer, Pedro Mexía, spoke truly in charging that the Junta had proceeded by "totally usurping the royal jurisdiction and preeminence and attributing them to itself in the name of the king."[107] In doing so, the Junta justified itself by such conceptions contained in Comunero statements as the commonwealth, common and public good, liberty, and the right of resistance to oppression and tyranny.

The Comunero revolution provides further refutation of the supposition that the "great" revolution constitutes a single type. Although in origin and foundation an urban rebellion, it generated a civil war and was a "great" revolution even in a European as well as a Spanish context. As in the case of the German peasant war, so also with the Comuneros, the "great" revolution is thus seen not as typologically sui generis but as a phenomenon that may appear in different forms, depending on background, circumstances, and the forces roused to action.

The revolution of 1520 was the last serious resistance to the progress of absolutism in Castile. Thenceforth, as the recent historian of Valladolid has written, "the practice of political liberty became impossible."[108] Although the cities retained some formal autonomy, royal control and supremacy under appointed *corregidores* was permanently reestablished. The

---

[107]Cited in Maravall, *Las comunidades*, 137.   [108]Bennassar, 534.

Cortes ceased to be capable of defiance or disregard of the crown's wishes. Castile never rose again, and Charles V and his son Philip II resumed and completed what Isabella and Ferdinand had begun.

There were some curious ironies, though, in the long sequel to the revolution of the Comuneros. If Castile succumbed to absolutism and had to share its king with alien realms, it also became the heart and paramount state of the Spanish monarchy. The Habsburg dynasty of kings of Spain became Castilianized and so, instead of remaining an equal union of crowns, did Spain's empire. Charles V returned to Spain in 1522 to abide eight years. He presently took his first wife from the Iberian world, a Portuguese princess and cousin, to Castilian satisfaction. Having come to feel a deep affection for his Spanish realm, he returned to Castile after his abdication to retire and die there in 1558. The succeeding rulers of the House of Austria were all thoroughly Spanish. Philip II, born and reared in Spain, hardly ever left Castile and the peninsula not at all after 1559. Many of the highest achievements of Spanish culture in the sixteenth and seventeenth centuries flowered in Castilian soil. In spite of the defeat of the Comuneros, Castile itself triumphed under Charles V and his heirs, although in the long historical reckoning it had to pay a ruinously high price for its ascendancy.

Index